Control System Design Using MATRIX$_X$®

BAHRAM SHAHIAN

California State University, Long Beach

MICHAEL HASSUL

California State University, Long Beach

PRENTICE HALL, Englewood Cliffs, New Jersey 07632

Library of Congress Cataloging-in-Publication Data

Shahian, Barry
Control system design using MATRIXx / Barry Shahian, Michael Hassul.
p. cm.
On t.p. last "x" in MATRIXx is subscript.
Includes bibliographical references and index.
ISBN 0-13-174095-4
1. MATRIXx 2. Automatic control--Data processing. 3. Control theory--Data processing. I. Hassul, Michael. II. Title.
TJ213.S425 1992
629.8'9'02855369--dc20 91-46911
CIP

Acquisitions editor: ***Pete Janzow***
Production editor: ***Jennifer Wenzel***
Cover design: ***Lundgren Graphics, Ltd.***
Prepress buyer: ***Linda Behrens***
Manufacturing buyer: ***Dave Dickey***
Supplements editor: ***Alice Dworkin***
Editorial assistant: ***Phyllis Morgan***

Printed in the United States of America

10 9 8 7 6 5 4 3 2

ISBN 0-13-174095-4

Prentice-Hall International (UK) Limited, *London*
Prentice-Hall of Australia Pty. Limited, *Sydney*
Prentice-Hall Canada Inc., *Toronto*
Prentice-Hall Hispanoamericana, S.A., *Mexico*
Prentice-Hall of India Private Limited, *New Delhi*
Prentice-Hall of Japan, Inc., *Tokyo*
Simon & Schuster of Asia Pte. Ltd., *Singapore*
Editora Prentice-Hall do Brasil, Ltda., *Rio de Janeiro*

To my parents, Saleh and Mahin
and my wife and daughter, Farahnaz and Bita

B. Shahian

To Laurie J. Spector

M. Hassul

Contents

Preface

This book has evolved both as an attempt to fully integrate Computer-aided Control System Design (CACSD) tools into our control curriculum and to devise an exciting and meaningful control system design course at CSULB.

Evolution of a control design course

Just a few years back, when we taught our design course, we would assign different textbook design problems to students. Most of the design work was done by hand. The difficult part was verification. Very few diligent students would actually compute the step response and plot it point by point using a calculator. Problems had to be limited to 2nd or 3rd order systems for obvious reasons. From the instructor's point of view, checking the results was also very tedious.

We then decided to ask the students to write computer programs to verify their work. This almost made things worse. We found that the students were spending most of the time writing, debugging and perfecting their programs. The control design aspects faded into the background. Good programmers turned in nice reports (we do not know if they learned any control design though), while those who were weak in programming were very frustrated. On our side, we still had problems with verification. Students were writing programs in different languages, so you had to check their results along with their programs.

Next, we decided to remove some of the programming burden on the students. We put together a collection of programs from Melsa's famous book [MJ73] and handed them out. Although this helped, it still was not very efficient. The Fortran programs were not user-friendly, to say the least, and students were still wasting a lot of their valuable time on the computer.

The situation remained the same for several terms until we discovered MATRIX_X® and MATLAB™. Our gut reaction to our first session with MATRIX_X can be summarized as " *where have you been all these years* ?! "

We immediately introduced MATRIXx to our classes. Manuals were made available in the labs, but we still had to spend significant class time going over necessary commands. The results, however, were fantastic. We were now able to assign more challenging problems, compare different design techniques, and expect better performance and full verification. On our side, we were able to write simple routines that would automatically regenerate their results and verify their work. We noticed improved performance in designs, better prepared reports, and better grasp of concepts.

The only problem was that students were still complaining about spending too much time paging through manuals (or looking for them because they were constantly disappearing). Valuable class time (or our own personal time) had to be spent answering questions about various commands. Eventually we wrote brief notes about using MATRIXx. The present book evolved from those notes.

Finally, we came to the conclusion that since we now have the computational tools, we can add a dimension of realism to our class by requiring full-scale hardware designs. The motivation behind this is that we believe that no amount of lecturing can substitute for the real experience of design. There are analysis and design issues that simply cannot be taught in the real sense in a traditional lecture format. Issues such as modeling, model uncertainties including nonlinearities and component tolerances, noise and disturbance effects, and a host of other implementation problems are issues that have to be experienced head-on and dealt with. Too many students leave the classroom without really knowing the true properties of feedback. If they do, they usually think that we use feedback to stabilize systems, not realizing that feedback itself can be a source of instability. Moreover, the interdisciplinary nature of control systems and control technology issues such as sensor and actuator technologies are subjects that can be better learned through actual experience.

We have selected for assignment some traditional problems in control: inverted pendulum on a cart, magnetic levitation of a globe, and balancing a ball on a beam. Other feasible projects might be the double tank problem or the sun tracker system. Samples of the projects are usually demonstrated at the beginning of the term to motivate the students. Groups of one to three (the larger the group size, the less likely they will finish the task) students pick any project they find interesting. Appropriate references and some good reports from previous years are available to them. Students are expected to obtain the mathematical models, gather data to get the parameters, search for and purchase the necessary parts (list of local vendors are available, we also recycle some components from unsuccessful projects from previous terms to reduce out of pocket expenditures), set the specifications, design the compensator, simulate, implement, test, prepare a report, and finally demonstrate their projects at the end of the term. Biweekly progress reports are also collected to obviate any future problems. A variety of designs from simple lead compensators to LQG type designs have been reported. After weeks of frustration over globes that defy stability, beams that over-react and hurl a metal ball into your face, carts that dance around the room, fried transistors and motors, the final day is a day to remember. The joy of learning and accomplishment, or the joy of learning and at least attempting to accomplish something real, is the true result of the course experience. A sense of appreciation for giving them the opportunity to prove their ingenuity and engineering skills has been the typical response from most students. This has been our reward.

Why we wrote this book

Our experience has indicated that we cannot spend valuable class time to discuss various commands or idiosyncrasies of any particular program. On the other hand, it is neither fair nor practical to expect students to pour over voluminous manuals (which are written to be comprehensive) when they have to study their main text, as well as study for other courses they happen to be taking. Therefore, we decided to write a user-friendly textbook that would include elements of a program manual and a control systems design book. It is not as comprehensive and thorough as a manual, but it has more examples targeted to a control audience. It is not a regular control text, because most concepts are not fully motivated or developed and there are no theorems or proofs. It instead is written in tutorial format. This should take the burden of teaching software off the instructor's shoulders without expecting too much of the students either. Most design techniques from classical to modern optimal control techniques are discussed, with an example for every method. We show, step by step, how the designs can be performed on the computer and how to verify them.

The book is divided into two parts. Part I is a quick, yet thorough introduction to MATRIXx. Most of the commands that we thought to be relevant to students in the systems area are quickly introduced and illustrated. The assumed background for the book is knowledge of classical control and some basic matrix theory. We have included a review of classical control in Chapter 1, and, for completeness, a brief introduction to state space in Chapter 5 . Part II is a collection of lessons in tutorial form for control design from classical to modern optimal control based techniques. We wanted the book to retain its usefulness for those students taking more advanced courses in controls and for the working engineer.

How this book can be used

We envision the following uses for this text.

- As a supplement to any control or signal processing course. Our experience has shown that the majority of students understand the basics in 5-8 hours (Chapters 2, 3 and 4). They learn the programming, Core commands, classical control, graphics and state space commands (Chapters 1-5) in 3-4 weeks. The use of System Build (Chapter 6) for block diagram simulation of linear/nonlinear systems takes 1-2 weeks. Within one semester, 15 weeks, Chapters 1-8 and 10 can be covered. Within that period, they have mastered most aspects of the program. For signal processing courses, Chapter 11 should also be covered.

As a textbook for a Control Systems Laboratory course. Part I of the book is fully covered. This is how we use the book at CSULB. The problems in Chapters 2, 3, 4 and 6 are intentionally written in Lab format to facilitate this use. Most of these problems are divided into two parts (Preliminary analysis and Lab work). All problems have a two-fold purpose: to practice using the program and to amplify important concepts in control. The approach is to learn and discover concepts and properties via simulation. Since many problems involve repeated computations and simulations, programming is introduced early.

The following concepts and properties are studied via simulation in the problems (problem numbers are indicated).

- dominant poles (3.3)
- *s*-plane regions satisfying transient response specifications (3.5)
- properties of the exponential map for s-plane to z-plane (3.6)
- effects of moving poles in a second order system (4.1)
- effects of adding poles and zeros to a second order system (4.2)
- effects of nonminimum phase zeros on the step response (4.3)
- effects of lead/lag compensators (4.4)
- disturbance rejection properties of feedback (4.5)
- effects of PI control (4.6) and PID control (4.7)
- differences between cascade and feedback compensators (4.8)
- discovering the problems faced using Bode plots for nonminimum phase systems (4.9)

By judiciously choosing problems in Chapters 2-4, one can clarify some properties that may be difficult to grasp for some students. At our school, we devote 2/3 of a semester to PC based simulations and 1/3 to analog servomotor control. Since the Control Systems Lab is a prerequisite to all subsequent control courses, we assume a working knowledge of the program in our control sequence.

- As a handy reference for working engineers. The tutorial format provides quick reviews without getting bogged down on theoretical details. This does not mean that theoretical issues are not important, but rather we assume that the reader is either familiar with them or can refer to any number of excellent controls textbooks. It has not been our intent to de-emphasize the importance of these books in the study of control theory. Important design formulas and equations are provided, properties are explained and demonstrated by examples. All design techniques are demonstrated by examples. We also verify the results by providing appropriate plots, data and tables. For instance, we have found that when some people perform state space design, they frequently have problems verifying the frequency response properties of their system, or misinterpret the results, or use the wrong transfer function (mixing up open loop and closed loop transfer functions). We have tried to point these out and explicitly derive the appropriate transfer functions. Most of the examples (like the problems) serve a two-fold purpose: to demonstrate the use of various commands, and to amplify important concepts in control.

Organization of the book

Part I of the book is devoted to familiarizing the reader with MATRIXx. Chapter 1 is a review of classical control. We also set our notation and terminology there. Chapter 2 introduces a selection of MATRIXx Core commands, 73 data structures, input/output, graphics, and some math commands. Chapter 3 discusses programming structures; sample programs are provided to illustrate the procedures. The programs can be used for data analysis in later chapters. Chapter 4 introduces classical control commands such as step response, root locus, and frequency response analysis. Chapter 5 is a quick introduction to state space analysis followed by appropriate commands. The packed matrix notation for system representation which is becoming popular in the robust control literature and is native to MATRIXx is also introduced. This is used to derive system interconnection commands. We also discuss how to deal with multi-input multi-output systems. Chapter 6 is a brief introduction to the System Build Module. This is one of the most important and useful features of MATRIXx. It is how the program is mainly used in industry. Thorough discussion of all simulation features available in System Build would double the size of the book, but we believe that this chapter will get the reader started. Several examples from simple lead compensation to simulating the chaotic behavior of the nonlinear Lorenz system are discussed.

Part II starts with Chapter 7, classical design. Design using root locus, Bode plots, and analytical formulas for PID, lead and lag compensation are discussed. All methods are demonstrated by examples. Simple programs that can be modified by the user are provided for all techniques to insure that the user concentrates on design rather than on programming. We give an example of ad-hoc design so the reader knows that classical design is also an art and not a cook book procedure that works for all systems. Chapter 8 discusses state feedback, observers, and reduced-order observers. We briefly introduce concepts of controllability and observability. The same example is used throughout for comparison. The chapter ends with programs for design and verification. Chapter 9 is a self contained and brief introduction to discrete systems and digital control. Appropriate commands are introduced and the effects of sampling, different discretization methods, and frequency warping are discussed. Classical digital design techniques are presented. The chapter ends with design programs. Algebraic, or polynomial, design is introduced in Chapter 10. Various methods for choosing desired closed loop transfer functions are discussed. The standard unity feedback, RST (two-parameter), and controller-observer (Input/Output) configurations are presented. Sample programs to implement various techniques are given at the end of the chapter. Chapter 11 is intended to prepare the reader for an introduction to Kalman-Bucy filtering, and to introduce various signal processing commands. We summarize basic terminology, facts, and important results from stochastic processes. An example is worked out in detail to demonstrate the signal processing commands, and to show how to interpret the results of the analysis. Optimal control methods (LQR/LQG) and the Kalman-Bucy filter are discussed in Chapter 12. Formulas and classical properties of LQ methods are presented and verified by examples. The famous stability margins of LQR and their subsequent loss when estimators are introduced are demonstrated by an example. These concepts and properties are usually discussed and proved in classroom lectures. We assign additional simulation homeworks. Our experience indicates that students retain the material better when they verify it by simulation.

Finally we wish to acknowledge our debt to all those who have somehow contributed to our knowledge and efforts. The first author wishes to thank Baxter Womack who first introduced him to the subject of control. David Luenbeger who showed him the beauty and magic of dynamic systems; Gene Franklin, who showed him that great teachers are not made overnight; Thomas Kailath whose great classic book has had, and still has, a great deal of influence on him; Cornelius Leondes who gave him the opportunity to explore and selflessly shared his years of experience with him. The second author wishes to thank his teachers in systems and controls: Leonard Shaw, Eliahu I. Jury, Pravin Varaiya, and particularly Ronald A. Rohrer, his graduate advisor who gave him his appreciation for computer-aided design. He also wishes to thank his university and industrial colleagues: Robert N. Clark, Wendy Svitil, Joseph Anselmi, Gerry Manke, and Eugene A. Lee.

We thank our colleagues, Raymond Stefani and Walter Walquist who suggested some changes in problems of Chapter 4, and Hung Vu who class tested our material. We thank the unknown soldiers, students in EE 471, who suffered through the early manuscripts and corrected many of our errors. We thank M. Hasan AlHafez, who contributed some of the programs in Chapters 7 and 10; Victoria Gilmore who developed a robust control module, and Freidoon Matin who helped in every way to put the book together.

From Prentice Hall, we thank Gerry Johnson, who encouraged us to write this book and wholeheartedly supported us throughout; Tim Bozik, who initially approved our project; Jennifer Wenzel and the production staff; and finally Pete Janzow, who supported us and put up with long delays.

Our thanks to the people at Integrated Systems, Inc., Andy Mills, Jeff Bach, Paul Schmidt, Umberto Milletti, Sinan Karahan, Martin Ratner, and Dhanunjay Vayugundla who generously donated copies of MATRIXx to our school and have supported us in every way they could.

B. Shahian thanks his little daughter, Bita. Her infatuation with the red "reset button" on his computer forced him to rewrite many sections; talk about harsh reviews! Finally, we wish to thank our wives. Surely, a couple of lines will not do justice to many of the sacrifices they have made over the time period we were working on this book. But certainly, big royalty checks and a diamond ring would!

Notation, Typography & Program Versions

Books that involve the use of computers require special attention with respect to typography. Please read this section so you can identify various changes from regular text to command entry to computer response. We have used the following typefaces in the book.

regular text is shown in 10 point Times Font

`commands you enter following the MATRIXx prompt < > are shown in size 8 Courier Font`

MATRIXx response to your commands are shown in size 8 Helvetica Font

MATRIXx command names and new words are shown in *italics.*

Example text is shown in size 9 Times Font.

When we started writing the book, we were using MATRIXx Version 5.2. We were later hit by updates to Versions 7.1, 7.2, 7.3 and now 8.0 (at the time of writing, still in beta testing stage). This forced us to rewrite major portions of the book and redo most of the examples to conform to the latest version. This is an inherent problem of writing a book tied to software, i.e. a matter of *time constants*. Software developers seem to have a much smaller time constant than authors!

Another important point worth noting is that the actual numbers and numerical values that you get may depend on which version of the program you are using. However, the final results and conclusions are identical. The algorithms used may be different and machine tolerances might vary. To be specific, we cite the following hypothetical examples. Suppose you have a transfer function with a pole at 1.002 and a zero at 1.001. The *minimal* command in MATRIXx performs pole-zero cancellation. If you are using the program on a PC platform, the cancellation may occur, while on a VAX platform they may not cancel. This has to do with the internal tolerance of each machine. Another example is transfer function to state space conversion. On earlier versions, one of the canonical forms was used, while in Ver. 8.0, a balanced realization is obtained. Other commands have also gone through changes in algorithms. Here is the lesson: if you are not getting the same answers in examples as we are, think again before you call it an error.

This book was typeset by the authors using Ventura Publisher 2.0, Professional Extension, on a PC-AT 286. All plots are generated by MATRIXx. They were sent to files using the HPGL Plotter format, then imported by Ventura. Block diagrams and plot annotations were done inside Ventura. The System Build Block Forms were captured by the Snipper program (a shareware utility), then converted to GEM format using Hijaak 2.0, and imported to Ventura. The graphics in Chapters 7 and 9 were done using Microsoft Windows Paint program and imported to Ventura. During the process of writing, converting, importing, cutting and pasting, errors might have been introduced. We have tried to detect and correct all errors. If any errors still remain, we apologize to the reader and would welcome your comments and corrections.

1

Review of Classical Control

1.1 Introduction

The Encyclopedia of Science and Technology (6th ed., McGraw Hill, 1987) defines control systems as

> "interconnections of components forming system configurations which will provide a desired system response as time progresses."

This definition is all encompassing, covering just about everything in the natural and man-made world. The universe, for example, is a system of planets, gasses, stars, etc. The desired response of the planetary system is a question best left for philosophers, however. Of more immediate concern to engineers are the systems composed of manufactured physical components (e.g., machines, electronics, and chemical processes) and to biomedical engineers, are the biological processes.

Control system design began in antiquity. The first cave man or woman who designed the bow and arrow combined two components to achieve the desired response of a more efficient means to hunt and to protect. This type of system is known as a ballistic, or open loop, system. Once set in motion, there is no further control of the behavior of the arrow. Feedback control is more sophisticated. System response is monitored and compared with the desired response. Corrective action can then be taken to minimize the difference between desired and actual response. The governor of a steam engine is an early example of feedback control.

Until this century, control systems were designed by artisans and crafts-people. They used their experience and insight. Mathematical modeling of the components of a system and their interconnections brought the engineer into the picture. With mathematics came predictability and increased sophistication of control system design.

The first great impetus that drove the development of control system mathematics was the telephone. Electronic feedback amplifiers were required to amplify the signals in a telephone system. World War II saw the extension of these feedback control techniques to the mechanical world. Oliver Heaviside (1850-1925) provided a mathematical framework that allowed the analysis and design of control systems. His technique, similar to the Laplace transform, takes the analysis and design of dynamic systems from the time domain of the differential equation and the convolution integral into the frequency domain of the transfer function. Transfer function techniques are to this day a mainstay in control system analysis and design.

An nth order linear time invariant (LTI) system can be described by a linear constant coefficient differential equation of the form

$$y^{(n)} + a_{n-1}\, y^{(n-1)} + \ldots + a_1\, \dot{y} + a_0\, y = b_m\, u^{(m)} + b_{m-1}\, u^{(m-1)} + \ldots + b_1\, \dot{u} + b_0\, u$$

where appropriate initial conditions are specified for the output, $y(t)$, of the system. Laplace transforming the above equation, we get

$$Y(s) = \frac{N(s)}{D(s)}\, U(s) + \frac{IC(s)}{D(S)} = G(s)\, U(s) + \frac{IC(s)}{D(s)}$$

where

$$G(s) = \frac{b_m s^m + b_{m-1} s^{m-1} + \ldots + b_1 s + b_0}{s^n + a_{n-1} s^{n-1} + \ldots + a_1 s + a_0} = \frac{N(s)}{D(s)}$$

and $IC(s)$ is a polynomial in s, a complex variable, containing the terms arising from the initial conditions. As you can see, the total response is the sum of the contributions from the initial conditions and the system input. If the system is unforced (i.e., the input is zero), we call the resulting response the *zero-input response* (ZIR) of the system. Likewise, if all initial conditions are zero, the forcing function produces the *zero-state response* (ZSR). The ratio of transform of output over transform of input of the system under zero initial conditions is the *transfer function*, denoted by $G(s)$ above.

Note that both terms in the output equation contain the same denominator polynomial, which is known as the *characteristic equation*. The roots of the common denominator $D(s)$ are the characteristic roots or the system *modes*.

The term *classical control* is applied to the body of techniques developed from the beginning of control theory to the early 1960s. It is characterized chiefly by the use of algebraic and graphical frequency domain techniques applied to single input-single output (SISO) systems. The use of computers was very limited. Classical control techniques are still in widespread use today. We will briefly review some of these methods in the following sections.

1.2 Transfer Functions

An open loop control system is composed of an input signal, a component that conditions the input signal (the controller), an actuator, the plant (or process), and the output signal. The control law, $G_1(s)$, the actuator, $G_2(s)$, and the plant, $G_3(s)$, are each modeled with transfer functions. The overall transfer function, $G(s)$, is given by

$$\frac{Y(s)}{X(s)} = G(s) = G_1(s)\, G_2(s)\, G_3(s)$$

Each individual transfer function is represented as a ratio of polynomials (or a rational function) in s, where s is a complex variable (interpreted as complex frequency). For example, $G(s)$ may be represented as

$$G(s) = K\frac{(s-z_1)(s-z_2)\,\dots\,(s-z_m)}{(s-p_1)(s-p_2)\,\dots\,(s-p_n)}$$

where we have assumed for simplicity that the polynomials have no repeated factors. If $\lim_{s \to \infty} G(s) = C < \infty$, $G(s)$ is said to be *proper*, otherwise it is called *improper*. If $C = 0$, $G(s)$ is *strictly proper*. Most physical systems have strictly proper transfer functions.

The set of frequencies at which transfer function " blows up, " i.e., approaches infinity, are the transfer function *poles*. The set of frequencies at which the transfer function approaches zero are the *zeros*, of the transfer function. As you know, the numerator roots are the finite zeros, and the denominator roots are the finite poles of $G(s)$ as long as there are no common factors among the numerator and denominator. Strictly proper transfer functions have $(n - m)$ zeros at infinity, and improper transfer functions have $(m - n)$ poles at infinity.

If there are no common roots between the numerator and denominator of $G(s)$, i.e., there are no pole-zero cancellations, we say $G(s)$ is *coprime* (or *irreducible*). Most properly modeled physical systems have strictly proper and coprime transfer functions; nevertheless, these definitions are needed later as constraints on physically realizable compensators or as mathematical solvability conditions.

1.2.1 Frequency Response

Because s is a complex variable ($s = \sigma + j\,\omega$), transfer functions like $G(s)$ are also complex. A complex number can be expressed with a magnitude and angle. Graphs of magnitude and angle of $G(s)$ versus s are three dimensional. Although it is possible to draw such graphs, particularly with the help of a computer, we typically limit ourselves to considering only values of s on the imaginary axis. This gives us the *sinusoidal steady state response*, which fully characterizes the system. Plots of magnitude and phase of a transfer function versus frequency are called *frequency response* plots.

At Bell Labs in the 1930s, H. W. Bode (1906-1982) developed a new method for displaying gain and phase. He plotted the logarithm of the gain (multiplied by 20) versus the logarithm of frequency and phase versus the logarithm of frequency. These plots have two immediate advantages over the linear plots. One is that using the log of frequency compresses that scale so that greater detail is available over a very wide range of frequencies.

More important, we are often analyzing systems in which transfer functions are multiplied together. A product of gains can be turned into a sum by taking logarithms. This is how we find the Bode magnitude plot of a product of transfer functions. We simply add the individual gain plots. Because the total phase of a product of complex numbers is already the addition of the individual phases, linear phase is plotted versus log frequency. The Bode magnitude and phase plots of the following transfer function are shown in Figure 1-1.

$$G(s) = \frac{1}{s\,(s+1)\,(s+2)}$$

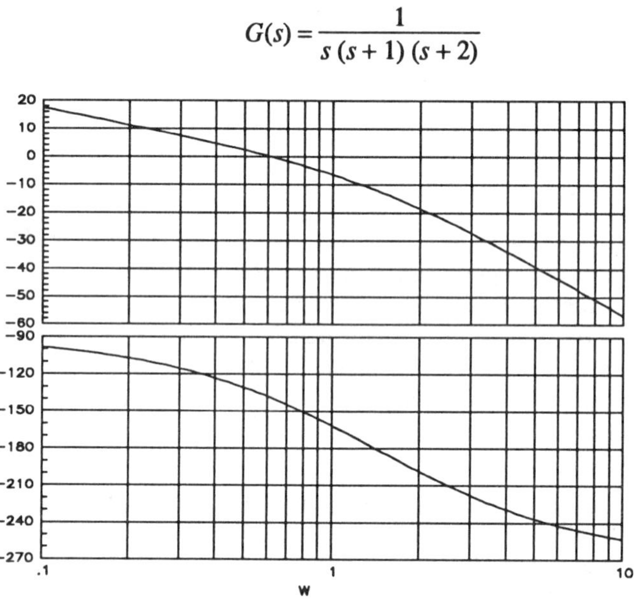

Figure 1-1 Bode magnitude and phase plot of $G(s)$.

Bode plots require two separate plots for each transfer function. If frequency is eliminated as a variable, then gain and phase can be shown on the same plot. There are many ways to present such data. Plots can be rectilinear or polar; gains can be linear or logarithmic. Before Bode's contribution, H. Nyquist (also of Bell Labs) published a paper on the use of linear magnitude polar plots in systems analysis. The polar, or Nyquist, diagram shows the frequency variations of the magnitude and phase of a transfer function as an ordered pair on the complex plane. At a given frequency, the gain and phase are found. The gain determines the distance from the origin of the complex plane, and the phase determines the angle from the positive real axis. Figure 1-2 shows the Nyquist plot for $G(j\omega)$. The Nyquist plot can also be constructed by plotting Im$G(j\omega)$ versus Re$G(j\omega)$, where $G(j\omega) = |G| \cos \angle G + j\,|G| \sin \angle G$.

We will discuss other plots as appropriate. A major benefit of the Bode and Nyquist plots is that they allow us to predict closed loop behavior by examining the open loop system. This will be discussed Section 1.8.

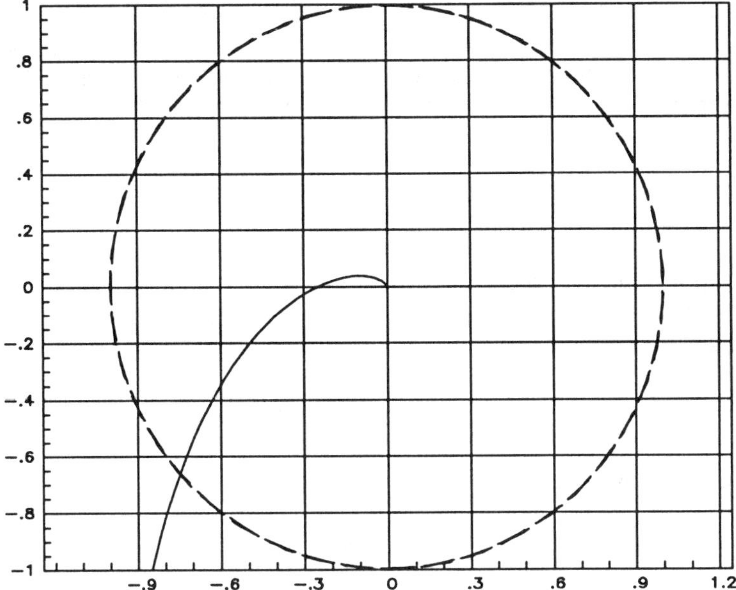

Figure 1-2 Nyquist plot of $G(s)$.

1.3 Convolution and the Impulse Response

Convolution is a fundamental concept in systems analysis. It is a time domain technique that provides the basis for transfer function analysis. Its use in a system of any complexity requires a computer; for this reason convolution has not been greatly used in classical control. Convolution is the basis for modern control analysis, however, and so will be reviewed here.

The zero-state response of a linear time-invariant system can be represented as

$$Y(s) = H(s)X(s)$$

where $H(s)$ is the system transfer function. The output, $Y(s)$, is the Laplace transform of

$$y(t) = \int_{-\infty}^{\infty} h(\tau)\,x(t-\tau)\,d\tau = \int_{-\infty}^{\infty} x(\tau)\,h(t-\tau)\,d\tau$$

The right-hand sides of the above equation are both known as the convolution integral. The equation can be abbreviated as

$$y(t) = h(t) * x(t) = x(t) * h(t)$$

where $x(t)$ is an arbitrary input (we will discuss $h(t)$ shortly). The convolution integral can also be used in time varying systems. Remember, we can not use Laplace transforms for time varying systems. This makes the convolution integral more applicable than transform techniques. For a time varying system, the convolution integral becomes

$$y(t) = \int_{-\infty}^{\infty} h(t,\tau)\, x(\tau)\, d\tau.$$

If we limit our discussion to time invariant systems, we can find $h(t)$ for a given system by using Laplace transforms. If the input to the system is an impulse, $\delta(t)$, then $X(s) = 1$ and

$$Y(s) = H(s) \cdot 1$$

The inverse Laplace transform leads to the impulse response

$$y(t) = h(t)$$

This leads to the very powerful conclusion that for a linear time invariant system, the system transfer function is the Laplace transform of its impulse response. This property is used in system identification. As an example of the use of the impulse response and the convolution integral, we will find the step response of the first order system represented by

$$H(s) = \frac{100}{s+3}$$

The impulse response of the system is $100\, e^{-3t}\, u(t)$. The step response is found as

$$y(t) = e^{-3t}\, u(t) * u(t) = \int_{-\infty}^{\infty} e^{-3\tau}\, u(\tau)\, u(t-\tau)\, d\tau$$

The unit steps change the limits of integration to 0 and t, so we get

$$y(t) = \int_{0}^{t} e^{-3\tau}\, d\tau = \frac{1}{3}(1 - e^{-3t}) \quad t \geq 0$$

The output of this system to any input can be found in a similar manner by replacing the unit step with the input of interest and using a table of integrals or a computer simulation program.

Higher order systems can also be analyzed using this technique. The transfer function of an nth order system can be expanded as

$$H(s) = \frac{R_1}{s-p_1} + \ldots + \frac{R_n}{s-p_n}$$

where p_i may be complex, and we assume, again for simplicity, that there are no repeated roots. The impulse response is, therefore,

$$h(t) = (R_1 e^{p_1 t} + \ldots + R_n e^{p_n t})\, u(t)$$

As you know, if there are a complex pair of poles, the corresponding impulse response is a damped sinusoid. Because integration is additive, it is a relatively simple matter to extend the first order example to the *n*th order example. An alternative approach is to represent the *n*th order system with a first order matrix equation. In this case, the impulse response is an exponential raised to a matrix power and, with certain modifications, similar equations discussed here can be used. This is the basis of state space analysis and will be discussed further in Chapter 5.

1.4 Stability

A control engineer must always consider the stability of a system under study or design. There are many definitions of stability; the *IEEE Standard Dictionary of Electrical and Electronics Terms* has 2 1/2 pages of definitions for stability. For now, however, we define a stable system as one in which the output of the system does not grow without bound for any initial condition (natural response) or for any bounded input. To avoid confusion, we will use stability to refer only to the behavior of the natural response. The second type is commonly known as *bounded-input bounded-output* (BIBO) stability.

1.4.1 Stability of the Zero-Input Response: Asymptotic Stability

Consider the ZIR of a system. This is determined only by the system's characteristic equation and its initial conditions. That is

$$Y(s) = \frac{IC(s)}{D(s)}$$

Recall that the roots of the characteristic equation are called system modes. There are three possibilities.

1. $\mathrm{Re}(p_i) < 0$ for all i

where p_i are the roots of the characteristic equation. In this case, $y(t) \to 0$ as $t \to \infty$ and the system is *asymptotically stable*.

2. $\mathrm{Re}(p_i) > 0$ for any i

Now, $y(t) \to \infty$ as $t \to \infty$, and the system is *unstable*.

3. $\mathrm{Re}(p_i) = 0$ for any i

This means that a root of the characteristic equation is zero or purely imaginary. In this case, the output either remains constant or is sinusoidal. Therefore, the output neither returns to zero nor goes to infinity. This is known as *marginal stability*. If the roots are repeated and have zero real parts, the system is unstable. This can be seen from the following examples:

$$H_1(s) = \frac{1}{s} \qquad H_2(s) = \frac{1000}{s^2 + 100} \qquad H_3(s) = \frac{1}{s^2}$$

Because the behavior of the ZIR is similar to the system's impulse response, we can examine stability by finding the impulse response of each system

$$h_1(t) = u(t) \qquad h_2(t) = 100 \cos 10tu(t) \qquad h_3(t) = tu(t)$$

The systems represented by $H_1(s)$ and $H_2(s)$ are marginally stable beacuse their impulse responses neither decay nor grow without bound. Conversely, the system represented by $H_3(s)$ is clearly unstable. This leads to the following: a system with a simple mode at the origin or single pairs of complex modes on the $j\omega$ axis is marginally stable. Multiple modes at the origin or on the $j\omega$ indicate an unstable system.

1.4.2 Stability of the Zero-state Response: BIBO Stability

We now consider the stability of ZSR of systems. The output of a linear time invariant system with general input $x(t)$ is given by the convolution integral

$$y(t) = \int_{-\infty}^{\infty} h(\tau)\, x(t-\tau)\, d\tau$$

If the input is bounded, i.e., $|\,x(t)\,| \le M < \infty$, then

$$|y(t)| = \left|\int_{-\infty}^{\infty} h(\tau)\, x(t-\tau)\, d\tau\right| \le M \left|\int_{-\infty}^{\infty} h(\tau)\, d\tau\right| \le M \int_{-\infty}^{\infty} |h(\tau)|\, d\tau$$

Therefore the system is BIBO stable if and only if

$$\int_{-\infty}^{\infty} |h(\tau)|\, d\tau < \infty$$

Mathematically this means the impulse response is absolutely integrable (also known as an L_1 function).

We state, without formal proof, that a system is BIBO stable if and only if all poles of the system lie in the open left half plane (LHP). If any pole lies in the right half plane (RHP), the system is unstable. Poles on the $j\omega$ axis require special attention. Is a marginally stable system BIBO stable? The answer is no. Consider the step response of $H_1(s)$

$$\frac{1}{s}H_1(s) = \frac{1}{s^2} \rightarrow tu(t)$$

Because the unit step is bounded and this system's output is unbounded, $H_1(s)$ is not BIBO stable.

It appears that the two definitions of stability (asymptotic and BIBO) are the same. This is a subtle point and needs some care. Asymptotic stability is determined by the modes, which are the roots of the characteristic equation. BIBO stability depends on the poles, however. In some cases, we may encounter a transfer function that is not coprime (i.e., there are pole-zero cancellations). Technically, poles are computed after the transfer function is reduced and any common terms are canceled out. Therefore, some of the modes may not appear as poles. We conclude that asymptotic stability implies BIBO stability but not vice versa. The definitions are equivalent only in the case of coprime transfer functions. The next example illustrates the point.

$$H(s) = \frac{(s-1)}{(s-1)(s+2)}$$

The modes are at $\{1, -2\}$, but the system has only one pole at $\{-2\}$. By the way, if you think the system has a pole at $\{1\}$, use L'Hospitals's Rule to verify that such is not the case. Therefore, the system is BIBO stable. Because of the RHP mode at $\{1\}$, however,it is not stable in the asymptotic stability sense. Such contradictory answers are common whenever we encounter transfer functions that are not coprime. We will later see that such cases are rare and pathological.

1.5 First and Second Order Systems

We will discuss time and frequency response characterization of first and second order systems in this section.

1.5.1 First Order Systems

The normalized (low frequency gain = 1) first order transfer function is

$$G(s) = \frac{a}{s+a}$$

This system has a single real pole at $(-a)$ and has the frequency response shown in Figure 1-3. The *bandwidth* of a low pass system (control systems are essentially low pass) is defined as the frequency where the magnitude drops by a factor of ($\frac{1}{\sqrt{2}} = 0.707 = -3$ dB) of its DC value (i.e., gain at zero or low frequency). As you can see from Figure 1-3, the bandwidth of the first order system is equal to the magnitude of the pole

$$BW = |a|$$

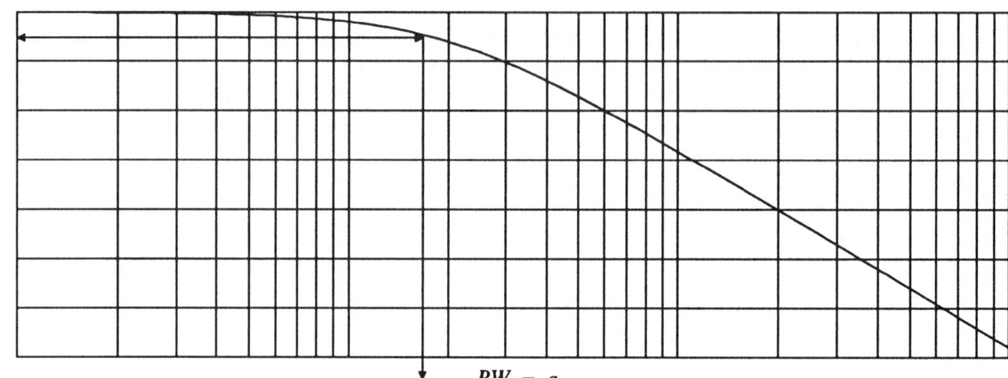

Figure 1-3 Magnitude response of first order system.

The time response of the output, $y(t)$, can be found by taking the inverse Laplace transform of $Y(s)$. When done by hand, we use the partial fraction expansion technique. The first order step response is given by

$$Y(s) = \frac{1}{s}\frac{a}{s+a} = \frac{1}{s} - \frac{1}{s+a}$$

The inverse Laplace transform yields the step response

$$y(t) = (1 - e^{-at})\, u(t)$$

The first order step response is plotted in Figure 1-4. We can see that the time constant of the first order step response ($\tau = 1/a$) is the inverse of the system bandwidth. The larger (smaller) the bandwidth, the faster (slower) the step response. Bandwidth is a direct measure of system susceptibility to noise. It is also an indicator of the system speed of response. The inverse relationship between bandwidth and speed of response also holds approximately for higher order systems. This demonstrates a design trade-off. A very fast system requires a large bandwidth. This means the system will be quite susceptible to high frequency noise, and unless additional filters are placed at appropriate points in the system, the noise may cause havoc in the system.

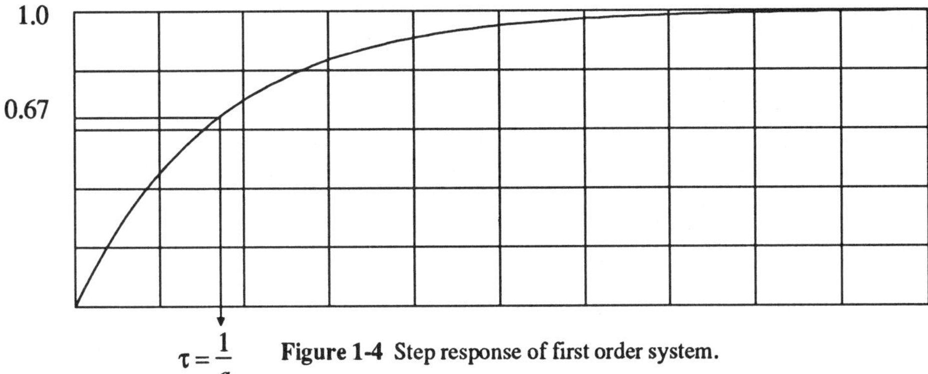

Figure 1-4 Step response of first order system.

There are two additional performance criteria that are used to describe the step response: *rise time* and *delay time*. Rise time, T_r , is a measure of the initial speed of the transient response and is defined as the time it takes the step response to go from 10% to 90% of its final, or steady-state value. Delay time, T_d, is defined as the time it takes the step response to reach 50% of its final value. Do not confuse delay time with a pure time delay ($f(t) = g(t-T)$). For the first order step response we can derive the following simple formulas for rise time and delay time:

$$T_r = \frac{2.2}{a} = 2.2\,\tau \quad \text{and} \quad T_d = \frac{0.69}{a} = 0.69\,\tau$$

1.5.2 Second Order Systems

The second order transfer function is very important in control design. System specifications are often given assuming that the system is second order. For higher order systems, we can use dominant pole techniques to approximate the system with a second order transfer function. Let us assume that

$$G(s) = \frac{\omega_n^2}{s^2 + 2\,\zeta\,\omega_n\,s + \omega_n^2}$$

where ζ is the damping ratio, and ω_n is the natural frequency of the system.

The poles are at

$$s_{1,2} = -\zeta\,\omega_n \pm j\,\omega_n\sqrt{1-\zeta^2}$$

Note that the poles can either both be real ($\zeta > 1$, overdamped), real and identical ($\zeta = 1$, critically damped), or complex conjugates ($0 < \zeta < 1$, underdamped).

The Bode magnitude plot of the underdamped case is shown in Figures 1-5. The plot shows a peak resonance at $\omega = \omega_r$, with a peak magnitude of M_r , where

$$\omega_r = \omega_n \sqrt{1 - 2\zeta^2} \qquad \text{for } \zeta \le \frac{1}{\sqrt{2}}$$

$$M_r = \frac{1}{2\zeta\sqrt{1-\zeta^2}} \qquad \text{for } \zeta \le \frac{1}{\sqrt{2}}$$

Note that the peak magnitude depends only on ζ.

The bandwidth, or 3-dB frequency, of the second order system is

$$BW = \omega_n [1 - 2\zeta^2 + (2 - 4\zeta^2 + 4\zeta^4)^{1/2}]^{1/2}$$

As ζ varies from 0 to 1, BW varies from $1.55\omega_n$ to $0.64\omega_n$. Control engineers, however, usually try to keep the damping ratio of their systems at approximately 0.707; for this value of ζ, $BW = \omega_n$. In fact, for most design considerations, we assume that the bandwidth of a second order all pole system can be approximated by ω_n.

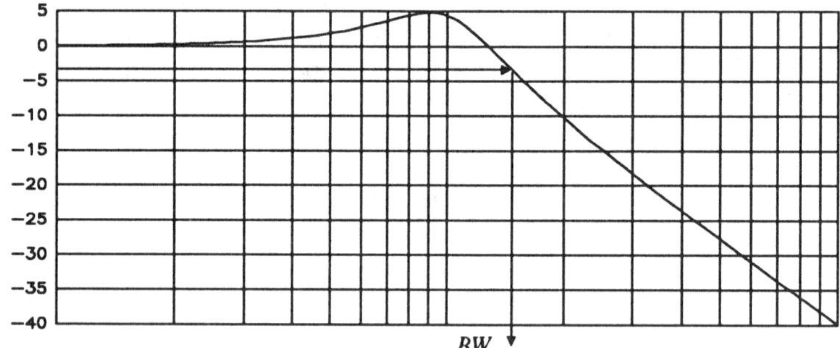

Figure 1-5 Bode magnitude plot of second order system.

The general all pole second order step response is

$$Y(s) = \frac{1}{s}\,G(s) = \frac{1}{s}\,\frac{\omega_n^2}{s^2 + 2\zeta\omega_n s + \omega_n^2}$$

Partial fraction expansion yields

$$Y(s) = \frac{1}{s} - \frac{s + 2\zeta\omega_n}{(s + \zeta\omega_n)^2 + \omega_n^2(1 - \zeta^2)}$$

This leads to the step response of $y(t)$

$$y(t) = 1 - \frac{e^{-t/\tau}}{\sqrt{1-\zeta^2}}\cos(\omega_d t - \varphi_d)\,, \qquad t \ge 0$$

where

$$|\sigma| = \zeta\,\omega_n \quad \text{and} \quad \tau = 1/|\sigma|, \qquad \omega_d = \omega_n\sqrt{1-\zeta^2}, \qquad \varphi_d = \sin^{-1}\zeta$$

Figure 1-6 shows an underdamped second-order step response with some important design criteria: overshoot, settling time, rise time, and delay time. To find overshoot (usually described as percent overshoot), determine the time of the first peak, T_p. The peak value of $y(t)$ is then found (denoted by M_p); finally the percent overshoot, POS, is calculated as $100\,[(M_p - y(\infty))/y(\infty)]$. The results are

$$T_p = \frac{\pi}{\omega_d} = \frac{\pi}{\omega_n\sqrt{1-\zeta^2}}, \quad M_p = 1 + \exp\left(\frac{-\zeta\pi}{\sqrt{1-\zeta^2}}\right)$$

$$\text{POS} = 100\exp\left(\frac{-\zeta\pi}{\sqrt{1-\zeta^2}}\right)$$

The overshoot is strictly a function of ζ; remember peak resonance in the magnitude frequency plot is also a function of ζ. The settling time is determined by the time constant of the envelope ($\tau = 1/\zeta\,\omega_n$). If we use the rule of thumb that an exponential decays in 4 to 5 time constants, then

$$T_s(\pm 2\,\%) \approx 4\tau = \frac{4}{\sigma} \quad \text{and} \quad T_s(\pm 1\,\%) \approx 4.6\,\tau = \frac{4.6}{\sigma}$$

If, as is often the case, overshoot and settling time are both given as desired system specifications, we first determine ζ from the allowable overshoot and then find ω_n from the settling time. There are no simple formulas for rise time and delay time; they are dependent on both ζ and ω_n. In addition, delay time is a function of the initial value of $\dot{y}(t)$; an output with an initial velocity will begin to rise before an output with zero initial velocity. For a damping ratio of 0.5, however, rise time is approximately equal to [FPE91]

$$T_r \approx \frac{1.8}{\omega_n} \qquad \text{for} \qquad \zeta = 0.5$$

Other approximations can be used also, but, as a general rule, we note that rise time is inversely proportional to ω_n.

Now that we have seen how ζ and ω_n affect such parameters as overshoot and settling time, we turn to the complex plane. In Figure 1-7, the vertical line is the contour of constant damping σ. Because the step response settling time is inversely proportional to σ, all second order systems that have poles along this contour will have the same settling time. To decrease (increase) the settling time, we must move the real part of the poles to the left (right).

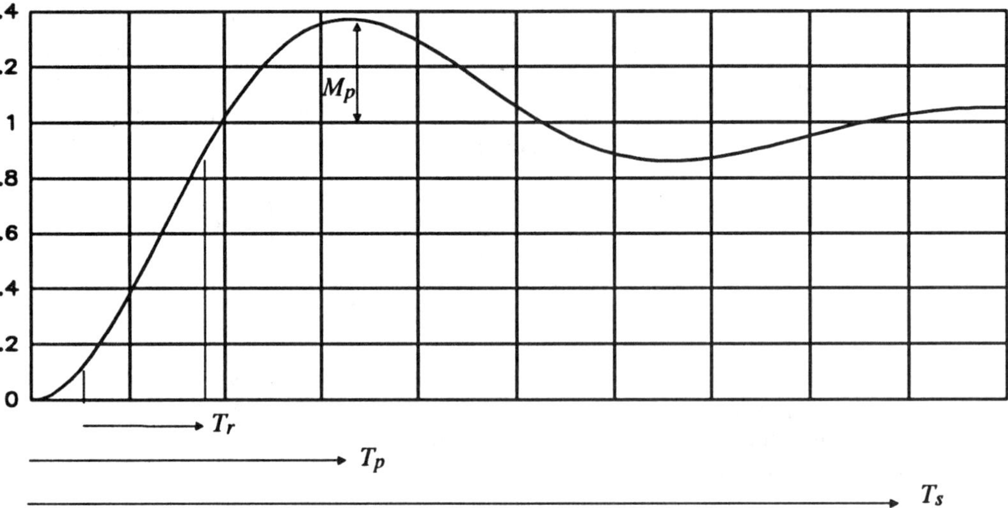

Figure 1-6 Step response of second order system.

The horizontal line in Figure 1-7 is the contour of constant ω_d, the oscillation frequency. It is sometimes important to control this variable to avoid exciting a resonant frequency of the structure being controlled.

The angle θ of the line from the origin through the pole in Figure 1-7 is the contour of constant ζ. This is easily shown by finding θ:

$$\theta = \tan^{-1}\frac{\sqrt{1-\zeta^2}}{\zeta} = \sin^{-1}\sqrt{1-\zeta^2} = \cos^{-1}\zeta$$

$$\zeta = \cos\theta$$

To increase (decrease) the damping of a second order system, decrease (increase) θ.

The radius in Figure 1-7 can be found from simple trigonometry to be ω_n. Therefore, the constant contour for ω_n is the circle shown. To increase (decrease) ω_n, increase (decrease) the radius of the circle.

To demonstrate the effects of varying pole locations in a canonical second order underdamped system, we consider the following:

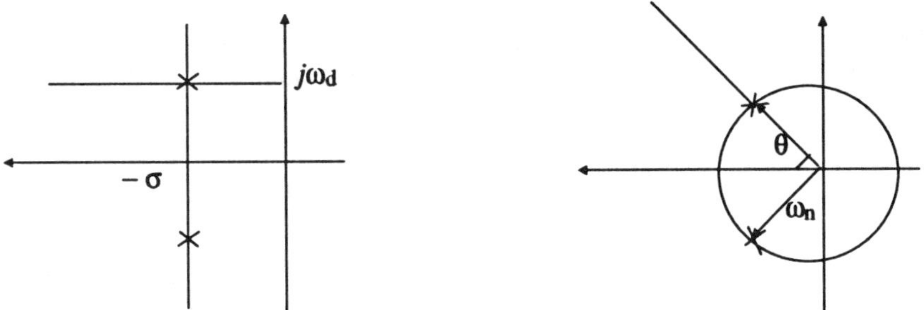

Figure 1-7 Complex plane showing different contours.

$$G(s) = \frac{\omega_n^2}{s^2 + 2\zeta\omega_n s + \omega_n^2} = \frac{\omega_d^2 + \sigma^2}{s^2 + 2\sigma s + (\omega_d^2 + \sigma^2)}$$

Case I: Effects of σ $\omega_d = 1, \sigma = \{0.5, 1, 5\}$

The poles move horizontally deeper into the LHP while keeping their imaginary parts fixed. We expect the following effects:

- Settling time decreases because it is inversely proportional to σ.
- Rise time decreases because the distance of the pole to origin increases and rise time is inversely proportional to this distance.
- Overshoot decreases because θ decreases, which means that ζ increases.
- Peak time remains fixed because ω_d is fixed.
- Bandwidth increases because it is proportional to ω_n. Note that bandwidth and rise time are inversely proportional.

The relevant step responses and Bode magnitude plots are shown in Figure 1-8.

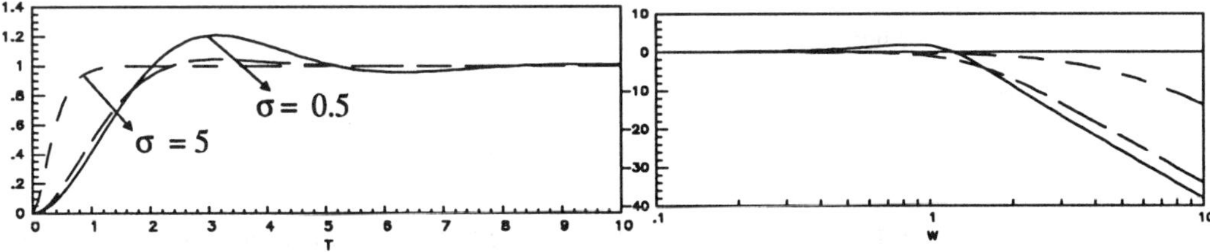

Figure 1-8 Step and magnitude responses for case I.

Case II: Effects of ω_d $\sigma = 1$, $\omega_d = \{0.5, 1, 5\}$

The poles move up vertically, whereas their real parts remain fixed at 1. In this case, settling time is fixed. Overshoot and bandwidth increase; peak time and rise time decrease. The plots are shown in Figure 1-9.

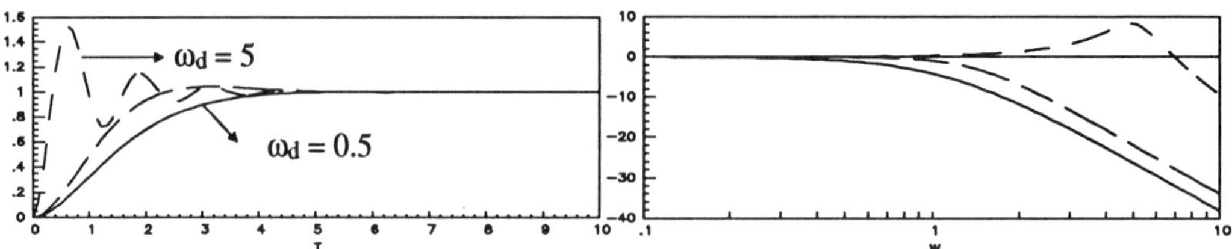

Figure 1-9 Step and magnitude responses for case II.

Case III: Effects of ω_n $\zeta = \frac{1}{\sqrt{2}}$, $\omega_n = \{\frac{\sqrt{2}}{2}, \sqrt{2}, 5\sqrt{2}\}$

The poles are moved radially outward along a line with angle of 45 degrees. Overshoot remains fixed while rise time, peak time, and settling time decrease. The bandwidth will increase. The plots are shown in Figure 1-10.

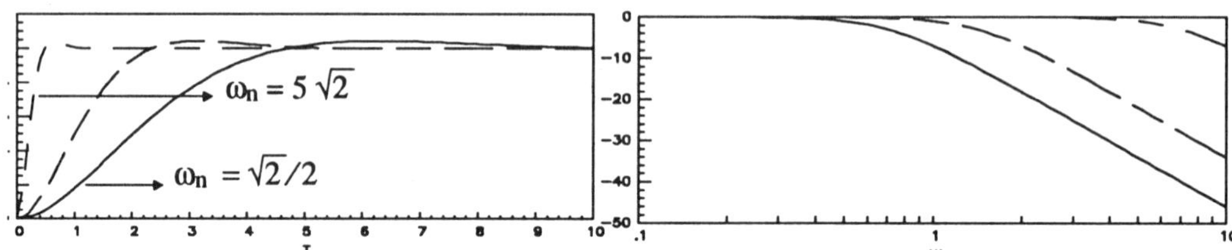

Figure 1-10 Step and magnitude responses for case III.

Case IV: Effects of ζ $\omega_n = \sqrt{2}$, $\theta = \{30, 45, 60 \text{ degrees}\}$

The poles are rotated along the perimeter of a circle of a fixed radius $\sqrt{2}$. Rise time is fixed, whereas overshoot and settling time increase and peak time decreases. The plots are shown in Figure 1-11.

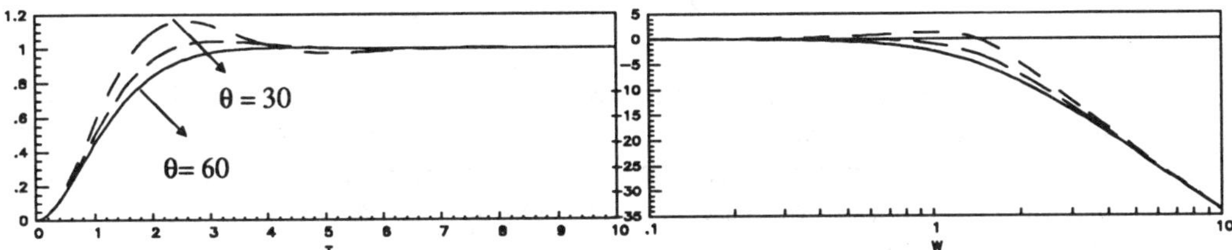

Figure 1-11 Step and magnitude responses for case IV.

1.5.3 Effects of Adding Poles and Zeros

The effects discussed earlier are limited to the case of second order systems in canonical form. It also holds for higher order systems with zeros as long as the system has a pair of dominant complex poles, i.e., all other poles and zeros are located deep in the LHP. Note that a system with RHP poles is unstable, and RHP zeros will cause spurious effects. What effect does a zero have on the second order step response? To determine this, we have plotted the step response of the following transfer function:

$$G(s) = \frac{zs+1}{s^2+s+1}$$

where values for z are $\{0.2624, 0.6122, 1.4286, 3.3333\}$. As you can see in Figure 1-12, as the zero approaches the origin (i.e., z approaches infinity), overshoot is increased dramatically, rise time and peak time decrease, and bandwidth and the resonant peak increase.

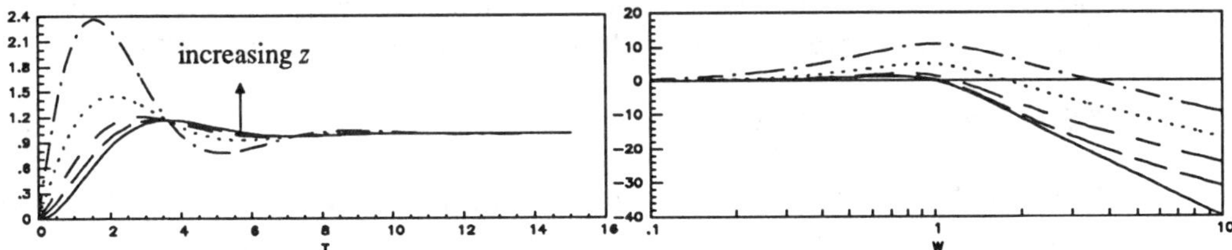

Figure 1-12 Step and magnitude response showing the effects of an added zero.

The effects of an added pole can be seen by examining

$$G(s) = \frac{1}{(ps+1)(s^2+s+1)}$$

The values of p are the same values as z earlier. As the pole approaches the origin, the real pole will dominate the response, and the system effectively behaves like a first order system. The overshoot decreases to zero, whereas rise time and peak time increase. The system bandwidth decreases, and the resonant peak disappears. These effects are shown in Figure 1-13.

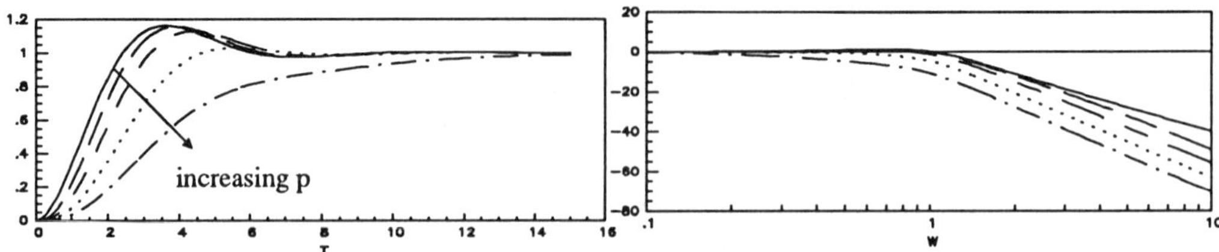

Figure 1-13 Step and magnitude response showing the effects of an added pole.

It is important for a control engineer to have a very good understanding of the effects of pole-zero locations in systems. A more extensive discussion of the effects of adding zeros and poles to transfer functions will be presented in Chapter 4 in Problem 4.2.

1.6 Feedback Control

Open loop systems only perform adequately if the model of the plant or process is very accurate, plant parameters change in a predetermined manner, and there are no external disturbances. Because these conditions are rarely met, most systems use feedback control. Feedback has many properties, some of which will be discussed in this section.

1.6.1 Feedback Properties

Simple feedback control systems are modeled in Figure 1-14. The controller is denoted by $K(s)$, and $G(s)$ denotes the plant. Models for actuators and other components in the forward path can be included in the plant model. The forward path transfer function, KG, is the *loop gain* (also called the *open loop transfer function* or *return ratio*). The system in general has several inputs.

r = reference input, which the system is desired to follow or track

d = disturbance inputs, known or unknown inputs that could be random or deterministic

Disturbances may represent actual physical disturbances acting on the system such as wind gusts disturbing aircrafts, disturbances owing to actuators such as motors, or uncertainties resulting from model errors in plant or actuator. Model uncertainties include neglected nonlinearities in plant or actuator, and neglected or unknown modes in the system.

n = sensor or measurement noise, which is introduced into the system via sensors that are usually random high frequency signals

A properly designed control system must track reference inputs with small error and reject disturbance and noise inputs. The contribution of general disturbances to the output must be small. The output of the closed loop system is

$$y(s) = \frac{K\,G(s)}{1+K\,G(s)}\,r(s) + \frac{1}{1+K\,G(s)}\,d(s) - \frac{K\,G(s)}{1+K\,G(s)}\,n(s)$$

If we define the tracking error as $e = r - y$, we get

$$e(s) = \frac{1}{1+K\,G(s)}\,r(s) - \frac{1}{1+K\,G(s)}\,d(s) + \frac{K\,G(s)}{1+K\,G(s)}\,n(s)$$

Finally, the actuator output (i.e., the plant input) is given by

$$u(s) = \frac{K}{1+K\,G(s)}\,(\,r(s) - d(s) - n(s)\,)$$

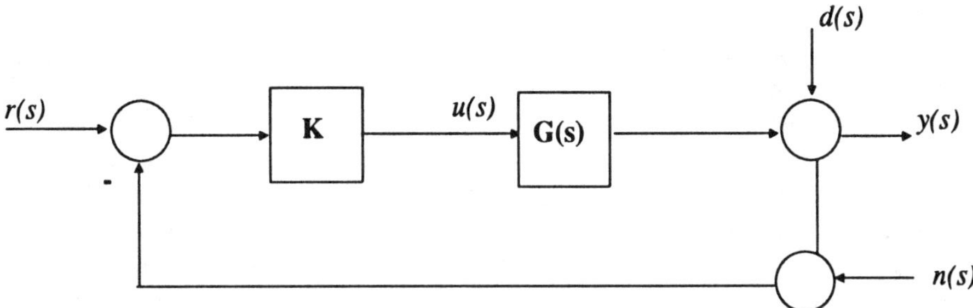

Figure 1-14 Block diagram of a feedback system containing disturbance and noise.

Several quantities appear frequently in the above relationships and are defined subsequently.

$$J(s) = 1 + K\,G(s) \qquad \textit{Return Difference}$$

$$S(s) = \frac{1}{1+K\,G(s)} = \frac{1}{J(s)} \qquad \textit{Sensitivity}$$

$$T(s) = \frac{K\,G(s)}{1 + K\,G(s)} \qquad \textit{Complementary Sensitivity}$$

It can be seen that for all frequencies

$$S(s) + T(s) = 1$$

To understand the concept of return difference, consider the block diagram in Figure 1-14. Break the loop at any point, and apply a unity input. At the output of the loop breaking point, we measure the returned signal as $-KG(s)$. The difference between the injected signal and the returned signal is the return difference, which is $1 - (-K\,G(s)) = 1 + KG(s)$. Bode introduced it as a quantitative measure of the amount of feedback.
Using the above notation, we can rewrite the output relationships as

$$y(s) = S(s)\,d(s) + T(s)\,[\,r(s) - n(s)]$$

$$e(s) = S(s)\,[\,r(s) - d(s)\,] + T(s)\,n(s)$$

$$u(s) = K\,S(s)\,[\,r(s) - d(s) - n(s)\,]$$

We are now ready to draw some general conclusions.

1. *Disturbance rejection*: The sensitivity must be small to reduce the effects of disturbances. This can be accomplished by keeping the loop gain large, i.e., $|KG(s)| >> 1$.

2. *Good tracking*: To keep e small, sensitivity must be small. Therefore, tracking and disturbance rejection are compatible specifications.

3. *Noise immunity*: For proper suppression of noise, we need to keep the complementary sensitivity small. Because S and T must add to unity, we conclude that noise immunity and the previous requirements are conflicting objectives.

4. *Bounded actuator signals*: All physical systems have limits on their inputs and outputs. Actuator outputs must be limited to avoid damage to the plant. Also, actuators can produce limited outputs (motors can produce a limited amount of torque, and amplifiers will saturate beyond certain limits). So generally, the signal $u(s)$ must be kept within certain specified limits. To keep the controller output within specified limits to prevent saturation problems, we need to limit $|K\,S(s)|$. If the loop gain is large, however, we get

$$K\,S(s) = \frac{K}{1 + K\,G(s)} \approx \frac{1}{G(s)}$$

Because most physical systems are strictly proper, their transfer functions roll off at high frequencies. This means that at high frequencies, $|G(s)|$ is small so the actuator signals can be large. Hence the gain at high frequencies must be adjusted to prevent saturation.

Typically we require the loop gain to be large at low frequencies to satisfy tracking requirements and rejection of low frequency disturbances. At high frequencies, the loop gain is kept low to suppress high frequency noise. Over the mid frequency range, the gain is shaped to satisfy stability margin requirements. The process of adjusting the loop gain to satisfy the above objectives is called *loop shaping.*

Sensitivity of the overall system to specific parameter changes can also be defined. This is called *differential sensitivity* and is defined by

$$S_x^y = \frac{\partial y/y}{\partial x/x} = \frac{x}{y}\frac{\partial y}{\partial x}$$

which is read as "the sensitivity of y with respect to x". This function measures the relative change in y owing to a relative change in x. For example, suppose we want to find the differential sensitivity of the closed loop system in Figure 1-14 with respect to changes in gain K.

The closed loop transfer function (same as complementary sensitivity defined earlier) and its sensitivity are given by

$$T(s) = \frac{K\,G(s)}{1 + K\,G(s)}$$

$$S_K^T = \frac{K}{T}\frac{\partial T}{\partial K} = \frac{1}{1 + K\,G} \quad \rightarrow 0 \;\text{ for }\; |K\,G| \text{ large}$$

Note that this quantity is the same as the sensitivity transfer function defined earlier. If K is located in the feedback path instead of the forward path, we get

$$S_K^T = \frac{K}{T}\frac{\partial T}{\partial K} = \frac{-K\,G}{1 + K\,G} \quad \rightarrow -1 \;\text{ for }\; |K\,G| \text{ large}$$

We conclude that feedback reduces the effects of parameter variations with respect to elements in the forward path. The overall system is still very sensitive to elements in the feedback path, however.

Another property of feedback is linearization. Given a nonlinear system, we can use feedback control to reduce the effects of nonlinearities within the system. If the nonlinearity is perfectly known, we can use a nonlinear controller to linearize the system and then use a linear controller to shape its response. This is called *feedback linearization*. Consider the example

$$\dot{x} = x^2 + x + u$$

using the following nonlinear controller

$$u = -x^2 + \bar{u}$$

we get a linear system

$$\dot{x} = x + \bar{u}$$

using the linear control law

$$\bar{u} = -kx \quad \rightarrow \quad \dot{x} = (1-k)x$$

we obtain a stable system for $k > 1$.

Feedback is also frequently used to stabilize unstable systems. You have to be aware, however, that feedback itself can destabilize otherwise stable systems. So use it with caution.

In summary, we emphasize that even though feedback has many other properties as well (modifies system gain, bandwidth, speed, etc.), the main reasons it is generally used are stabilization, disturbance rejection, and protection against model uncertainties.

1.6.2 Closed Loop Stability

We have already seen how the stability of a system depends on the location of the system's poles. The closed loop poles can be found using the computer. In parametric cases, in which the location of the closed loop poles depends on some parameter like K, we can use root locus (described later) to find all of them for all values of the parameter. The *Routh-Hurwitz* test is a technique for determining how many closed loop poles are located in the RHP. Although its use is outdated if control system computer programs are available, it is still an effective and easy method for hand calculations.

Routh-Hurwitz Stability Test

We demonstrate the Routh-Hurwitz technique with the following example

$$K\,G(s)\,H(s) = \frac{K}{s^4 + s^3 + 11\,s^2 + s + 0.5}$$

The characteristic equation is given by

$$s^4 + s^3 + 11\,s^2 + s + K + 0.5 = 0$$

The Routh array is

$$\begin{array}{c|lll} s^4 & 1 & 11 & K+0.5 \\ s^3 & 1 & 1 & \\ s^2 & 10 & K+0.5 & \\ s^1 & -K+9.5 & & \\ s^0 & K+0.5 & & \end{array}$$

The number of poles in the RHP is equal to the number of sign changes in the first column. For stability, there must be no sign changes. From row 4, $K < 9.5$, whereas from row 5, $K > -0.5$. Therefore, $-0.5 < K < 9.5$ would lead to a stable system. If $9.5 < K$, there would be two sign changes and, therefore, two poles in the RHP. If, conversely, $K<-0.5$, there would one sign change and one pole in the RHP. The Routh array occasionally leads to zeros in the first column or an all-zero row. Consult a control textbook in the references to see how to deal with these situations.

1.6.3 Steady State Error

In many control system designs, we are specifically interested in the final, or steady state, value of the output. This is known as steady state accuracy. Ideally, in the steady state, the output, $y(t)$, equals the command signal, $r(t)$, and the error is zero. This ideal situation is rarely met, and so we need to be able to determine the steady state error for any system. The steady state error is defined as

$$e_{ss} = \lim_{t \to \infty} e(t) = \lim_{t \to \infty} [r(t) - y(t)]$$

For unity feedback systems, and only for unity feedback systems, the error is the comparator output signal. For non-unity feedback systems, this is not the case. For unity feedback systems, we can determine the steady state error by examining the open loop transfer function $KG(s)$. For unity feedback, we can write

$$E(s) = R(s) - Y(s) = R(s) - G(s)E(s)$$

so

$$E(s) = \frac{1}{1 + G(s)} R(s)$$

The final value theorem tells us that (assuming closed loop stability)

$$e_{ss} = \lim_{s \to 0} sE(s) = \lim_{s \to 0} \frac{s}{1 + G(s)} R(s)$$

We are interested in the steady state error for step, ramp, parabolic, and higher order polynomial inputs, i.e.,

$$r(t) = \frac{t^n}{n!} \rightarrow R(s) = \frac{1}{s^{n+1}}, \quad n = 0, 1, 2, \ldots\ldots$$

Therefore

$$e_{ss} = \lim_{s \to 0} \frac{1}{s^n + s^n G(s)}$$

For a unit step input $(n = 0)$, $e_{ss} = \dfrac{1}{1 + G(0)}$

For higher order polynomial inputs, $e_{ss} = \lim\limits_{s \to 0} \dfrac{1}{s^n G(s)}$

The steady state error obviously depends on the structure of $G(s)$. For example, if $G(s)$ has no poles at the origin, then $G(0)$ is finite, which means that the step response error is finite, and all other response errors are infinite. We define the system *Type* as the order of the input polynomial that the closed loop system can track with finite error. If $G(s)$ has no poles at the origin, the closed loop system is Type 0 and can track a constant; one pole at the origin results in a Type 1 system that can track a ramp, two poles at the origin results in a Type 2 system that can track a parabola, etc.

Because we deal with many electromechanical systems, control engineers also define a position, velocity, and acceleration error constants as follows

$$K_p = G(0), \qquad K_v = \lim_{s \to 0} sG(s), \quad K_a = \lim_{s \to 0} s^2 G(s)$$

Table 1-1 shows the steady state errors for Type 0, 1, and 2 systems.

Table 1-1 Steady State Errors for Polynomial Inputs

System Type ⇒ Polynomial Degree ⇓	0	1	2
0	$\frac{1}{1+K_p}$	0	0
1	∞	$\frac{1}{K_v}$	0
2	∞	∞	$\frac{1}{K_a}$

System type and steady state errors can also be found directly from the closed loop transfer function. If the closed loop transfer function is given by

$$T(s) = \frac{b_m s^m + b_{m-1} s^{m-1} + \dots + b_1 s + b_0}{s^n + a_{n-1} s^{n-1} + \dots + a_1 s + a_0}$$

Then the steady state error to a unit step is given by

$$e_{ss} = \lim_{s \to 0} [1 - T(s)] = \left| \frac{a_0 - b_0}{a_0} \right|$$

For a Type 1 system, $e_{ss} = 0$, so $a_0 = b_0$. Likewise for a Type 2 system we can find the condition to be : $a_0 = b_0$ and $a_1 = b_1$.

1.7 Root Locus

Let us examine the effect of feedback on pole and zero location. We assume that $G(s) = N_1(s)/D_1(s)$ and $H(s) = N_2(s)/D_2(s)$ so that the closed loop transfer function can be written as (refer to Figure 1-15)

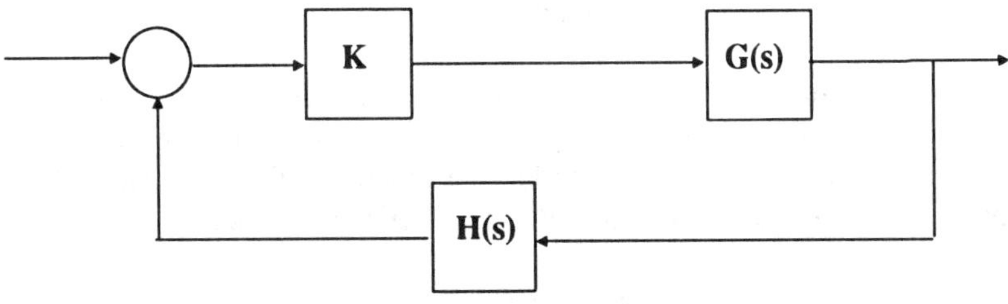

Figure 1-15 Block diagram of a feedback control system.

$$T(s) = \frac{KN_1(s)/D_1(s)}{1 + K [N_1(s)/D_1(s)] [N_2(s)/D_2(s)]}$$

or

$$T(s) = \frac{K N_1(s) D_2(s)}{D_1(s) D_2(s) + K N_1(s) N_2(s)}$$

The poles of the closed loop system, therefore, are found from

$$1 + K G(s) H(s) = D_1(s) D_2(s) + K N_1(s) N_2(s) = 0$$

We will be describing several techniques to find information about closed loop behavior given the open loop transfer function. The closed loop zeros are another matter. They are clearly the zeros of the plant and poles of the feedback transfer functions assuming there are no pole-zero cancellations.

The root locus is a plot of the poles of closed loop transfer function, $T(s)$, as any parameter, e.g., K, varies from 0 to ∞. The most straightforward method, used by many computer programs, is to simply vary K and use a polynomial root solver to find the poles. Techniques developed early in control analysis history, however, still give important insights into the design of closed loop systems. For this reason, we will describe some of them here.

The characteristic equation of $T(s)$ is

$$1 + K\,G(s)\,H(s) = 0 \quad \rightarrow \quad D_1(s)\,D_2(s) + K\,N_1(s)\,N_2(s) = 0$$

For K small, the right side yields

$$D_1(s)D_2(s) = 0$$

These solutions are the poles of $G(s)H(s)$. For K large, we get

$$KN_1(s)N_2(s) = 0$$

The solutions of which are the zeros of $G(s)H(s)$. Hence, we have our first rule. The root locus begins at the poles of $G(s)H(s)$ and ends at the zeros of $G(s)H(s)$. The obvious starting point, therefore, is the pole-zero plot of the loop gain $G(s)H(s)$. Most of the other rules can be derived if we first rearrange the characteristic equation as

$$KG(s)H(s) = -1$$

This implies that

$$|KGH| = 1 \quad \text{and} \quad \angle GH = \pm(2k+1)\pi$$

The properties in this equation are the basis of most stability studies. For a point, s^*, in the s-plane to be part of the root locus, the total angle from the poles and zeros of $G(s)H(s)$ to s^* must be $\pm(2k+1)\pi$. The gain K that corresponds to this point is found by $K = 1/|G(s^*)H(s^*)|$.

A partial listing of root locus rules sufficient for quick sketches is given subsequently for $0 < K < \infty$.

1. Loci start at poles and end at zeros of $G(s)H(s)$, where poles and zeros at infinity are also included.
2. Loci exist on the real axis only to the left of an odd number of poles and zeros.

3. Loci approach asymptotes with angles of $\frac{(2k+1)\pi}{(n-m)}$, where n is the number of finite poles, and m is the number of finite zeros of $G(s)H(s)$.
4. The asymptotes originate from a centroid on the real axis, σ, where

$$\sigma = \frac{\sum_i p_i - \sum_j z_j}{n-m}$$

As an example, the root locus of the open loop transfer function of the system shown below appears in Figure 1-16.

$$K\,G(s) = \frac{K}{s\,(s+1)\,(s+2)}$$

For $K > 6$, the root locus is in the RHP, indicating closed loop instability for these gains.

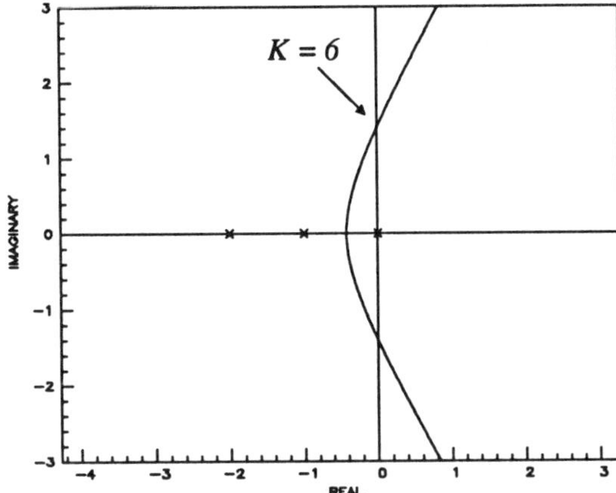

Figure 1-16 Root locus of $K\,G(s)$.

The changes in closed loop pole locations owing to changes in other system parameters can also be analyzed with the root locus technique. Consider a unity feedback system with a second order closed loop transfer function

$$T(s) = \frac{10}{s^2 + bs + 20}$$

We can rearrange $T(s)$ as

$$T(s) = \frac{10}{s^2 + 20 + bs} = \frac{10/(s^2 + 20)}{1 + bs/(s^2 + 20)}$$

We can now treat $bs/(s^2 + 20)$ as $KG(s)H(s)$ and plot the root locus with b as the gain parameter.

WARNING

It is important to note that the correct pole-zero plot that is used to construct the root locus is the pole-zero plot of the open loop transfer function (i.e., the loop gain) KGH and not the closed loop transfer function ($T= KG/(1+KGH)$). It has been observed many times that students learn the mechanics of root locus plotting, but do not quite understand the concept behind it and, hence, use the wrong transfer function. These types of conceptual errors may become accentuated when computer programs are used to plot root locus. An important aspect of classical control is to use the open loop transfer function to predict closed loop behavior.

1.7.1 Zero Degree Root Locus

There are instances in which we are interested in the closed loop poles as a parameter ranges over negative numbers. An equivalent situation is when we have positive feedback loops where the characteristic equation becomes

$$1 - KG(s)H(s) = 0$$

Rearranging this, we get

$$KG(s)\,H(s) = 1$$

Hence, the angle of GH becomes 0 or any multiple of 2π. This changes rules 2 and 3 and all other rules related to the angle criterion. Loci on the real axis now exist to the left of an even number of poles and zeros. Poles or zeros at positive infinity are now numbered as the zero position where zero is considered as an even number.

1.8 Frequency Response Analysis

Frequency response analysis has been at the heart of classical control. The fact that frequency response can be measured in the laboratory and used for analysis without relying on mathematical models (empirical models are frequently obtained from frequency response data) has been their traditional advantage. Time delays, ever present in process control applications, can also be easily handled by these techniques. Their graphical nature together with physical and intuitive appeal, their ability to predict closed loop response from open loop analysis, and many years of successful applications are the primary reasons frequency response techniques have survived and have now been generalized to handle multivariable systems.

1.8.1 Bode Plot

Bode plots have several uses. They are used to determine stability, relative stability, and for design purposes. Again, the warning about the use of root locus is in order here. We can obtain the Bode plot of any transfer function, but we distinguish between open loop and closed loop Bode plots. You have to know how to interpret each plot and use them correctly. The Bode plot of the open loop transfer function (i.e., KGH) can be used to determine relative stability margins of closed loop stable systems. For ease of use, it is necessary that the open loop system itself be stable and *minimum phase*. By minimum phase, it is meant that the system has no zeros in the RHP (some authors define it as no poles or zeros in the RHP). The Bode plot should not be used to determine closed loop stability for nonminimum phase systems. System Type can be determined by looking at the low frequency slope of the magnitude plot. For example, if the slope is -20 dB/dec, then the system is Type 1 (assuming unity feedback). Open loop Bode plots are also used for compensator design as described in Chapter 7. In fact, this is one of their main uses in control systems. Because gain and phase plots are additive, the effects of a compensator, H, can easily be determined. The Bode plots are shaped until desired specifications are met.

Bode plots of the closed loop transfer function ($T = KG/(1+KGH)$) can be used to determine the system bandwidth, which is a measure of both the filtering properties and speed of response of the system. The peak in the closed loop Bode plot is a reliable indicator of relative stability. The use of closed loop Bode plots in classical design has been very limited, however, because of the way H enters the equation.

The open and closed loop Bode plots provide complementary information provided they are interpreted correctly.

1.8.2 Nyquist Plot and Stability Criterion

The Nyquist plot provides a powerful tool for determining the stability of systems. It is the plot of imaginary versus the real part (or a polar plot of magnitude and phase) of the *open loop transfer function*. However, the derivation of this technique is quite involved. We will present a brief review here.

Consider the gain $D(s)$. Without proof, we state the following

$$Z_D = P_D + \vec{N}$$

where $\vec{N}$ is the number of *clockwise* encirclements of the origin, P_D is the number of poles of $D(s)$ in the RHP, and Z_D is the number of zeros of $D(s)$ in the RHP. For a counterclockwise traversal of the origin, $\vec{N}$ is negative. You should be aware that some authors reverse this definition. Note that poles and zeros of $D(s)$ that are in the LHP, or on the $j\omega$ axis, do not affect the above equation.

Now, reconsider the closed loop transfer function (with $K = 1$)

$$T(s) = \frac{G(s)}{1 + G(s)\,H(s)}$$

Define the denominator of $T(s)$ as

$$T(s) = \frac{G(s)}{D(s)} \qquad \text{so} \qquad D(s) = 1 + G(s)\,H(s)$$

The poles of $T(s)$ are equal to the zeros of $D(s)$. We can now use the Nyquist plot of $D(s)$ and the previously stated result to find the zeros of $D(s)$. Note that the poles of $G(s)H(s)$ are the same as the poles of $D(s)$. We can now rewrite our result as

$$P_T = P_{GH} + \vec{N}$$

Rather than examine $D(s)$, we can examine $G(s)\,H(s) = D(s) - 1$. The point of interest is shifted from the origin to the (-1, 0) point. We draw the Nyquist plot of $G(s)H(s)$ and count the number of clockwise encirclements of the (-1, 0) point. The number of poles of $T(s)$ in the RHP is equal to the number of encirclements plus the number of RHP poles of $G(s)H(s)$. We remind you that N is positive for a clockwise traversal and negative for a counterclockwise traversal.

Figure 1-2 shows the Nyquist plot for our example transfer function

$$K\,G(s) = \frac{1}{s\,(s+1)\,(s+2)}\ , \quad K = 1$$

For this system, there are no open loop RHP poles, so that any encirclement of (-1, 0) indicates an unstable closed loop system. As you can see, for $K=1$ there is no encirclement of (-1, 0) so the closed loop system is stable.

1.8.3 Gain and Phase Margins

Because of model uncertainties, it is not merely sufficient for a system to be stable, but rather it must have adequate stability margins. Stable systems with low stability margins only work on paper, and when implemented in real time, they are frequently unstable. The way uncertainty has been quantified in classical control is to assume that either gain changes or phase changes occur. Typically systems are destabilized when their gain exceeds certain limits or if there is too much phase lag (i.e., negative phase associated with unmodeled poles or time delays). These tolerances of gain or phase uncertainty are called gain and phase margin.

Suppose a system is stable for $K < K_{max}$, then *gain margin* (GM, or more properly *upper* GM) is defined as

$$GM|_{dB} = 20 \log \frac{K_{max}}{K}$$

In some cases, such as systems that are open loop unstable, the system may become destabilized for low gain, so for stability we may have $K > K_{min}$. We can likewise define a *lower gain margin* (or *gain reduction margin* [GRM]) as

$$GRM|_{dB} = 20 \log \frac{K_{min}}{K}$$

Note that according to our definition, GM is positive, and GRM is negative for stability. GM is the factor by which the gain can be increased before the onset of instability. Note that these measures can be computed using the Routh-Hurwitz test or from the root locus. They can also be measured from open loop Bode and Nyquist plots as shown for our example plant in Figures 1-17 and 1-18. The GM can be read off the Bode plot by measuring the distance to unity gain (i.e., 0 dB) when the phase is -180 degrees. The frequency where the phase is -180 degrees is called the *phase crossover frequency* and denoted by ω_{pc}.

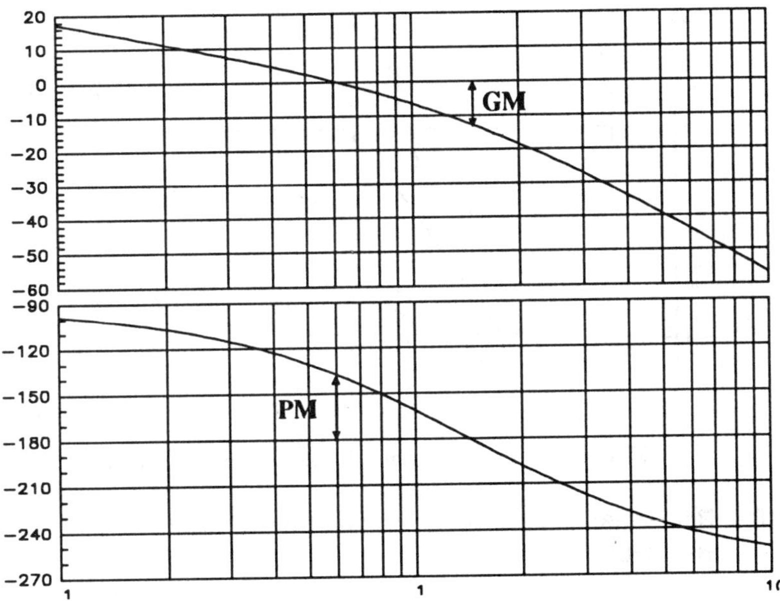

Figure 1-17 Bode plots showing gain and phase margins.

Phase margin is defined as the minimum amount of phase lag that can be added to the system to destabilize it. This happens when

$$1 + KG(s)H(s) = 0\ , \text{ or } \ KG(s)H(s) = -1$$

$$\text{i.e., } |KG(j\omega)H(j\omega)| = 1 \quad \text{and} \quad \angle KG(j\omega)H(j\omega) = \pm\pi$$

The angular distance to $-\pi$ when the magnitude is unity is the phase margin, i.e.,

$$PM = \pi + \angle KG(j\omega_{gc})H(j\omega_{gc}) \quad \text{when} \quad |KG(j\omega_{gc})H(j\omega_{gc})| = 1$$

where ω_{gc} is the *gain crossover frequency*. This is where the magnitude of the loop gain is unity. On the Bode plot, we can determine the phase margin at the frequency where the gain crosses the 0 dB line. On a Nyquist plot (Figure 1-18), we look at the point where the plot intersects the unit circle.

For a stable minimum phase system, the system is closed loop stable if the gain is below the 0 dB line (i.e., GM > 0), and the phase is above the -180 degree line (i.e., PM > 0).

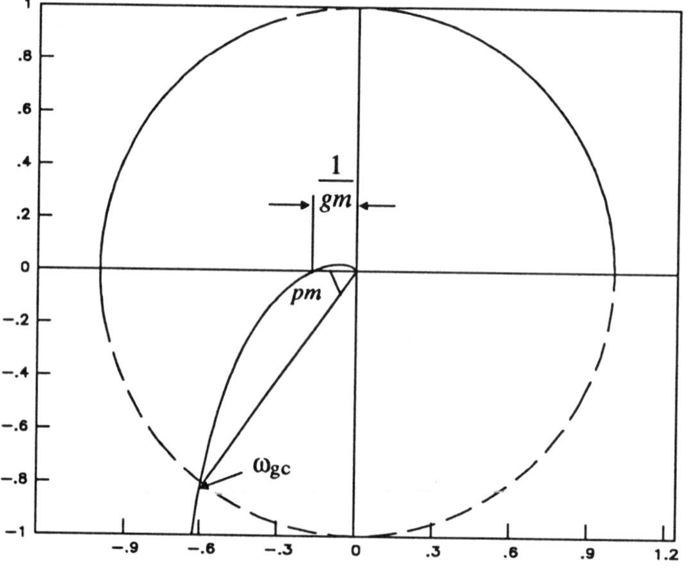

Figure 1-18 Nyquist plot showing gain and phase margins.

1.8.4 Relationship between Open and Closed Loop Behavior

Unless otherwise noted, we assume that $H(s) = 1$, i.e., unity feedback. For the first order case, $KG(s) = Ka/(s + a)$. The open loop Bode magnitude plot is shown in Figure 1-3. We already know that the open loop bandwidth is a; the open loop gain is K. We define a *gain-bandwidth product* for this system

$$GBW = Ka$$

The closed loop transfer function for this system is

$$T(s) = \frac{KG(s)}{1 + KG(s)} = \frac{Ka}{s + a\,(1 + K)}$$

The closed loop gain is $K/(1 + K)$, and the closed loop bandwidth is $a(1 + K)$. We can see that the closed loop gain is lower than the open loop gain, and the closed loop bandwidth is greater than the open loop bandwidth. Because of the increased bandwidth, the closed loop system is faster than the open loop system (closed loop $\tau = 1/a(1 + K)$. The closed loop gain-bandwidth product is still Ka! In fact, for first order systems, the gain-bandwidth product is a constant.

What can we tell about the closed loop system from the open loop plot of Figure 1-3? To find out, let us solve for the gain crossover frequency, $\omega_{gc} = a\,K$. Comparing this answer to the closed loop bandwidth of $a(1 + K)$, we see that for large K, $\omega_{gc} \approx BW_{CL}$.

We now assume that

$$K\,G(s) = \frac{K\,\omega_n^2}{s^2 + 2\,\zeta\,\omega_n\,s + \omega_n^2}$$

The open loop Bode magnitude plot for $K = 1$ is shown in Figure 1-5. If we assume that $BW \approx \omega_n$, then the open loop gain bandwidth product for this system is

$$GBW = K\omega_n$$

The closed loop transfer function is

$$T(s) = \frac{K\,\omega_n^2}{s^2 + 2\,\zeta\,\omega_n\,s + (K + 1)\,\omega_n^2} = \frac{K\,\omega_n^2}{s^2 + 2\,\zeta_{CL}\,\omega_{n_{CL}}\,s + \omega_{n_{CL}}^2}$$

Therefore, the closed loop natural frequency, damping ratio, and gain-bandwidth product are given by

$$\omega_{n_{CL}} = \omega_n\sqrt{K + 1}\,, \qquad \zeta_{CL} = \frac{\zeta}{\sqrt{K + 1}}\,, \qquad GBW_{CL} \approx \frac{\omega_n\,K}{\sqrt{K + 1}}$$

Note that the gain bandwidth product is not constant for a second order system. We can still make the general statement, however, that as the gain is decreased, the bandwidth is increased. Also, the gain crossover frequency ($\omega_{gc} \approx \omega_n \sqrt{K}$ for K large) still gives an accurate measure of the closed loop bandwidth.

The damping ratio of the closed loop system is approximately $1/\sqrt{K}$ of the open loop damping ratio. The closed loop system will therefore be faster and have greater overshoot than the open loop system. Can the closed loop damping ratio (ζ_{CL}) be predicted from the open loop frequency response? From the definition of phase margin in the Nyquist plot, using simple geometry, we obtain

$$PM = 2 \sin^{-1} \frac{1}{2\,|T(j\omega_{gc})|}$$

Because $\omega_{gc} \approx \omega_n \sqrt{K}$, then

$$PM \approx 2 \sin^{-1}(\zeta_{CL}) \quad \text{or} \quad \zeta_{CL} \approx \sin\left(\frac{PM}{2}\right)$$

Some authors [FPE91] use the following approximation:

$$\zeta_{CL} \approx .01\, PM \text{ (degrees)}$$

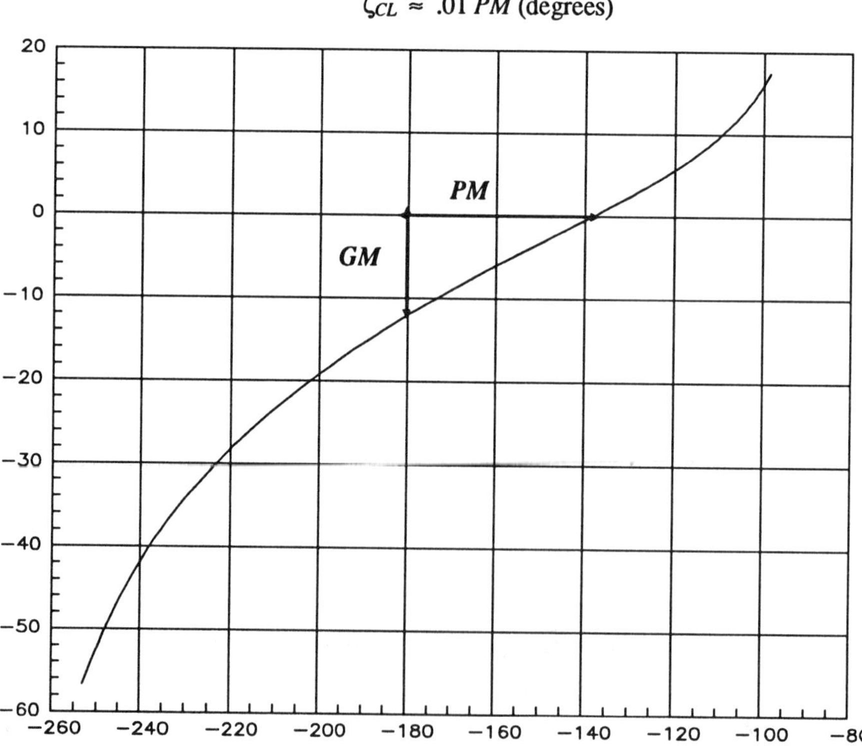

Figure 1-19 Nichols plot showing gain and phase margins.

If we are just interested in stability, rather than compensator design, the *Nichols plot* is very convenient (see Figure 1-19). As you can see, the 180 degree point, the gain margin, and phase margin are quite clear. Neither ω_{gc} nor ω_{pc} are obvious, however. The Nichols plot is actually more sophisticated than shown in this figure and can be used to determine closed loop behavior. Consult the references for more details on the use of the Nichols plot.

Remember, neither the Bode nor Nichols plots should be used to determine stability if the system is nonminimum phase. In this case, use either the root locus or Nyquist plot.

1.9 Computer-aided Control System Design

Engineers and physicists have been using mechanical and electrical aids for the analysis and design of systems since William Thompson (Lord Kelvin) invented a mechanical integrating device (a primitive analog computer) in 1876 that could be used to solve ordinary differential equations. The mechanical analog computer was greatly improved during World War I and was successfully applied to naval gunfire control systems. The electronic differential amplifier was invented in the early part of the twentieth century; was improved during World War II; and led to the development of the operational amplifier in 1947. The operational amplifier made possible the development of electronic circuits that would add, subtract, multiply, and integrate. Thus was born the electronic analog computer, which can be used for the simulation of a vast class of systems.

With the introduction of digital computers and languages such as FORTRAN and BASIC, the engineer was able to write numerical routines to simulate integration. One could, therefore, model and simulate dynamic systems. The earliest prewritten, or canned, programs such as CSMP were based on these techniques. Additional programs increased the efficiency of the control engineer, which led to the tackling of ever-more complex systems using more sophisticated techniques.

As systems grew in complexity from single-input single-output to multi-input multi-output systems, the classical techniques became cumbersome, or even impossible, to use. In the 1960s, control engineers turned to linear algebra techniques of state space modeling for these systems. The matrix-based mathematics of state space analysis and design drove the need for more sophisticated computer analysis. Fortunately, the numerical analysis community had been busy. Packages such as LINPACK and EISPACK were made commonly available. It was still left to the mathematician or engineer, however, to write the main body of the analysis program, while making subroutine calls to LINPACK or EISPACK.

To relieve some of this burden, C. B. Moler of the University of New Mexico wrote an interactive program called MATLAB that provided easy access to the routines of LINPACK and EISPACK. The introduction of MATLAB was a phenomenal success, as it revolutionized computer-aided analysis and design of control systems. Although MATLAB provided an easy-to-use environment for mathematics, specially matrix-based mathematics, it still lacked the additional algorithms needed for control system analysis and design. Soon after its introduction, many companies developed commercially available software for control systems based on the MATLAB environment, for example, MATRIXx (by Integrated Systems, Inc.), MATLAB (by The Mathworks, Inc.), and Ctrl-C (by Systems Control Technology). All of the preceding programs provide easy access to control, signal processing, and mathematics algorithms.

Programs based on the MATLAB environment can be considered as sophisticated matrix calculators with specialized toolboxes or modules for control systems. There are also other programs available, not based on MATLAB, that are more specialized. Program CC (by Systems Technology Inc.) and EASY5 (by Boeing Computer Services) are control systems programs. SIMNON (by Lund Institute of Technology), a differential equation calculator (according to its manual), is suited more for simulation of linear and nonlinear systems. ACSL (by Mitchell & Gauthier Associates, MGA) and CSMP are among other simulation programs. There are many other programs, and we refer the reader to [JH85], [F91].

Further progress in computer hardware and software, along with recent developments in control theory, are bringing in new tools. For instance, new generations of EISPACK and LINPACK are being made available that take advantage of parallel processing capabilities of computers. Object Oriented Programming (OOP) has been incorporated into Xmath (next generation of MATRIXx). New data types are also being introduced into MATLAB for expert system development (see [P91]) and μ-synthesis (see [CS 91] and [BPDGS 91]).

In the following chapters, we will describe the operations and uses of MATRIXx. A companion volume describes MATLAB.

1.10 Problems

1.1 Consider a system represented by the following differential equation.

$\ddot{y} + \dot{y} - 2y = \dot{u} - u \qquad \text{with} \qquad y(0^-) = a \;,\; \dot{y}(0^-) = b \;,\; u(0^-) = c$

a. Find the characteristic equation and the system modes. Determine asymptotic stability.

b. Find the system transfer function and its poles. Determine BIBO stability.

c. Find the zero-input response (ZIR).

d. Find the zero-state response (ZSR).

e. Determine for what set of initial conditions the ZIR approaches zero. Conclude that for all other initial conditions, the ZIR goes to infinity.

f. Explain the specific feature of this system that has resulted in conflicting answers relating to stability.

1.2 Find and sketch the impulse and step responses of the following transfer functions.

a. $G_1(s) = \dfrac{1000}{5s + 20}$

b. $G_2(s) = sG_1(s)$, compare to part a

c. $G_3(s) = \frac{1}{s}G_1(s)$, compare to part a

d. $G_4(s) = \frac{100}{s^2 + 20s + 100}$

e. $G_5(s) = \frac{100}{s^2 + 4s + 100}$

f. $G_6(s) = (s+5)G_5(s)$

g. $G_7(s) = (s^2 + .2s + 100)G_4(s)$

1.3 Consider the system, $G(s)$, and a cascade compensator, $K(s)$, in unity feedback

$$G(s) = \frac{1}{s+2}, \qquad K(s) = k\,\frac{s+a}{s}$$

a. Discuss the effects of $K(s)$ on the steady state error properties of the system.

b. Consider three range values for a: $a < 0$, $0 < a < 2$, and $a > 2$. Draw the root locus for each range and decide which ones are stabilizing.

c. Which range gives the fastest settling time? Why?

1.4 Consider the following transfer functions (assume unity feedback):

$$G_1(s) = \frac{1}{s}, \quad G_2(s) = \frac{1}{s(s+1)}, \quad G_3(s) = \frac{1}{s(s+1)(s+5)}$$

$$G_4(s) = \frac{1}{s^3}, \quad G_5(s) = \frac{s+1}{s^3}, \quad G_6(s) = \frac{(s+1)(s+5)}{s^3}$$

Note that in the first set of transfer functions (G_1, G_2, G_3), poles are added to G_1, whereas in the second set, zeros are added to G_4.

a. Obtain the root locus in each case.

b. How does adding poles affect the shape of the root locus and stability?

c. Same question as in part b, but now comment on the effects of adding zeros.

1.5 Repeat the preceding problem using Bode plots. Obtain gain and phase margins in each case, and comment on how adding poles and zeros affect the margins.

1.6 In this problem, you will compare the differences between cascade and feedback compensation. Consider the plant $G(s)$ and compensator $K(s)$

$$G(s) = \frac{4}{s(s+2)}, \qquad K(s) = \frac{s+1}{s}$$

a. Show that if $K(s)$ is in series with $G(s)$, with unity feedback, the system will be stable and can track step and ramp inputs with zero error. Find the closed loop zeros.

b. Show that if $K(s)$ is placed in the feedback path, these properties are lost, even though both systems have the same closed loop poles. Find the closed loop zeros, and compare with part a.

c. Show that we can recover the tracking properties of part a using feedback compensation, by placing an additional compensator outside the loop. Find this compensator and call it $K_f(s)$.

d. Suppose during implementation, or due to component tolerances, we instead use

$$K_2(s) = \frac{s+0.5}{s}$$

Repeat part a with this incorrect compensator. Are the tracking properties lost?

e. Repeat part b with the incorrect compensator.

f. Use the same $K_f(s)$ as in part c, show that you lose the tracking properties of part c.

1.7 Consider the following plant, $G(s)$, and compensator, $K(s)$. Assume the plant and compensator are in series with unity feedback around them.

$$G(s) = \frac{1}{s^2} \quad , \quad K(s) = K_c \frac{s+a}{s+b} \quad \text{and} \quad a > 0\,, b > 0\,, K_c > 0$$

a. Use the Routh-Hurwitz test to determine for what values of a and b the system will be stabilized.

b. Verify your answer in part a using root locus with K_c as the root locus parameter.

c. Set b = 5 and K_c = 1. Obtain the root locus with a as the root locus parameter. Confirm the conclusion in part a by determining for what values of a the system will be stable.

d. Draw the Nyquist plot for value of K_c in part b, and show that the system is stable. Also find the gain crossover frequency, gain margin and phase margin.

1.8 Consider the plant $KG(s)$ in unity feedback

$$KG(s) = \frac{K(s+0.8)}{s(s-1)}$$

a. Find the stabilizing value of K.

b. Find value of K for a critically damped response.

c. Using the value of K in part b, find the steady state errors to unit step and ramp inputs.

1.9 The purpose of this exercise is to show how closed loop bandwidth and gain crossover frequency can be estimated by the location of dominant closed loop poles. Consider the plant, $KG(s)$, in unity feedback

$$KG(s) = \frac{K}{s(s+1)}$$

a. Find exact analytical formulas for ω_n , ω_d , BW , ω_{gc} , T_p.

b. Using your formulas, what are the effects of increasing K on the system?

c. Compute the above quantities for $K = 1, 10$.

d. Determine how well BW and ω_{gc} are approximated by ω_d and ω_n.

1.10 Consider a plant containing time delay in unity feedback, i.e.,

$$K\,G(s) = \frac{K\,e^{-Ts}}{s+1}$$

Analytically find the gaincrossover frequency of the system, and determine for what value of T = time delay, the system becomes unstable for a given gain.

1.11 The open loop transfer function of a system is given by

$$K\,G(s) = \frac{K}{(s+2)^2\,(s+3)}$$

Find an acceptable range of values for K to simultaneously satisfy the following specifications.

$K_p \geq 2$ and $GM \geq 20 \log_{10} 3$ dB

1.12 Consider the following plant in unity feedback

$$G(s) = \frac{1}{(s-1)^2}$$

The specifications are closed loop stability and zero steady state error to unit step input. Discuss in each case, using root locus, whether both specifications can be met by a cascade compensator. Give full explanations. If any of the compensators work, you must specify for what range of values the specifications are met. Remember that the system must be stabilized first before you consider steady state errors.

a. Proportional control: $K(s) = k$

b. PI : $K(s) = a + (b / s)$

c. PD : $K(s) = a + b\,s$

d. Lead : $K(s) = (s + a) / (s + b)$, $a < b$

e. Lag : $K(s) = (s + a) / (s + b)$, $a > b$

f. PID : $K(s) = a + (b / s) + c\,s$

g. Suppose, in addition, all closed loop poles are to be placed at $s = -1$. Determine the compensator parameters to achieve this. Also, plot the root locus and step response for the compensated system for this case.

1.13 The system $G(s)$ in unity feedback is

$$G(s) = \frac{1}{s^2+1}$$

a. Draw the root locus and discuss the system's stability.

b. Suppose we try to compensate the system using $K(s) = k\dfrac{s+a}{s+b}$

Using root locus or the Routh Hurwitz test, determine for what values of a and b the system is stable.

c. Let $a = 1, b = 5$, find k to get less than 10% steady state error to a unit step input.

d. Discuss the effects of increasing k on the following system characteristics:

i. Relative stability measured by the distance of the closest pole to the $j\omega$ axis

ii. Per cent overshoot.

iii. Sensitivity with respect to modelling errors.

iv. Steady state errors.

v. Frequency of oscillation in the transient step response.

vi. Settling time.

In each case, give adequate reasons for your answer.

1.14 Consider the following plant, $G(s)$, and assume unity feedback.

$$G(s) = \frac{1}{s\,(s+1)}$$

It is desired to track unit ramp inputs with a maximum steady state error of 10%. This must be achieved while maintaining an overshoot of less than 20%.

a. Suppose an amplifier with gain K is placed in series with the plant. Determine the value of K that meets the tracking requirement. Find the closed loop transfer function and estimate the resulting overshoot. Is the design satisfactory? Explain.

b. Suppose a compensator of the form $K(s) = (s+a)/(s+b)$ is proposed. This compensator will be placed in series with the plant. Determine the ratio a/b that meets the tracking requirement.

c. Set $a = 0.1$ and find value of b (this is called a *lag* compensator). Find the closed loop transfer function; plot the root locus; find the closed loop poles; and estimate the resulting overshoot. Is this design satisfactory? Explain.

d. Compare the design in part a with part c. Compare other step response characteristics such as settling time and peak time.

1.15 This problem will take you through the steps for lead compensation using root locus. Consider the plant, $G(s)$, and the following specifications

$G(s) = \dfrac{1}{s^2}$ specifications: $T_s \le 4$ sec and POS $\le 20\%$

a. Show that if the dominant closed loop poles of the system are at $s^* = -1 \pm j\,2$, the system will meet the specifications.

b. Find the angle of $G(s)$ at s^*.

c. Suppose a compensator of the form $K(s) = K_c\,(s+a)/(s+b)$ is placed in series with the plant in a unity feedback configuration. Compute the angle of $K(s)$ such that the root locus of $K(s)G(s)$ passes through the point s^*.

d. Set $b = 3$. Find the value of a such that $K(s)$ will have the angle obtained in part c.

e. Determine the value of K_c for the compensated system at the point s^*.

f. Find the closed loop transfer function, closed loop poles, and determine if the specifications are met. If the specifications are not met, explain why.

Notes and References

The recent survey by A. Feliachi [F91] reports the following as the most frequently used textbooks (in frequency of usage) in a first course in automatic control (we are listing the latest editions): [Do89], [K91], [O90], [PH88], [HSS88], [FPE91], [M84], [DH88], [SM67], [H88]. For further study, we refer the reader to any of the above texts. See the Bibliography for more details.

2

Introduction to MATRIXx

MATRIXx is a sophisticated simulation environment that can be used to model dynamic systems. It handles continuous, discrete, linear, or nonlinear systems. As the name implies, it has extensive features for matrix manipulations. It is broken into several modules that we will refer to as MATRIXx Core, Control, and System Build. Other modules such as Optimization and Robust Control plus other products are available, but the emphasis of this textbook is on the Core, Control, and System Build. The Core module contains the core MATLAB commands (refer to Section 1.9) with some modifications and extensions, and signal processing commands. The Control module contains classical and modern control commands. The System Build module is menu driven (or mouse driven) and allows the user to simulate systems by building on the screen the block diagram of the system. It is the Build package that allows insertion of nonlinear and other elements to perform realistic simulations.

The MATRIXx Core and Control modules are command driven, and you have to know the various commands available. Because on-line help is available and the syntax structure of most commands are very similar, there is no need to memorize the commands. You will learn them very quickly as you use the program. In this chapter, we will introduce most of the MATRIXx Core commands.

The MATRIXx prompt is < > and the command you enter is shown in `COURIER` font after the prompt.

2.1 On-screen Help

You can get on-screen information about MATRIXx commands with `what` and `help`. Typing

```
< > what
```

produces a listing of all MATRIXx commands (includes commands related to all modules available on your version of the program), as shown subsequently. The commands in this list are grouped by function.

Mathematical operations ...

+ - * / \($) .* ./ .*. ./. .** '

Mathematical functions ...

ABS ACOS ACOSH ASIN ASINH ATAN ATAN2
ATANH CONDITION CONJG CONVOLVE COS COSH COT
COTH CSC CSCH DET DIAGONAL EXP EYE
HILBERT IMAGINARY INV KRONECKER LOG LOG10 MAX
MIN MOD NORM ONES PINV POLY POLYVAL
PRODUCT RANDOM RANK RAT RCOND REAL ROOTS
ROUND SEC SECH SIN SINH SIZE SORT
SORTVALUE SPLINE SQRT SUM TAN TANH TRIL
TRIU

Matrix decomposition functions ...

CHOLESKY EIG HESSENBERG LU ORTH PVA QR
QZ RREF SCHUR SVD

Linear system interconnection functions ...

AFEEDBACK APPEND CONNECT CONVOLVE FEEDBACK PARALLEL SERIES

Frequency response functions ...

BODE DBODE DNICHOLS DNYQUIST DPSD NICHOLS NYQUIST
PSD PVAFREQ

Time response functions ...

DINITIAL DLSIM DSTEP FILP IMPULSE INITIAL LSIM
PULSE STEP TIMR

Control design functions...

ALTFREQ CLSYS DESTIMATOR DISCRETIZ DLINFNORM DLYAPUNOV
DPERFPLOTS DREGULATOR DRLOCUS DRMS DSMARGIN DSVPLOT
DWCBODE ESTIMATOR FREQ FSESTI FSLQGCOMP FSREGU HINF_CONTR
INTEXT LINFNORM LININT LQELTR LQGCOMP LQRLTR LYAPUNOV
MARGIN MIN_DIST OPT_SCALE OPT_SUBG OS_SCALE PERFPLOTS
PF_SCALE POLEPLACE REGULATOR RESIDUES RICCATI RLOCUS RMS
SINGRICCAT SMARGIN SPLIT SPLIT4 SPLIT9 SSV SVPLOT WCBODE
WCGAIN ZEROS

Model reduction functions ...

BALANCE CNTRLABLE DBALANCE DMREDUCE MINIMAL MODAL
MREDUCE OBSERVABL STAIR

System identification functions ...

AML MAXLIKE MSD RLS RML RPEM

Signal processing functions ...

CORRELATE DETREND FFIR FFT FIIR FILP FWIN

HISTOGRAM IFFT SPECTRUM SPLINE

Optimization functions ...

LPOPT OPTIMIZE QPOPT

System build functions ...

LIN SIM SIMIN SIMOUT TRIM

Programming functions ...

CHK_VAR EXECUTE EXIST GET_INFO INDEX MENU USER

Display functions ...

BASE CHARACTER CLOCK DIARY DISPLAY LINES PLOT STRING

Miscellaneous functions ...

CHOP OSCMD SFORM SIZ_LIMIT TFORM

Programming commands ...

DEBUG DEFINE EDIT ELSE ELSEIF END EXIT

FOR IF INQUIRE PAUSE RETF RETURN WHILE

Display commands ...

DOTDOT ERASE LONG PRINT SEMI SHORT

Miscellaneous commands ...

BRIEF BUILD CHDIR CLEAR DEMO DIM DIR EDTSAV EXIT
FSAVE HELP KEEP LOAD SAVE

SYNTAX WHAT WHO

Typing

```
< > help
```

also produces a list of all available commands. This list, however, is arranged alphabetically. Information about a specific command is obtained by typing

```
< > help "function name"
```

For example, note the result of typing

```
< > help impulse
```

IMPULSE

Purpose: Compute the impulse response of a linear continuous time system.

Syntax: < T,Y > = IMPULSE(S,NS,TMAX,NPTS)

—or—

< T,Y > = IMPULSE(NUM,DEN,TMAX,NPTS)

Inputs: S - System matrix.

NS - Number of states in S.

TMAX - Maximum time for response to be calculated.

NPTS - Number of points to be calculated in response (default: 100).
NUM - Vector of numerator coefficients of transfer function in order of descending power.
DEN - Vector of denominator coefficients 73 of transfer function in order of descending power.

Outputs: T - Time vector for calculated responses.
Y - Matrix of impulse responses at T.

Remarks: Y contains p*q (number-of-outputs * number-of-inputs) columns. The first q columns are the response of the first output to each of the q inputs, the second q columns are the response of the second output to each of the q inputs, etc.

Related topics: TIMR, PULSE

The general syntax of MATRIXx commands is the following:

[output1, output2, ...] = command name (input1, input2, ...)

where the command outputs are enclosed within square brackets and inputs within parantheses. If there is only one output, brackets are optional.

To obtain brief information about a command or to recall simply the syntax of a command, use the *brief* or *syntax* commands (available in Version 7.1 and above). For example, try

```
< > brief impulse
< > syntax impulse
```

2.2 File Management

To create a record of all **inputs and outputs** in a MATRIXx session and save it under a given name in **ASCII format**, use the *diary* command below. Note that this command does not save your data, just what you type and what you see on screen. It is used for report generation and writing programs. **It is recommended that you use it at the start of every session to keep track of your work.** To save your session record, you should close the diary. For different diaries, use different names, otherwise you will write over the previous one.

```
< > diary('a:\filename')
```

Opens a diary with a given name directed to drive " a ". To write to a different drive or subdirectory, include the path. When you are done, you should close the diary using

```
< > diary(0)                 // close the diary
```

To create a record of your **inputs** only, use diary with option " 1 ". This option is used to create MATRIXx executable programs (see Chapter 3). It has to be closed with an option " 1 " as shown below.

```
< > diary('a:\filename,1) // open executable diary in the "a" drive
< > diary(0,1)                       // close executable diary
```

The double slash (//) shown above allows you to add comments to your programs. To enter comment lines, type

```
< > //  (everything to its right on that line is ignored and not executed)
```

```
< > save 'a:\filename'
< > fsave 'a:\filename'
```

Saves the data stack (including System Build block diagrams) to a file with a given name in MATRIXx format in drive " a ". Note that this saves the data stack (variables you have defined or results of operations), while *diary* saves inputs and outputs records only and not the actual data. You can also perform partial save, i.e., save some of the data. For example,

```
< > save 'a:\filename'  x y z       (save variables x, y, and z to file)
< > save 'a:\filename' x*
< > save 'a:\filename' x%
```

Note the use of *wildcards* (*, %), where * stands for any **set of characters** and % stands for any **single character**. For example, using x* will save variables such as x1, x2, xbar, xmin, etc. Saving x% saves all variables with names that start with " x " and end with any singlecharacter such as x1, x2, xa, xy, etc.

The data saved using the *save* command is not readable by other programs or machines, or even different versions of MATRIXx. You can save your data, however, in formatted files that can be read across machines or by other programs using the *fsave* command. The only cost is that file sizes are larger using this command. The file will include a list of the variables, their dimensions, type, and the actual data stored in E25.17 format.

```
< > print 'a:\filename'  a b c
```

saves data vectors or matrices (a, b, c, etc.) in the given file in the same format (ASCII) you see on screen. This can be imported into other programs for further processing or plotting.

```
< > load 'a:\filename'
```

loads a data file with a given name from drive " a ". You can also load partial data in a file by specifying the variables you want as in the *save* command.

```
< > clear  a b c
< > clear  *
```

The first command will clear specified variables (a, b, c) from the data stack. The second command will clear the entire data stack. You have to use this with caution or you will lose all your data. The use of wildcards is allowed as in the *save* command.

```
< > keep a b c
```

This command is the opposite of clear. It will clear everything except the listed variables.

There are two ways to correct data entry mistakes. If you have not yet hit the RETURN (ENTER or ↵) key, use the BACKSPACE (←) key. More generally (in Version 7.1 and above), you can use the *multiline buffer* to correct errors in lines above (below) your present line. Simply press the UP or DOWN ARROW (↑ or ↓) key until you reach the line of interest. You may scroll xx lines this way.

To exit MATRIXx, type

```
< > exit
```

2.3 Data Structures: Vectors and Matrices

The basic element in MATRIXx is a double-precision complex matrix. This is quite general and includes real and complex vectors and scalars. It indirectly includes polynomials and transfer functions. Row vectors are entered using square brackets where you can separate the elements using either blanks or commas. To create a column vector, we transpose the vector using the single quote key " ' ". For example,

```
< > x=[1, 2, 3], y=[1+jay, 2+pi*jay, -jay]

 X       =
   1.  2.  3.
```

```
Y        =
  1.0000 + 1.0000j  2.0000 + 3.1416j  .0000 - 1.0000j

< >   z=[1+jay 2+pi*jay -jay]'

Z        =
  1.0000 - 1.0000j
  2.0000 - 3.1416j
  0000 + 1.0000j
```

Note that we can create several vectors on a single line of code by separating them using commas or semicolons. Also, *pi* (=3.1416...) and *jay* ($=\sqrt{-1}$) are reserved variable names. Note that when you transpose complex vectors, you get the *conjugate transpose* as can be seen from the signs of the imaginary parts of Z.

The *colon* " : " is a powerful command and has many uses. For example, it can be used to generate sequential data such as

```
< > t=[0:0.1:10];
```

which generates a row vector t, with values increasing from 0 to 10 in increments of 0.1. If the increment is negative, you will get a decreasing sequence.

To suppress the immediate display of data, end each command with a semicolon

```
;
```

You will soon discover that if you forget to end your commands with the semicolon, you will be forced to watch lines and lines of data. So, use it often. You can always examine the value(s) of a variable by simply typing its name.

Very long variables or commands may require more than a single line for data entry. To continue a long command to the next line, type

```
...
```

at the end of the current line.

Matrices are entered row by row, separated by semicolons (you can also hit the RETURN key). To enter the matrix

$$A = \begin{pmatrix} 1 & 2 & 3 \\ 4 & 5 & 6 \\ 7 & 8 & 9 \end{pmatrix}$$

type

```
< > A=[1 2 3; 4 5 6; 7 8 9]
```

Addressing: elements of matrices are addressed by A(m,n); for example, A(2,3) gives the (2,3) element. A(:,2) gives the second element in all rows, i.e., the second column. A(1:2,1:3) gives rows 1 through 2 and columns 1 through 3. Note the use of " : " as a wildcard in these cases.

Two special matrices can be very useful and have reserved names.

```
< > eye(m)
```

returns an m by m *identity* matrix, *eye(A)* returns an identity matrix the same size as the matrix *A*, and *eye(m,n)* creates the largest identity matrix it can and fills the rest of the matrix with zeros.

```
< > ones(m,n)
```

returns an m by n matrix of " 1's ", and *ones (A)* returns a matrix of "1's " the same size as the matrix *A*. This is quite useful, e.g., *ones (t)*, where *t* is a vector generates the " *unit step* " function. To create an m by n matrix of zeros, enter

```
< > 0*ones(m,n)
```

For example, to create the function { y(t) = 3 + t , for t = 0, 1, 2, ... , 10 }, we enter

```
< > t=[0:1:10]; y=3*ones(t)+t
```

Another useful matrix command is

```
< > diag(v)
```

which returns a *diagonal matrix* with elements of the vector *v* on its diagonal. If *v* is a matrix, then this command returns the diagonal of *v* as a column vector; *diag(v,*1*)* returns the first superdiagonal, and *diag(v,*- 1*)* returns the first subdiagonal.

Two commands, *who* and *dim*, provide information on the variables in use in a MATRIXx session. Typing

```
< > who
```

lists all the variables you have defined and the reserved names. You can also ask for subsets of data by using wildcards as in the *save* command. In addition, *who* displays the number of bytes used by the variables. There are limits to the number of variables and the stack size. These are 148 variables for a total stack size of about 7,000 bytes in Version 7.1, 888 variables and 32,000 bytes in Version 7.2, and 888 variables and 100,000 bytes in Version 8.0. If you define many large vectors and matrices, you will eventually reach these limits. In this case, you can save your data and clear some variables. In Version 7.1 and later, you can also use the *siz_limit* command (get on-line help or see the manual).

Typing

```
< > dim
```

displays all data and their dimensions and *dim (' filename')* does the same for the given filename. This is useful when you approach the limits mentioned earlier. You also may wish to eliminate unnecessary variables, otherwise you will end up with so many variable names that bookkeeping will be difficult.

Some additional commands related to data display are given below.

```
< > [m,n]=size(A)
```

returns the size of the matrix A as a vector. This is a very useful command. Matrix algebra requires that dimensions of vectors and matrices satisfy certain compatibility conditions. The *size* command can be used to make sure these conditions are met. To see if a variable exists, we use

```
< > [m,n]=size('a',1)
```

If the variable does not exist, the program returns [0. 0.].

```
< > long
```

displays data in long format using fifteen digits, and *long e* will display in scientific notation. This is useful when small numbers appear as zeros, and switching to long format will display the correct value. To get back to the default format, use *short* or *short e*. You can also enter data in scientific notation, e.g., 2000 is entered as *2E3*.

```
< > display ('text string')
```

Text strings can be assigned to vectors or matrices, and are entered inside single quotes. Text strings can be displayed using the preceding command. For example,

```
< > A=['this is a' ; 'text string']
< > display A
```

```
this is a
text string
```

2.4 Plotting and Graphics

```
< > plot(t,y)
```

Plots the vector y versus the vector t. The vectors must have the same size. When a plot command is issued, MATRIXx switches to " graphics mode " and will not display ordinary text. To return to text mode, you erase the screen with the command

```
< > erase
```

This command will not affect the data stack.

```
< > plot(x,y,z)
```

produces a three-dimensional plot of the three vectors.

```
< > plot(t,[y1,y2,y3])
```

creates multiple (i.e., simultaneous) plots of vectors y1, y2, and y3 versus t. Try entering the following sequence of commands.

```
< > t=[0:100]'; x=sin(t); y=sin(2*t); z=sin(3*t); plot(t,[x,y,z])
```

You can customize your plots with a title, and labels for the X and Y axes. You can also size your plots or split the screen into two or four portions, and send them to a printer. These are *options* and are placed inside single quotes separated by blank spaces. For instance, the following command plots x (response) versus t (time) , sets up labels for the X and Y axes, titles it (output), and sends it to the printer.

```
< > plot(t,x,'ylabel response xlabel time title output printer')
```

Many other options are available; check the manual, and do some of the problems at the end of this chapter. You can get on-line help on the various plot options by typing

```
< > help plotoptions
```

Some classical control commands like root locus, Bode, Nyquist, and Nichols automatically generate plots; to obtain the printout of these commands, special commands are required and will be explained later in Chapter 4.

2.5 Mathematical Operations

Basic algebraic operations (+, -, *, /, **), standard trigonometric functions, hyperbolic functions, transcendental functions (*log* = *base* e *log*, *log10* = *base* 10 *log*, *exp*), and *sqrt*

($\sqrt{\ }$) are supported (the arguments can be scalars or matrices). Other functions such as *det* (determinant), *inv* (inverse), *eig (eigenvalue), A′ = transpose, rank, norm* are standard matrix operations. Other obvious functions are *min, max, real, imag, sum, product, abs* (absolute value or magnitude of complex quantities), *norm*, and *conj* (complex conjugate). There are also element-by-element operations that are very useful but are not part of standard linear algebra and will be demonstrated below. A complete list is available using the *what* command.

matrix division

```
< > A/B
< > B\A
< > inv(A)
```

A\B is equivalent to $A^{-1}B$ or *inv(A)*B*. It solves the problem : Ax= B. *B/A* is equivalent to BA^{-1}or *B*inv(A)*. It solves the problem xA=B. If A is rectangular, *A\B* and *B/A* automatically find the least squares solution, whereas *inv(A)* is only valid for square matrices.

element-by-element operations

```
< > A.*B
< > A./B
< > A.\B
```

A . B* is the element-by-element product and returns a matrix $c_{ij} = a_{ij}\, b_{ij}$.

A ./ B and *A .\ B* return $\frac{a_{ij}}{b_{ij}}$ and $\frac{b_{ij}}{a_{ij}}$, respectively. For example,

```
< > a=[1 2;3 4]; b=[5 6;6 8];
< > a.*b

ANS =

5  12
18 32


< > a.\b

ANS =

5 3
2 2
```

You can verify the identity { sin (2t) = 2 sin(t) cos(t) } by

```
< > t=[0:100]'; x=sin(2*t);  y=2*sin(t).*cos(t); [x  y]
```

Kronecker product

```
< > A.*.B
< > kron(A,B)
```

$C = A .*. B$ or $C = kron\ (A,B)$ is a matrix where the ij-th partition is $C_{ij} = a_{ij} B$. For A and B given above we get

```
< > a.*.b

ANS =
5   6   10  12
6   8   12  16
15  18  20  24
18  24  24  32
```

vector and matrix functions

The results of matrix functions such as *log, log10, exp, sin*, etc., depend on whether the argument is a vector or matrix. For example, If the argument is a vector, *sin(x)* returns the sine of the individual elements. If A is a matrix, *sin (A)* returns the matrix sine function defined by $\sin(A) = M \sin(\Lambda) M^{-1}$, where Λ is the matrix of eigenvalues and M is the modal matrix (matrix of eigenvectors).

```
< > sum(A)
< > prod(A)
```

return the sum (product) of all elements. They are useful in programming and eliminate unnecessary loops.

```
< > B=min(A)
< > B=min(A,x)
< > [B,C]=min(A)
```

Min (*max*) return the smallest (largest) element of A. For complex data, only the real part is considered. The optional form *min*(A,x), compares the elements of A with the scalar x and returns a matrix containing the elements $\min(a_{ij}, x)$. This is useful for picking the positive or negative elements of A by assigning x to be zero. The third form will return the smallest element for the first argument, and the corresponding location (row and column index) for the second argument.

```
< > sortval(A)
< > sortval(A,'magn')
```

The *sortvalue* command will sort vectors in increasing order of the real part. If the input is a matrix, each column will be sorted individually. In the second syntax, the sorting will occur according to the magnitudes rather than the real parts.

Polynomials

Polynomials are represented as vectors containing the polynomial coefficients in descending order. For example, the polynomial $s^3 + 2\,s^2 + 3\,s + 4$ is entered as

```
< >  p=[1 2 3 4];
< > roots(p)
```

returns the roots of a polynomial with coefficients given by the row vector p. The roots are stored as a column vector. The result of the above command is

```
ANS     =
-.1747-1.5469j
-.1747+1.5469j
-1.6505-.000j
```

```
< > poly(x)
```

creates a row vector representing the polynomial with roots given by the vector x. It is the inverse of the roots command. For example, to generate $(s+1)(s+2) = s^2 + 3\,s + 2$, enter

```
< > poly([-1  -2])
```

```
ANS  =
1.
3.
2.
```

```
< > polyval(P,s)
```

returns the value of the polynomial P, at a given complex point s, where s can be a vector. (This command is available in Version 7.1 and above).

```
< > conv(x,y)
```

stands for discrete convolution, which may be used for multiplying polynomials. For example, to multiply the following polynomials $(s+1)(s+2) = s^2 + 3s + 2$, enter

```
< > conv([1  1],[1  2])
```

```
ANS  =
1.0  3.0  2.0
```

2.6 Examples

We will demonstrate some of the commands and graphics capabilities in the following examples.

Lissajous figures

Lissajous figures are frequently used as a method of determining the frequency and phase of an unknown signal by using a known signal as reference.

Let us define x(t) and y(t) as

$$x(t) = \sin(8t), \quad y(t) = \sin(10t)$$

and plot x versus y. The plot is shown in Figure 2-1.

```
< > t=[0:pi/200:pi]';
< > xl=sin(8*t); yl=sin(10*t); plot(xl,yl, 'nogrid noxlab noylab');
```

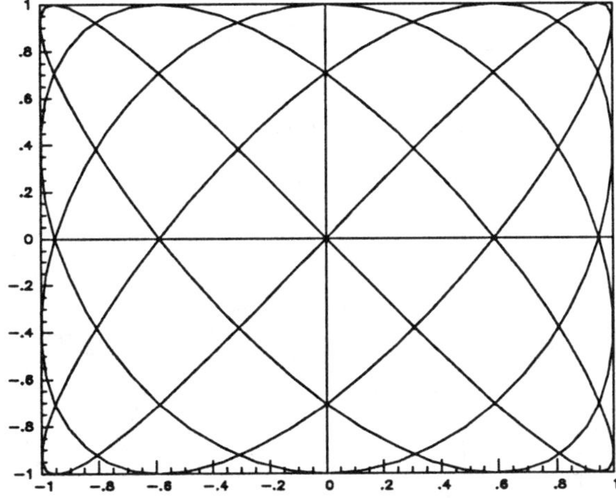

Figure 2-1 Lissajous figure.

Polar plots

The equation of a four-leaf figure in polar coordinates is $r = \cos(4\theta)$
We plot this in polar coordinates in Figure 2-2.

```
< > th=[pi/200:pi/200:2*pi]'; dth=th*180/pi; r=cos(4*th);
< > plot(dth,r,'full polar noxlab noylab')
```

The equation for the Archimedes spiral is given by $r = k\theta$, $k > 0$. The plot is shown in Figure 2-3.

```
< > sa=th/(2*pi);      // th defined above
< > plot(dth,sa,'polar full noxlab noylab')
```

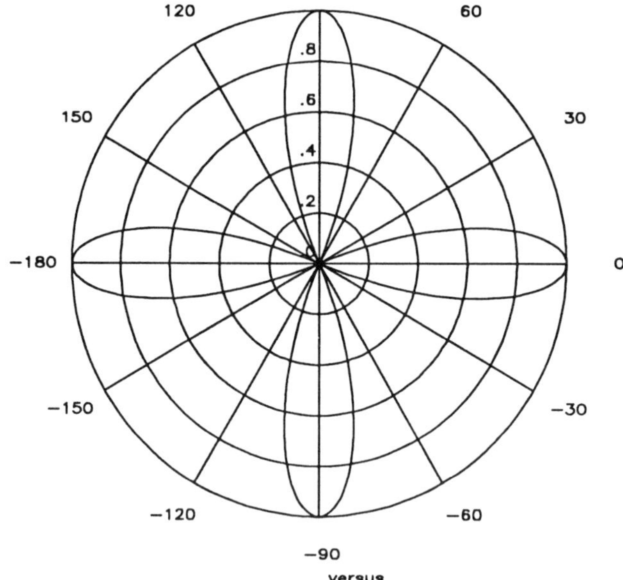

Figure 2-2 The four-leaf figure.

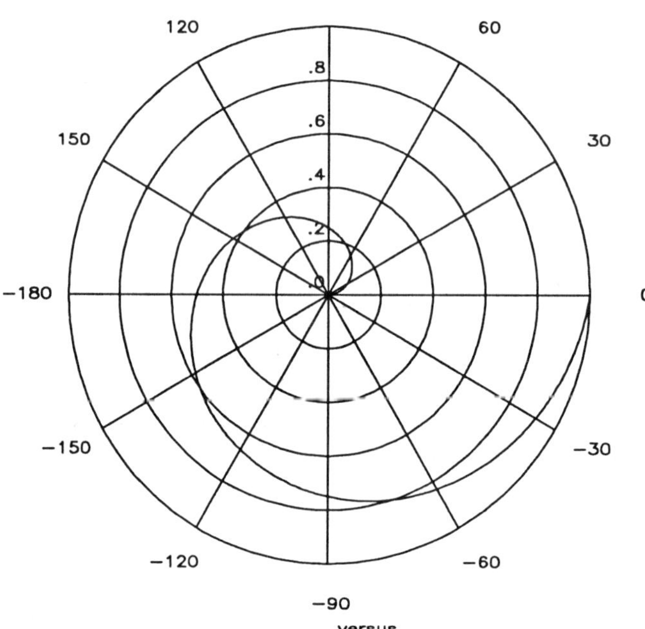

Figure 2-3 Archimedes spiral.

Drawing circles

The parametric equations of a circle with radius r and center at (a, b) are given by

$$x(t) = r\cos(t) + a \quad , \quad y(t) = r\sin(t) + b$$
$$(x - a)^2 + (y - b)^2 = r^2$$

We will plot two unit circles; one centered at the origin and the other centered at (1,1). Plotting X versus Y produces the circles.

```
< > t=[0:0.1:2*pi]';
< > x=cos(t); y=sin(t);
< > x2=cos(t)+ones(t); y2=sin(t)+ones(t);
< > plot([x,x2],[y,y2],'xmin=-3 xmax=4 ymin=-3 ymax=4 noxlab,...
 noylab noygrid coscale');
```

Note the use of (. . .) on the long plot command to continue on the next line. We are also using the *coscale* option to get round circles (available in Version 7.1 and above). The plot is shown in Figure 2-4.

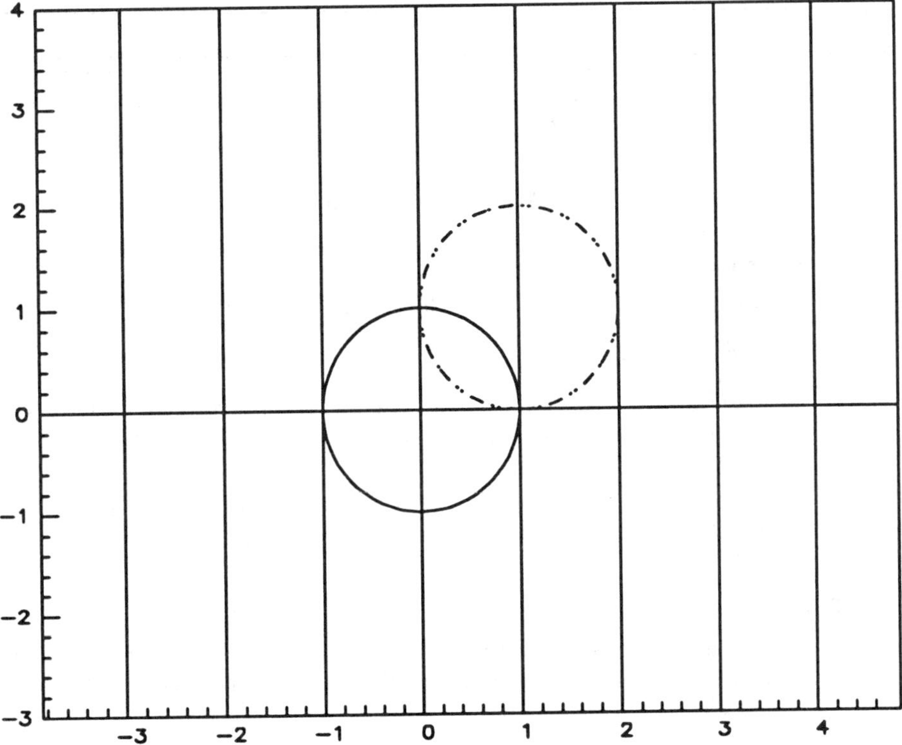

Figure 2-4 Two circles.

Generating a pulse train

The Kronecker product is used to duplicate a long series of 1's and -1's for the pulse train. It is then plotted in the upper half of the screen with no labels or X axis gridlines, the Y axis is also set between -2 to 2 for clarity. The plot is shown in Figure 2-5.

```
< > u=[1;-1;1;-1].*.ones(30, 1);       // the pulse train
< > su=prod(size(u));tt=0.1*[0:su-1]';  // the time axis
< > plot(tt,u,'upper noxlab noylab ymin=-2 ymax=2 noxgrid')
```

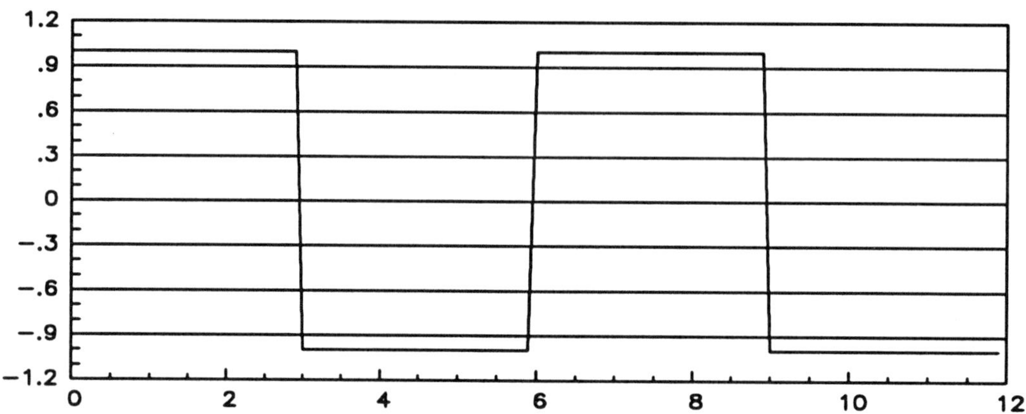

Figure 2-5 Pulse train.

Three-dimensional plots

We now plot the famous " sombrero hat ", which is a plot of

$$z = \frac{\sin(x)}{x} \cdot \frac{\sin(y)}{y}$$

To generate this, we define two vectors x and y and a matrix z. Note the use of element-by-element division to divide *sin(x)* by x. The plot is shown in Figure 2-6.

```
< > xs=[-2*pi:0.4:2*pi]'; ys=xs; zs=sin(xs)./xs*(sin(ys)./ys)';
< > plot(xs,ys,zs,'nolegend ')
```

Triangles

It is possible to draw lines and generate geometric figures. All one needs to do is to enter the X coordinates in one vector and the Y coordinates in another, and plot Y versus X. To produce closed figures like triangles, the first and last coordinates must be the same.

```
< > a=[1 ; 1]; b=[3 ; 1]; c=[2.5 ; 2];          //  the vertices
< > tx=[a(1),b(1),c(1),a(1)]                    // X coordinates
< > ty=[a(2),b(2),c(2),a(2)];                   // Y coordinates
```

We will now define a rotation matrix, which will rotate the vertices of the triangle by 45 degrees and plot the rotated triangle (see Problem 2.7).

```
< > aa=[cos(pi/4),sin(pi/4);sin(pi/4),cos(pi/4)]; //rotation matrix
< > b1=aa*b; a1=aa*a; c1=aa*c;    // new vertices
< > tx1=[a1(1) b1(1) c1(1) a1(1)];  // new X coordinates
< > ty1=[a1(2) b(2) c1(2) a1(2)];   // new Y coordinates
< > plot(tx,ty,' xmin=-1 xmax=4 ymin=0 ymax=4 noxlab, ...
noylab nogrid');...
plot(tx1,ty1,'xmin=-1 xmax=4 ymin=0 ymax=4 noxlab, ...
noylab nogrid keep');
```

Note the use of the continuation between plot commands and the *keep* option, which allows two separate plots to be overlaid. The plot is shown in Figure 2-7.

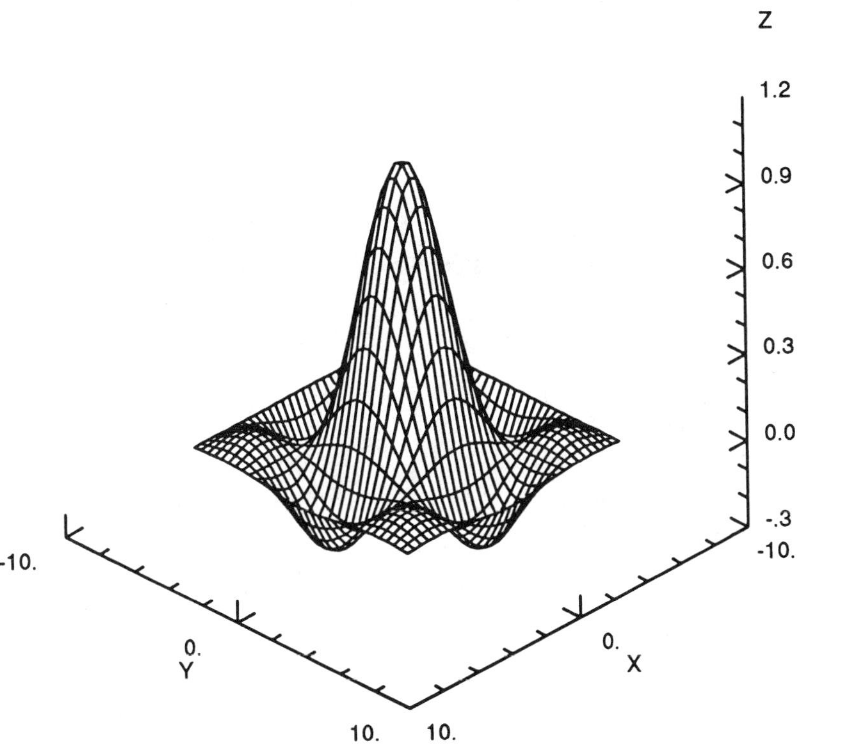

Figure 2-6 The sombrero hat plot.

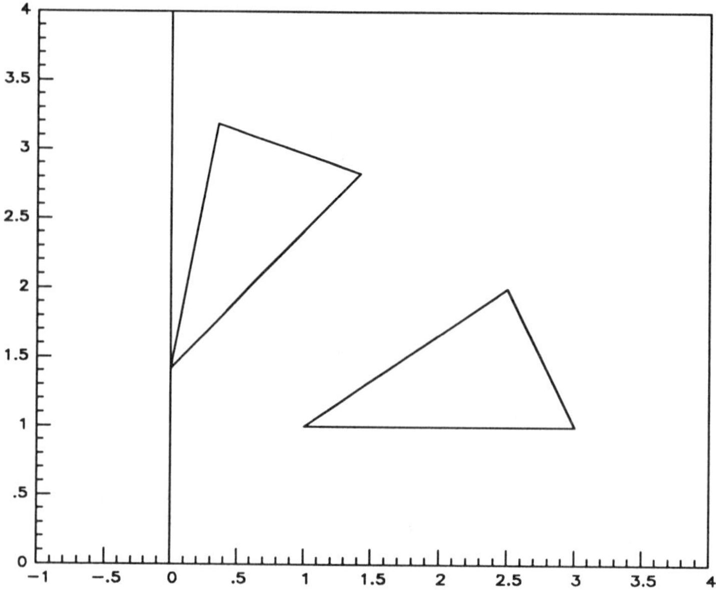

Figure 2-7 Plot of triangles.

2.7 Problems

2.1 The purpose of this exercise is to demonstrate different ways of addressing elements of matrices. Consider the following matrix A

$$A = \begin{bmatrix} 11 & 12 & 13 & 14 \\ 21 & 22 & 23 & 24 \\ 31 & 32 & 33 & 34 \\ 41 & 42 & 43 & 44 \end{bmatrix}$$

You are to predict the result of the following operations and later check your predictions on the computer.

a. Use minimum number of operations to enter the matrix A.
b. A(: , 1)
c. A (2 , :)
d. A (: , 2 : 3)
e. A (2 : 3 , 2 : 3)
f. A (: , 1 : 2 : 3)
g. A (2 : 3)
h. A (:)
i. A (: , :)

j. ones (2 , 2)
k. eye (2)
l. B = [A , [ones (2 , 2) ; eye (2)]]
m. diag (A)
n. diag (A , 1)
o. diag (A , -1)
p. diag (A , 2)

2.2 The purpose of this exercise is to demonstrate matrix functions, e.g., the matrix sine function.
a. Enter the following matrix A.

$$A = \begin{bmatrix} 0 & \frac{\pi}{3} \\ \frac{\pi}{6} & \frac{\pi}{2} \end{bmatrix}$$

b. Find the sine of the individual elements; call this B1.
c. Find the cosine of the individual elements; call this B2.
d. Find $B1^2 + B2^2$. Note that this is not the identity matrix.
e. Find the eigenvalues and eigenvectors of A; call the eigenvector matrix M and the eigenvalue matrix L.
f. Find $M \sin(L) M^{-1}$.
g. Find sin (A). You must get the same answer as in part f.
h. Find cos(A).
i. Show $\sin(A)^2 + \cos(A)^2 = I$.

2.3 The purpose of this exercise is to demonstrate the use of the matrix division (\) command.
a. Use the *rand* command to generate five random 2 by 2 matrices, A, B, C, D, E.
b. Without the use of the *inv* command, compute F in one line.
$F = A^{-1}\ [B + C^{-1}(D^{-1}E)]$
c. Without the use of the *inv* command, find the first column of A^{-1} using one command. Check your answer in both parts using the *inv* command.

2.4 The purpose of this exercise is to demonstrate the use of element-by-element operations and Kronecker products. Do each part by hand, and compare your answer with the computer.

$$A = \begin{bmatrix} 1 \\ 1 \\ 1 \end{bmatrix} \quad \text{and} \quad B = [\,2 \;\; 3 \;\; 4\,]$$

a. A .*. B ′
b. A .*. B
c. A ′.*. B
d. A′ .*. B ′
e. A .* B ′
f. A .\B′
g. A ′.\B

2.5 The purpose of this problem is to practice some of the graphic features.

a. Plot the following in polar coordinates for $0 \le \theta \le 2\pi$. Note that for polar plots, θ must be expressed in degrees not radians.

i. $r = 3\,(1 - \cos\theta)$ cardioid

ii. $r = 2\,(1 + \cos\theta)$

iii. $r = 2\,(1 + \sin\theta)$

iv. $r = \cos 3\theta$ three-leaf rose

v. $r = e^{\frac{\theta}{4\pi}}$ logarithmic spiral

b. Obtain the three-dimensional plot of the function z for the given range of values $-5 \le x \le 5$, $-5 \le y \le 5$, $-2 \le z \le 2$.

$$z = \frac{1}{(x+1)^2 + (y+1)^2 + 1} - \frac{1.5}{(x-1)^2 + (y-1)^2 + 1}$$

2.6 The purpose of this problem is to practice graphics along with some MATRIXx math functions.

a. Obtain a plot of

$y(t) = 1 - 2\,e^{-t}\sin(t)$, where $0 \le t \le 8$

Label the X axis "Time", the Y axis "Amplitude", and title the graph "Decaying-oscillating Exponential".

b. Obtain a plot of

$y(t) = 5e^{-0.2t}\cos(0.9t - 30^{\circ}) + 0.8e^{-2t}$, where $0 \le t \le 30$

c. For $0 \le t \le 10$, obtain a graph of

$y(t) = 1.23\cos(2.83t + 240^{\circ}) + 0.625$ and $x(t) = 0.625$

Plot the functions on the same graph, and find $y(t{=}0)$ and $y(t{=}10)$. Watch out for radians and degrees.

d. For $0 \le t \le 20$, plot the following functions on the same graph.

$y_1(t) = 2.62\,e^{-0.25t}\cos(2.22t + 174^{\circ}) + 0.6$
$y_2(t) = 2.62\,e^{-0.25t} + 0.6$
$y_3(t) = 0.6$

Limit your graph to values of y between -2 and +3. Find the minimum value of y_1, the maximum value of y_1, and the values of the second maximum and minimum of y_1.

e. For $0 \le t \le 25$, plot the following functions on the same graph.

$y_1(t) = 1.25\, e^{-t}$

$y_2(t) = 2.02\, e^{-0.3t}$

$y_3(t) = 2.02\, e^{-0.3t} \cos(0.554t - 128^\circ) + 1.25\, e^{-t}$

Limit the Y axis to -0.2 and +1 and your X axis to 0 and 16. Also find the following values for $y_3(t)$: $y(t{=}0)$, y_{max}, y_{min}, and $y(t{=}12)$.

2.7 The purpose of this problem is to demonstrate the effects of linear transformations. A point in the two-dimensional plane can be represented as a vector (an element of R^2 vector space). A matrix is geometrically a linear transformation or a map from R^2 to R^2. Therefore, $y = A\,x$ is another point or vector in the plane. Different matrices have different effects. They may expand, shrink, reflect, rotate, or perform other geometric operations on the vector.

You are to consider the following matrices and determine by analysis their effects on the triangle shown in the examples and then check your work using the computer. In each case, plot the original triangle and the transformed triangle on the same plot using appropriate scales for the x and y axis. (In MATRIXx: issue the *plot* command for the first triangle, continue to next line, issue the plot command for the second triangle, and use the *keep* option).

a. $A1 = \begin{bmatrix} 1 & 0 \\ 0 & -1 \end{bmatrix}$

b. $A2 = \begin{bmatrix} -1 & 0 \\ 0 & 1 \end{bmatrix}$

c. $A3 = \begin{bmatrix} 2 & 0 \\ 0 & 1 \end{bmatrix}$

d. $A4 = \begin{bmatrix} 1 & 2 \\ 1 & 0 \end{bmatrix}$

e. $A5 = \begin{bmatrix} \cos(\frac{\pi}{2}) & -\sin(\frac{\pi}{2}) \\ \sin(\frac{\pi}{2}) & \cos(\frac{\pi}{2}) \end{bmatrix}$

Note: Make sure you use appropriate scaling of the axes to fit both plots on the same screen.

3

Programming in MATRIXx

MATRIXx supports some basic programming structures that allow looping and conditioning commands. The syntax and use of these structures is very similar to those found in other high level languages such as C, BASIC, and FORTRAN. These new commands combined with ones we have discussed earlier can be put together to form programs or new functions that can be added to MATRIXx. These features are discussed in this chapter. First, we will briefly introduce the simple MATRIXx editor.

3.1 MATRIXx Editor

The MATRIXx editor is a last line editor that can be used to correct mistakes or create macros (macros are discussed in 3.3). It is often more convenient, however, to use the multiline buffer (available in Version 7.1 and above) to correct mistakes. The editor is invoked with a single backslash (\ ). The backslash is also used to exit the editor. Once inside the editor, there are two commands available: *change* and *overlay*. The syntax for *change* is

```
< >  c/string1/string2/n
```
or
```
< >  c/string1/string2/all
```

This changes the *n*th occurrence (or all occurrences) of string1 to string2. The default for n is 1. The strings are any nonblank characters. If string1 is null, then string2 is inserted at the beginning of the line. If string2 is null, then string1 is deleted.
For example, consider the vector *A*

```
< > a = [1  2  3  4  5  6  6  8]

A     =
  1.  2.  3.  4.  5.  6.  6.  8.
```

Invoke the editor and change 6 to 7 in its second occurrence

```
< > \c / 6 / 7 / 2
```

```
A       =
  1.  2.  3.  4.  5.  6.  7.  8.
```

Delete 8 by setting string2 to null

```
< > \c\8\

A       =
 1.  2.  3.  4.  5.  6.  7.
```

The second command available is *overlay*. This is invoked by entering the editor and typing " O " followed by carriage return. The last line will be displayed and any nonblank characters typed in the overlay line will replace characters in the original line. For instance,

```
< > a=[1  2  3  4]

A       =
  1.  2.  3.  4.
< >  \              (invoke the editor)

a= [1 2 3 4 ]           (the last line is displayed)
Edit: o                 (invoke overlay)
        a=[1 2 3 4]            (the original line is displayed)
Overlay: b                     (change a to b)
b=[1 2 3 4]                    (the new line is displayed)
Edit: \                  (exit the editor)
B       =
  1.  2.  3.  4.
```

Within *overlay* there are three operations available.

- % delete character and force a blank
- # delete character without forcing a blank
- ^ insert text before the indicated character

Let us practice using the editor.

```
< > a=[2 3 4 5]

A       =
  2.  3.  4.  5.
```

```
< > edit

 a=[2   3  4  5]
Edit: o
         a=[2 3 4 5]
Overlay:           ^ 6          (to insert a space and 6 before the bracket, type ^ 6 after 5)

 a=[2 3 4 5 6]
Edit: o
          a=[2 3 4 5 6]
Overlay:     %              (to delete 3 and force a blank, put % directly under 3)
 a=[2  4 5 6]               (note the extra blank between 2 and 4)
Edit: o
         a=[2  4 5 6]
Overlay:        #       (to delete 5,  put # directly under 5)
 a=[2  4  6]
Edit: o
          a=[2  4  6]
Overlay:     3      (to replace blank with 3, type 3 directly under the blank)

 a=[2 3 4  6]
Edit:   o
         a=[2 3 4  6]
Overlay:        ^5         (to insert 5 before 6, type 5 under 6 with ^ in front of it)
 a=[2 3 4 5 6]
Edit: \                 (exit the editor)
  A      =
   2.   3.   4.   5.   6.
```

3.2 Loops and Conditional Structures

Three commands are available that allow you to write loops, conditional loops, and conditional statements. They are *for*, *while*, and *if-else-elseif* commands. These commands must be entered as a single MATRIXx command line containing up to 4096 characters. By a command line, we mean any set of statements ending with a carriage return (when you hit the ENTER key). Command lines can be continued across the display line by the use of the continuation symbol (" . . . ") for ease of reading. If you use more than the number of characters allowed, you can get unpredictable results. Therefore, it is recommended that you avoid long and complex nested loops.

for

The *for* command is used to execute a series of statements iteratively. Its syntax is shown below

```
< > for  variable=expression, statement,..., statement, end
```

The expression is a vector or matrix, or valid MATRIXx command resulting in a vector or matrix. *The statements are executed once for each element of the row vector or column of the matrix.* Loop variables cease to exist once the loop has terminated. From the beginning until the end of the loop, you may have several statements. It is important to remember to end each line with the continuation symbol ("..."). *For* loops can be nested, but try to avoid complex nested structures. They tend to be very slow and error prone. You can instead take advantage of vector and matrix operations like *sort, sortvalue*, and various matrix-addressing operations.

The following example gives squares of numbers from 1 to 10. Note the use of "..." at the end of each line to continue from line to line.

```
< > for i=1:10;...
< > a(i)=i**2;...
< > end;
```

The following example[1] will demonstrate how to avoid *for* loops. Suppose we wish to exchange elements between two matrices systematically (a very common operation). In particular, given matrices A and B, we wish to set every other row of A equal to the last seven elements of every other row of B.

```
< > a =[ 1, 3, 5, 7, 9, 11, 13 ];
< > a =[ a ; a ; a ; a ; a ; a ; a ]

A    =
1.  3.  5.  7.  9.  11.  13.
1.  3.  5.  7.  9.  11.  13.
1.  3.  5.  7.  9.  11.  13.
1.  3.  5.  7.  9.  11.  13.
1.  3.  5.  7.  9.  11.  13.
1.  3.  5.  7.  9.  11.  13.
1.  3.  5.  7.  9.  11.  13.

< > b =[ 0, 2, 4, 6, 8, 10, 12, 14, 16, 18 ];
< > b =[ b ; b ; b ; b ; b ; b ; b ; b ; b ; b ]
```

1 Example taken from programming notes provided at the first I.S.I. (Integrated Systems, Inc.) Users' Conference, Santa Clara, CA, October 1990.

```
B      =

0.  2.  4.  6.  8.  10.  12.  14.  16.  18.
0.  2.  4.  6.  8.  10.  12.  14.  16.  18.
0.  2.  4.  6.  8.  10.  12.  14.  16.  18.
0.  2.  4.  6.  8.  10.  12.  14.  16.  18.
0.  2.  4.  6.  8.  10.  12.  14.  16.  18.
0.  2.  4.  6.  8.  10.  12.  14.  16.  18.
0.  2.  4.  6.  8.  10.  12.  14.  16.  18.
0.  2.  4.  6.  8.  10.  12.  14.  16.  18.
0.  2.  4.  6.  8.  10.  12.  14.  16.  18.
0.  2.  4.  6.  8.  10.  12.  14.  16.  18.
```

This is how **not** to solve the problem!

```
< > a2=a; for i=1:2:7;...
< > for j=1:7;...
< > a2(i,j)=b(i+1,j+3),...
< > end;...
< > end;
```

```
A2     =

6.  8.  10.  12.  14.  16.  18.
1.  3.   5.   7.   9.  11.  13.
6.  8.  10.  12.  14.  16.  18.
1.  3.   5.   7.   9.  11.  13.
6.  8.  10.  12.  14.  16.  18.
1.  3.   5.   7.   9.  11.  13.
6.  8.  10.  12.  14.  16.  18.
```

The following command uses matrix addressing and produces the same result.

```
< > a2=a; a2([1:2:7],[1:7])=b([2:2:8],[4:10])
```

while

This command allows conditional looping in which statements within the loop are executed as long as the condition is true. Its syntax is

```
< > while  expression,  statement, . . ,statement,end;
```

The "expression" is of the form: X operator Y
where X and Y are scalars or expressions that yield scalars. The"operator" is any of the following relational operators { < , > , = , >=, <= , <> }, where the last operator stands for " not equal to ", and the others are obvious.

For example, to compute and display the famous Fibonacci numbers, defined by

$$f(n+2)=f(n+1)+f(n) \qquad f(0)=1,\ f(1)=1$$

we write:

```
< > f=[1 , 1]; i=1;              // initialization
< > while  f(i+1)+f(i)<100;...
< > f(i+2)=f(i+1)+f(i);...
< > i=i+1;...
< > end;f
```

if, else, elseif

These commands are also used for conditional execution of a set of commands. The syntax is

```
< > if  expression1, statement,...statement,...
    elseif  expression2,  statement,...,  statement ,... ,
    else  statement,... ,end
```

If expression1 is true, the first set of statements is executed; if expression2 is true, then the next set of statements is executed; otherwise, the statements after *else* are executed. Expression has the same form as the *while* statement. The *elseif* or the *else* portions are optional. Note that all the three commands above can also be nested.

There are also other programming commands such as *pause*, *inquire*, and *menu* available for making custom menus and interactive programs. Some utilities and error-checking commands such as *clock*, *get_info* and *exist* are also available. Use on line help or refer to the manual for further information.

3.3 Programming Structures

Four different programming tools are available.

- Macros
- Command files (EXEC FILES)
- User-defined functions (UDFs)
- User-defined commands (UDCs)

3.3.1 Macros

Macros are a short sequence of MATRIXx commands used often in a session. They can be saved for use in future sessions as part of other files. There are two ways to define a macro.

1. As a text *string*

```
< > macname='macro definition';
```

For example, the following macro will compute and plot the step response of a transfer function with numerator *n* and denominator *d*. (*Note*: *n* and *d* must be defined before you define the macro).

```
< > stepmac='[t,y]=step(n,d,10); plot(t,y)';
```

For multiline macros, use " . . . " to continue on the next line.

2. Using the *Editor* and *Overlay*

We will create the previous macro using the Editor and Overlay.

```
< > edit stepmac
```

Edit: o

Overlay: `[t,y]=step(n,d,10);plot(t,y);`

[t,y] = step(n,d,10) ; plot(t,y);

Edit: \

To invoke a macro, enclose the name of the macro within reverse brackets as shown below.

```
< > ]macname[
```

The following invokes our previously defined macro to compute and plot the step response.

```
< > n=1; d=[1 2 3];
< > ]stepmac[
```

The contents of a macro can be checked with the *display* command. For example,

```
< > disp(stepmac)
```

[t,y] = step(n,d,10) ; plot(t,y);

3.3.2 Command Files (Exec Files)

Command files (exec files) are stored as executable ASCII files that are accessible to other users. Exec files are generally a more complex set of commands than macros, and in fact may contain macros within them. There are two ways to create exec files. One is to leave the program and use any local editor or word processor capable of producing ASCII format files. The second method is the "*diary*" command with *option* 1.

```
< > diary('name',1)
```

The above creates an "executable" file that is closed by typing *diary(*0,1*)*. Using diary with option 1, only the inputs will be printed and not the outputs. The last line of an exec file should be " *return* ".
Here is a simple example.

```
< > diary('example',1)
< > n=1; d=[1   2   3]; [t,y]=step(n,d,5); plot(t,y); return
< > diary(0,1)
```

To execute an exec file type

```
< > exec('filename',n)
```

where n is an optional parameter that allows you to pause between commands, etc. (see on-line help on *exec* for details).

3.3.3 User-defined Functions

UDFs are like Fortran Subroutines or Pascal Procedures. They are used for complex tasks and allow parameter passing by value and use local variables. This is the main difference between a UDF and an exec file. In an exec file, all variables must either be defined within it or must be on the stack, and all defined variables will remain on the stack after execution. In a UDF, only the input arguments must be passed by value, and all variables defined within the UDF are local and will be destroyed after execution unless they are passed as output arguments. Local variables in a UDF will not affect the stack. UDFs must be created outside the program using your local text editor. It must be given a name and stored as an ASCII file. The syntax is

```
//[out1,out2, ... ]=funname(in1,in2, ... )
// Help and comments (optional)
      .
      .                      list of MATRIXx commands
      .
retf
```

The total number of inputs and outputs is limited by the number of characters on the function definition line (80 characters, approximately 35 total input and output arguments).[1] A total of 84 UDFs can be created in a session.[2] You can override this limit dynamically by clearing some UDFs and defining others. In future versions, these limits may increase. The first line is a required comment line that gives the program name and its syntax. The last line, " *retf* ", distinguishes it from an exec file. All variables are local, and only the output variables are stored. If there is only one output, the brackets can be omitted. To use a UDF, you need to define it by using the *define* command as follows

```
< > define 'funname'
```

Drive specifications and paths are also allowed as part of the filename definition. After being defined, the UDF can be used like any other MATRIXx command. If you use many UDFs in a session, you can create a separate UDF to define all the other UDFs; otherwise, defining large numbers of UDFs all the time can be a chore. Starting with Version 7.1 and up, help utilities such as *brief*, *syntax*, and *help* are also available for UDFs. An example of a UDF follows.

This program, " STAT ", finds the mean and standard deviation of data stored in a vector x. Recall that

$$\text{mean} = \frac{\sum_{i=1}^{N} x_i}{N} \quad \text{and} \quad \sigma^2 = \frac{\sum_{i=1}^{N} (x_i - \bar{x})^2}{N-1}$$

where $\bar{x}$ = mean and σ = standard deviation

```
// [MEAN,SD]=STAT(X)
//Compute the mean and standard deviation of data in a vector.
n=max(size(x));
mean=sum(x)/n;
xbar=mean*ones(x);
var=(sum((x-xbar).*(x-xbar)))/(n-1);
sd=sqrt(var);
retf;
```

After creating the above program in your text editor, you should define it inside MATRIXx by the *define* command.

1 This limit was 5 inputs and 7 outputs in earlier versions like Version 5.2.

2 This limit was 10 in Version 5.2.

```
< > define 'stat'
```

You can now define any vector and find its statistics with this function. If you forget its syntax, you can type

```
< > help stat
```

This will display the comment lines in your program (the first two lines in our example).

3.3.4 User-defined Commands

UDCs are a variation of UDFs. The syntax for UDC[1] is

```
// commandname inp1  inp2 inp3   . . .
// Help and comments (optional)
       .
       .                       list of MATRIXx commands
       .
return
```

The input arguments in a UDC are optional. To use a UDC, it be must be defined using the *define* command as for a UDF. The main differences between UDFs and UDCs (except for a different syntax) are the following:

1. A UDC requires no input argument (optional) whereas a UDF must have at least one input argument.

2. A UDC accepts inputs by reference; and has access to and operates on variables on the stack. A UDF accepts inputs by value and has access only to variables passed to it via the input arguments. It also operates only on local variables. This is an important distinction.

For example, suppose variable " x " with a value of 10 is on the stack. Consider the following UDF and UDC.

```
// y=udf(x)                                // UDC
x=100;                                     x=100;
y=x+100;                                   y=x+100;
retf                                       return
```

After we run the UDF, the values of x and y on the stack are x = 10 and y = 200. The values in the UDC are x = 100 and y = 200. Therefore, a UDC changes the values on the

1 UDCs are available in Version 7.1 and above.

stack, whereas in the UDF, x retains its value on the stack even though it was changed within the body of the UDF.

The following is a simple UDC, called " CLTF ", that assumes transfer functions G(s) and H(s) are in series in unity feedback configuration. It gives the open loop, GH(s), and closed loop, T(s), transfer functions. You can rewrite the program as a UDF or use state space commands discussed in Chapter 5. Note the use of various commands like *size*, *prod*, and others.

```
//  CLTF    ng dg nh dh
ngh=conv(ng,nh); dgh=conv(dg,dh) ;
dimngh=prod(size(ngh)); dimdgh=prod(size(dgh));
nc=[0*ones(1,dimdgh-dimngh),ngh];
dt=nc+dgh;
nt=ngh;
retf;
```

3.4 Debugging Facilities

There are limited debugging facilities available. The *debug* and *semi* commands are toggle commands.

```
< > semi
```

Typing *semi* reverses the role of the " ; " command and will display lines that had been suppressed previously (you normally end command lines with " ; " to suppress display and speed up execution). This helps you catch unexpected results or values.

```
< > debug
```

The debug command is also a toggle. Typing *debug* will turn it on. When you execute your program, every line will be displayed; when you call another function within your program, its lines will also be displayed. If there is an error, the line containing the error will be displayed, and the approximate location of the error is indicated. The program stops, and all local variables (normally destroyed) will be saved on the stack. This allows you to examine the variables (use *who* or *dim*) that have been computed.

Sometimes, you do not see anything wrong with the indicated line, but you may have incompatible dimensions in previous lines that will cause an error (e.g., adding matrices of different size).

Every time you define and enter a UDF, you go down an extent level. If you use another UDF within a UDF, you go down another extent level. If *debug* is on and you type *who*, only the local variables within that level are shown. To see the variables on the previous level, you must type *retf*, which destroys the local variables and brings you one level up. If you later wish to examine the variables, you must save them to a file before you type *retf*. To correct mistakes in your programs, you must leave MATRIXx, enter your local editor, fix the errors, and return. (You can also type \\ on some systems to leave the program temporarily without losing your data, which is called "*spawning* ").

3.5 Program Examples

1. The following is a simple exec file that will compute the step response of a second order system for values of ζ ranging from 0.2 to 1 and will create a three-dimensional plot of the step responses.

```
n=1;
for zeta=1:5;...
d=[1,0.2*zeta,1];...
[t,ytemp]=step(n,d,20);...
y(:,zeta)=ytemp;...
end;
plot(t,[1 2 3 4 5],y,'nolegend   web=1')
return
```

Note that the vector `ytemp` is a temporary vector that holds the step response data for each iteration. These column vectors are then passed to the matrix `y`, which will contain all responses. The output of the program is shown in the Figure 3-1.

Caution

Avoid including comments (using //) within loops, as this will direct the program to ignore all lines following the comment line, resulting in an error message.

2. This program is a slight generalization of the first program. Suppose we want to obtain the step response of a system for three different values of damping ratio and undamped natural frequency, i.e.,

$$G(s) = \frac{b}{s^2 + a\,s + b}$$

where a = { 1, 2, 4 } and b = { 1.25, 2, 29 }. The following program accomplishes the task.

```
a=[1 2 4]; b=[1.25 2 29];
for j=1:3, num=b(j), den=[1 a(j) b(j)],...
[t,ytemp]=step(num,den,10);...
y(:,j)=ytemp;...
end
```

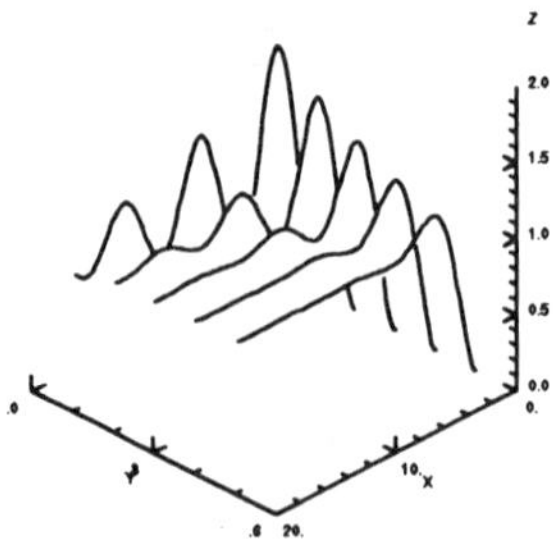

Figure 3-1 Family of step responses.

The responses can be displayed in various ways.

a. Separate plots by splitting the screen as

```
< > plot(t,y(:,1),'upper left');...
 plot(t,y(:,2),'upper right');...
 plot(t,y(:,3),'lower left')
```

b. One simultaneous plot with responses overlaid as

```
< > plot(t,y)
```

c. Three separate strip chart plots as

```
< > plot(t,y,'strip')
```

3. This program is a UDF that will compute the step response characteristics of a system. It computes percent overshoot (POS), rise time (T_r), peak time (T_p) and 2% settling time (T_s). You can modify it for your own use. It is also meant to demonstrate the use of *if* and *while* structures. You will find this program useful for many of the exercises and simulations in Chapter 4 because it simplifies data analysis by automating it.

```
//[POS,TR,TS2,TP]=STEPCHAR(T,Y)
//finding  POS
mp=max(y); sizet=size(t); dimt=sizet(1); yss=y(dimt);
pos=100*(mp-yss)/yss;
//finding rise time
i=1;j=1;k=1;q=1;
while y(i)<0.1;...
i=i+1;...
```

```
end;
t1=t(i);
while  y(j)<0.9;...
j=j+1;...
end;
t2=t(j);tr=t2-t1;
//finding settling time (two percent)
i=dimt+1;n=0;
while n=0,...
i=i-1;...
if i=1,n=1;else...
if y(i)>=1.02, n=1;...
end;
t1=t(i); i=dimt+1; n=0;
while n=0,...
i=i-1;...
if y(i)<=0.98, n=1;...
end; t2=t(i);
if t1>t2, TS2=t1, else TS2=t2;
//finding  peak time
while y(q)<mp;...
q=q+1;...
end;
tp=t(q);
retf;
```

4. Here is the same program using the *for* and *if-elseif* structures.

```
//[POS,TR,TS2,TP]=STEPCHAR2(T,Y)
sizet=size(t); dimt=sizet(1); mp=max(y); yss=y(dimt);
pos=100*(mp-yss)/yss;
for i=1:dimt,...
if mp=y(i), tp=t(i);...
for i=1:dimt,...
if  y(i)>1.02*yss, ts2=t(i);...
elseif y(i)<0.98*yss, ts2=t(i);
end;
for i=1:dimt,...
if  y(i)<0.1*yss,  t1=t(i);...
elseif  y(i)=mp, exit;...
end;
for i=1:dimt,...
if  y(i)<0.9*yss, t2=t(i);...
elseif  y(i)=mp, exit;...
end;
tr=t2-t1;
retf
```

3.6 Problems

Note: The problems denoted by * require many simulations and are time consuming.

3.1 The purpose of this problem is to illustrate the use of *for*, *sum* and *prod* commands.

a. Write a program to generate the sine of the individual elements of a random four by four matrix.

b. Use the *prod* command to generate and list N factorial (N !) and test it for N ranging from 1 to 10.

c. Repeat part b using the *for* command instead of *prod* command.

d. Use the *sum* command to find and list in tabular form the consecutive sum of N numbers and test it for N ranging from 1 to 10.

e. Repeat part d using the *for* command instead of *sum* command.

f. Write a program to generate and tabulate the sum of the squares for the first N integers and test it for N ranging from 1 to 10.

Note: for the following problems, you might note that the step response and frequency response of a transfer function, $G = num/den$, are obtained as shown below.

```
< > [time,y]=step(num,den,tmax);
< > [omega,mag,phase]=bode(num,den,omegamin,omegamax);
```

3.2 Modify the program in Example 3 or 4 so that the UDF computes characteristics of several step responses simultaneously. Note that in the examples, the step response data is a column vector, here you want to feed in several responses simultaneously, so the response data is a matrix (each column corresponds to a different step response data).

3.3 The purpose of this problem is to compare the step response of a system with a pair of dominant complex poles versus systems that have non-dominant poles.

a. Find the poles of the following transfer functions. Use the program developed in Problem 3.2 to compute the step response characteristic features (POS, T_r, , T_s, T_p) of the following systems:

$$T_1 = \frac{2}{s^2+2s+2} \quad , \quad T_2 = \frac{4s+2}{s^2+2s+2} \quad , \quad T_3 = \frac{1}{2s^3+3s^2+3s+1}$$

b. Write a program that will take as its inputs the closed loop frequency response data (ω, Mag, Phase) and will output its characteristic features (M_r,BW). Test it on the above systems.

c. Use the above programs and obtain the required data.

d. Comment on the effects of an added zero (as in T_2) or an added pole (as in T_3) on the time and frequency response characteristics of the systems.

3.4 Write a program that will take the numerator and denominator of a transfer function as its input and finds its poles, isolates the *dominant* complex poles, and computes its step response characteristic features. Note that in the program of Problem 3.2 you used actual data to find response features, while here you use the dominant poles and *formulas*. It is expected that while the poles are dominant, the results of both programs should be fairly close, otherwise the formulas give inaccurate results. Use the transfer function in Problem 3.3 for data. Note that T_2 and T_3 have an extra pole or zero and it is expected that the results will be inaccurate for these cases.

***3.5** Write a program that will take two step response specifications and produces a set of five desirable complex pole locations that meet the specifications. It should also compute the other remaining features and tabulate them along with the pole locations. Note that this program is almost " inverse" of the program you prepared for Problem 3.4. For example the inputs might be $10 \le POS \le 30$, and $1 \le T_r \le 3$. Your program should search over the appropriate region of the complex plane and choose five pole locations, and for each pole it should compute the expected T_r, T_s, T_p and tabulate them alongside the corresponding poles. Test your program for the following specifications and tabulate your results. Before writing the program, show geometrically in the complex plane the regions satisfying the following specifications. You should also obtain the step response of a canonical second order transfer function having your computed poles and actually verify that your poles meet the specifications by finding the resulting step responses and their characteristics.

a. $10 < POS < 30$, $5 < Tr < 10$

b. $5 < POS < 15$, $1 < Tr < 2$

c. $5 < POS < 20$, $2 < Tp < 3$

d. $1 < Tp < 2$, $5 < Ts < 10$

***3.6** Consider the exponential mapping between two complex planes: $z = e^{sT}$
This map plays an important part in digital control (see Chapter 9), e.g., it shows the relation between poles of a continuous system and and its sampled version. Let $T = 1$ for simplicity. Remember, the complex variable of the Laplace transform, s, is
$s = -\sigma + j\,\omega_d \;\rightarrow\; z = e^{-\sigma + j\omega_d} = e^{-\sigma} e^{j\omega_d}$ where $\sigma = \zeta\,\omega_n$, $\omega_d = \omega_n\sqrt{1-\zeta^2}$

We would like to investigate how various lines in the s-plane are mapped into the z-plane. For example, lines of constant σ are mapped into circles of radius e^{σ} as shown next.

When σ is fixed, $|z| = e^{\sigma}$ and $\angle z = \omega_d$. Therefore as ω is varied, a circle is swept out. In particular, the $j\omega$ axis ($\sigma = 0$) is mapped onto the unit circle.

a. Let $\omega_d = [0 : 0.1 : 2]$, plot the map of constant σ for $\sigma = [1 : 5]$. Use the *keep* option to get five concentric circles in one plot.
b. Let $\sigma = [0 : 0.05 : 5]$, plot the map of constant ω_d, for $\omega_d = [\,0 : \pi/6 : \pi\,]$. Use the *keep* option to get seven lines emanating from the origin in one plot.
c. Let $\zeta = [0 : 0.05 : 1]$, plot the map of constant ω_n, for $\omega_n = [\,\pi/20 : \pi/10 : \pi]$. Use the *keep* option to get ten logarithmic curves in one plot.
d. Let $\omega_d = [0 : \pi/60 : \pi]$, plot the map of constant ζ, for $\zeta = [\,0 : 0.2 : 0.8]$. Use the *keep* option to get five spirals in one plot.

To get the correct plots, you will have to express z in terms of the appropriate sweep variables. For instance, in part c, you have to write z in terms of ζ and ω_d.
Refer to [FPW91], [O87], or other references given in Chapter 9 to see samples of these contours.

4

Classical Control Commands

In this chapter we will demonstrate some of the commands available for classical control analysis. We are interested in finding impulse response, step response, response to general inputs, frequency response, and root locus of a system represented by a transfer function. A transfer function *G(s)* is entered by defining separately its numerator and denominator as polynomials. MATRIXx commands interpret these polynomials internally as a transfer function.

4.1 Time Domain

The step response, *y(t)*, of a system with transfer function $G(s) = num(s)/den(s)$, can be obtained by the *step* command. Its syntax is

```
< > [t,y]=step(num,den,tmax,npts)
```

The final desired time for simulation is *tmax* and *npts* is the number of desired points, which is optional (default is 100). The outputs are a time vector and an output matrix. The time vector ranges from 0 to *tmax*. For SISO systems, the output will be a vector with the same size as the time vector.

For multi-input multi-output systems (MIMO systems), the output is a matrix. It will have the same number of rows as the time vector. For a system with *p* inputs and *m* outputs, *y* will have *p*m* columns. The first *p* columns are the response to the first input, the second *p* columns are the response to the second input, etc.

For example, to compute and plot the step response from $t = 0$ to $t = 20$ of

$$G(s) = \frac{10}{s^2 + 2\,s + 10}$$

we enter

```
< > num=10; den=[1,2,10]; [t,y]=step(num,den,20); plot(t,y)
```

The impulse response is obtained by the *impulse* command. Its syntax is similar to the *step* command, i.e.,

```
< > [t,y]=impulse(num,den,tmax,npts)
```

The system response to general inputs can also be obtained. The appropriate command is called *lsim* with the following syntax:

```
< > [t,y]=lsim(num,den,u,deltat)
```

The input is the vector *u*. The number of rows of *u* controls the number of output points computed. For single input systems *u* is a column vector. (For multi-input systems the number of columns of *u* equals the number of inputs). The time increment between points in the *u* vector is *deltat*. For example, to generate the unit ramp, we can define it as a 100-point column vector and use it as the input *u* in the *lsim* command to find the ramp response for a 100-sec record as shown below.

```
< > ramp=[0:1:100]' ; [t,y]=lsim(num,den,ramp,1)
```

We can find the response to random uniform noise using the *rand* function. Note that *rand(m, n)* generates an *m* by *n* matrix of uniformly distributed random numbers between 0 and 1. The noise response is found for a record of 10 sec by choosing *deltat*=0.1.

```
< > noise = rand(100,1) ; [t,y]=lsim(num,den,noise,0.1);
```

4.2 Frequency Domain

The frequency response of systems can be obtained using *bode*, *nyquist*, and the *nichols* commands. These commands automatically generate plots, so you do not have to issue any *plot* commands. In addition, the nyquist and nichols commands are interactive (explained later). The syntax for the *bode* command is

```
< > [w, mag, phase]=bode(num,den,wmin,wmax,npts, 'options')
< > [w, mag, phase]=bode(num,den,omega, 'options')
```

The first syntax produces on a split screen, the Bode magnitude (in dB) and phase (in degrees) plots from radian frequency *wmin* to *wmax* (logarithmically spaced). Do not forget to issue the *erase* command after it is done. The default number of points is 100. In the alternate syntax, you can evaluate the frequency response for a given frequency vector *omega*. The plotting options available are *plot*, *noplot*, *wrap*, and *nowrap*. The *wrap* option produces discontinuous phase plots where phase is limited to ± 180 degrees. The *noplot* option is useful when the command is part of a loop, so no time will be wasted for plotting. For MIMO systems, frequency response between all inputs and outputs are generated. The interpretation is similar to the *step* command. For other options and syntactical information, either refer to your manual or get on-line help on *bode*. The *nyquist* and *nichols* commands have the following syntax.

```
< > [w,re,im]=nyquist(num,den,wmin,wmax,' options' )
< > [w,mag,phase]=nichols(num,den,wmin,wmax,' options ')
```

The *nyquist* command computes the real and imaginary parts of $G(j\omega)$ and plots the imaginary versus the real part. The *nichols* command plots the magnitude in dB versus phase in degrees. If you have already issued the *bode* command, you can get this by plotting magnitude versus phase directly.

Interactive Tracking in Plots

Starting with MATRIXx Version 7.1, *nyquist* and *nichols* commands became interactive. Once the command is entered, the plot is drawn, and a cursor becomes available. Using the up (↑) or down (↓) arrows on your keyboard, you can track the plot to see the corresponding frequency. This is important because the frequency is an implicit variable in these two plots. How fast the cursor moves on the plot is chosen by the program. You can override this by entering jump increments in powers of 10 (you actually enter the power). For example, typing *2* causes the cursor to move in increments of 100, whereas typing *-2* causes increments of 0.01. You can go to any desired frequency directly by typing *E*. The program responds by asking you to enter the desired value, and the cursor will jump accordingly. You can quit the interactive session by typing *Q*. (In some platforms, typing *R* will redraw the plot and *H* produces a hardcopy output. This is not available on the PC version). In summary, the interactive specific commands are

```
E Enter desired value
Q Quit
↑ or U ( ↓ or D )        Move cursor up (or down)
H Hardcopy
R Redraw
```

Starting with MATRIXx Ver. 7.2, M circles and N circles are automatically drawn on the above two plots. These features can be overridden by specifying *nopattern* in the options strings. Unless they are needed, you may want to override this feature, because it causes delays in display and printing.

Hardcopy

The *bode*, *nyquist*, and *nichols* commands automatically generate plots, i.e., we do not issue a *plot* command. One method of getting hardcopy of these plots is using the *plot* command.

Once the data is generated, you can customize your plots by using the *plot* command and its options (among the option strings are *printer* and *plotter* strings). The second method is to get the hardcopy of these plots directly by issuing the following commands, which will direct all plots to the printer.

```
< > plot('printer hold')              // directs all plots to printer
< > [w,mag,phase]=bode(....)           // issues the appropriate command
< > plot('display hold')              // returns to screen mode
```

Note: Getting graphics hardcopy is hardware specific and depends on how your system is configured. The above is for a PC platform. Consult your manual or the system manager for specifics.

Stability Margins

Classical notions of relative stability as measured by gain and phase margin are obtained using the *margin* command. Its syntax is

```
< > [gm,pm,wpc,wgc] = margin(w,mag,phase)
```

The inputs are the magnitude, phase, and frequency vectors obtained from the *bode* or *nichols* command. The outputs are the gain margin (in dB), phase margin (in degrees) and their corresponding frequencies. If there are multiple crossings of the frequency axes (which may occur when the corresponding transfer function has RHP poles or zeros), all frequencies and margins will be displayed. It is important that these numbers be interpreted correctly. This can be done by obtaining the Nyquist plot and examining the encirclements.

4.3 Root Locus

Root locus of continuous SISO systems can easily be obtained using the *rlocus* command. There are two varieties of this command. Interactive and non-interactive.

Non-Interactive Root Locus

The non-interactive command plots root locus of *G(s)* for a specified range of gain values, where the gain is entered as a row vector. Its syntax is

```
< > clpoles=rlocus(num,den,k,'options')
```

The output is the matrix of closed loop poles. Each row corresponds to the closed loop poles for a given gain. For example, if k = [0 : 0.1 : 1], we get root locus for values of k from 0 to 1 in increments of 0.1 (i.e., 10 points). Make sure k does not have a lot of elements unless you enjoy long waits! The options (available in Version 7.2 and above) will be described shortly.

As mentioned in Chapter 1, be sure to enter the correct transfer function. The underlying configuration is the standard feedback configuration with negative feedback. The transfer function you enter is the open loop transfer function (i.e., the product of transfer functions around the loop). If you have positive feedback or if you want the complementary root locus (also called zero degree or inverse root locus), you should multiply the numerator by {- 1 }.

For a printout, follow the similar steps explained under Hardcopy explained in Section 4.2.

Interactive Root Locus

The " *interactive* " root locus has the following syntax.

```
< > gain=rlocus(num,den,'options')
```

In the interactive mode, you can vary the gain by using the up or down arrow keys on your keyboard a explained in the previous section under Interactive Tracking in Plots. You view the closed loop poles move along the locus. The corresponding gain is displayed in the bottom left portion of the screen. The output of the command is the last gain.

The following useful options are available:

Noplot: To suppress plotting in non-interactive mode.

Nopattern: To suppress the overlay of lines of constant damping ratio (ζ) and natural frequency (ω_n). These lines will be drawn by default and can cause very long delays in printing; it is recommended that you use the *nopattern* option for printing purposes unless you need them.

Zeta, Omega, Ts: To highlight the specified line of ζ, ω_n, or settling time. This is very useful for root locus design (see Chapter 7) as it allows you to see clearly the region meeting your specifications.

Zooming: You can also zoom on any region in the complex plane by specifying values for *xmin*, *xmax*, *ymin* and *ymax*. Here is an example.

```
< > gain=rlocus(num,den,'xmin=-5 xmax=0 ymin=0 ymax=5 ...
zeta=0.7 omega=2')
```

The above zooms on the second quadrant, and highlights the lines for damping ratio of 0.7 and natural frequency of 2.

The interactive root locus (in Version 7.1 and above) also allows specification of time delays for systems of the form $G(s)\, e^{-T\,s}$. The syntax is

```
< > gain=rlocus(num,den,T,'options')
```

We will demonstrate some of the above commands using the following example.

4.4 Examples

Example 4.1

To demonstrate how the above commands can be used in analysis of control systems, we will consider the following third order plant with unity feedback configuration.

$$G(s) = \frac{1}{s\,(s+1)\,(s+2)}\,, \qquad K = 1.5$$

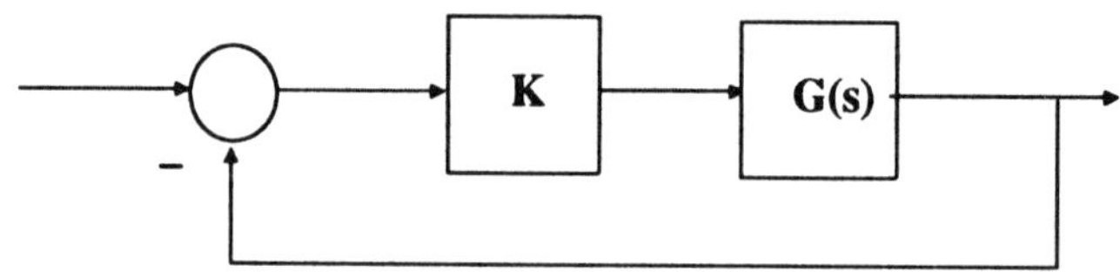

Figure 4-1 Block diagram for Example 4.1.

Frequency response analysis

First, we enter the open loop transfer function, G(s) = ng/dg, and obtain the Bode plot with gain $K = 1.5$. To print this plot, we use the first method for getting hardcopy. Initially we use the *noplot* option in the *bode* command, then we use the *plot* command directly to customize the plot. The options we have used are the following. Magnitude and phase are plotted as a *strip* plot with the *log* option for magnitude (to get log-log plot) and the *logx* option for phase (to get a semi-log plot). The y-axis label is suppressed, and the plot is sent to the printer.

```
< > k=1.5; ng=1*k; dg=[1 3 2 0];
< > [w,m,p]=bode(ng,dg,0.1,10,100,'noplot');
< > plot(w,[m,p],'log|logx strip noylab printer')
```

From the plots in Figure 4-2, we observe that the gain and phase margins are approximately 10 dB and 45 degrees. We can verify this using the *margin* command.

```
< > [gm,pm,wpc,wgc]=margin(w,m,p)
```

```
WGC =
.6118
WPC =
1.4143
PM =
41.5332
GM =
12.0416
```

The Nyquist plot with the unit circle superimposed on it can be obtained using

```
< > [w,r,i]=nyquist(ng,dg,0.1,10,'noplot');
< > t=[0:0.1:10]';x1=sin(t); x2=cos(t);  // parametric equation of a circle
< > plot([r,x1],[i,x2],'xmin=-1 xmax=1 ymin=-1 ymax=1 noxlab ...
noylab coscale printer')
```

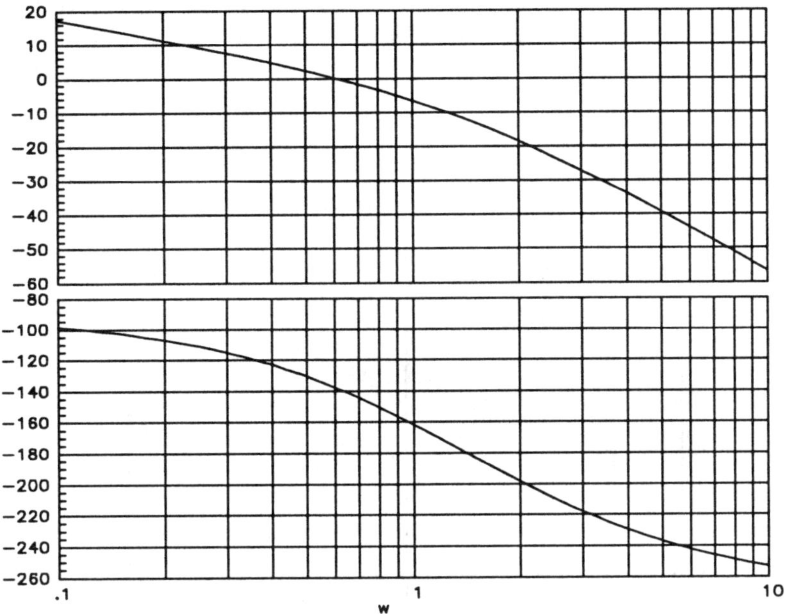

Figure 4-2 Bode magnitude and phase plot of *KG(s)*.

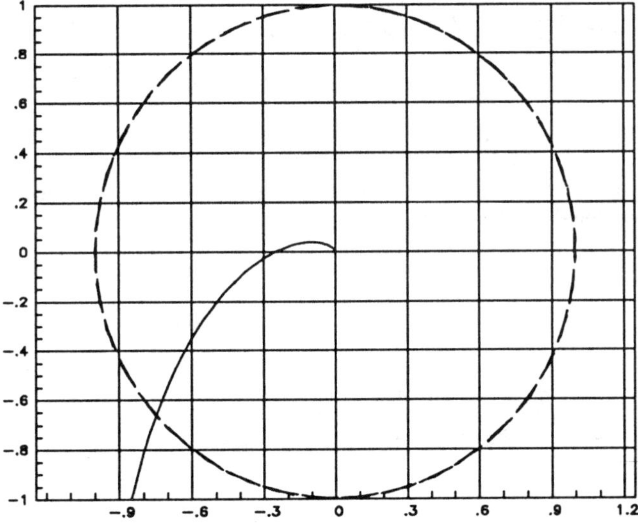

Figure 4-3 Nyquist plot for Example 4.1.

The plotting options use axes scaling to position the plot in a unit box, and the *coscale* option produces a true circle. The axis labels are suppressed.

The Nyquist plot in Figure 4-3 confirms closed loop stability and the stability margins.

We will obtain the Nichols plot next. This can be done using the *nichols* command. Note, however that because we have already issued the *bode* command, we have all the data required to obtain the Nichols plot (plot of magnitude in dB versus phase in degrees). The plot is shown in Figure 4-4.

```
< > plot(p,m,'noxlab noylab')
```

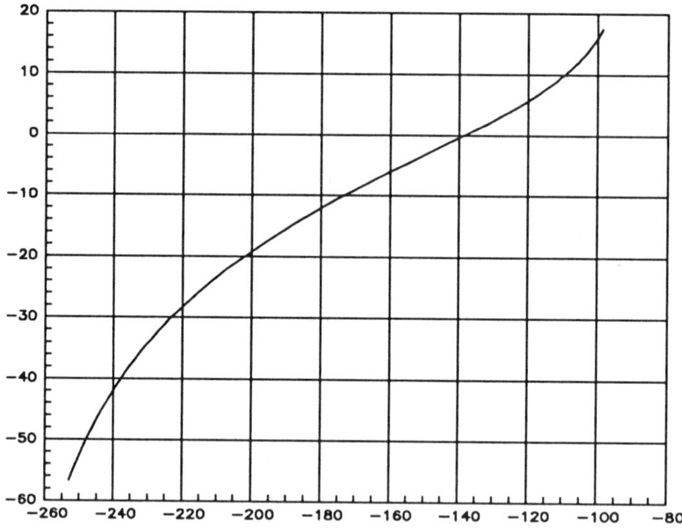

Figure 4-4 Nichols plot of *KG(s)* .

You can again verify the margins from the Nichols plot.

The closed loop Bode plot is also obtained to find the bandwidth and the peak resonance. Let *T(s)* denote the closed loop transfer function

$$T(s) = \frac{K\ G(s)}{1 + K\ G(s)}$$

Let $G(s) = \frac{ng}{dg}$, then $T(s) = \frac{K\,ng}{dg + K\,ng} = \frac{nt}{dt}$

Because dg and K*ng are vectors of different sizes, they cannot be added, but we will use a simple trick

```
< > dt=dg+[0  0  0  K*ng];
```

You see the idea; we have converted K*ng to a third order polynomial by padding it with enough leading zero coefficients.

```
< > nt=1.5; dt=dg+[0 0 0 1.5];
< > [w,mc]=bode(nt,dt,0.1,10,100,'noplot');
< > plot(w,mc,'log upper ymin=-30 printer')
```

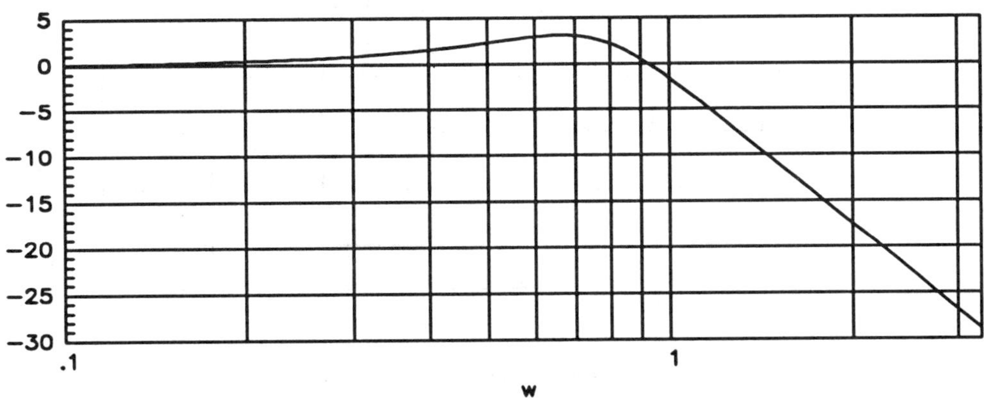

Figure 4-5 Closed loop Bode magnitude plot.

From Figure 4-5, we observe a peak resonance of 3 dB and a bandwidth of about 1 rad/sec.

Root locus analysis

Next we will use the interactive root locus to predict the response types for various gains.

```
< > r=rlocus(ng,dg,'nopattern')
```

After the plot is obtained, use the arrow keys on the numeric keypad as explained before, and make the following observations:

Case 1: For $0 < K < 0.4$, the poles are distinct and real, implying an overdamped response.

Case 2: The breakaway point occurs for $K = 0.4$; therefore, the response is critically damped.

Case 3: For $0.4 < K < 6$, the dominant poles are complex, resulting in an underdamped response.

Case 4: For $K = 6$, the system has a pair of imaginary poles and is marginally stable.

Case 5: For values of $K > 6$, the poles enter the RHP, and the system is unstable.

To verify the above observations, we will find the closed loop transfer function and obtain the five responses. Instead of repeating this procedure five times, you can write a UDF or a UDC

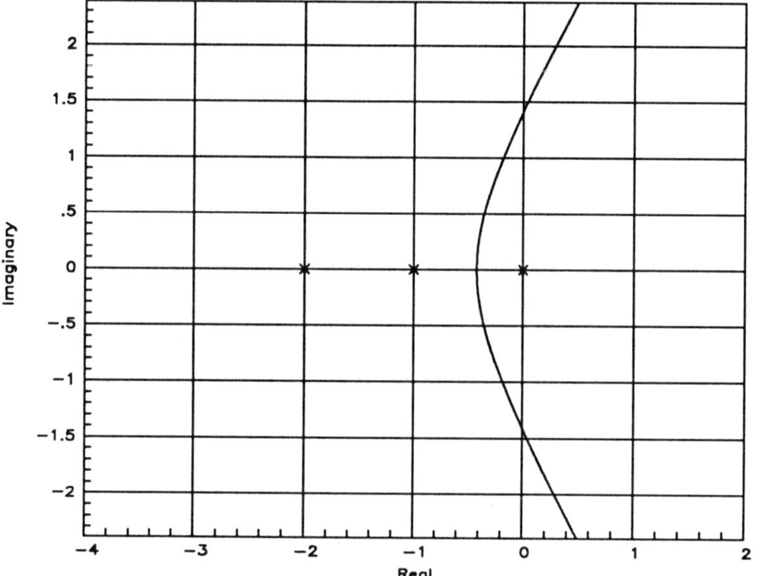

Figure 4-6 Root locus for Example 4.1.

to simplify the task. Our simple UDF is called "cstep" and is shown below. Recall that the UDF has to be created outside of MATRIXx ahead of time.

```
// [nt,dt,t,yc]=cstep(ng,dg,nh,dh,tf)
// Closed loop step response: T= GH/ (1+GH ), T=nt/dt, G=ng/dg , H=nh/dh
ngh=conv(ng,nh); dgh=conv(dg,dh);
dimngh=prod(size(ngh)); dimdgh=prod(size(dgh));
nc=[0*ones(1,dimdgh-dimngh), ngh];
dt=nc+dgh;
nt=ngh;
[t,yc]=step(nt,dt,tf);
retf
```

To invoke this UDF, we need to define it first using

```
< > define 'cstep'
```

We then invoke it five times. For example, for the underdamped case (Case 3) we use

```
< > [nt3,dt3,t,y3]=cstep(1,dg,1.5,1,20);
```

The plots for the three stable responses and two non-stable responses are shown in Figure 4-7. The values of K that were used for the simulations are { 0.25, 0.4, 1.5, 6, 8}.

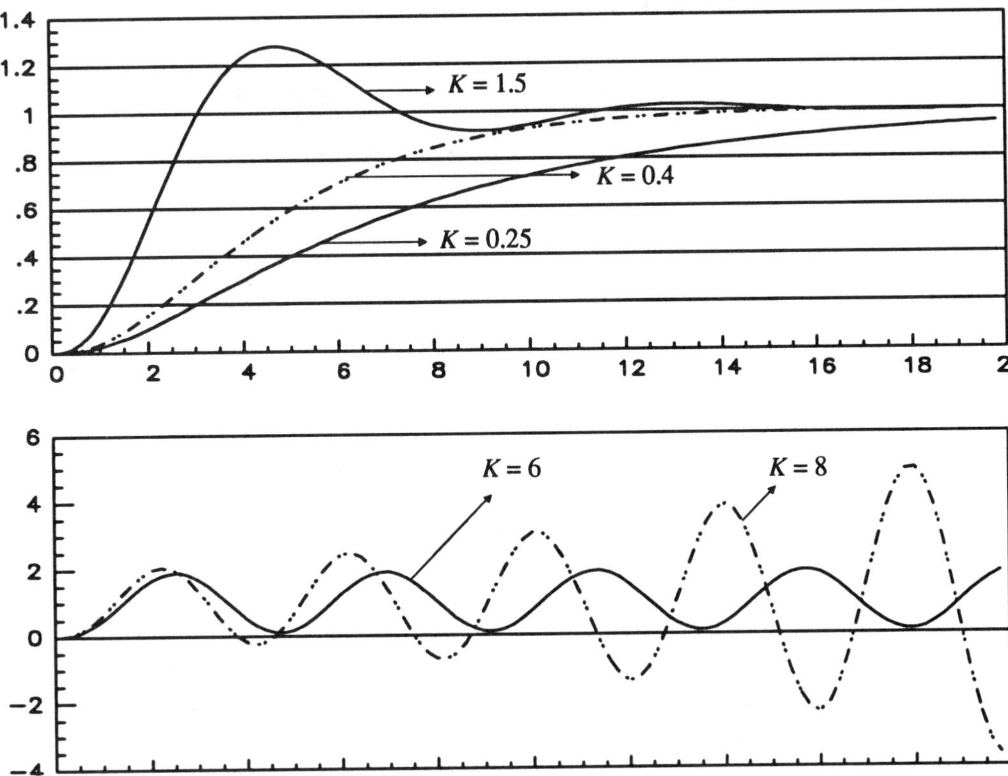

Figure 4-7 Step responses for Example 4.1.

From now on, we will concentrate on the underdamped response, i.e., K=1.5. We can compute the percent overshoot as the percentage difference between peak value M_p (maximum value) and steady state response yss:

```
< > Mp=max(y3); yss=y3(100); POS=100*(Mp-yss)/yss

 POS     =
27.8585
```

Steady state error analysis

We will next study the steady state error properties of the system. Because the unity feedback system has a pole at the origin, it is Type 1, and the steady state error (e_{ss}) to a step input is zero. The error to a unit ramp input is given by ($1/K_v$), where K_v is the velocity error coefficient

$$K_v = \lim_{s \to 0} s\,G(s) = \frac{1.5}{2} = 0.75\,,\quad \text{hence}\,,\quad e_{ss} = 1.33$$

We will use the *lsim* command to find the ramp response and verify our result. An easy way to find the ramp response is to find the step response of the closed loop system multiplied by 1/s. This is done by adding an extra 0 to the denominator polynomial vector as shown below.

```
< > dtt=[dt , 0];
< > [t2,yramp]=step(nt,dtt,10);
< > plot(t2,[t2 yramp],'noxlab noylab nogrid upper ')
```

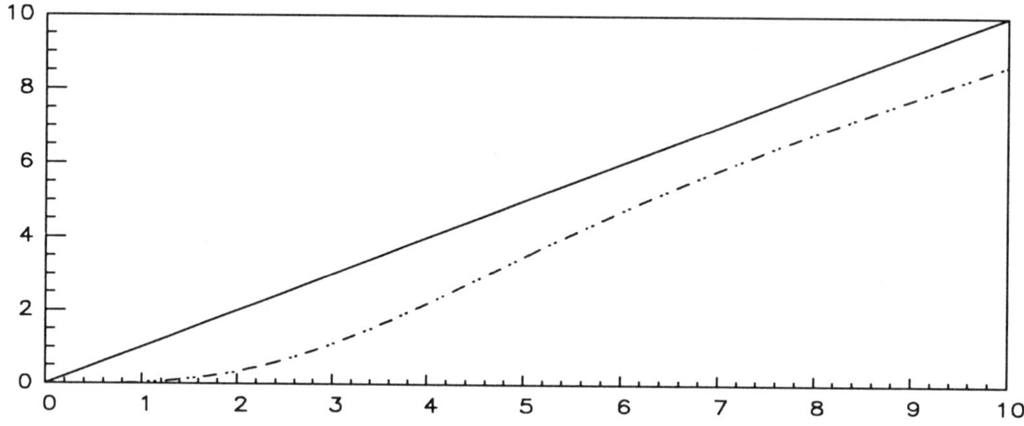

Figure 4-8 Ramp response for Example 4.1.

We can easily verify the steady state error from

```
< > ess=t2-yramp;
< > ess(100)

ANS =

  1.3307
```

Filtering properties

From the closed loop Bode plot (Figure 4-5) we can see that the system acts as a low pass filter. Most control systems have low pass characteristics. This means the system rejects high frequency signals outside of its bandwidth. We will verify this by finding the response of the underdamped system to random noise. The *rand* command is used to add uniform noise to a step input, and the *lsim* command is used to find the response.

```
< > t=[0:0.1:10]'; noise=ones(t)+rand(t);
< > [t,ynoise]=lsim(nt3,dt3,noise,0.2);
```

Note that t is a vector, *ones(t)* creates a step input of the same size, and *rand(t)* creates a random vector of the same size with elements between 0 and 1, so the input is a noisy step. We have plotted the input and output on the same plot for comparison in Figure 4-9. As expected, the system suppresses high frequency signals such as noise. Noise creates an offset error in this case. The offset occurs because the noise has an average magnitude of 0.5. Usually random noise has smaller magnitude relative to the input, and in that case its effect is barely noticeable.

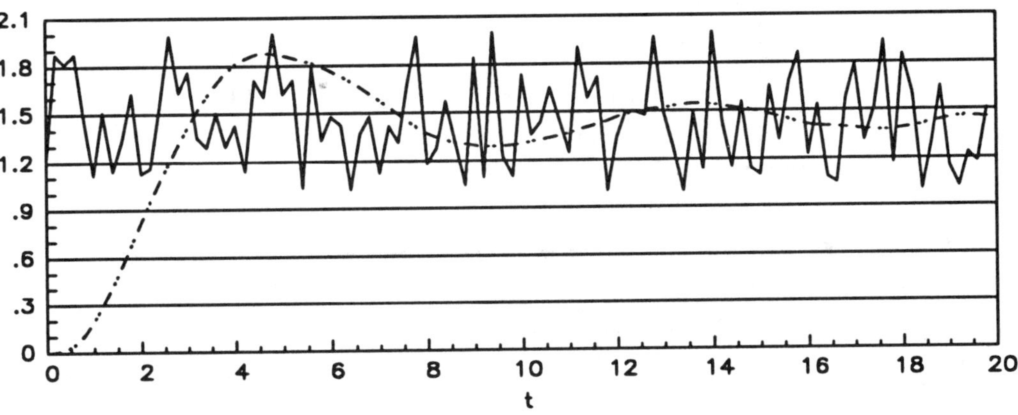

Figure 4-9 Response of system in Example 4.1 to random noise.

Example 4.2 : Effects of Time Delay

Time delays exist in many applications of control systems such as process control, manufacturing systems, transportation, deep space applications, and others. In linear time invariant continuous systems, time delay is represented by e^{-sT}. Systems with time delay can be conveniently analyzed using frequency response methods.

Note that $e^{-j\omega T} = 1 \angle -\omega T$.

Therefore, time delay leaves the magnitude unchanged and simply adds phase lag. The phase lag associated with time delay tends to be destabilizing.

For simulation purposes, if we use the *bode* command, all we have to do is to subtract the phase of time delay from the phase of *G(s)*.

Let $G(s) = \dfrac{2}{s+1}$ and T = 1 , the Bode plot of the system is obtained as follows:

```
< > n=2; d=[1   1]; delay=1;
< > [w1,m,p]=bode(n,d,0.01,5,100,'noplot');
< > pd=p-(delay*w1*180/pi);       // subtract the phase in degrees
< > plot(w1,m,'log upper noylab noxlab');
< > plot(w1,[p,pd],'logx lower noylab noxlab');
```

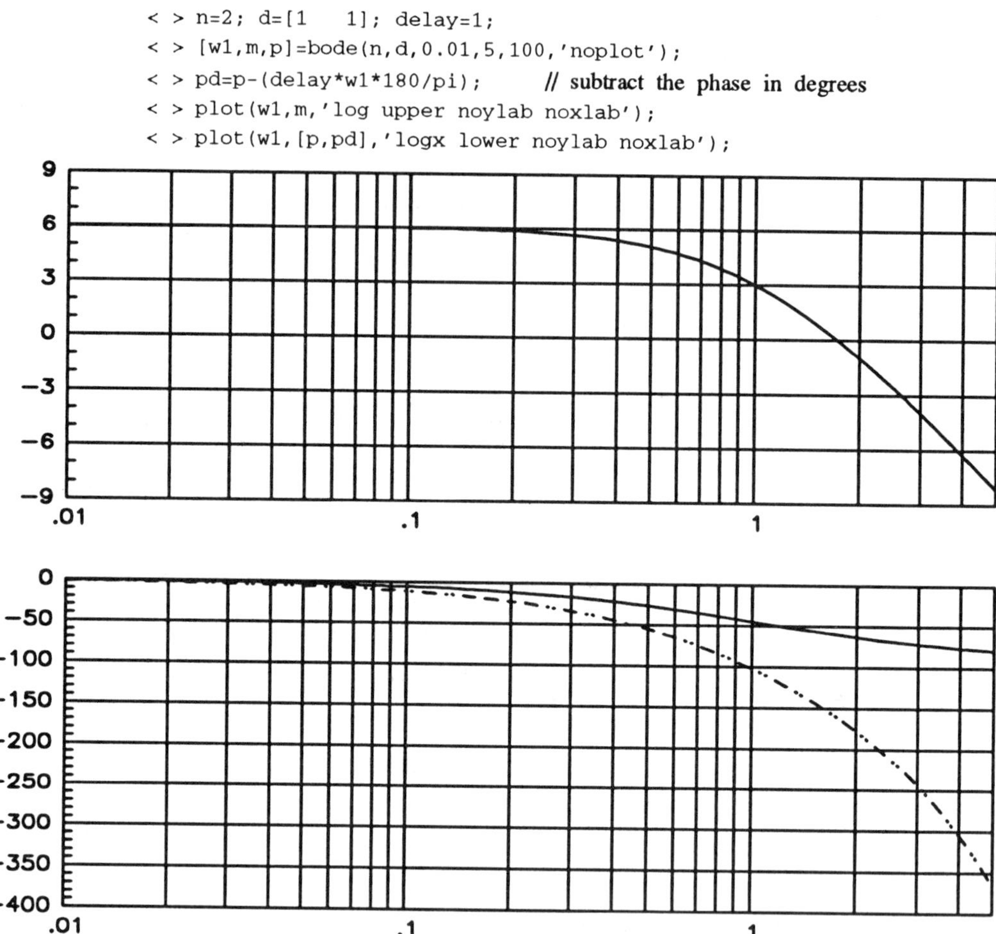

Figure 4-10 Bode plot of the system showing the effects of time delay.

Observe from Figure 4-10 that even though the original system has infinite gain margin and about 120 degrees of phase margin, time delay reduces these margins to almost 2 dB and 30 degrees. Hence, the destabilizing effects of time delay can be quite drastic.

The Nyquist plot can be obtained by observing that

$G(j\,\omega)e^{-j\,\omega\,T} = [R(\omega) + j\,I(\omega)]\,e^{-j\,\omega\,T}$ where $R(\omega) = \mathrm{Re}\,[\,G(j\,\omega)\,]$, $I(\omega) = \mathrm{Im}\,[\,G(j\,\omega)\,]$

Hence, we can compute the real and imaginary parts of the frequency response of the system with time delay. The plot of the imaginary versus the real part is the Nyquist plot.

```
< > [w2,r,i]=nyquist(n,d,0.01,20,200,'noplot');
< > rd=real((r+jay*i).*exp(-jay*w2*delay));
< > id=imag((r+jay*i).*exp(-jay*w2*delay));
```

```
< > plot([r, rd], [i, id],'noxgrid noylab noxlab')
```

Note the use of *real, imag*, and *exp* commands. The Nyquist plot in Figure 4-11 clearly shows the small stability margins.

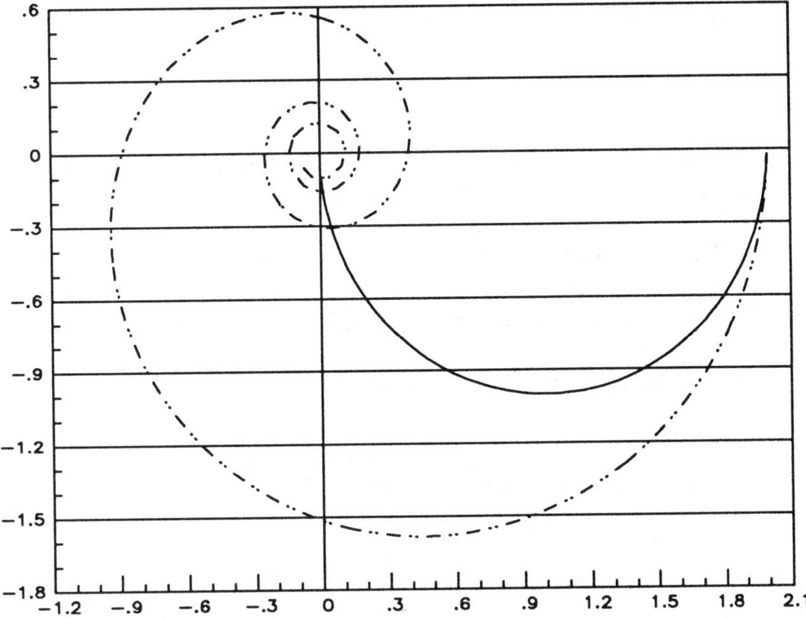

Figure 4-11 Nyquist plot of the system showing the effects of time delay.

4.5 Problems

***4.1** The purpose of this exercise is, to investigate the effects of varying the pole locations of a second order underdamped system, and to observe some well known relationships between the step response and Bode plot of the system.
The canonical form of an underdamped second order system is

$$G(s) = \frac{\omega_n^2}{s^2 + 2\zeta\omega_n s + \omega_n^2} = \frac{(\omega_d^2 + \sigma^2)}{s^2 + 2\,\sigma\, s + (\,\omega_d^2 + \sigma^2\,)}$$

where the poles are located at

$$s = -\,\sigma \pm j\,\omega_d \quad \text{where} \quad \sigma = \zeta\,\omega_n \;\;,\quad \omega_d = \omega_n\sqrt{1-\zeta^2} \quad \text{and} \quad \zeta = \cos(\theta)$$

Preliminary analysis

Using the properties and formulas for second order systems, discuss the effects of varying each parameter, σ, ω_d, ω_n, and ζ (the other three fixed) on the step response parameters (POS, T_r, T_s, T_p) and Bode plot parameters (M_r, BW). For terminology, formulas, and notation, refer to Chapter 1.

Laboratory

For each of the following parts, the step responses are from $t = 0$ to 10, plotted simultaneously, and Bode plots are from $\omega = 0.1$ to 10. Magnitude plots are log-log, plotted in the upper half of the screen, simultaneously; phase plots are semi-log, plotted on the lower half of screen, simultaneously. You must turn in a total of twelve plots containing the results of thirty six simulations (there are some duplications, only twenty seven simulations are needed). Because of the large number of repetitive simulations, you are far better off writing a simple program using *for* loops (see Chapter 3) to automate the process and save a lot of time.

a. Let $\omega_d = 1$, obtain the step response and Bode plots when $\sigma = 0.5, 1, 5$.
b. Repeat part a for $\sigma = 1$ and $\omega_d = 0.5, 1, 5$.
c. Repeat part a for $\zeta = \frac{1}{\sqrt{2}}$ and $\omega_n = \frac{\sqrt{2}}{2}, \sqrt{2}, 5\sqrt{2}$.
d. Repeat part a for $\omega_n = \sqrt{2}$ and $\theta = 30, 45, 60$ degrees. Note $\zeta = \cos(\theta)$.
e. From your data and the plots, compute all of the above six response parameters, and tabulate your results. Use the data to draw conclusions about the effects of varying the parameters on response characteristics (increase, decrease or no change).

The following questions are about some relationships between step and frequency responses.

f. What relation do you observe between M_r and POS? Can you obtain a numerical relation between them?
g. What about T_r and BW?
h. What about ω_n and BW? Can BW be approximated by ω_n?

***4.2** The purpose of this exercise is to investigate the effects of adding poles and zeros to a second order transfer function. The pole and zero are added separately. We also distinguish two cases: adding a pole (or zero) within the loop, or outside the loop. Because in classical design using Bode or root locus, we usually add poles and zeros—lag-lead compensators— to modify system dynamics, it is important to have a good understanding of these effects.

The nominal system is $G(s)$ in unity feedback structure with a closed loop transfer function given by $T(s)$.

Case I: Feedback **Case II: Open Loop**

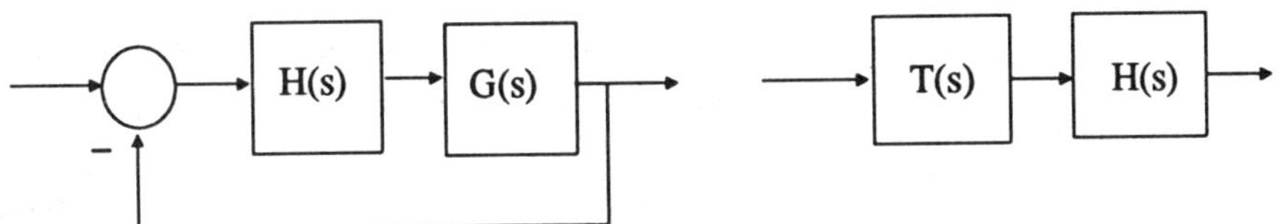

Preliminary analysis

Using rough manual root locus and Bode sketches and some analysis, predict the effects of adding pole (or zero) in both cases I and II. Comment on any increase or decrease in speed of response, overshoot, bandwidth, and relative stability of the system (gain and phase margins).

Laboratory

Let $H(s) = \dfrac{1}{p\,s+1}$ for the case of adding a pole and $H(s) = z\,s + 1$ for the zero case. Note that the actual pole and zero locations are $1/p$ and $1/z$ respectively. Similar to problem 4.1, you will obtain some plots (16 of them) and perform data analysis. Plots are again simultaneous with the same format as before. Since the number of simulations are large (43), it is important to choose good mnemonic names for variables and jot them down for later reference. Also since the number of data vectors generated are large, you may run out of memory locations depending on your hardware platform. To solve this problem, you may have to do the experiment in two steps. For example, do the simulations for the case of adding pole, save your data, and clear the data stack. Then do the case of adding zero and save it under a different name. All step response simulations are from $t = 0$ to 10. Bode plots are from $\omega = 0.05$ to 20. A simple program is a must because of the large number of simulations. Both p and z take the following values: {0.2624, 0.6122, 1.4286, 3.3333}. These values can be generated by the following commands:

```
< > b=log(7/3);a=(10/3)exp(-4*b);
< > for i=1:4,p=a*exp(b*i),end;
```

For each case, the following simulations and the corresponding data must be obtained and tabulated.

Case I: Closed loop step response (POS, T_r, and T_s), open loop Bode plot (ω_{gc} and PM), closed loop Bode plot (M_r and BW).

Case II: Step response and Bode plot (since there is no loop, there is only one kind of Bode plot).

a. Obtain the step response and Bode plot of *T(s)*, and Bode plot of *G(s)*. Note that this is the nominal system, i.e., no pole or zero added, against which all other responses are compared with.

b. Case I, add a pole to *G(s)*: let *p* take the specified values, obtain the appropriate responses. Plot the responses simultaneously with the one in part a for comparison. For instance, your step response plot should consist of five plots, four of them generated here, the fifth one was obtained in part a.

c. Case II, add a pole to *T(s)*: same comments as in b.

d. Case I, add a zero to *G(s)* : same comments as in b.

e. Case II, add a zero to *T(s)*: same comment as in b.

You should now be able to answer the following questions. Note that adding a pole or zero to the transfer function, *T(s)*, does not change its stability, it changes its other properties, however. Adding a pole or zero to the open loop transfer function, *G(s)*, changes both the stability and other response parameters. In general, adding zeros have stabilizing effects and adding poles may be destabilizing. This is one of the reasons compensators are added inside the loop. We will see later how to choose these pole and zero locations to satisfy certain specifications.

f. Based on analysis of your data, what is the effect of adding a pole to *G(s)* on POS, T_r, PM, and BW?

g. What about adding a pole to *T(s)* ?

h. What about adding a zero to *G(s)* ?

i. What about adding a zero to *T(s)* ?

These questions relate to some correspondence between step response and frequency response parameters.

j. What relation do you observe between POS and PM?

k. What about ω_{gc} and BW ?

4.3 This problem investigates the effects of nonminimum phase zeros (i.e. zeros in the right half plane). Systems with RHP zeros or time delays are commonly referred to as nonminimum phase systems. Consider the system

$$G(s) = \frac{n(s)}{s^2 + 0.5s + 1.5}$$

a. Let $n(s) = 1.5$, using formulas for step response of a second order system, estimate POS, peak time, and settling time of the system. Find the step response using the computer and compare your results.

b. Let $n(s) = (-s + \alpha)/\alpha$, find the step response for $\alpha = \{1, 3, 6\}$.

c. Let $n(s) = (s + \alpha)/\alpha$, find the step response for $\alpha = \{1, 3, 6\}$.

Report your work in two plots and tabulate your results. Each plot in case a is overlayed with the simulation plots on b and c.

d. Based on your data, what are the effects of LHP and RHP zeros on the step response? Observe that when the system has RHP zeros the step response "goes in the wron direction" first. This phenomenon can be shown to occur whenever the system has an odd number of RHP zeros.

4.4 The purpose of this problem is to introduce *lag* and *lead* compensators and show their effects on an unstable system. Consider the following double integrator system, $G(s)$, and compensators.

I) *Proportional* compensator : $K(s) = K_c$

II) *Lead* compensator: $K(s) = K_c \dfrac{s+1}{s+5}$

III) *Lag* compensator : $K(s) = K_c \dfrac{s+5}{s+1}$

Preliminary analysis

Using both root locus and Bode plots, drawn manually, answer the following questions.

a. Can the system be stabilized in case I? What are the effects of increasing K_c on the step response in case I?

b. Can the system be stabilized in case II? What are the effects of increasing K_c on the step response in case II?

c. Can the system be stabilized in case III? What are the effects of increasing K_c on the step response in case III?

Laboratory

d. Simulate the step response in each case using three values for $K_c = \{0.1, 0.5, 1\}$. Three simultaneous step response plots in each case are required. Analyze the plots and confirm your conclusions with your preliminary analysis. Convenient final times for simulation in each case are $\{10, 50, 5\}$.

4.5 The purpose of this problem is to demonstrate disturbance rejection properties of feedback systems as compared with open loop systems. You must first analyze the problem and answer the questions, then confirm your results via simulations.

Preliminary analysis

Consider the first order system: $G(s) = \dfrac{1}{s+1}$

a. Open Loop Control: Find a compensator, $K(s)$, that has poles at $\{-1 \pm j\}$ and achieves zero steady state error to step and ramp inputs.

b. Feedback Control: Assume the compensator is in series with the plant in a unity feedback configuration. Find the compensator to satisfy the specifications in part a.

c. Assume that there is a unit step disturbance entering between $K(s)$ and $G(s)$. Find the steady state response of both systems to this disturbance. Which one is suppressing the disturbance better?

d. Determine the filtering properties of each case by looking at rough Bode plots. Which system is better able to suppress high frequency noise or disturbance ?

Laboratory

e. Find the step response in each case to verify your results in part c. Make sure you use the correct transfer function.

f. Generate "normal/Gaussian" noise and let the input be $n(t) = 0.01*\text{rand}(t)$. Simulate the noise response using *lsim* command. In each case, plot the noise input and its response together. Does your simulation confirm your analysis? Does there seem to be a conflict between suppressing low frequency disturbance and high frequency noise?

4.6 The purpose of this problem is to introduce *Proportional plus Integral (PI)* control, and investigate its effects. Consider a canonical second order system $G(s)$ and a cascade PI compensator $K(s)$:

$$G(s) = \frac{\omega_n^2}{s(s+2\zeta\omega_n)} \quad , \quad K(s) = K_p + \frac{K_I}{s} = K_c \frac{s+z}{s}$$

Preliminary analysis

a. Determine for what values of K_c and z, the closed loop system is stable.

b. What are the effects of PI on the steady state error properties of the system?

c. Let $\zeta = 0.5$, $\omega_n = 2$, $K_c = 1$, and $z = 1$. Draw the root locus before and after compensation, determine the effects of PI on rise time and POS.

d. Using open and closed loop Bode plots, determine the effects of PI on peak resonance, closed loop bandwidth, and phase margin.

Laboratory

e. Use root locus to find closed loop poles for the values specified in part c.

f. Obtain step response before and after compensation. Compare rise time, and POS.

g. Obtain open loop Bode plots before and after compensation and compare phase margins and gain crossover frequencies.
h. Obtain closed loop Bode plots before and after compensation to compare bandwidths and peak resonance values. *Note*: all before and after plots must be displayed together for comparison.

4.7 The purpose of this problem is to introduce *Proportional plus Integral plus Derivative* (*PID*) control and perform a simple ad-hoc design. Consider the following unstable plant:

$$G(s) = \frac{1}{(s-1)^2}$$

The specifications are: closed loop stability, and zero steady state error to unit step inputs.

Preliminary analysis

a. Use the Routh-Hurwitz test and root locus arguments to show that a cascade PID compensator, $K(s)$, can meet both specifications. Remember that the system must be stabilized first before you consider steady state errors. Assume unity feedback configuration.

PID compensator: $K(s) = K_p + \dfrac{K_I}{s} + K_D\, s$

Laboratory

b. Use trial and error to select the PID parameters to meet the above specs. Obtain the step response of the system and plot it. Note that the PID introduces two zeros. These zeros can be complex or real. Try both cases.
c. Suppose, in addition, all closed loop poles are to be placed at $s = -1$. Determine the compensator parameters to achieve this. Also, plot the root locus and step response for the compensated system for this case.

4.8 The purpose of this problem is to compare cascade and feedback compensation. Consider the plant $G(s)$ and a PI compensator $K(s)$

$$G(s) = \frac{4}{s\,(s+2)}, \qquad K(s) = \frac{s+1}{s}$$

Preliminary analysis

a. Show that if $K(s)$ is in series with $G(s)$ with unity feedback, the system will be stable and can track step and ramp inputs with zero error.

b. Show that if $K(s)$ is placed in the feedback path, these properties are lost, even though both systems have the same closed loop poles.

c. Show that we can recover the tracking properties of part a using feedback compensation by placing an additional compensator outside of the loop. Find this compensator and call it $K_f(s)$.

d. Suppose that during implementation, or due to component tolerances, we instead use the following incorrect compensator, $K_2(s) = \frac{s+0.5}{s}$. Repeat part a with this compensator. Are the tracking properties lost?

e. Repeat part b with the incorrect compensator.

f. Using the same $K_f(s)$ as in part c, show that the tracking properties of part c are now lost.

There are three lessons here. First, the location of the compensator (i.e., cascade or feedback), seriously affects the tracking properties of the system. Second, tracking requirements can be met by using compensators outside of the feedback loop, i.e., you do not need feedback to satisfy tracking, or even response shape requirements. The third lesson is that feedback reduces the sensitivity of the closed loop system with respect to changes in elements in the forward path. That is why tracking properties of part a are maintained in part d, but they are lost in part f. When properties of the system are maintained in spite of parameter variations, we call that system property *robust.* Hence, using a PI cascade compensator is a robust method of meeting tracking requirements while the design procedure in part c is not. The actual robustness comes from the fact that PI increases the system Type. If instead, we had used another compensator, such as lag (i.e., a pole at 0.001 instead of at the origin), the steady state error to ramp would also increase in part c but not as much as in part f.

Laboratory

g. Obtain and plot the step and ramp responses in each case (there are a total of eight plots). In all cases, f ind the steady state errors to step and ramp inputs, and compare with the results of your preliminary analysis.

***4.9** The purpose of this problem is to show that using Bode plots can lead to misleading or confusing answers when applied to nonminimum phase systems. The plants to be studied in the problem are

i. $KG_1(s) = \frac{10\,(-1+s)}{s\,(1+10\,s)}$ for $K = 1$.

ii. $KG_2(s) = \frac{K\,(s-1)}{s\,(2\,s+1)}$ where $K = -0.5, -1, 1$

iii. $KG_3(s) = \frac{K\,(4s-1)}{s\,(3s-1)\,(2s+1)\,(s+1)}$ where $K = -0.5, -1, 1$

iv. $KG(s) = \dfrac{7K}{(s-1)(s+2)(s+4)}$ for $K = 1$

Preliminary analysis

a. Use the Routh-Hurwitz test and root locus to find the stable range of K. Use this information to find the lower and upper gain margin(s) for the specified gain(s).

b. Obtain the Nyquist plots and use Nyquist stability criterion to verify your answer in part a. In addition, find the phase margin(s).

Laboratory

c. Obtain the Bode plot(s) for the specified gain(s) and use the *margin* command to find the gain and phase margins. Compare the results with parts a and b. Comment on the validity of using Bode plots to determine stability of nonminimum phase systems.

4.10 Consider the following plants, and in each case perform the requested analysis.

i. $G_1(s) = \dfrac{0.485}{s^2 + 0.3s + 1}$

ii. $G_2(s) = \dfrac{7(s+2)}{s(s^2 + 2s + 12)}$

a. Use the open loop Bode plots to obtain the gain and phase margins.

b. Use the closed loop Bode plot to obtain the peak resonance.

c. Find the closed loop poles (unity feedback) and compute the damping ratio.

d. Obtain the closed loop step response; find POS, T_r, and T_s; comment on the quality of the transient response.

e. Based on the information from the above data, which quantity best describes the poor quality observed in the step response?

5

Introduction to State Space Analysis

5.1 Introduction

Mathematical analysis of systems requires that the system be represented by a mathematical model that captures its essential features. An electrical circuit can usually be adequately modeled using Kirchoff's laws, whereas mechanical systems can be modeled by Newton's laws. These models are combinations of algebraic and differential equations. A linear time invariant (LTI) system can be represented equivalently by its impulse response or its Laplace transform, the transfer function. We may also use graphical models such as circuit diagrams, free body diagrams, block diagrams, or signal flow graphs. These different "realizations" of the same system are equivalent means of system representation. In the early 1960s, a new system representation was developed: the state space representation. Roughly speaking, any *Nth order* differential equation can be converted to N simultaneous *first order* differential equations. Some of the advantages of state space representation over transfer function models are the following:

- The equations are written directly in the time domain and, hence, are more amenable for computer solutions.
- The equations are first order and, hence, conceptually simpler. Simultaneous equations involve the use of matrices for which a wealth of robust numerical routines such as EISPACK/LINPACK are available. Programs such as MATRIX$_X$ and MATLAB are based on these core of routines.
- Multiple-input multiple-output (multivariable or MIMO) systems and advanced optimal and robust control techniques are usually formulated in state space and use state space based numerical routines for their numerical solutions.
- Time varying and nonlinear systems are more naturally represented in state space.

5.2 State Space Realizations

We will demonstrate the idea of state space realizations with a simple example. Consider the following second order differential equation (possibly representing a RLC circuit)

$$\ddot{y} + 3\,\dot{y} + 2\,y = u\,(t) \qquad \text{where } \dot{y} = \frac{d\,y}{d\,t}$$

the transfer function of the above system is given by

$$G\,(s) = \frac{Y(s)}{U(s)} = \frac{1}{s^2 + 3\,s + 2}$$

Let us introduce the following variables: $x_1 = y \; ; \; x_2 = \dot{y}$.
Using the original differential equation and the above definitions we get

$$\dot{x}_1 = x_2$$

$$\dot{x}_2 = -\,2x_1 - 3x_2 + u$$

Now defining the vector x with components x_1 and x_2, we can write the above two equations in vector matrix form as

$$\dot{x} = \begin{bmatrix} 0 & 1 \\ -2 & -3 \end{bmatrix} x + \begin{bmatrix} 0 \\ 1 \end{bmatrix} u$$

$$y = [\,1 \quad 0\,]\,x + [\,0\,]\,u$$

In general, any linear differential equation can always be put into the above form. Now let us denote the above matrix and vectors as

$$A = \begin{bmatrix} 0 & 1 \\ -2 & -3 \end{bmatrix}; \quad B = \begin{bmatrix} 0 \\ 1 \end{bmatrix}; \quad C = [1 \quad 0]; \quad D = 0$$

We get the general state space realization as

$$\dot{x} = A\,x + B\,u$$

$$y = C\,x + D\,u$$

The vector x is the *state vector,* and its components are called *state variables*; u and y are input and output vectors, respectively. State space representation applies equally to systems that have multiple inputs and outputs. In this case, u and y will be column vectors, and B, C, and D will be matrices. In general if the system is nth order with m outputs and p inputs, the dimensions of the matrices become

$$A = n \times n\,,\ B = n \times p\,,\ C = m \times n\,,\ D = m \times p$$

Note that the state space form is not unique and if we relabel the state variables, we get different matrices. For example, let us denote

$$x_2 = y\ ;\ x_1 = \dot{y}$$

We obtain another realization

$$\dot{x} = \begin{bmatrix} -3 & -2 \\ 1 & 0 \end{bmatrix} x + \begin{bmatrix} 1 \\ 0 \end{bmatrix} u$$

$$y = [0 \quad 1]\ x + [\,0\,]\,u$$

We can also derive two other forms as follows. Let

$$x_1 = y \quad \text{and} \quad x_2 = \dot{y} + \alpha y$$

then $\dot{x}_1 = x_2 - \alpha x_1$, and $\dot{x}_2 = \ddot{y} + \alpha\dot{y} = -3\dot{y} - 2y + u + \alpha\dot{y}$

To eliminate $\dot{y}$ from the equation, set $\alpha = 3$. We get

$$\dot{x} = \begin{bmatrix} -3 & 1 \\ -2 & 0 \end{bmatrix} x + \begin{bmatrix} 0 \\ 1 \end{bmatrix} u$$

$$y = [1 \quad 0]\ x + [\,0\,]\,u$$

Note that we can again exchange the labels of x_1 and x_2 to get a fourth realization

$$\dot{x} = \begin{bmatrix} 0 & -2 \\ 1 & -3 \end{bmatrix} x + \begin{bmatrix} 1 \\ 0 \end{bmatrix} u$$

$$y = [0 \quad 1]\ x + [\,0\,]\,u$$

The above four forms are called *canonical realizations*. The first two are *controllable forms I* and *II* and the last two are, *observable forms I* and *II*. Note, however, that these names are not standard.

Now suppose a system with transfer function $G(s)$ has distinct poles. We can perform partial fraction expansion and write it as a sum of first order transfer functions; if the expanded system is converted to state space form, the A matrix will be in diagonal form. The diagonal elements of A will be the poles of $G(s)$, which are also eigenvalues of A and are referred to as system *modes*, hence, the name *modal form.* We also recall that the system will be stable if and only if the poles have negative real parts, i.e., modes are in the LHP. This form is quite useful for analysis, because the system is effectively decoupled. Let us obtain the modal form of our example.

$$G(s) = \frac{1}{(s^2+3s+2)} = \frac{1}{s+1} - \frac{1}{s+2} = \frac{Y(s)}{U(s)} = G_1(s) - G_2(s)$$

Hence, $Y(s) = G_1(s)\,U(s) - G_2(s)\,U(s) = X_1(s) - X_2(s)$

where $U(s) = (s+1)\,X_1(s)$ and $U(s) = (s+2)\,X_2(s)$

This leads directly to

$$\dot{x}_1 = -x_1 + u\,,\quad \dot{x}_2 = -2x_2 + u\,,\quad \text{and}\quad y = x_1 - x_2\,,\quad \text{or}$$

$$\dot{x} = \begin{bmatrix} -1 & 0 \\ 0 & -2 \end{bmatrix} x + \begin{bmatrix} 1 \\ 1 \end{bmatrix} u$$

$$y = [1 \quad -1\,]\,x + [\,0\,]\,u$$

Note that even though the matrices of the various realizations above look different, they are similar in a mathematical sense, and they all represent the same system with a unique transfer function $G(s)$ given by

$$G(s) = \frac{1}{s^2+3s+2}$$

To transform one realization to another, we have to find a similarity transformation matrix T, which is nonsingular and then proceed as shown below.

Let $x = T\,z$, where z represents the states in the new coordinate system. The state equations in the new coordinate system are

$$\dot{z} = T^{-1}\dot{x} = (T^{-1}A)\,x + (T^{-1}B)\,u = (T^{-1}A\,T)\,z + (T^{-1}B)\,u$$

$$y = C\,x + D\,u = (C\,T)\,z + D\,u$$

Hence, the new realization becomes $\{\,\bar{A}, \bar{B}, \bar{C}, \bar{D}\,\}$ where

$$\bar{A} = T^{-1}A\,T\;,\quad \bar{B} = T^{-1}B\;,\quad \bar{C} = C\,T\;,\quad \bar{D} = D$$

Note that $\bar{A}$ and A have the same eigenvalues. The canonical forms discussed above can be generalized. Consider the transfer function

$$G(s) = \frac{b_1 s^{n-1} + \ldots + b_{n-1} s + b_n}{s^n + a_1 s^{n-1} + \ldots + a_n}$$

The Observable Form II is given by

$$A = \begin{bmatrix} 0 & . & . & 0 & | & -a_n \\ - & - & - & & | & . \\ . & . & . & . & | & . \\ . & I_{n-1} & . & & | & . \\ . & . & . & . & | & -a_1 \end{bmatrix} , \quad B = \begin{bmatrix} b_n \\ . \\ . \\ . \\ b_1 \end{bmatrix} , \quad C = [\,0 \ldots 0 \;\; 1\,] , \quad D = [\,0\,]$$

The controllable form I is given by

$$A = \begin{bmatrix} 0 & | & . & . & . & . \\ 0 & | & I_{n-1} & . & . & . \\ . & | & . & . & . & . \\ - & & - & . & - & - \\ -a_n . & & -a_{n-1} & . & . & -a_1 \end{bmatrix} , \quad B = \begin{bmatrix} 0 \\ . \\ . \\ 0 \\ 1 \end{bmatrix} , \quad C = [\, b_n \;\; b_{n-1} \ldots \;\; b_1 \,] , \quad D = [\,0\,]$$

The other two forms can likewise be obtained (see the Problems). We can obtain the transfer function directly by Laplace transforming the state equations:

$$s\,X(s) = A\,X(s) + B\,U(s) \;\rightarrow\; X(s) = (s\,I - A\,)^{-1}\,B\,U(s)$$

$$Y(s) = C\,X(s) + D\,U(s) = [\,C\,(s\,I - A\,)^{-1}\,B + D\,]\,U(s) = G(s)\,U(s)$$

Hence, $G(s) = C\,\Phi(s)\,B + D$ where $\Phi(s) = (s\,I - A\,)^{-1}$

The solution of the linear time invariant state equations can be shown to be

$$x(t) = e^{A\,t}\,x_0 + \int_0^t e^{A\,(t-\sigma)}\,B\,u(\sigma)\,d\sigma \qquad \text{where } e^{A\,t} = L^{-1}\{\,\Phi(s)\,\} = \phi(t)$$

where $\phi(t)$ is called the *state transition matrix*, and $\Phi(s)$ is called the *resolvent matrix*. Needless to say, analytical solution of state equations can be very cumbersome; therefore, we use computer programs to solve them numerically.

5.3 Asymptotic Stability

An important property of systems is the notion of stability. Consider the unforced equation

$$\dot{x} = A\,x \qquad\qquad x(0) = x_o$$

We say the system is *asymptotically stable* if the states asymptotically approach zero with time, i.e., $x(t) \rightarrow 0 \quad as \quad t \rightarrow \infty$.

It can be shown that this happens when all eigenvalues of the matrix A have negative real parts, i.e., they are strictly in the LHP. It can also be shown that in the absence of pole-zero cancellations in the transfer function, system eigenvalues and transfer function poles are identical. This can be seen from the following:

$$G(s) = \frac{n(s)}{d(s)} = \frac{C\,Adj\,(s\,I - A)\,B}{\det\,(s\,I - A)}$$

The poles of $G(s)$ are the roots of $d(s)$, and the eigenvalues of A are the roots of the characteristic polynomial of A (i.e., $\det\,(s\,I - A)$).

5.4 State Space Analysis Using MATRIXx

State space representation requires specifying four matrices $\{A, B, C, D\}$. MATRIXx combines these matrices into one partitioned matrix referred to as the *System Matrix*, *S*.

$$S = \begin{pmatrix} A \mid B \\ \text{——} \\ C \mid D \end{pmatrix}$$

This representation is also known as the *packed matrix* notation and is used to denote the transfer function of the system. For any state space realization of a given system, there is a unique transfer function that is defined once the state space quadruplet, $\{A, B, C, D\}$, is specified. Therefore, the following are equivalent

$$S = \begin{pmatrix} A \mid B \\ \text{——} \\ C \mid D \end{pmatrix} = G(s) = C\,(\,s\,I - A\,)^{-1}\,B + D$$

If these matrices are predefined, we define S by

```
< > S=[A , B;C , D]
```

We need to specify the number of states (size of A) so the program will know how to partition S; let us denote the number of states by *NS*. From now on we specify state space equations by *[S, NS]*. Given *[S, NS]*, we can recover the four matrices using the *split* command

```
< > [A, B, C, D]=split(S,NS)
```

We can check for asymptotic stability by finding the eigenvalues of A

```
< > eval=eig(a)
```

This can also be done directly on the S matrix (in Version 7.1 and above)

```
< > eval=eig(S,NS)
```

We can also easily convert from transfer function to state space form and vice versa using *sform* and *tform* commands, respectively

```
< > [num, den]=tform(S,NS)
< > [S,NS]=sform(num,den,q)
```

The argument, q, in the *sform* command is for multivariable systems (in Version 7.1 and above). It corresponds to the number of inputs and is not needed for SISO systems. The state space form obtained using the *sform* command is not in any of the standard forms, because these forms do not have good numerical properties. Instead it returns a *balanced realization* of the system, which is numerically superior to other forms. We will not discuss this issue any further because it is beyond the scope of this text.

The modal (or diagonal) form of a system can be obtained using the *modal* command. Its syntax is

```
< > sm=modal(S,NS)
```

If a transfer function of a system has pole-zero cancellations, we can obtain the *minimal realization* (i.e., cancel the common poles and zeros) using the *minimal* command.

```
< > [min_num,min_den]=minimal(num,den)
< > [s_min,ns_min]=minimal(S,NS)
```

The transfer function version is available in Version 7.1 and above. The main power of this command is in the state space form, because pole-zero cancellations are not apparent in state space. You should especially use this when you combine systems using the interconnection commands (discussed in the next section) to ensure the overall system is of minimal order. This is important because minimality of the system realization is often one of the requirements of modern design techniques.

All of the simulation commands like *step, bode, lsim,* etc. also have equivalent state space forms. Some commands, however, have special features available only in their state space form, for example, *lsim* with nonzero initial conditions. Some commands have state space forms only like the *freq* command. Most commands internally use state space operations, so it is more efficient to use the state space representations in most commands instead of transfer function forms. Also, for numerical reasons such as round-off error and conditioning, it is strongly advised that you use the state space forms of the commands as much as possible.

5.5 System Interconnections

MATRIXx has several interconnection commands that make it possible to connect systems in various configurations directly in state space. Of course it is also possible to connect systems using System Build (discussed in Chapter 6), but for LTI systems, it is much easier and faster to use state space commands. We use System Build for nonlinear systems and more complicated block diagrams. We will explain these commands and demonstrate their features via examples.

5.5.1 Series (Cascade) Connection

Suppose systems S_1 and S_2 are given

$$S_1 = \left[A_1, B_1; C_1, D_1\right] \quad \text{and} \quad S_2 = \left[A_2, B_2; C_2, D_2\right]$$

We want to find the state space realization of $S = \{A, B; C, D\}$, the series connection of S_1 and S_2 (see Figure 5-1).

Of course we can always find transfer functions $G_1(s)$ and $G_2(s)$ and multiply their numerators and denominators to obtain $G(s)$ using the *convolve* command, and then transform the result back to state space. This is a slow five-step process that will also introduce numerical errors. In state space, it can be done in one step without introducing any numerical errors.

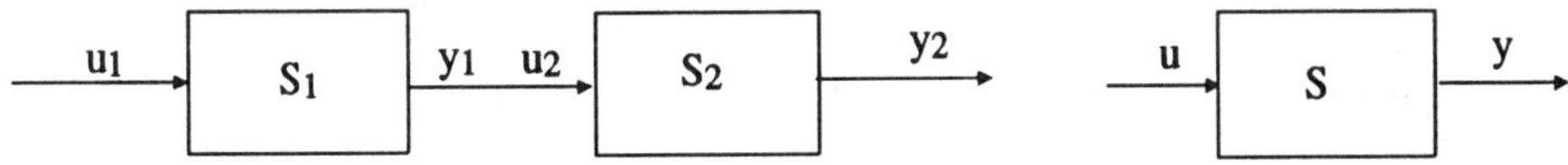

Figure 5-1 Series connection.

$$\dot{x}_1 = A_1 x_1 + B_1 u_1 , \quad y_1 = C_1 x_1 + D_1 u_1$$

$$\dot{x}_2 = A_2 x_2 + B_2 u_2 , \quad y_2 = C_2 x_2 + D_2 u_2$$

Note from the block diagram that $u_2 = y_1$, $y = y_2$, and $u = u_1$, so substitute y_1 in the state and output equations for S_2:

$$\dot{x}_2 = A_2 x_2 + B_2 y_1 = A_2 x_2 + B_2 (C_1 x_1 + D_1 u_1) = B_2 C_1 x_1 + A_2 x_2 + B_2 D_1 u_1$$

$$y_2 = C_2 x_2 + D_2 y_1 = C_2 x_2 + D_2 (C_1 x_1 + D_1 u_1) = D_2 C_1 x_1 + C_2 x_2 + D_2 D_1 u_1$$

Now define the combined state x for the S system with components x_1 and x_2, and write the two state equations together

$$\begin{bmatrix} \dot{x}_1 \\ \dot{x}_2 \end{bmatrix} = \begin{bmatrix} A_1 & 0 \\ B_2 C_1 & A_2 \end{bmatrix} \begin{bmatrix} x_1 \\ x_2 \end{bmatrix} + \begin{bmatrix} B_1 \\ B_2 D_1 \end{bmatrix} u_1$$

$$y_2 = [\, D_2 C_1 \quad C_2 \,] \begin{bmatrix} x_1 \\ x_2 \end{bmatrix} + [\, D_2 D_1 \,]\, u_1$$

Note that the order of the series system is the sum of the orders of S_1 and S_2, i.e., $NS = NS1 + NS2$, and S is given by:

$$S = \text{series}\,(S_2, S_1) = \left[\begin{array}{c|c} A_2 & B_2 \\ \hline C_2 & D_2 \end{array}\right] \cdot \left[\begin{array}{c|c} A_1 & B_1 \\ \hline C_1 & D_1 \end{array}\right] = \left[\begin{array}{cc|c} A_1 & 0 & B_1 \\ B_2 C_1 & A_2 & B_2 D_1 \\ \hline D_2 C_1 & C_2 & D_2 D_1 \end{array}\right]$$

The above result is shown in packed matrix notation and requires further clarification. By a series connection of two systems, we actually mean the product of their transfer functions, i.e.,

$$G(s) = G_2(s)\, G_1(s) \quad \text{is represented by} \quad S = \text{series}\,(\, S_2, S_1 \,)$$

where the S matrix is the state space representation of $G(s)$.
The command to find S is

```
< > [S,NS]=series(S1,NS1,S2,NS2)
```

Let us demonstrate this technique with an example.

Find the series connection of S_1 and S_2 , and verify the result with transfer functions.

$$S1=\begin{bmatrix}2&1&1\\2&3&0\\1&0&0\end{bmatrix}\ ;\ S2=\begin{bmatrix}-2&-18\\1&5\end{bmatrix}\ ;\ NS1=2\ ,\ NS2=1$$

First define the systems, next use *tform* on S_1 and S_2 to get $G_1(s)$ and $G_2(s)$, then apply the *series* command to get S, and use *tform* to get $G(s)$. You can use *convolve* on numerators and denominators of $G_1(s)$ and $G_2(s)$ to verify $G(s)$.

```
< > s1=[2 1 1; 2 3 0; 1 0 0]; ns1=2; s2= [-2 -18;1 5]; ns2=1;
< > [ng1,dg1]=tform(s1,ns1)

DG1    =
   1.  -5.  4.
NG1    =
  1.0000  -3.0000

< > [ng2,dg2]=tform(s2,ns2)

DG2    =
  1.  2.
NG2    =
  5.  -8.

< > [ss,nss]=series(s1,ns1,s2,ns2)

NSS    =
  3.
SS     =
   2.  1.  0.  1.
   2.  3.  0.  0.
 -18.  0. -2.  0.
   5.  0.  1.  0.

< > [ngs,dgs]=tform(ss,nss)

DGS    =
  1.  -3.  -6.  8.
NGS    =
  5.0000 -23.0000  24.0000
```

In summary, we have

$$S=\begin{bmatrix}2&1&0&1\\2&3&0&0\\-18&0&-2&0\\5&0&1&0\end{bmatrix}\ \rightarrow\ G(s)=\frac{5\,s^2-23s+24}{s^3-3s^2-6s+8}$$

$$G(s) = G_1(s)\ G(_2(s) = \left(\frac{s-3}{s^2-5s+4}\right)\left(\frac{5s-8}{s+2}\right)$$

5.5.2 Parallel Connection

In the parallel connection, the output of two systems with possibly different inputs are added as shown in Figure 5-2. The system matrix S is easy to derive and is left as an exercise. The command to obtain S is given by

```
< > [SP,NSP]=parallel(S1,NS1,S2,NS2)
```

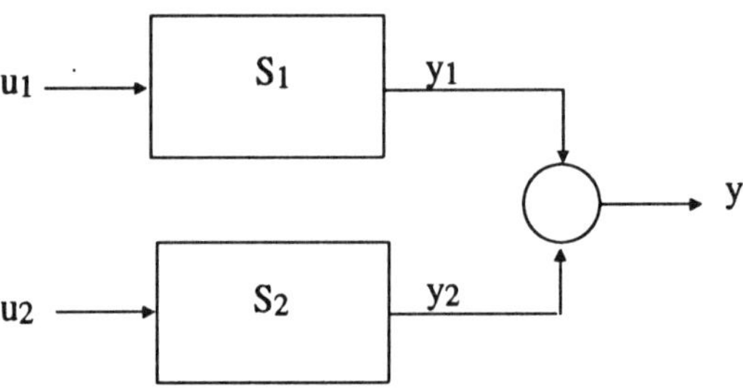

Figure 5-2 Parallel connection.

Continuing with our example, for S_1 and S_2 , we get

```
< > [sp,nsp]=paral(s1,ns1,s2,ns2)

  NSP    =
   3.
  SP     =
2.  1.  0.  1.  0.
2.  3.  0.  0.  0.
0.  0. -2.  0. -18.
1.  0.  1.  0.  5.
```

```
< > [ngp,dgp]=tform(sp,nsp)

 DGP     =
  1. -3.  -6.  8.
 NGP     =
  .0000  5.0000  1.0000 -33.0000  -1.0000  60.0000  -6.0000 -32.0000
```

Note the appearance of NGP. It seems to have too many elements. Actually it does not, this is simply the way MATRIXx displays transfer functions of MIMO systems. The parallel connection is a two-input-one-output system. Its transfer function (which is a vector) in general is obtained as

$$T(s) = [\ T_1(s) \quad T_2(s)\ ] = [\ \frac{n_1}{d_1} \quad \frac{n_2}{d_2}\ ] = \frac{1}{d_1\, d_2}\left[n_1\, d_2 \quad n_2\, d_1 \right]$$

$$T(s) = \frac{[0.\ s^3 + s^2 - s - 6 \qquad 5\,s^3 - 33\,s^2 + 60\,s - 32\,]}{s^3 - 3\,s^2 - 6\,s + 8}$$

Now note that the first two columns of NGP are the coefficients of s^3, next two columns are those of s^2, etc.

If the system has a common input (i.e., $u_1 = u_2 = u$), $G(s)$ becomes a scalar transfer function. As an exercise, you can derive the formula for the S matrix in general and show that you get the following result for the same S_1 and S_2:

$$S = \begin{bmatrix} 2 & 1 & 0 & 1 \\ 2 & 3 & 0 & 0 \\ 0 & 0 & -2 & -18 \\ 1 & 0 & 1 & 5 \end{bmatrix} \quad \rightarrow \quad G(s) = \frac{5\,s^3 - 32\,s^2 + 59\,s - 38}{s^3 - 3\,s^2 - 6\,s + 8} = G_1(s) + G_2(s)$$

5.5.3 Feedback Connection

The feedback configuration appears frequently as shown in Figure 5-3. We will obtain the system matrix, S, for the feedback configuration. The key to this derivation is to note that

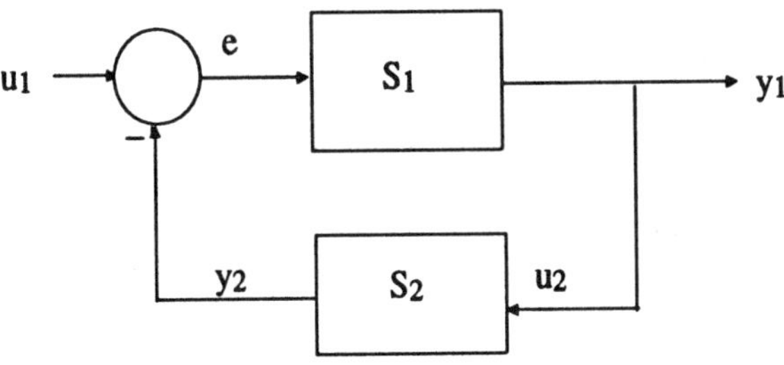

Figure 5-3 Feedback connection.

the input to S_2 is y_1, and the input to S_1 is (u_1 - y_2). We then make these substitutions in the state space equations. For simplicity, we will assume that D_1 is equal to zero.

$$\dot{x}_2 = A_2\, x_2 + B_2\, u_2 = A_2\, x_2 + B_2\, y_1 = B_2\, C_1\, x_1 + A_2\, x_2$$

$$y_2 = C_2\, x_2 + D_2\, u_2 = C_2\, x_2 + D_2\, y_1 = C_2\, x_2 + D_2\, C_1\, x_1$$

$$\begin{aligned}\dot{x}_1 = A_1\, x_1 + B_1\,(u_1 - y_2) &= A_1\, x_1 + B_1\, u_1 - B_1\, C_2\, x_2 - B_1\, D_2\, C_1\, x_1 \\ &= (A_1 - B_1\, D_2\, C_1)\, x_1 - B_1\, C_2\, x_2 + B_1\, u_1\end{aligned}$$

Therefore, the S matrix becomes

$$S = \begin{bmatrix} A_1 - B_1\, D_2\, C_1 & -B_1\, C_2 & B_1 \\ B_2\, C_1 & A_2 & 0 \\ C_1 & 0 & 0 \end{bmatrix}$$

The following commands produce S for various feedback configurations

```
< > [SF,NSF]=feedback(S1,NS1,S2,NS2)
< > [SF,NSF]=feedback(S1,NS1,S2)
< > [SF,NSF]=feedback(S1,NS1)
```

(constant gain feedback S_2) (for unity feedback)

Going back to our example, we get

```
< > [sf,nsf]=feedback(s1,ns1,s2,ns2)

NSF =
  3.

SF =
-3.   1.  -1.  1.
 2.   3.   0.  0.
-18.  0.  -2.  0.
 1.   0.   0.  0.

< > [ngf,dgf]=tform(sf,nsf)

DGF =
  1.0000   2.0000  -29.0000  32.0000]

NGF =
1.0000  -1.0000  -6.0000
```

$$SF = \begin{bmatrix} -3 & 1 & -1 & 1 \\ 2 & 3 & 0 & 0 \\ -18 & 0 & -2 & 0 \\ 1 & 0 & 0 & 0 \end{bmatrix} \rightarrow G(s) = \frac{s^2 - s - 6}{s^3 + 2\, s^2 - 29\, s + 32} = \frac{G_1(s)}{1 + G_1(s)\, G_2(s)}$$

5.5.4 Afeedback Connection

This is the generalization of the feedback configuration that is useful for studying the effects of disturbances, measurement noise, or modeling errors on the system. It has the same syntax as the feedback command. The derivation of the system matrix S is left as an exercise. Its block diagram is shown in Figure 5-4. One interesting feature of this configuration is that it is a two-input-two-output system, i.e., a *multivariable* system, and its transfer function is a 2×2 matrix. We will go in detail through our example to show how to make sense of transfer function matrices. As you will observe, it is a generalization of the discussion we had in the parallel connection case.

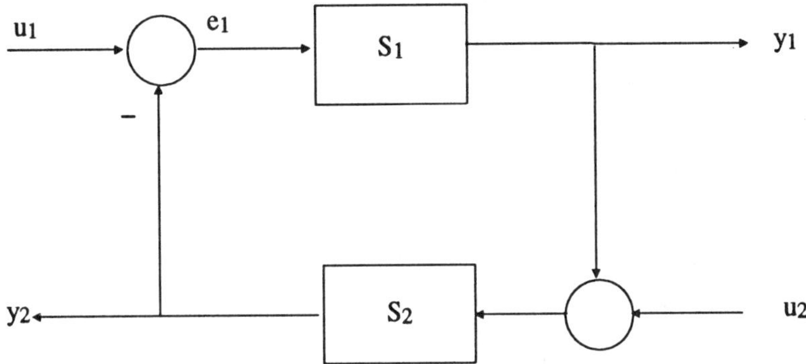

Figure 5-4 Afeedback connection.

First we recall that, in general, the transfer function between the ith output and the jth input, is obtained by setting all other inputs equal to zero and considering one output at a time, i.e.,

$$G_{ij}(s) = \frac{Y_i(s)}{U_j(s)} \quad \text{where} \quad U_k(s) = 0 \quad k \neq j \text{, and } Y_i \text{ is the selected output}$$

$$G(s) = \frac{1}{1 + G_1(s)\,G_2(s)} \begin{bmatrix} G_1 & -G_1\,G_2 \\ G_1\,G_2 & G_2 \end{bmatrix}$$

let $G_1 = \frac{n_1}{d_1}$, $G_2 = \frac{n_2}{d_2}$ then

$$G(s) = \frac{1}{d_1\,d_2 + n_1\,n_2} \begin{bmatrix} n_1\,d_2 & -n_1\,n_2 \\ n_1\,n_2 & n_2\,d_1 \end{bmatrix}$$

For our example, $G(s)$ becomes (you can do this manually)

$$G(s) = \frac{1}{s^3 + 2\,s^2 - 29\,s + 32}\begin{bmatrix} s^2 - s - 6 & -5\,s^2 + 23\,s - 24 \\ 5\,s^2 - 23\,s + 24 & 5\,s^3 - 33\,s^2 + 60\,s - 32 \end{bmatrix}$$

We now write the numerator of *G(s)* as a polynomial with matrix coefficients in the form shown below. This is the form that MATRIXx displays transfer function matrices.

$$G(s) = \frac{\begin{pmatrix} 0 & 0 \\ 0 & 5 \end{pmatrix} s^3 + \begin{pmatrix} 1 & -5 \\ 5 & -33 \end{pmatrix} s^2 + \begin{pmatrix} -1 & 23 \\ -23 & 60 \end{pmatrix} s + \begin{pmatrix} -6 & -24 \\ 24 & -32 \end{pmatrix}}{s^3 + 2\,s^2 - 29\,s + 32}$$

Checking this on the computer, we get

```
< > [saf,nsaf]=afeedb(s1,ns1,s2,ns2)


 NSAF    =
   3.


 SAF    =
-3.   1.  -1.   1.  -5.
 2.   3.   0.   0.   0.
-18.  0.  -2.   0. -18.
 1.   0.   0.   0.   0.
 5.   0.   1.   0.   5.

< > [ngaf,dgaf]=tform(saf,nsaf)


 DGAF    =
 1.0000   2.0000 -29.0000  32.0000

 NGAF    =
   .0000    .0000   1.0000  -5.0000  -1.0000  23.0000  -6.0000 -24.0000
   .0000   5.0000   5.0000 -33.0000 -23.0000  60.0000  24.0000 -32.0000
```

In summary, we get

$$S = \begin{bmatrix} -3 & 1 & -1 & 1 & -5 \\ 2 & 3 & 0 & 0 & 0 \\ -18 & 0 & -2 & 0 & -18 \\ 1 & 0 & 0 & 0 & 0 \\ 5 & 0 & 1 & 0 & 5 \end{bmatrix} \rightarrow G(s) = \frac{\begin{pmatrix} 0 & 0 & | & 1 & -5 & | & -1 & 23 & | & -6 & -24 \\ 0 & 5 & | & 5 & -33 & | & -23 & 60 & | & 24 & -32 \end{pmatrix}}{[1 \quad 2 \quad -29 \quad 32\,]}$$

For the denominator we get a vector as expected, and for the numerator we get a matrix as shown above.

Interpreting Transfer Function Matrices

In general, if a system has p inputs and m outputs, the numerator matrix of G will have the following dimensions:
m rows corresponding to the number of outputs
$p \times (n+1)$ columns where p is the number of inputs, and n is the degree of the denominator
First p columns are coefficients of the s^n term, next p columns are the coefficients of the s^{n-1} term, etc.

5.5.5 Append and Connect

These two commands are usually used together to create very general interconnections. The *append* command simply puts two systems together in a decoupled form, and the *connect* command is used to interconnect them with appropriate gain matrices. Let S_1 and S_2 be represented by (see Figure 5-5)

$$\dot{x}_1 = A_1 x_1 + B_1 u_1 \quad , \quad y_1 = C_1 x_1 + D_1 u_1$$
$$\dot{x}_2 = A_2 x_2 + B_2 u_2 \quad , \quad y_2 = C_2 x_2 + D_2 u_2$$

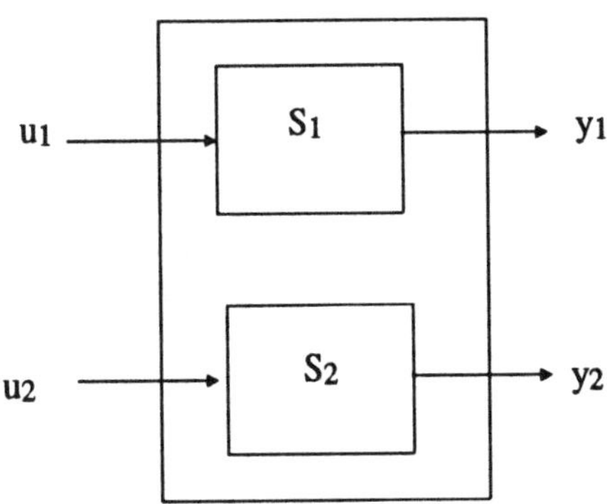

Figure 5-5 Append connection.

Then *append* will combine the two systems into one decoupled system as

$$\begin{bmatrix} \dot{x}_1 \\ \dot{x}_2 \end{bmatrix} = \begin{bmatrix} A_1 & 0 \\ 0 & A_2 \end{bmatrix} \begin{bmatrix} x_1 \\ x_2 \end{bmatrix} + \begin{bmatrix} B_1 & 0 \\ 0 & B_2 \end{bmatrix} \begin{bmatrix} u_1 \\ u_2 \end{bmatrix}$$

$$\begin{bmatrix} y_1 \\ y_2 \end{bmatrix} = \begin{bmatrix} C_1 & 0 \\ 0 & C_2 \end{bmatrix} \begin{bmatrix} x_1 \\ x_2 \end{bmatrix} + \begin{bmatrix} D_1 & 0 \\ 0 & D_2 \end{bmatrix} \begin{bmatrix} u_1 \\ u_2 \end{bmatrix}$$

The system matrix S is clearly given by

$$S = \begin{bmatrix} A_1 & 0 & B_1 & 0 \\ 0 & A_2 & 0 & B_2 \\ C_1 & 0 & D_1 & 0 \\ 0 & C_2 & 0 & D_2 \end{bmatrix}$$

The syntax for the *append* command is given by

```
< > [S,NS]=append(S1,NS1,S2,NS2)
```

Connect

Figure 5-6 shows the block diagram for the *connect* command. Its syntax is given by

```
< > [S,NS]=connect(S1,NS1,K,M,N)
< > [S,NS]=connect(S1,NS1,K,M)          (unit output gain)
< > [S,NS]=connect(S1,NS1,K)      (unit input and output gain)
```

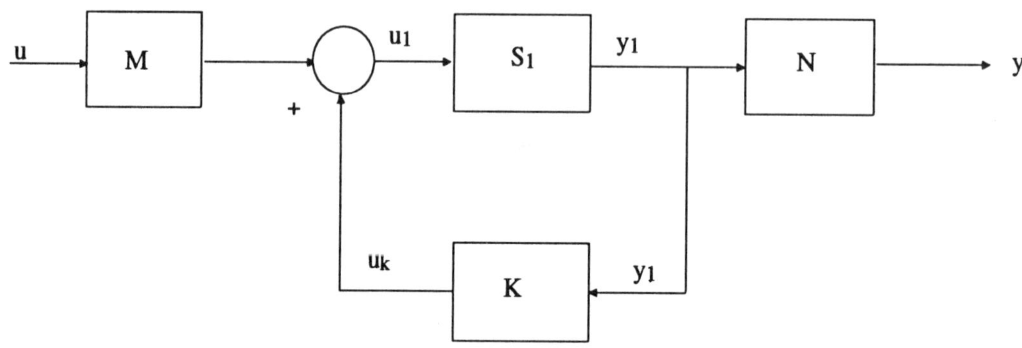

Figure 5-6 Connect connection.

where M, N, and K are input, output and feedback gain matrices, respectively. The basic equations defining the final system follow from Figure 5-6 and are given by

$$\dot{x}_1 = A_1 x_1 + B_1 u_1 , \quad y_1 = C_1 x_1 + D_1 u_1$$

$$y = N\,y_1\,,\quad u_k = K\,y_1\,,\quad u_1 = u_k + M\,u$$

Note: The *connect* command uses *positive* feedback, whereas the *feedback* command uses *negative* feedback convention.

The derivation of the system matrix for the *connect* command is left as an exercise. We will demonstrate these two commands by the following example.

Consider the block diagram in Figure 5-7, where

$$G_1(s) = \frac{1}{s+1} \quad \text{and} \quad G_2(s) = \frac{1}{s-1}$$

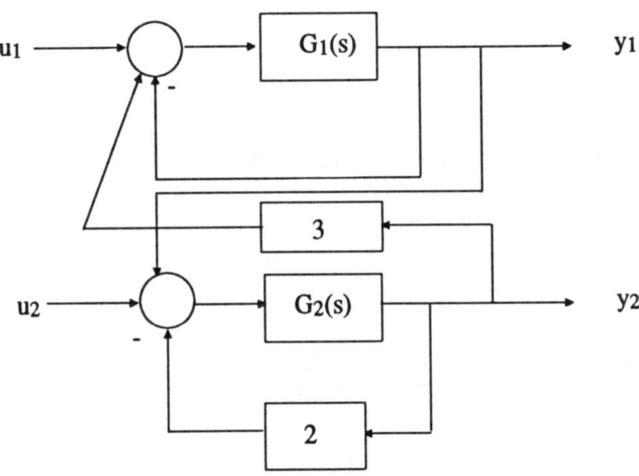

Figure 5-7 The append/connect example diagram.

The first step is to define G_1 and G_2 and append them.

```
< > [S1,NS1]=sform(1,[1, 1]); [S2,NS2]=sform (1,[1, -1]);
< > [SA,NSA]=append(S1,NS1,S2,NS2);
```

```
 NSA    =
  2.
 SA     =
  -1.  0.  1.  0.
   0.  1.  0.  1.
   1.  0.  0.  0.
   0.  1.  0.  0.
```

The feedback connection matrix, K, is defined by

```
< > K = [ -1 , 3 ; 1 , -2 ];
```

The first row of K are feedbacks from Y_1 and Y_2 to the first summing junction, the second row are feedbacks from Y_1 and Y_2 to the second summing junction. Both inputs and outputs have unity gain, so that M and N are identity matrices, and because this is the default, they do not have to be defined. The systems are now connected.

```
< > [SC,NSC]=connect(SA,NSA,K);
< > [NC,DC]=tform(SC,NSC);

NSC      =
 2.
SC       =
-2.  3.   1.  0.
 1. -1.   0.  1.
 1.  0.   0.  0.
 0.  1.   0.  0.
```

One can easily verify that the state equations and the transfer function matrix of the connected system are given by

$$\dot{x}_1 = -2x_1 + 3x_2 + u_1, \quad y_1 = x_1$$
$$\dot{x}_2 = -x_2 + x_1 + u_2, \quad y_2 = x_2$$

$$G(s) = \begin{bmatrix} s+1 & 3 \\ 1 & s+2 \end{bmatrix} \frac{1}{s^2+3s-1}$$

$$NC = \begin{bmatrix} 0 & 0 & 1 & 0 & 1 & 3 \\ 0 & 0 & 0 & 1 & 1 & 2 \end{bmatrix} \quad \text{and} \quad DC = [1 \;\; 3 \;\; -1]$$

To verify this on computer

```
< > [nc,dc]=tform(sc,nsc)

DC       =
  1.0000  3.0000  -1.0000
NC       =
  .0000   .0000  1.0000   .0000  1.0000  3.0000
  .0000   .0000   .0000  1.0000  1.0000  2.0000
```

Let us see what happens when we convert this transfer function to state space form using the *sform* command

```
< > [sc2,nsc2]=sform(nc,dc,2)
```

```
NSC2    =
 4.
SC2     =
-3.0000    .0000   1.0000    .0000   2.0000    .0000
  .0000 -3.0000     .0000   1.0000    .0000   2.0000
 1.0000    .0000    .0000    .0000    .0000    .0000
  .0000   1.0000    .0000    .0000    .0000    .0000
  .5000    .0000    .5000   1.5000    .0000    .0000
  .0000    .5000    .5000   1.0000    .0000    .0000
```

Note that two extra states are added. Indeed this may happen when we use the *sform* command (it is a property of the algorithm used), i.e., it may result in a nonminimal realization. Therefore, we recommend that you use the *minimal* command when using connection commands or when using *sform* and the number of states appears to be nonminimal.

```
< > [sc22,nsc22]=minim(sc2,nsc2)

MINIMAL— THE SYSTEM HAS UNOBSERVABLE STATES

NSC22    =
 2.
SC22     =
-2.9091   1.1245   -1.0238   1.6088
 1.1245  -0.0909     .6030    .0000
  .0000   1.6583     .0000    .0000
  .6216   1.0553     .0000    .0000
```

Note that the new system matrix is different from the previous one (SC2). As mentioned previously, however, they both represent the same transfer function as can be seen below.

```
< > [nc2,dc2]=tform(sc22,nsc22)

DC2    =
 1.0000  3.0000  -1.0000
NC2    =
  .0000   .0000  1.0000   .0000  1.0000  3.0000
  .0000   .0000   .0000  1.0000  1.0000  2.0000
```

5.6 Feedback and Sensitivity Measures

The above transfer function matrices were introduced in Chapter 1 and are used to measure stability robustness and most other feedback properties, such as disturbance rejection, noise suppression, and effects of parameter variations. The system matrices of these transfer functions can be obtained using the connection commands as presented below. The derivations are left as exercises.

Return Difference is defined by : $J(s) = I + L(s)$

The system matrix for J is given below (assuming that $L(s)$ is square, i.e., it has the same number of inputs and outputs). Note that $L(s)$ is the loop transfer function matrix (also called the loop gain, or open loop transfer function in classical control, and shown in Figure 5-8).

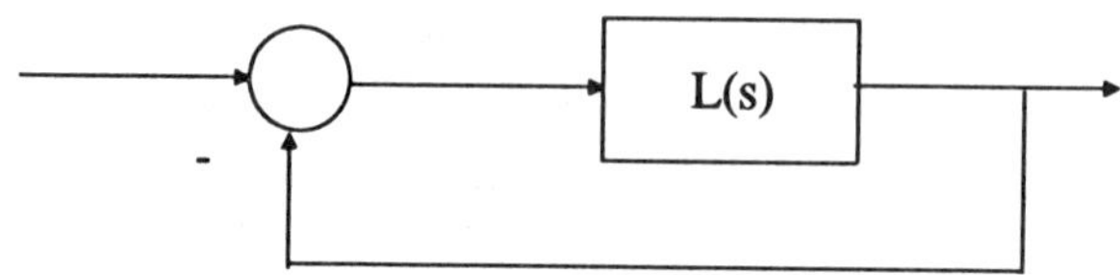

Figure 5-8 Feedback diagram showing the loop transfer function.

$$L(s) = \begin{bmatrix} A & B \\ C & D \end{bmatrix}, \quad J(s) = \begin{bmatrix} A & B \\ C & D + I \end{bmatrix}$$

$L(s)$ is also used to define the so-called *inverse return difference*

$$R(s) = I + L^{-1}$$

Note that this is not the " inverse " of the return difference matrix. Its system matrix is given by (assuming that L is invertible, i.e., square and biproper, which ensures D has an inverse)

$$R = \begin{bmatrix} A - B\,D^{-1}\,C & B\,D^{-1} \\ -D^{-1}\,C & D^{-1} + I \end{bmatrix}$$

Sensitivity transfer function (matrix) is defined by

$$S\,(s) = (I + L)^{-1}$$

Its system matrix is given by (assuming square L)

$$S\,(s) = \begin{bmatrix} A - B\,V\,C & -B\,V \\ V\,C & V \end{bmatrix} \quad \text{where} \quad V = (\,I + D\,)^{-1}$$

Complementary sensitivity transfer function (matrix) is defined by

$$T\,(s) = L\,(I + L)^{-1}$$

Note that $S + T = I$, or $T = I - S$. Therefore its system matrix is given by

$$T = \begin{bmatrix} A - B\,V\,C & -B\,V \\ V\,C & V - I \end{bmatrix}$$

5.7 Problems

5.1 Consider the following system

$\ddot{y}_1 + \dot{y}_1 + 2\,y_1 + 3\,\dot{y}_2 + 4\,y_2 = u_1$
$\ddot{y}_2 + \dot{y}_2 + 2\,y_2 + 3\,\dot{y}_1 + 4\,y_1 = u_2$

a. Find a state space representation for the above system. (Let $x_1 = y_1$, $x_2 = \dot{y}_1$, etc.)

b. Find the system transfer function, poles and zeros

c. Determine the stability of the system.

5.2 Consider the following system

$$G(s) = \frac{2\,(s+4)}{s\,(s+1)\,(s+2)}$$

a. Obtain the four canonical form realizations for $G(s)$.

b. Obtain a diagonal realization for $G(s)$.

c. Discuss stability of the system.

5.3 Consider the following transfer function matrix

$$G(s) = \begin{bmatrix} \dfrac{1}{(s+1)^3\,(s+10)} & \dfrac{1}{s+10} \\ \dfrac{1}{s+1} & 0 \end{bmatrix}$$

a. Obtain a state space realization for the system.

b. Determine its poles, zeros, and stability.

5.4 Show that the system matrix for the parallel representation (or sum) of two systems is given by

$$S = \begin{bmatrix} A_1 & 0 & B_1 & 0 \\ 0 & A_2 & 0 & B_2 \\ C_1 & C_2 & D_1 & D_2 \end{bmatrix}$$

5.5 Show that the system matrix for the feedback connection in the general case in which D_l is nonzero is given by

$$S = \begin{bmatrix} A_1 - B_1 V D_2 C_1 & -B_1 V C_2 & B_1 - B_1 V D_2 D_1 \\ B_2 W C_1 & A_2 - B_2 D_1 V C_2 & B_2 W D_1 \\ W C_1 & -D_1 V C_2 & W D_1 \end{bmatrix}$$

where $V = (I + D_2 D_1)^{-1}$ and $W = (I + D_1 D_2)^{-1}$

5.6 Derive the system matrix for the Afeedback Connection given below

$$S = \begin{bmatrix} A_1 - B_1 V D_2 C_1 & -B_1 V C_2 & B_1 V & -B_1 V D_2 \\ B_2 W C_1 & A_2 - B_2 W D_1 C_2 & B_2 W D_1 & B_2 W \\ W C_1 & -D_1 V C_2 & D_1 V & -D_1 D_2 W \\ D_2 W C_1 & V C_2 & D_2 D_1 V & D_2 W \end{bmatrix}$$

where $V = (I + D_2 D_1)^{-1}$ and $W = (I + D_1 D_2)^{-1}$

5.7 Show that the system matrix for the connect command is given by

$$S = \begin{bmatrix} A + B V K C & B V M \\ N W C & N D V M \end{bmatrix}$$

where $W = (I - D K)^{-1}$ and $V = (I - K D)^{-1}$

5.8 The Inverse of a system is defined as follows: If $y = G u$, then $u = G^{-1} y$. If the system matrix of G is given by the quadruplet $\{ A , B , C , D \}$, and assuming that G is square and D is invertible, show that the system matrix for G^{-1} is given by

$$G^{-1} = \begin{bmatrix} A - B D^{-1} C & -B D^{-1} \\ D^{-1} C & D^{-1} \end{bmatrix}$$

5.9 Derive the system matrices for the return difference, inverse return difference, sensitivity, and complementary sensitivity transfer function matrices defined in Section 5.6. In addition, show how the above system matrices can be computed using standard system connection commands.

5.10 The loop transfer function, *L(s)*, of a *full order observer* (defined in Chapter 8) or a *Kalman-Bucy filter* (defined in Chapter 12) is given by

$$L(s) = C\,\Phi(s)\,L = C\,(sI - A)^{-1}\,L$$

Compute the return difference, sensitivity, and complementary sensitivity transfer function matrices for this system.

Notes and references

According to the survey [F91], the most frequently used books in linear systems/state variable analysis are: [B91], [C84], [F86], [K80], and [De89]. Other books mentioned for graduate level linear systems courses are: [FPE91], [DH88], [Do89], and [L79].

6

Introduction to System Build/PC

System Build is an interactive menu-driven graphical environment that allows us to "build" system models in block diagram form. Simulation is then performed by the MATRIXx Core. Due to the fact that Build is menu driven and interactive, the best way to learn it is to work with it. Build is an extensive product on its own. It has many capabilities, menus, commands, shortcuts, tricks, etc. It would take much more than a brief chapter to fully describe its power. Therefore, this chapter is written as a hands on guided tour of Build. We will describe the basic concepts and some of the commands you will be using to simulate dynamic systems. We will take you step by step through a simple example and show you all the actual menus. After working through Example 6.1, you should try the other examples on your own. For your convenience, we have included the appropriate menu selections in the Appendix, and show you the block diagrams and results of simulations in the body of the examples.

How you physically interact with the program depends on the particular hardware (PC, Workstation or Mainframe) and the version of System Build you are using. The look of the screen, interface, and some of the available utilities and menu items also vary with these factors. The System Build interface in the PC version has gone through major changes in the past few years. The PC Version 5.2 was completely menu driven. The menu items appeared in the lower portion of the screen, and the upper portion was reserved for the block diagrams. The block diagram region was internally divided into 6 super-blocks (explained in the next section), numbered clockwise starting with the northwest corner of the screen. The next update, PC Version 7.1 improved the graphics of the screen and increased the number of super-blocks from 6 to 99. It also introduced block forms, where descriptions of individual blocks could be entered on a one page form, hence, avoiding the chore of choosing several menu items and going through several layers of menus. Block forms also provided the means for documenting block diagrams. The major improvement in the latest PC Version 8.0 is that System Build is now mouse driven. This makes the PC version very similar to the more powerful workstation version. Even though the interface of System Build has gone through major changes, the actual process of model building still remains the same.

6.1 Hierarchical Super-Blocks

Build is accessed within MATRIXx by typing

```
< > build
```

The screen switches to graphical mode where the lower portion contains the first menu (referred to as the *Top Menu*). The upper portion is where the model will appear and is called a *super-block* (see Figure 6-1). The screen containing the super-block has grid coordinates or position numbers. There can be at most 99 blocks within each screen. However, due to limited memory on PCs and too much clutter on the screen, the number of blocks should be limited to less than 30.

Each block may contain transfer functions, gains, summing junctions, nonlinearities and various other elements. Although it appears that we can only model systems that

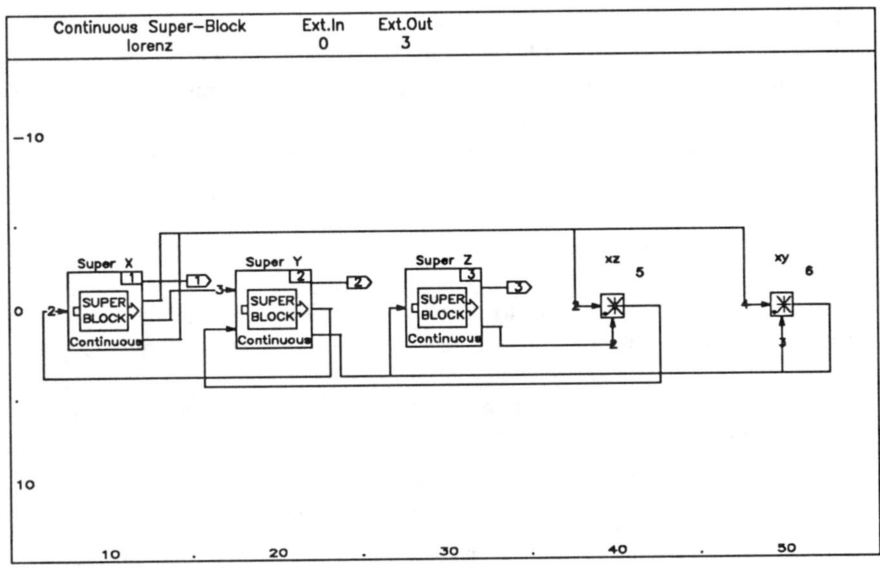

< SystemBuild >

1 Catalog	2 Edit SuperBlock	3 Copy SuperBlock
4 Delete SuperBlock	5 Rename SuperBlock	6 Analyze SuperBlock
7 Save/Load SuperBlock	8 Exit SystemBuild	9 Detail SuperBlock

Figure 6-1 Sample super-block screen with the Top Menu.

contain a few elements this is not the case. Each numbered block itself is a super-block, consisting of many other blocks which are themselves super-blocks, consisting of more blocks, etc. This is what is meant by hierarchical super-blocks. It enables one to create large models by building them piece by piece and connecting them together. Let us take a look at an example of a typical super-block screen shown in Figure 6-1.

Basic identification of the super-block is displayed on top of the screen. Here we note that we have a super-block named "lorenz", which is continuous, has 3 external outputs and no external inputs. There are 5 blocks here. The first three are super-blocks. This means that they are defined separately and contain other elements within them. The last two are multiplication blocks. Each block is identified either by a position number or grid coordinates. For instance, the first block here has position number "1", or grid coordinates [0,10]. You can read the grid coordinates on screen and the position number is displayed in the upper right hand corner of the block.

Blocks can be named (e.g., Super X for block # 1). You can also view the connections. For example, note that the output of the first multiply block (xz) is fed back to the second super-block (Super Y). The three pointed boxes from blocks numbered 1, 2, and 3 are the external outputs. This means that we have chosen to observe the outputs of these blocks. You also see numbers on some of the connection lines. For instance, the first input of super-block # 2 is labeled as "3". This indicates that it is coming from output # 3 of the first super-block. This is useful for keeping track of the connections. As you can see, even in a relatively simple system (this is the model of a third order nonlinear system described in Example 6.4), you can get complicated simulation diagrams. You can make these diagrams manageable by breaking them up into simpler super-blocks. Keep in mind that a complex and cluttered diagram is hard to debug, and is of no value to others viewing it.

6.2 Basic Steps in Model Building

You may have to go through many steps and several layers of menus to build a model of a dynamic system, but the following steps are typically the minimum required.

- 1. *System Build* (*Top menu*): edit a new super-block, assign a name to it and specify whether it is continuous or discrete.
- 2. *Describe Blocks*: *Define* a block and specify its location.
- 3. *Type of Block* : select dynamic system, nonlinearity, algebraic equation, etc.
- 4. *Dynamic System* : select transfer function, state space equation, integrator, etc.
- 5. *Block Forms* : these are special fill-in forms that will appear and allow you to specify the name of block, number of inputs, outputs, parameters, etc.
- 6. Back to *Describe Blocks* menu to define more blocks and repeat the above steps until all blocks are defined.
- 7. Back to *Describe Blocks* menu and choose *Connect* to connect the blocks together.

- 8. Back to the *Top* menu where all blocks are connected. Choose *Analyze* in this menu; this checks to see if any errors have been made. If the errors are minor, it gives warnings, exits Build, and enters MATRIXx. If the errors are fatal, it returns to Build for corrections.
- 9. Use the *Lin* and/or the *Sim* commands to linearize and simulate the system represented by the model created by Build.

6.3 Menus, Mouse, and Basic Navigation

There are several ways to choose menu items. Let us take a look at the first menu.

< SystemBuild >

1 Catalog	**2 Edit SuperBlock**	3 Copy SuperBlock
4 Delete SuperBlock	5 Rename SuperBlock	6 Analyze SuperBlock
7 Save/Load SuperBlock	8 Exit SystemBuild	9 Detail SuperBlock

There are nine items here. To build your first block diagram, you must select the second item, which is "Edit SuperBlock". To do this, or in general to select any menu item, you can do any of the following:

- Click the left mouse button on the item and press Enter.
- Use the arrow keys on the numeric keypad until you reach the item, press Enter.
- Type the item number, and press Enter.
- Type the first few letters of the item, press Enter.

If you have a mouse, the first method may be the fastest.

We need to mention an important fact about keystrokes and mouse clicks. Inside Build, keystrokes and mouse clicks are interpreted differently in the menu area (lower part of screen) and the display area (upper portion). This means the position of the mouse cursor is important when using the keyboard. If you want to make a keyboard entry, make sure the mouse cursor is in the menu area. The reason for this is that Build has some keyboard shortcuts for experienced users. For instance, suppose the mouse cursor is pointing to a block in the display area. If you now type E, this block gets enlarged, because E is the keyboard shortcut for Enlarge a block. If the mouse cursor is in the menu area, however, and you type E, a menu item that starts with this letter will be highlighted.

Several MATRIXx Core commands are available in Build (see the manual for a list). Also, data can be defined in MATRIXx and simply called upon in Build. Note that if you make mistakes during data entry, you can correct them by using the *Cancel* or *Undo* commands. The *Cancel* command takes you to the previous data inquiry prompt or menu. If you use *Cancel* successively, you will eventually lose your block diagram. The *Undo* command backs up to the menu above the current prompt or menu.

The following example illustrates all steps in a simulation. It is recommended, that for maximum understanding, you follow the example on your computer .

6.4 Examples

Example 6.1

Consider the double integrator system *G(s)*, which is open loop unstable. To stabilize the system, we use a lead compensator, *K(s)*, as shown in Figure 6-2.

$$G(s) = \frac{1}{s^2}, \quad K(s) = 10\frac{(s+1)}{(s+5)}$$

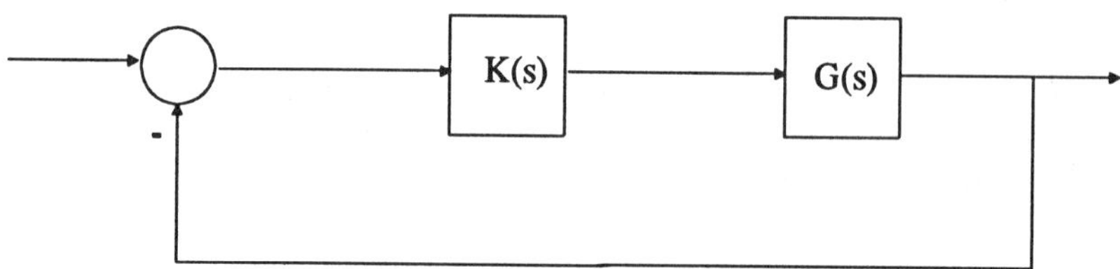

Figure 6-2 Block diagram for Example 6.1.

We start a Build session by typing

```
< > build
```

You will then get the following Top menu. (*Note*: the selected menu items appear in **bold**).

< SystemBuild >

1 Catalog **2 Edit SuperBlock** 3 Copy SuperBlock
4 Delete SuperBlock 5 Rename SuperBlock 6 Analyze SuperBlock
7 Save/Load SuperBlock 8 Exit SystemBuild 9 Detail SuperBlock

To start a new diagram, select *Edit SuperBlock*. You will then be presented with a *Block Form*. All operations dealing with defining a block or super-block are followed by a *Block Form*. This is simply a fill-in form, in which all items necessary for defining a block are displayed. Some items have defaults, such as: number of inputs/outputs (default = 1), color (default = black), orientation of blocks (default = left to right), etc. If the defaults are acceptable, you can skip these items. Other items are optional, such as: block names, labels on inputs/outputs, comments, etc. The exception is that all super-blocks must be named. To navigate through the form, use the TAB key, or use the mouse. When you are done, either hit the Return key, or click the left mouse button on DONE.

The first Block Form is shown in Figure 6-3; select *Edit New SuperBlock*.

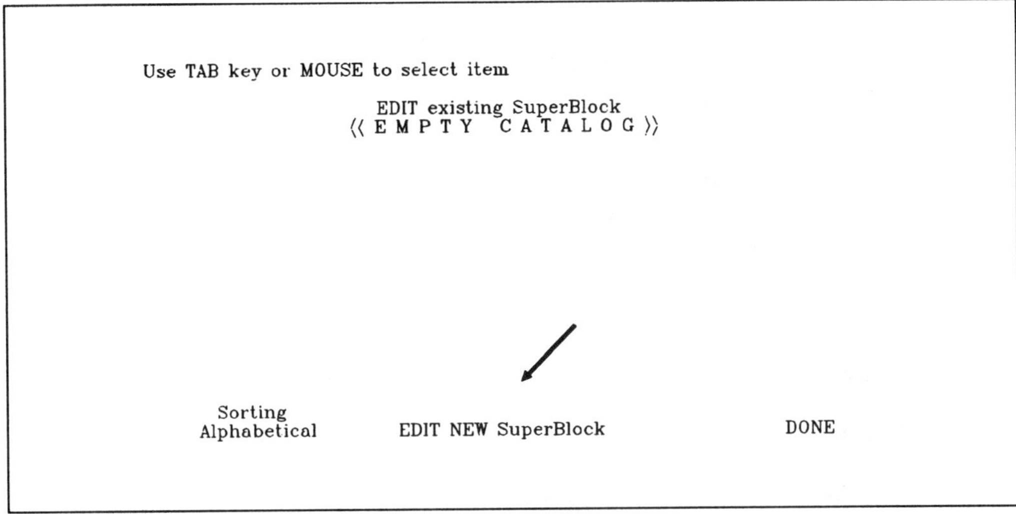

Figure 6-3 The Edit New SuperBlock form.

You will get the first super-block form, shown in Figure 6-4.

Write the name of the super-block (we call it "example", here). Change the number of external inputs and outputs from 0 to 1. You can either write this in, or by double clicking on the numbers, they will automatically increase by one. The super-block Type is Continuous by default. For discrete systems, change this to Discrete; Build will ask you for the sampling period information. Click on DONE when finished. These choices are marked in Figure 6-4.

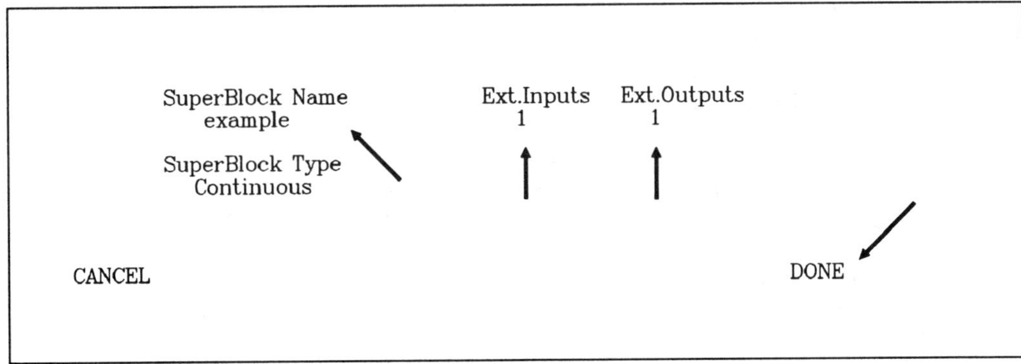

Figure 6-4 The Edit SuperBlock form.

The next menu allows you to define your individual blocks.

< DESCRIBE BLOCKS >

1 — Next Menu —	**2 Define Block**	3 Remove Block(s)
4 Examine-Modify Block	5 Copy - Paste Block(s)	6 Connect Blocks
7 Duplicate Block(s)	8 Flip Block(s)	9 Exit to TOP Menu

Select 2, then click on the upper portion of screen for a block location. You will get the next menu asking for the type of block. We will put a summing junction there. This choice appears under option 4, *Algebraic Equations.*

< TYPE OF BLOCK >

1 — Next Menu —	2 Gain Block	3 SuperBlock
4 Algebraic Equations	5 Piece-Wise Linear	6 Dynamic Systems
7 Trig Functions	8 User Code Block	9 — Previous Menu —

You will now get the appropriate sub-menu. Choose 2, *Sum of Vectors.*

< ALGEBRAIC EQNS >

1 General Expression	**2 Sum of Vectors**	3 Polynomial in 1 Var
4 Elem by Elem Product	5 Dot or Inner Product	6 Cross Product
7 Elem by Elem Divide	8 Signal Conversion	9 — Previous Menu —

You get the appropriate Block Form. All the defaults (2 inputs, one output) are acceptable here. Note that the signs on the summing junction are [1 , -1]. The default form assumes the typical two-input case with negative feedback. The summing inputs are numbered counter-clockwise, starting with the horizontal input pointing to the right. Keep in mind that the first input is positive and the second one is negative. This is important when you want to make connections. Select DONE.

< DESCRIBE BLOCKS >

1 — Next Menu —	**2 Define Block**	3 Remove Block(s)
4 Examine-Modify Block	5 Copy - Paste Block(s)	6 Connect Blocks
7 Duplicate Block(s)	8 Flip Block(s)	9 Exit to TOP Menu

Click on the screen for another location. We want to put the compensator here. Transfer functions and state space equations are under *Dynamic Systems* option.

< TYPE OF BLOCK >

1 — Next Menu —	2 Gain Block	3 SuperBlock
4 Algebraic Equations	5 Piece-Wise Linear	**6 Dynamic Systems**
7 Trig Functions	8 User Code Block	9 — Previous Menu —

Choose 4 to enter transfer function in numerator/denominator form.

< DYNAMIC SYSTEMS >

1 — Next Menu —	2 Nth Order Integrator	3 State-Space System
4 Num - Den Coeffs.	5 Gain Zeros - Poles	6 Gain Damps - Freqs
7 Hysteresis Block	8 Time Delay: exp(-kTs)	9 — Previous Menu —

You will now get the following default Block form, shown in Figure 6-5.

```
Use TAB key or MOUSE to select item
          BLOCK NAME                INPUTS     OUTPUTS      STATES
                                       1          1            1

  Order of NUMerator : 0
  NUMerator Coeffs : 1.

  Order of DENominator : 1
                       1-by-2 DENominator Coeffs
    1.       0.

          Input External-Signals                  Output Labels
  1                                    1 ""



                              COMMENTS

          VIEW-INPUT      COLOR    ICON    IN-PINS  OUT-PINS  LABELS
  External-Signals  0    Special  Show-All Show-All   OFF
  CANCEL                                                  DONE
```

Figure 6-5 The transfer function definition "Num-Den Coeffs" Block form.

The number of states is the number of poles. Change the Order of NUM to 1, the NUM Coeffs to [10 10], and the DEN Coeffs to [1 5]. The rest of the defaults are acceptable. Finally, we can define the plant as a double integrator, which is also under *Dynamic Systems*.

< DESCRIBE BLOCKS >

1 — Next Menu —	**2 Define Block**	3 Remove Block(s)
4 Examine-Modify Block	5 Copy - Paste Block(s)	6 Connect Blocks
7 Duplicate Block(s)	8 Flip Block(s)	9 Exit to TOP Menu

< TYPE OF BLOCK >

1 — Next Menu —	2 Gain Block	3 SuperBlock
4 Algebraic Equations	5 Piece-Wise Linear	**6 Dynamic Systems**
7 Trig Functions	8 User Code Block	9 — Previous Menu —

< DYNAMIC SYSTEMS >

1 — Next Menu —	**2 Nth Order Integrator**	3 State-Space System
4 Num - Den Coeffs.	5 Gain Zeros - Poles	6 Gain Damps - Freqs
7 Hysteresis Block	8 Time Delay: exp(-kTs)	9 — Previous Menu —

After filling in the corresponding form, we can now connect the blocks. This is done using the *Connect Blocks* option in the < DESCRIBE BLOCKS > menu.

< DESCRIBE BLOCKS >

1 — Next Menu —	2 Define Block	3 Remove Block(s)
4 Examine-Modify Block	5 Copy - Paste Block(s)	**6 Connect Blocks**
7 Duplicate Block(s)	8 Flip Block(s)	9 Exit to TOP Menu

The most widely used options are 1, 2, and 3. The *Internal Path* option is used for connecting individual blocks. A block diagram may also have external inputs. These are selected via option 2. The output of any block we wish to observe can be passed on as external output via option 3. It goes without saying that you must have at least one external output. External inputs are not necessary, however, because the system may be driven by initial conditions, or signal sources that are available inside Build under the *Next Menu* option in the <TYPE OF BLOCK> menu. Standard inputs such as step, ramp, and sinusoids are available.

To connect internal blocks (*From* one block *To* another), use the following three-step procedure:

1. Choose Internal Path.

2. Click the left mouse button on the northeast corner (where the block number is shown) of the From block.

3. Click the left mouse button on the northeast corner of the To block.

If the blocks are not aligned, the connection will not be a straight line. If you would like to straighten it out, you can move the blocks to align them by the following procedure. Click the left mouse button on the block, and hold the button down, then drag the mouse. This moves the block and its connections.

We will make the connections in the following order: summing junction to compensator, compensator to plant, plant to summing junction, external input to summing junction, external output from the plant output.

< CONNECT BLOCKS >

1 Internal Path	2 External Input	3 External Output
4 Examine Connection	5 Disconnect Blocks	6 Describe Blocks
7 Exit to TOP Menu	8 — Previous Menu —	

Click on the summing junction location number, then click on the NE corner of the compensator; the connection line will be drawn.

< CONNECT BLOCKS >

1 **Internal Path**	2 External Input	3 External Output
4 Examine Connection	5 Disconnect Blocks	6 Describe Blocks
7 Exit to TOP Menu	8 — Previous Menu —	

Click on NE corner of compensator, then click on NE corner of plant.

Before we connect the plant to the summing junction, we need to make the following observation. A summing junction has at least two inputs. When you connect a block to a multi-input block, we need to specify which one of these inputs will be selected. This is done through a *Connection Editor*, which graphically shows the connections. You will specify the connection as shown below and enter (0,0) when done. For our example, input # 2 of the summing junction is coming from the feedback loop (it has been specified in its Block form), and input # 1 is coming from the external input.

< CONNECT BLOCKS >

1 **Internal Path**	2 External Input	3 External Output
4 Examine Connection	5 Disconnect Blocks	6 Describe Blocks
7 Exit to TOP Menu	8 — Previous Menu —	

Click on NE corner of plant, then click on location number of the summing junction. This is shown in Figure 6-6, which shows the final block diagram.

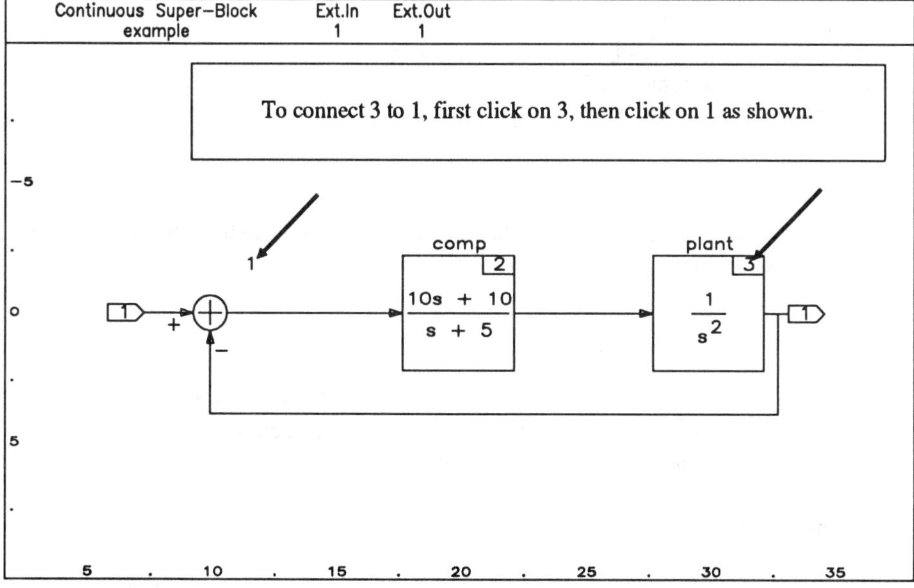

Figure 6-6 The final block diagram for Example 6.1.

CONNECTIONS: Enter I,J to connect from I to J
Enter I,0 or 0,J to remove all from I or to J
Enter 0,0 when complete.

From, To : `[1,2];0,0`

Note that summing junction inputs are numbered counter-clockwise. So, the horizontal arrow pointing east is #1, the vertical arrow pointing up is #2, etc. If you make a mistake, select *Disconnect Blocks* in the <CONNECT BLOCKS > menu and try again.

We will now connect the *External Inputs* and *External Outputs.* If you have a three-button mouse, you can, without menus, do the following to connect an external input to a block. Click the middle button in an empty area of the screen, click the middle button again in the position number of the block. For an external output, follow the reverse procedure; first click inside the block, then click outside. If you have a two-button mouse, use the menus as shown below.

< CONNECT BLOCKS >

1 Internal Path	**2 External Input**	3 External Output
4 Examine Connection	5 Disconnect Blocks	6 Describe Blocks
7 Exit to TOP Menu	8 — Previous Menu —	

Click the position number of the summing junction; you will get the *Connection Editor* again. You will get a prompt for the dimension of the external input in case there are more than one inputs. Type 1 for the response.

Ext input vector dim [0] : `1`
CONNECTIONS: Enter I,J to connect from I to J
Enter I,0 or 0,J to remove all from I or to J
Enter 0,0 when complete.

From, To : `[1,1];0,0`

To create External Outputs, either use the above procedure for a three-button mouse, or the menu as shown below.

< CONNECT BLOCKS >

1 Internal Path	2 External Input	**3 External Output**
4 Examine Connection	5 Disconnect Blocks	6 Describe Blocks
7 Exit to TOP Menu	8 — Previous Menu —	

Ext output vector dim [0] : `1`

Type the dimension of the external output and click the NE corner of the plant.

Our block diagram is now finished; you should have a diagram roughly similar to Figure 6-6. If you wish to get a printout of your diagram, this can be done using the *Hardcopy* option in the < ENVIRONMENT > menu. This is a special menu, which contains some screen utilities; it can be accessed directly at almost any menu or data inquiry prompt.

< CONNECT BLOCKS > `Environment`

1 Internal Path	2 External Input	3 External Output
4 Examine Connection	5 Disconnect Blocks	6 Describe Blocks
7 Exit to TOP Menu	8 — Previous Menu —	

< ENVIRONMENT >

1 — Next Menu —	2 Return	3 PLOT or REDRAW
4 Drag	5 Reduce	6 Window to Fit
7 Enlarge	8 Normal Window	**9 Hardcopy**

< AVAILABLE DEVICES >

1 Plotter	**2 Printer**	3 Cancel Hardcopy

To return to the previous menu, select the *Return* option.

< ENVIRONMENT >

1 — Next Menu —	**2 Return**	3 PLOT or REDRAW
4 Drag	5 Reduce	6 Window to Fit
7 Enlarge	8 Normal Window	9 Hardcopy

We are now finished with our block diagram, and we need to get back to the Top Menu. This option is available in most menus. Moreover, *TOP* is a *global command*. This means that it can be invoked by typing it at any point. Another useful global command is *MAT*, which returns you to the MATRIXx prompt. For other global commands, see the manual.

< CONNECT BLOCKS >

1 Internal Path	2 External Input	3 External Output
4 Examine Connection	5 Disconnect Blocks	6 Describe Blocks
7 Exit to TOP Menu	8 — Previous Menu —	

The final step before we leave Build, is to select *Analyze SuperBlock* option. This will check the diagram for any errors. It either issues warnings for non-fatal errors, or returns to Build if there are fatal errors. A shortcut for this is to type A at any menu; this will analyze the block.

< SystemBuild >

1 Catalog	2 Edit SuperBlock	3 Copy SuperBlock
4 Delete SuperBlock	5 Rename SuperBlock	**6 Analyze SuperBlock**
7 Save/Load SuperBlock	8 Exit SystemBuild	9 Detail SuperBlock

```
SuperBlock Reference Map :
  example
System Built with 0 error(s) and 0 warning(s).
Use  SIM('IALG') to set the integration algorithm
```

We are now ready to simulate the system using the *Sim* command. Note that the *Sim* command is similar to the *Lsim* command, but it can only be used in conjunction with a Build simulation. *Lsim* is only for linear systems, but as you might have noticed, Build can contain many kinds of nonlinearities, logical functions, time delays, etc, therefore, *Sim* is more general. In addition, using the command *Sim('ialg')*, one can choose among seven different integration algorithms. The default is the Variable Step Kutta-Merson algorithm.

Let us find the step response of the above system. First, we will generate the time axis as a column vector (this must be a column, otherwise you will get an error message), and a step input using the *ones* command.

```
< > t=[0:0.1:10]'; u=ones(t);
< > y=sim(t,u);
```

As we can see from Figure 6-7, the compensator, *K(s)*, is able to stabilize the unstable system. This type of compensator is called a lead compensator. Classical compensator designs such as lead and lag are discussed in Chapter 7.

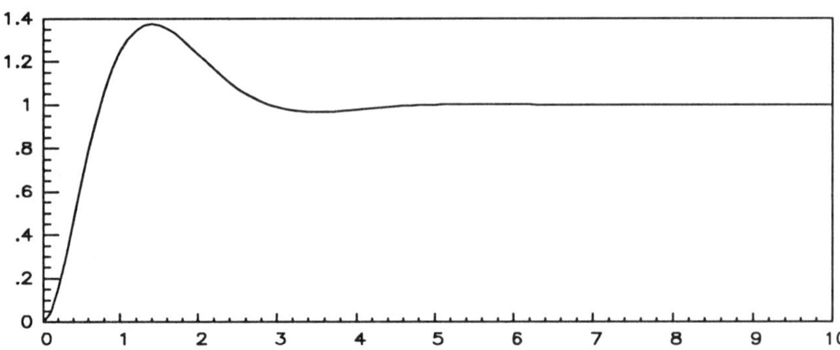

Figure 6-7 Step response for Example 6.1.

For your information, Figure 6-8 shows all the blocks available in Build. Make sure you browse through the different block menus to see what is available. Before we move to the next example, we point out the documentation option in Build. This option is available in the first < System Build > menu under option 9, *Detail SuperBlock*. This will allow you to fully document your diagram for future reference. It essentially puts together all the selected Block forms in an ASCII file. If another person wishes to recreate your simulation, all he or she needs is the diagram and the documentation file. Another useful capability is that once you become experienced enough and know the menu items, and their sequences, you can program all the menu selections and data entries in an executable file (exec file). Anyone wishing to recreate your diagram can run this exec file. For your convenience, we have included such exec files

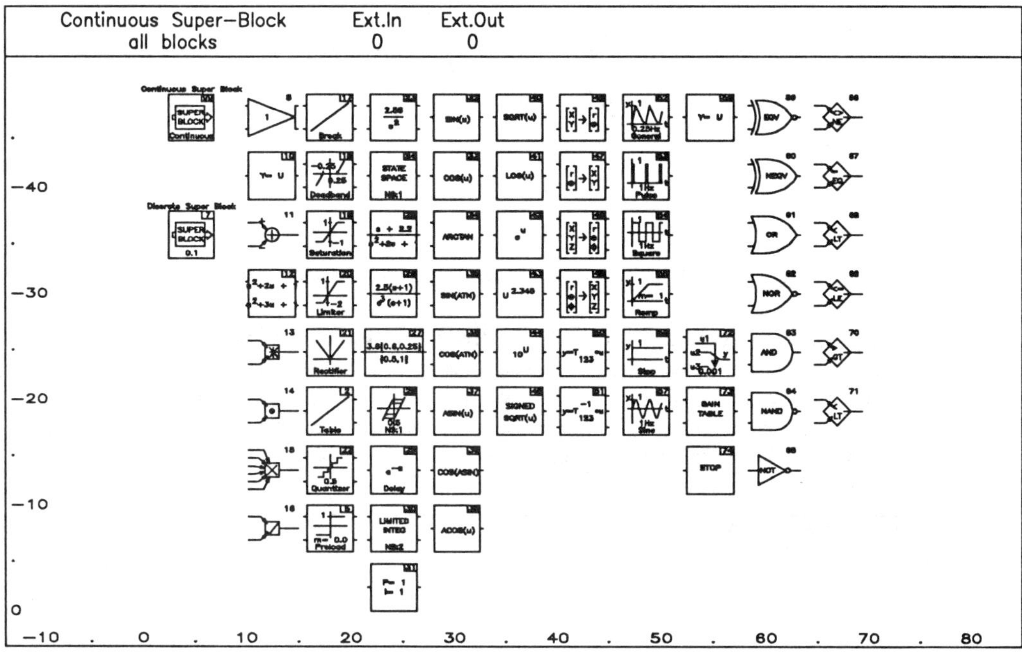

Figure 6-8 All blocks in System Build. The data to generate this diagram is available in the MATRIXx Demo directory.

for all the subsequent examples in the Appendix. No instructions are given within the body of the examples; only the diagrams and the results are shown. Try to recreate our examples by yourself. If you run into problems, either execute the programs, or simply examine our exec files.

Example 6.2 Effects of Saturation

We will investigate the effects of saturation in the previous example. Saturation is a nonlinear phenomenon which is very common in control systems. For instance, electronic amplifiers have almost linear gain up to a certain range, beyond which the output saturates. It occurs in electric motors due to saturation of magnetic fields, and it is present in almost every real physical system. Although saturation effects can be analyzed using "describing functions" and other approximate nonlinear methods, we will examine their effects using simulation. The input-output characteristic of a nonlinear saturation element is shown in Figure 6-9.

The gain of the nonlinear element is M/E for input signals with a magnitude less than E, and has a fixed gain of M for input magnitudes greater than E. The overall result is that the "effective gain" of the amplifier decreases as the amplitude of the external input increases.

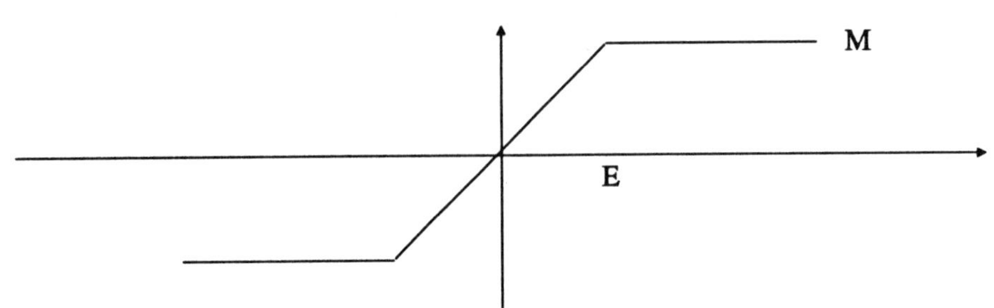

Figure 6-9 Input-Output characteristic of a saturation element.

This gain reduction generally has stabilizing effects, and makes the system more sluggish. Of course, for conditionally stable systems that become unstable for lower gains, saturation can be destabilizing. It is worth noting that during saturation, the system temporarily becomes open loop; the system must tolerate this mode. The bottom line, is that for real systems, simulation incorporating all nonlinear effects must be performed to ensure proper performance.

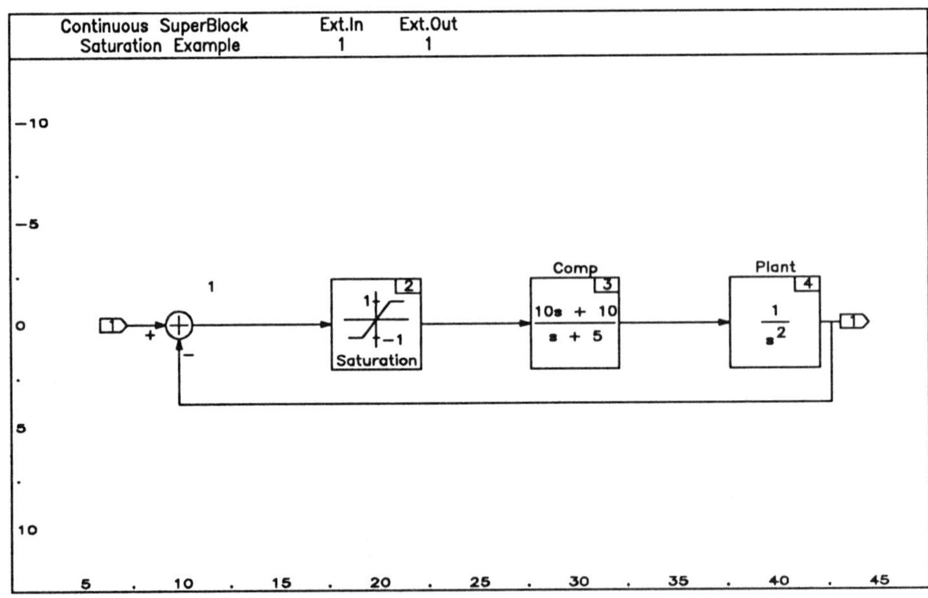

Figure 6-10 System Build block diagram for Example 6-2.

After building the system shown in Figure 6-10, we are ready for simulation. We vary the input level from one to six, simulate the system, and compute the overshoot six times. To do this in one step, we will write a simple *for* loop as shown next.

```
< > t=[0:.1:10]'; input=ones(t);
< > for i=1:6; ui=i*input; ysat(:,i)=sim(t,ui); i=i+1; end;
< > for i=1:6; pos(1,i)=100*(max(ysat(:,i))-ysat(100,i))/ysat(100,i); end
```

POS = [37.5 34.4 31.3 29.4 29.6 30.6]

The simulation result is shown in Figure 6-11. From the plot, we observe that the settling time increases with larger inputs. Notice that in linear systems, when the input level changes, the output level changes accordingly—system dynamic behavior, however, does not change. With saturation, dynamic characteristics, such as settling time and overshoot, are dependent on input levels. This is strictly a nonlinear phenomenon. The root locus of *K(s)G(s)*, shown in Figure 6-12, will shed some light on the above results.

Since the effective gain decreases, the real part of the complex root decreases. Because the settling time is inversely proportional to this real part, we expect longer settling time for larger input values. Also note that the damping ratio (ζ) initially increases but then decreases. This explains the initial reduction in POS and the final slight increase.

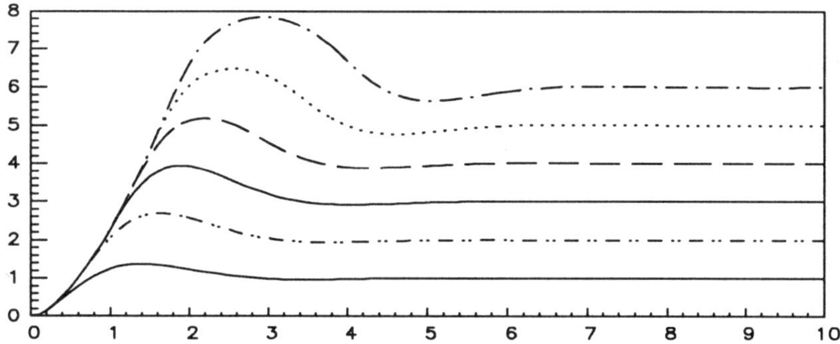

Figure 6-11 Step response for Example 6-2 showing the effects of saturation.

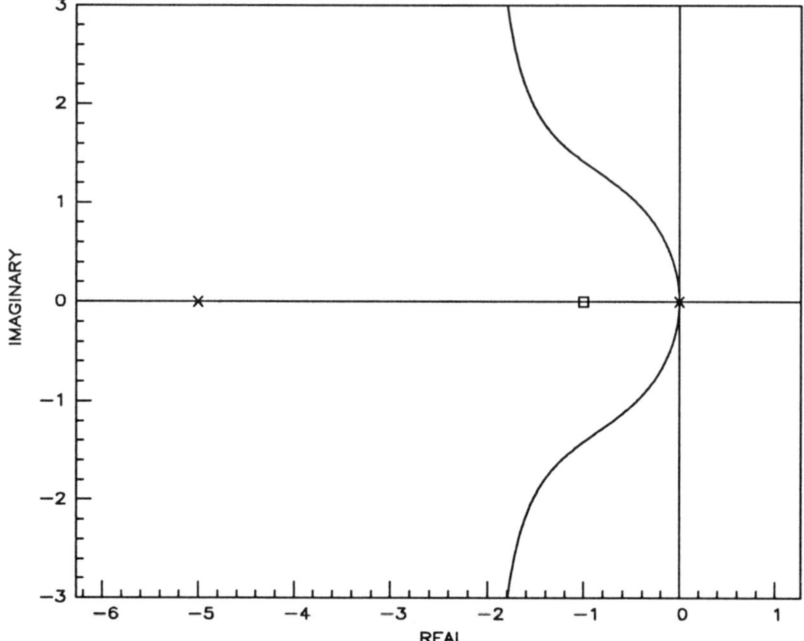

Figure 6-12 Root locus for Example 6-2.

Example 6.3 Pole-Zero Cancellation Effects

We will investigate the effects of pole-zero cancellation. Stable pole-zero cancellation is a very common and effective design strategy. It is also referred to as "pole shifting", in which stable poles are cancelled with zeros, and replaced with poles in more desirable locations. It is also the idea behind notch filter design. Although it has to be noted that exact pole-zero cancellation is not possible in practice, due to component tolerances in continuous systems, and finite word length effects in digital systems, it is still a very popular and effective strategy. The main point of this example is to demonstrate, through analysis and simulation, the effects of *unstable* pole-zero cancellation, and explain why it must not be done.

We will consider the following example adapted from [K80]

$$G(s) = \frac{1}{s-1} \quad \text{and} \quad K(s) = \frac{s-1}{s+1}$$

where $G(s)$ is the plant, and $K(s)$ is the cancellation compensator. The product $G(s)K(s)$ is, of course, stable in the bounded-input bounded-output sense (i.e., BIBO stable). Because the system is now second order, we can represent it as a set of two first order differential equations and solve for the step response (the details are left as an exercise).

$$\dot{x}_1 = x_1 + u$$
$$\dot{x}_2 = -2x_1 - x_2$$
$$y = x_1 + x_2$$

The System Build block diagram corresponding to these equations is shown in Figure 6-13.

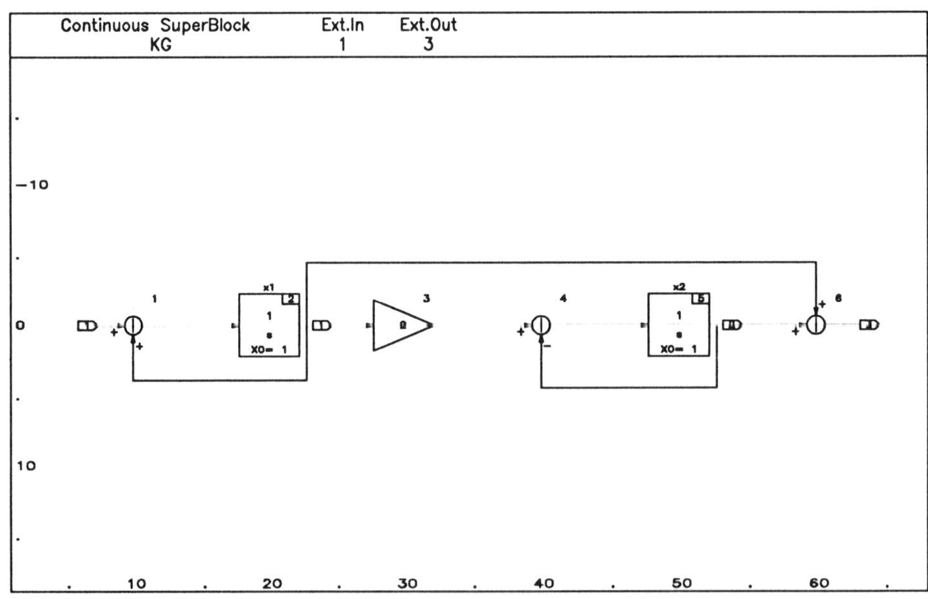

Figure 6-13 Build block diagram for $G(s)K(s)$.

Solving for the states and the output, we get

$$x_1(t) = (\alpha + 1)\, e^{t} - 1 \qquad \text{where } x_1(0) = \alpha$$
$$x_2(t) = 2 + (\alpha + \beta - 1)\, e^{-t} - (\alpha + 1)\, e^{t} \qquad \text{where } x_2(0) = \beta$$
$$y(t) = x_1 + x_2 = 1 + (\alpha + \beta - 1)\, e^{-t}$$

Now, note that as $t \rightarrow \infty$, $x_1 \rightarrow \infty$, $x_2 \rightarrow -\infty$, and $y \rightarrow 1$

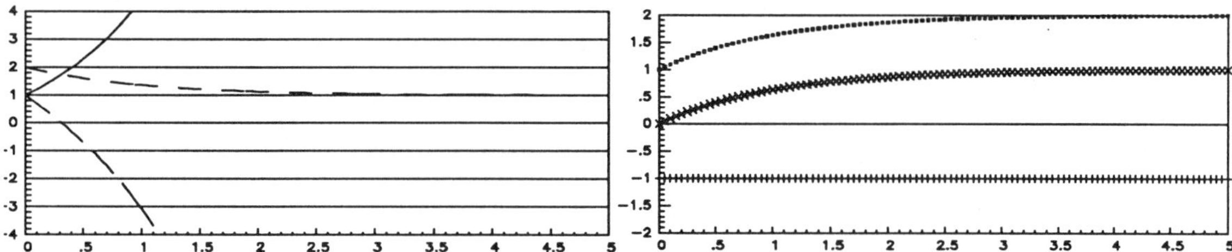

Figure 6-14 Step response of $G(s)K(s)$ for (1,1) initial conditions.

Figure 6-15 Step response of $G(s)K(s)$ for (-1,1) initial conditions.

Therefore, even though the internal variables within the system are unbounded, the output somehow masks this information and, in fact, approaches one for any initial condition. We define a system to be *internally stable* if all possible transfer functions between all inputs and outputs are stable. Hence, the above system, although BIBO stable, is not internally stable. Also, note that the system has two "modes", e^t and e^{-t}, and the unstable mode gets cancelled. The cancelled mode is called a "hidden mode", and corresponds to the pole at $s = 1$, which is precisely the pole that was cancelled.

In summary, when a pole is canceled by a zero, it creates hidden modes within the system; if the pole is unstable, it leads to a system which is not internally stable, which is unacceptable. For those familiar with state space concepts, we say that the system becomes unobservable (or undetectable if the mode is unstable). It is worth noting, however, that when $\alpha = -1$, all variables remain bounded. For all other initial conditions, we get the previous result. The plots for initial conditions of (-1,1) and (1,1) are shown in Figures 6-14 and 6-15.

We will now analyze the case where the compensator precedes the plant, i.e., $K(s)G(s)$. In a transfer function sense, there should not be any difference, because the closed loop transfer function is the same in both cases (GK and KG are the same). In the time domain, however, we will see some differences due to the effects of initial conditions. It can be shown that the following set of differential equations represents the system (this is left as an exercise). The Build block diagram is shown in Figure 6-16.

The equations and the step response calculation results are shown below

$$\dot{x}_1 = -x_1 - 2u$$

$$\dot{x}_2 = x_1 + x_2 + u$$

$$y = x_2$$

$$x_1(t) = -2 + (\alpha + 2)\, e^{-t}$$

$$y(t) = x_2(t) = 1 + \left(\frac{\alpha + 2\beta}{2}\right) e^{t} - \left(\frac{\alpha + 2}{2}\right) e^{-t}$$

We note, again, that for values of $\alpha = -2\beta$, the unstable mode is cancelled, and

$$x_1 \rightarrow -2 \quad \text{and} \quad y = x_2 \rightarrow 1$$

For all other initial conditions the output is unbounded. From the state space point of view, the present realization is not controllable, or rather not stabilizable, because the hidden mode is unstable. For the particular choice of initial conditions (-2, 1) we have $x_1(t) = -2$ and $x_2(t) = y(t) = 1$ as shown in Figure 6-17. The plot for initial conditions of (1,1) is shown in Figure 6-18.

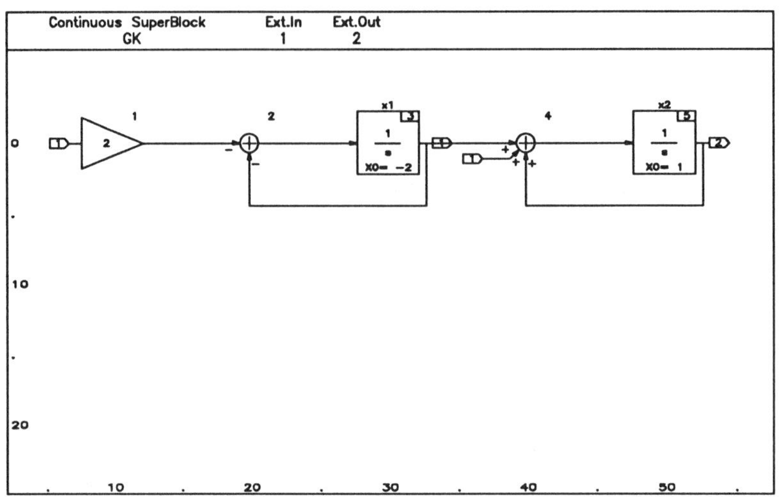

Figure 6-16 Build block diagram for $K(s)G(s)$.

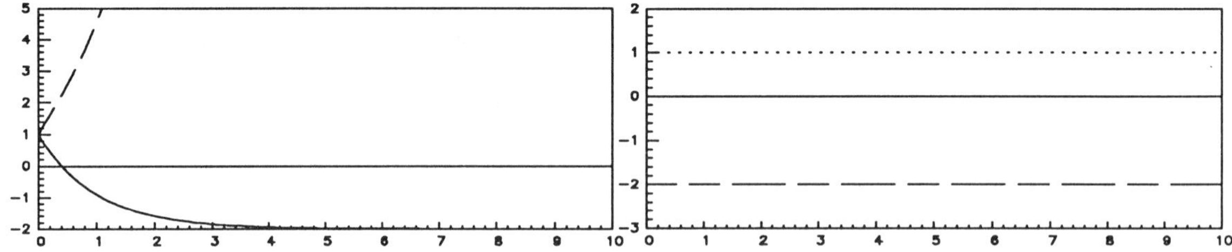

Figure 6-17 Step response of $K(s)G(s)$ for (1,1) initial conditions.

Figure 6-18 Step response of $K(s)G(s)$ for (-2,1) initial conditions.

Example 6.4 Simulation of a Chaotic System: The Lorenz System

The Lorenz system is a set of three first-order nonlinear differential equations. They were first presented in 1963 by E. N. Lorenz, whose motivation for the problem was weather forecasting. For more details, see Thompson and Stewart [TS86]. The equations are given below.

$$\dot{x} = a(y - x)$$

$$\dot{y} = x(b - z) - y$$

$$\dot{z} = cz + xy$$

Lorenz realized the exponential divergence of nearby initial conditions, and concluded that the fundamental problem of long term weather forecasting is imprecise knowledge of initial conditions. The strong dependence of solutions of nonlinear dynamic systems on their initial conditions has been long recognized. The term "*chaos*" commonly refers to the fact that it is impossible to exactly predict the behavior of the system in the long run, even though the underlying phenomenon is deterministic and represented by a simple set of differential equations.

We will simulate the above system using Build. To demonstrate the use of the super-block concept, we will limit ourselves to not more than six blocks per screen. It should be noted that the use of super-blocks, and their proper connection, is the most challenging aspect of using Build for the novice user.

Before using Build, you must have a plan. You must first draw a draft version of the diagram on paper, and carefully number all inputs and outputs. Our plan is to build each equation separately as a super-block, and then connect them, along with the required products, in a main super-block. We are following an outward approach to building, i.e., we are building the system from inside out. It is also possible to take an inward approach and build the main system first, and then the other subsystems.

The simulation parameters are: $\{ a = 10, b = 28, c = -2.67, x(0) = y(0) = z(0) = 5 \}$

X Super-Block : This is to build the first equation. Note that this equation requires an input of y. The output x appears as an input to the Y Super-Block, and in the xz and xy terms. To view x, we also need a separate output as an external output. Therefore, the X Super-Block has one input and four outputs. Its draft version is shown in Figure 6-19.

Y Super-Block : This builds the second equation. This equation has two inputs: 28x and -xz. The output y appears as an input in the X Super-Block, and in the xy term. Hence, this super-block has two inputs and three outputs (one output is to view y). Its draft version appears in Figure 6-20.

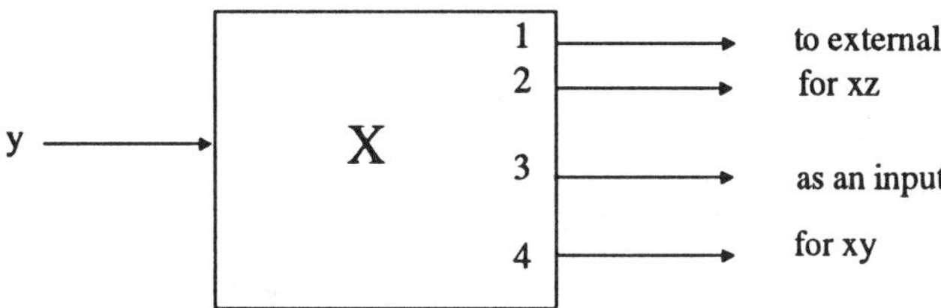

Figure 6-19 Draft version of the X Super-Block.

Z Super-Block : This builds the third equation. Following the same reasoning above, it has one input and two outputs. Its draft version is shown in Figure 6-21.

Lorenz Super-Block : The role of this super-block is to create the needed products and connect the above three super-blocks together. It is the main super-block.

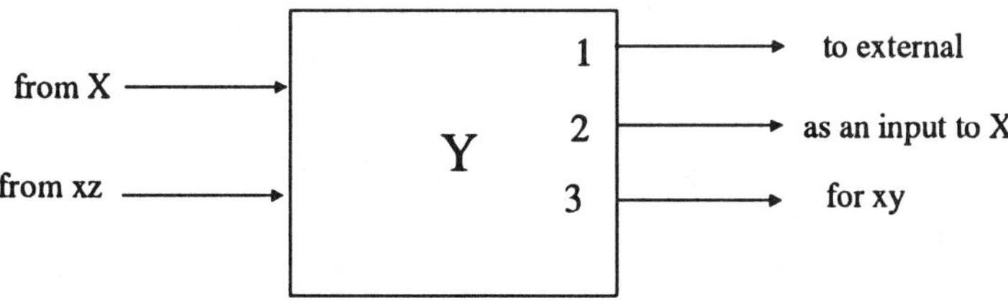

Figure 6-20 Draft version of the Y Super-Block.

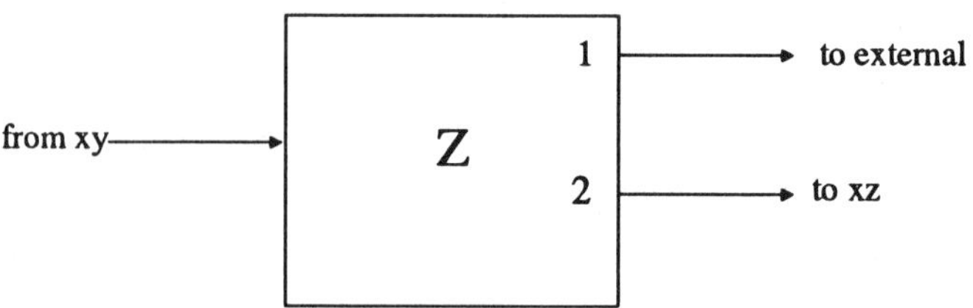

Figure 6-21 Draft version of the Z Super-Block.

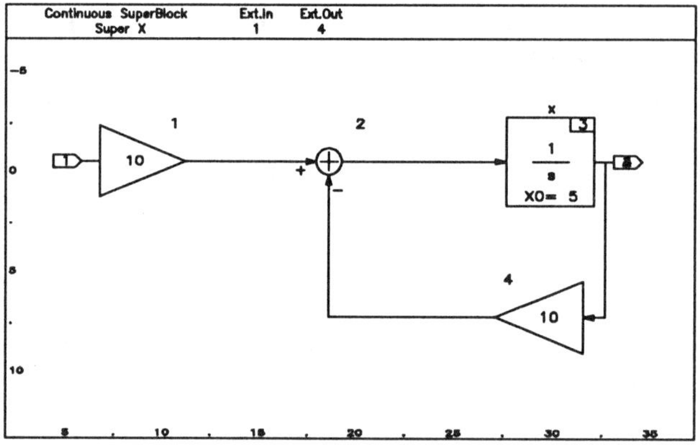

Figure 6-22 The X Super-Block.

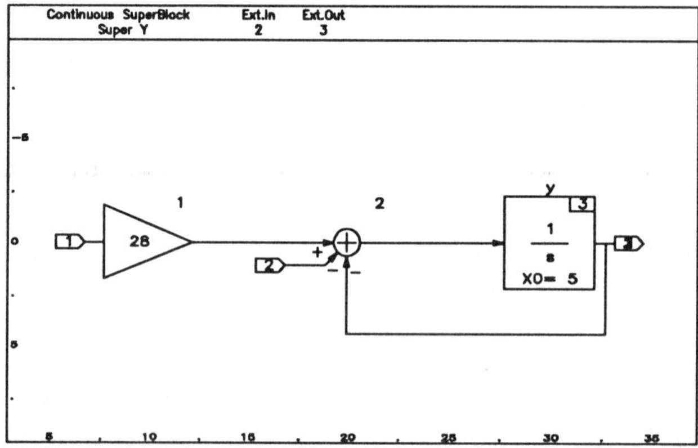

Figure 6-23 The Y Super-Block.

The System Build diagrams for the three super-blocks and the main super-block are shown in Figures 6-22 to 6-25. *Note*: Figure 6-25 is the same as Figure 6-1, except the blocks were repositioned, using the mouse, for better presentation. To show that the equations can be simulated using only one super-block, we show the diagram in Figure 6-26 (its exec file is not included). As you can see, your simulation diagrams can become very cluttered if you do not break them up into super-blocks. The results of simulation are shown in Figures 6-27 to 6-30.

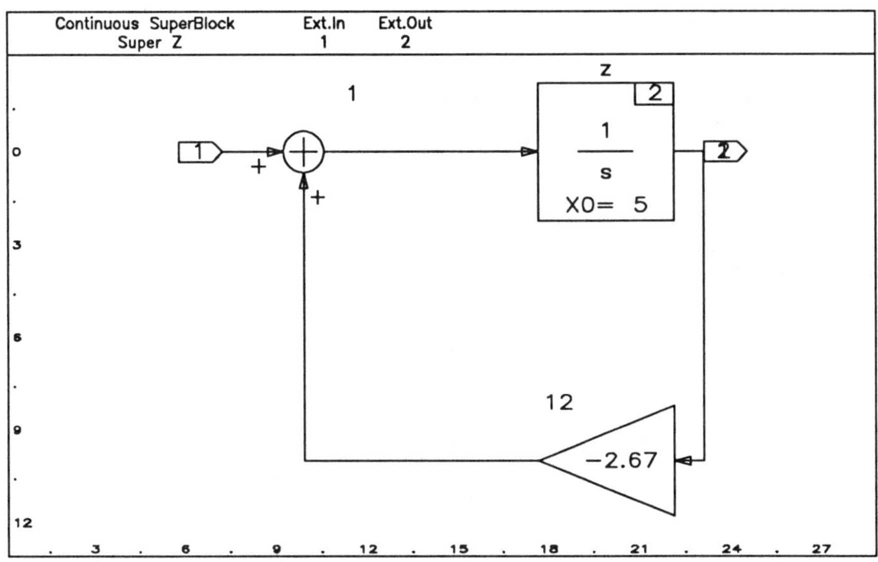

Figure 6-24 The Z Super-Block.

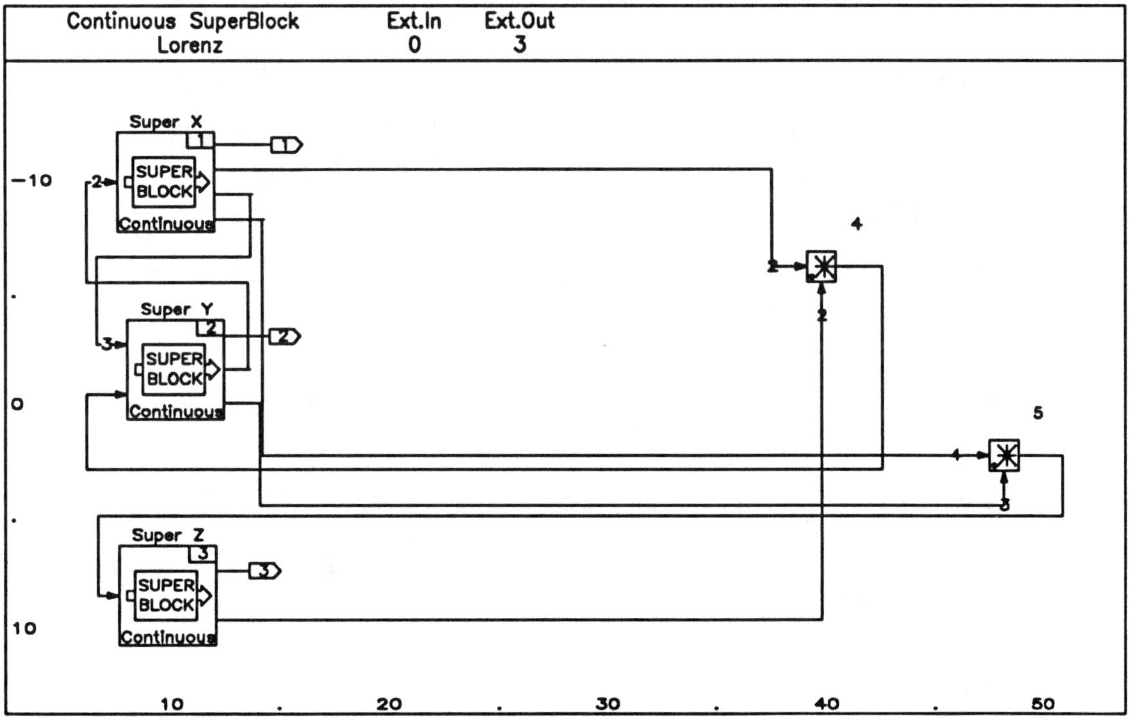

Figure 6-25 The Lorenz Super-Block.

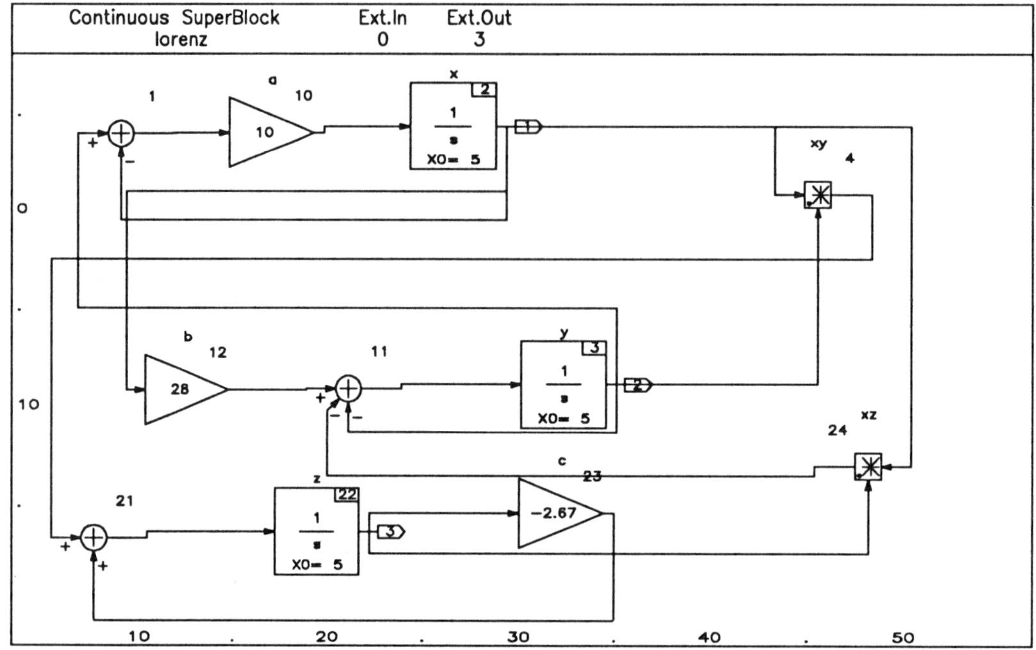

Figure 6-26 The Lorenz Super-Block without using nested super-blocks.

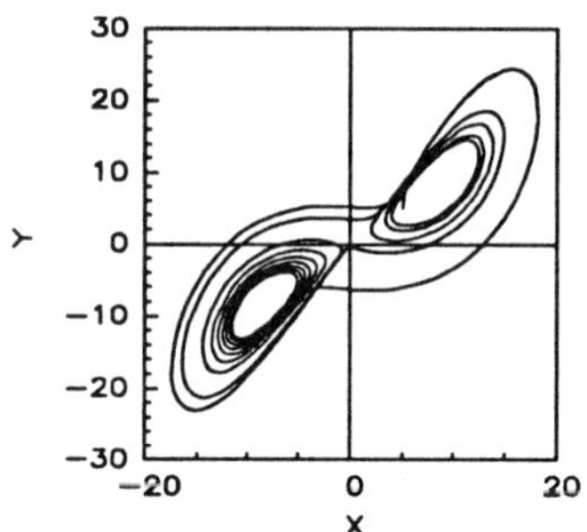

Figure 6-27 Plot of y versus x.

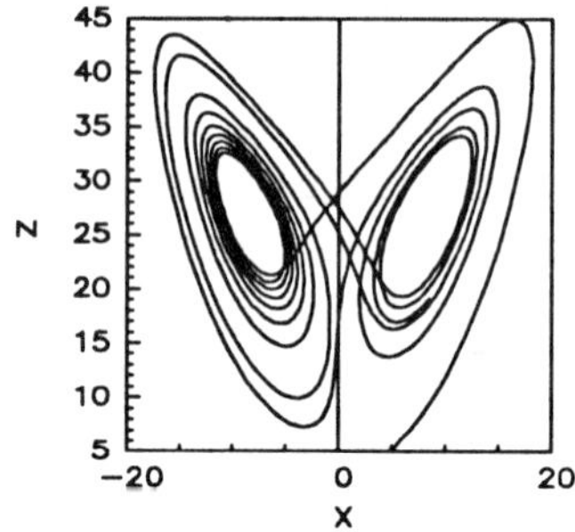

Figure 6-28 Plot of z versus x.

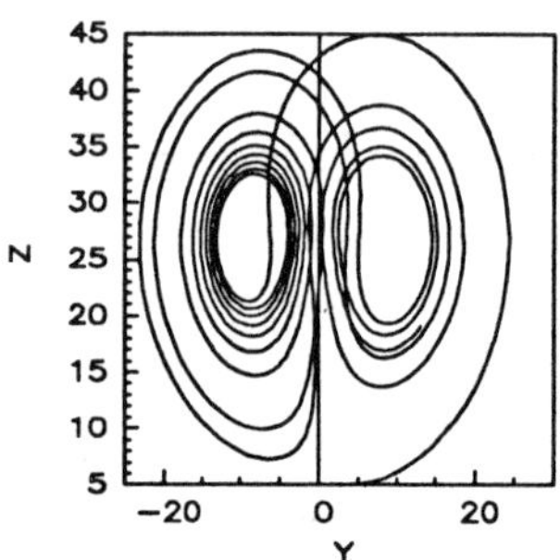

Figure 6-29 Plot of z versus y.

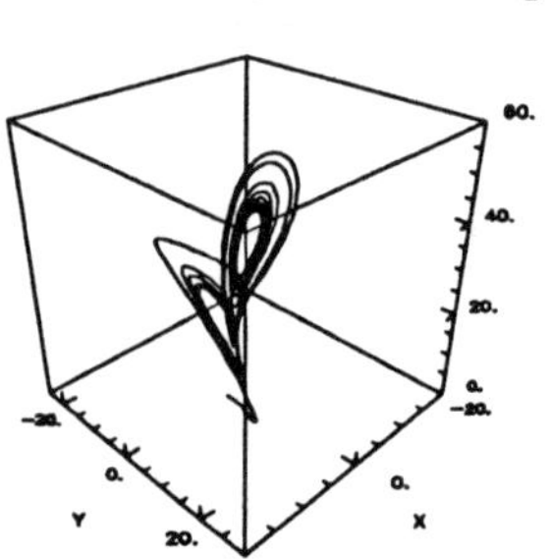

Figure 6-30 Three dimensional plot of x, y, and z.

6.5 Appendix: System Build Programs

Example 6.2 Effects of Saturation

```
build
 Edit, Saturation Example, 0;
 Define, 4, dyn, num, Name, Plant, Parameter, 0, 1, 2, [1,0,0];
 Define, 3, dyn, num, Name, Comp, Parameter, 1, [10,10], 1, [1,5];
 Define, 2, Piece-Wise Linear, Absolute Satur, Parameter, 1;
 Define, 1, Algeb, Sum, Parameter, 2, 1, -1;
 Connect, Internal,1,2, Internal,2,3, Internal,3,4, Internal,4,1,1,2;0,0;
 Input, 1, 1, 1,1;0,0;
 Output, 1, 4;
top, analyze, Saturation Example;
//************ Finished System Build, return to MATRIXx ***********
t=[0:.1:10]';input=ones(t);
 for i=1:6;ui=i*input;ysat(:,i)=sim(t,ui);i=i+1;end;
 for i=1:6; pos(1,i)=100*(max(ysat(:,i))-ysat(100,i))/ysat(100,i);end
plot(t,ysat,'nogrid')
return
```

Example 6.3 Pole-Zero Cancellation Effects

```
//*********** Building the G(s)K(s) system *******************
build, Edit, GK, 0;
 def, 1, alge, sum, Parameter, 2, 1,1;
 def, 2, dyn, Nth Order Int, Name, x1, Parameter, 1, 1, n, 1;
 def, 3, Gain, Parameter, -2;
 def, 4, alg, sum, Parameter, 2, 1,-1;
 def, 5, dyn, Nth Order Int, Name, x2, Parameter, 1, 1, n, 1;
 def, 6, alg, sum, Parameter, 2, 1,1;
 Connect, Internal, 1,2, Internal, 2,3, Int, 4,5;
 Int,2,1,1,2;0,0; Int,5,4,1,2;0,0; Int,3,4,1,1;0,0;
 Int,5,6,1,1;0,0; Int,2,6,1,2;0,0;
 Output,3,2,1,1;0,0; Output,3,5,1,2;0,0; Output,3,6,1,3;0,0;
 Input, 1,1,1,1;0,0;
top, anal, GK;
t=[0:.05:5]';u=ones(t);ygk11=sim(t,u);
plot(t,ygk11,'repo1 noxgrid noxlab noylab ymin=-4 ymax=4 upper')
// Return to Build the change initial conditions
build, Edit, GK, 0, Examine, 2, Initial, n, -1, Done;
top, anal, GK;
ygk_11=sim(t,u);
plot(t,ygk_11,'nogrid repo1 noxlab noylab ymin=-2 ymax=2 symbol...
mark 4 5 6 upper ')
return
//**************** Building the K(s)G(s) system *****************
build, ed, KG, 0;
 Def, 1, Gain, Parameter, 2;
```

```
 Def, 2, Alg, Sum, Parameter, 2, -1,-1;
 Def, 3, Dyn, Nth Order Int, Name, x1, Parameter, 1,1,n,1;
 Def, 4, Alg, Sum, Parameter, 3, 1,1,1;
 Def, 5, Dyn, Nth Order Int, Name, x2, Parameter, 1,1,n,1;
 Connect, Int,1,2,1,1;0,0; Int,2,3,Int,3,2,1,2;0,0; Int,3,4,1,1;0,0; Int,4,5;
 Int,5,4,1,3;0,0;
 Input, 1,4,1,2;0,0; Input, 1,1;
 Output, 2,5,1,2;0,0; Output, 2,3,1,1;0,0;
top, ana, kg;
t=[0:.1:10]';u=ones(t); ykg11=sim(t,u);
plot(t,ykg11,'noxgrid repol ymin=-2 noylab noxlab upper ')
// Return to Build the change initial conditions
build, ed, kg, 0, Examine, 3, Initial, n, -2, Done;
top, ana, kg;
ykg_21=sim(t,u);
plot(t,ykg_21,'nogrid ymax=2 ymin=-3 noylab noxlab upper ')
return
```

Example 6.4 The Lorenz System

```
a=10;b=28;c=-2.67;
//****************** Building X ***********************
build, Edit, Super_X, 0;
 Def, 1, Gain, Parameter, a;
 Def, 2, Alg, Sum, Parameter, 2, 1,-1;
 Def, 3, Dyn, Nth Order Int, Name, x, Parameter, 1, 1, n, 5;
 Def, 13, Gain, Parameter, a;
 Connect, Int, 1,2,1,1;0,0; Int, 2,3, Int, 3,13, Int, 13,2,1,2;0,0;
 Input, 1,1;
 Output, 4, 3, 1,1;1,2;1,3;1,4;0,0
top
//******************* Building Y ********************
ed, Super_Y, 0;
 Def, 1, Gain, Parameter, b;
 Def, 2, Alg, Sum, Parameter, 3, 1,-1,-1;
 Def, 3, Dyn, Nth Order Int, Name, y, Parameter, 1, 1, n, 5;
 Connect, Int, 1,2, 1,1;0,0; Int, 2,3, Int, 3,2,1,3;0,0;
 Input, 2, 1, 1,1;0,0; Input, 2,2,2,2;0,0;
 Output, 3, 3, 1,1;1,2;1,3;0,0;
top
//************************ Building Z ****************
ed, Super_Z, 0;
 Def,1, Alg, Sum, Parameter, 2, 1,1;
 Def, 2, Dyn, Nth Order Int, Name, z, Parameter, 1, 1, n, 5;
 Def, 12, Gain, Parameter, c;
 Connect , Int, 1,2, Int, 2,12, Int, 12,1,1,2;0,0;
 Input, 1, 1, 1,1;0,0;
 Output, 2, 2, 1,1;1,2;0,0;
```

```
top
//******************* Building Lorenz ********************
ed, Lorenz, 0;
 Def, 1, SuperBlock, Name, Super_X, Input, 1, Output, 4, Parameter;
 Def, 2, SuperBlock, Name, Super_Y, Input, 2, Output, 3, Parameter;
 Def, 3, SuperBlock, Name, Super_Z, Input, 1, Output, 2, Parameter;
 Def, 4, Alg, Elem by Elem Prod, Parameter;
 Def, 5, Alg, Elem by Elem Prod, Parameter;
 Connect,Int,1,2,3,1;0,0;Int,1,5,4,1;0,0;Int,2,5,3,2;0,0;Int,1,4,2,1;0,0;
 Int,3,4,n,2,2;0,0;Int,4,2,1,2;0,0;Int,5,3,Int,2,1,2,1;0,0;
 Output, 3,1,1,1;0,0; Output, 3,2,n,1,2;0,0; Output, 3,3,1,3;0,0;
top, ana, Lorenz;
//******************* Back to MATRIXx *******************
t=[0:.01:10]';xyz=sim(t);clear t;x=xyz(:,1);y=xyz(:,2);z=xyz(:,3);clear xyz
plot(x,y,'nogrid repo1 upper left')
plot(x,z,'nogrid upper left repo1')
plot(y,z,'nogrid upper left repo1');
plot(x,y,z,'nolegend')
return
```

6.6 Problems

6.1 The purpose of this problem is to investigate the behavior of two famous nonlinear systems that exhibit chaotic behavior. Simulate the systems for the given parameters and initial states. Plot the states versus time, and also plot all combinations of one state versus another (e.g., see Example 6.4). You may vary the parameters or the initial states to see vastly different behavior.

a. The Rossler system

$$\dot{x} = -y - z \qquad x(0) = 5$$

$$\dot{y} = x + \frac{1}{5}\, y \qquad y(0) = 5$$

$$\dot{z} = \frac{1}{5} + z\,x - 5.7\,z \qquad z(0) = 5$$

b. The Duffing system

$$\dot{x} = y \qquad x(0) = 5$$

$$\dot{y} = -(x^3 + x + y) + \cos\theta \qquad y(0) = 5$$

$$\dot{\theta} = \omega \qquad \theta(0) = 3$$

6.2 The purpose of this problem is to illustrate the effects of computational errors in a nonlinear system. Repeat the simulations in Example 6.4 and Problem 6.1, but use a different integration algorithm (e.g., Euler). Plot the responses and plot the difference between the states obtained using different algorithms. Observe that the errors build up and the systems are very sensitive to computational errors.

6.3 The purpose of this problem is to demonstrate that systems with identical gain, or phase, margin can have step responses with vastly different qualities. Hence, good margins do not necessarily imply good time responses [AH84].

a. For each transfer function given, obtain the Nyquist or Bode plot, and compute and compare gain and phase margins.

$$G_1(s) = \frac{1.4\,(1+0.5s)\,e^{-0.4s}}{s^2}, \qquad G_2(s) = \frac{0.072\,e^{-5s}}{s\,(1+5s)^2}, \qquad G_3(s) = \frac{1.65\,e^{-12s}}{1+20s}$$

$$G_4(s) = \frac{1.25\,e^{-15s}}{(1+5s)^2}, \qquad G_5(s) = \frac{0.1}{s\,(1+5s)^2}, \qquad G_6(s) \frac{1.4\,(1+1.2s)\,e^{-0.2s}}{s^2}$$

b. Assuming unity feedback, obtain closed loop step response and compute POS and T_s, and also obtain closed loop Bode magnitude plot and compute peak resonance, M_r.

c. Tabulate your responses and draw conclusions about the relationships between stability margins and time response. Determine which one of the frequency response measures (GM, PM, M_r) is the most reliable indicator of the quality of the step response as measured by POS.

6.4 Consider the systems in Example 6.3. Analytically solve for the states and the outputs in both cases, and verify that the stated results and conclusions are correct.

6.5 [Problem suggested by B. Torby] A standard problem in mechanical vibrations is the two-degree-of-freedom problem. There are two masses; the first mass is connected to a fixed wall via springs and dashpots, there is a spring and a dashpot between the masses as shown in Figure 6-31. A sinusoidal input force is applied to the second mass. The problem is to find the resulting positions and velocities of the masses. The equations of motion and the parameters are

$$M_1\,\ddot{x}_1 + (k_1 + k_2)\,x_1 + (c_1 + c_2)\,\dot{x}_1 - k_2\,x_2 - c_2\,\dot{x}_2 = 0$$
$$M_2\,\ddot{x}_2 + k_2\,x_2 + c_2\,\dot{x}_2 - c_2\,\dot{x}_1 - k_2\,x_1 = F \sin(20\,t)$$

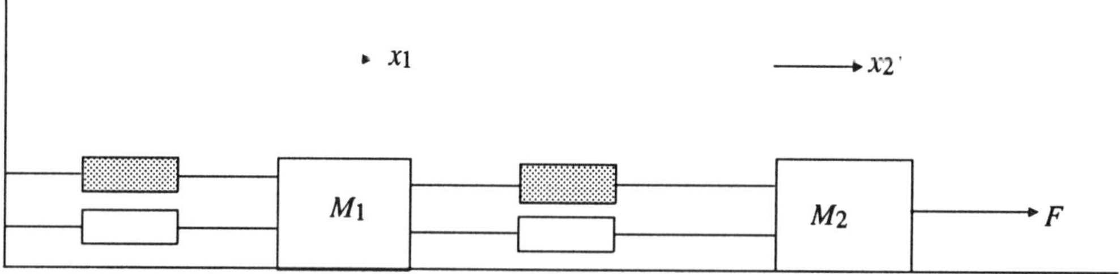

Figure 6-31 Two-degree-of-freedom problem. The filled (hollow) boxes represent dashpots (springs).

$$M_1 = 10\,kg,\; M_2 = 20\,kg,\; k_1 = 1000\,N/m,\; k_2 = 200\,N/m,\; c_1 = c_2 = 120\,N.s/m,\; F = 100.$$

Build the above system by using a super-block for each system, and a main super-block for connecting them. Simulate the system for 4 sec. Plot the four states (positions and velocities) versus time. Plot x_1 versus x_2, $\dot{x}_1$ versus x_1, $\dot{x}_2$ versus x_2.

7

Classical Design

7.1 Introduction

Classical control system design is usually performed using transfer function descriptions; the two most popular techniques are root locus and Bode plot design. Closed loop specifications are most often given in terms of steady state error and such desired system step response parameters as rise time, peak time, settling time, peak overshoot, etc. Steady state error, system type, and step response parameters are discussed in Chapter 1. The step response parameters are used to derive the desired open loop frequency domain characteristics of gain and phase margin. Remember that these relationships are derived assuming the system can be described with a pair of dominant poles. Zeros and additional poles close to the dominant poles affect the step response of the system. These effects were described and simulated in Chapter 1.

An advantage of using the computer to aid in control system design is that the complete closed loop system can be modeled and analyzed. Always treat the techniques we describe here as the initial design procedure. Close the loop and perform a time domain and frequency domain analysis and adjust your design as needed. Before discussing specific design strategies, we will review how the root locus and Bode plots can be used to predict closed loop behavior.

Root Locus

The root locus plot shows the location of the closed loop poles as a particular transfer function parameter, usually its gain, is varied. The root locus is an excellent technique for determining closed loop stability and relative stability. Even if the Bode plots are used in the design process, the root locus can be used for stability analysis.

Constant contours in the s-plane for settling time (T_s), damped frequency (ω_d), damping ratio (ζ), and (undamped) natural frequency (ω_n) can be determined for a second order system. The roots of the second order characteristic equation are given by

$$s = -\zeta\,\omega_n \pm j\sqrt{1-\zeta^2}\;\omega_n = -\sigma \pm j\,\omega_d$$

The standard zero-state step response is described mathematically below

$$y(t) = 1 - \frac{1}{\sqrt{1-\zeta^2}} e^{-\zeta \omega_n t} \cos(\omega_d t - \sin^{-1} \zeta)$$

Settling time is usually taken to be between 4 and 5 time constants, so

$$4\tau < T_s < 5\tau, \quad \text{where} \quad \tau = \frac{1}{\sigma} \quad \text{and} \quad \sigma = \zeta \omega_n$$

Although there are no exact relationships for rise time, T_r, and delay time, T_d, they both are inversely proportional to ω_n . Peak overshoot (POS) as a percentage is given by

$$POS = 100\, e^{\frac{-\pi\zeta}{\sqrt{1-\zeta^2}}} \qquad 0 \le \zeta < 1$$

As an example, consider the following system requirements

overshoot < 25%
settling time < 5 sec
From these specifications we determine that

$\zeta > 0.4 \rightarrow \theta < 66^o$
$T_s < 5 \rightarrow \sigma < -1$

The allowable region in the s-plane for the give n specification is shaded dark in Figure 7-1.

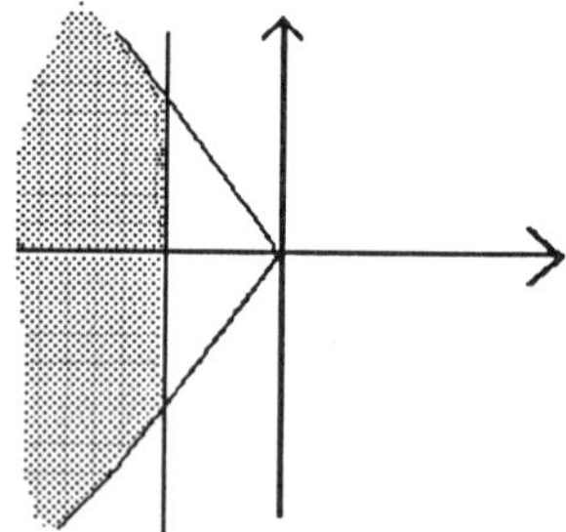

Figure 7-1 Region of allowable pole locations.

Again, all of the foregoing assumes that we are dealing with a system that is adequately described with a single pair of complex conjugate poles. If the actual system has poles or zeros close to these complex poles, then the closed loop response will not be as predicted.

Bode Plots

The Bode plots can be used to determine closed loop steady state error, damping ratio, natural frequency (for a dominant pole system), and stability margins. The use of Bode plots to determine the stability of nonminimum phase systems (i.e., poles or zeros in the RHP) is not recommended; instead, use Nyquist stability criterion.

Let us assume that the plant in a unity feedback configuration is described by

$$KG(s) = \frac{K\,\omega_n^2}{s^2 + 2\zeta\omega_n s + \omega_n^2}$$

We can determine immediately from the Bode plot of the open loop system what the system Type is. In this case, the initial slope is zero, so $KG(0)$ is finite. This implies that the system is Type 0 with $K_p = KG(0) = K$, the low frequency gain. An initial slope of -20n dB/dec indicates a Type n system.

The closed loop transfer function for this system is

$$T(s) = \frac{K\,\omega_n^2}{s^2 + 2\,\zeta\,\omega_n\,s + (K+1)\,\omega_n^2} = \frac{K\,\omega_n^2}{s^2 + 2\,\zeta_{CL}\,\omega_{nCL}\,s + \omega_{nCL}^2}$$

where $\omega_{n\,CL} = \omega_n\sqrt{K+1}$ and $\zeta_{CL} = \dfrac{\zeta}{\sqrt{K+1}}$

For large K, the gain crossover frequency ($\omega_{gc} \approx \omega_n\sqrt{K}$) gives an accurate measure of the closed loop natural frequency. The closed loop bandwidth is also approximated by ω_{gc}, however, the actual closed loop bandwidth may vary by as much as 100% of this value.

The damping ratio of the closed loop system is approximately $1/\sqrt{K}$ of the open loop damping ratio. The closed loop system will therefore be faster and have greater overshoot than the open loop system. Can the closed loop damping ratio (ζ_{CL}) be predicted from the open loop Bode plots? From the definition of phase margin (PM) in Nyquist plots and using simple geometry, we obtain

$$\text{PM} = 2\sin^{-1}\frac{1}{2\,|T(j\,\omega_{gc})|}$$

Because $\omega_{gc} \approx \omega_n\sqrt{K}$, then

$$\text{PM} \approx 2\sin^{-1}(\zeta_{CL}) \quad \text{or} \quad \zeta_{CL} \approx \sin\left(\frac{\text{PM}}{2}\right)$$

Some authors [FPE91] use the following approximation

$$\zeta_{CL} \approx .01\ \text{PM (degrees)}$$

Relative stability can be determined from both the phase margin and the gain margin (GM), which is defined as

$$\text{GM} = -|G(j\omega_{pc})|_{dB}, \quad \text{where} \quad \angle G(j\omega_{pc}) = -180^{\circ}$$

Either the root locus or the Bode plots can be used to predict closed loop behavior. The root locus gives a very accurate picture of the closed loop poles, whereas the Bode plots can be used to determine closed loop steady state error, bandwidth, and stability margins easily.

7.2 Compensation

There are various configurations that can be used for compensation. Among them are series (cascade), feedback, and combination of both. In series compensation, the compensator is placed in cascade with the plant. In the feedback configuration, the compensator is placed within the feedback path. In both cases the open loop transfer function and the closed loop poles are identical. Therefore, they have the same root locus and Bode plots, hence, the stability properties are similar. The closed loop zeros are different, however, so the steady state errors are different. Because feedback reduces the effects of parameter variations with respect to elements in the forward path, the series configuration has better sensitivity properties. It is also easier to control the error constants in the unity feedback case. As a result, the cascade configuration has traditionally been more popular.

It is also possible to place filters outside of the loop for filtering out extraneous signals. Notch filters that damp out specific known frequencies are commonly used. Because these filters are placed outside of the loop, they do not benefit from feedback properties. Hence, their use is recommended only when the frequencies they are supposed to attenuate are accurately known.

A compensation technique that is often used in the classroom is pole-zero cancellation. The dominant poles (zeros) of the plant are canceled with a compensator that has zeros (poles) at the same locations. The desired system loop gain poles are then added to the denominator of the compensator.

Although this technique may be feasible for canceling LHP plant poles and zeros, it should never be used to cancel plant poles or zeros in the RHP. Another problem with pole-zero cancellation is that we never really know where the plant poles and zeros are. Our plant transfer function is only a model for plant behavior. It is never absolutely accurate. If pole-zero cancellation is used, the designer must be sure to examine how sensitive closed loop response is to variations in plant pole and zero locations.

Two commonly used controllers are *proportional-integral-derivative (PID)* and *lead-lag*. The transfer functions of these controllers are

$$\textit{PID} \qquad K_p + K_d s + \frac{K_i}{s}$$

$$\textit{Lead (or Lag)} \qquad K\,\frac{s+a}{s+b}$$

7.3 Proportional-integral-derivative Control

The proportional-integral-derivative (or PID) controller can take several forms: *proportional* only, $K_d = K_i = 0$; *proportional plus derivative (PD)*, $K_i = 0$; *proportional plus integral (PI)*, $K_d = 0$; full PID. Proportional only control is the simplest control scheme. It allows the designer, however, to satisfy only one closed loop specification, e.g., GM, PM, steady state error, etc. The addition of derivative control increases the damping in the closed loop system while integral control increases the system type and, hence, decreases steady state error. PID is usually effective in meeting most specifications. It is by far the most widely used controller in the process industry. It is also widely available in various forms (analog, digital, and adaptive).

7.3.1 Ziegler-Nichols Method

Because three parameters must be adjusted in the design of PID controllers, root locus and Bode design techniques are usually not used directly. Ziegler and Nichols [ZN42] developed a method for tuning a PID controller, which is based on a simple stability analysis. First set $K_d = K_i = 0$, and then increase the proportional gain until the system just oscillates (i.e., closed loop poles on the $j\omega$ axis). The proportional gain is then halved, and the other two gains are calculated as

$$K_p = 0.6\,K_m \qquad K_d = \frac{K_p\,\pi}{4\,\omega_m} \qquad K_i = \frac{K_p\,\omega_m}{\pi}$$

where K_m is gain at which the proportional system oscillates, and ω_m is the oscillation frequency. Note that this technique does not design to any specifications. Rather, Ziegler and Nichols found that this design procedure provided "good" behavior for process controllers. Years of experience by process control engineers have indicated that it is indeed a good technique.

Either the root locus or the Bode plots can be used to determine K_m and ω_m. For example, a root locus is obtained for the given plant transfer function. The gain at which the root locus crosses the $j\omega$ axis is K_m and the frequency on the $j\omega$ axis gives us ω_m. Alternatively, Bode plots are plotted for the given plant transfer function. The GM is determined at the frequency ω_{pc}: $K_m = 10^{(GM/20)}$ and $\omega_m = \omega_{pc}$. Be aware that the Bode technique gives approximate answers only.

Example 7.1 PID Control—Ziegler-Nichols Method

Given the plant

$$G(s) = \frac{400}{s\,(s^2 + 30s + 200)}$$

The above transfer function will be used in all subsequent examples for PID, PD, and lead design. It has the following characteristics:

Closed loop poles = {- 4.2 ± j0.93, -21.59}
Gain crossover frequency = 1.95 rad/sec
GM = 23 dB
PM = 73 degrees

The closed loop step response has no overshoot, and the steady state error to a unit ramp input is 0.5. The root locus for this plant is shown in Figure 7-2. The interactive root locus is used to find the crossover gain of $K_m = 14$ and crossover frequency of $\omega_m = 14$ rad/sec. We can now use Ziegler-Nichols equations to find the gain parameters

$$K_p = 9 \qquad K_d = 0.5 \qquad K_i = 40$$

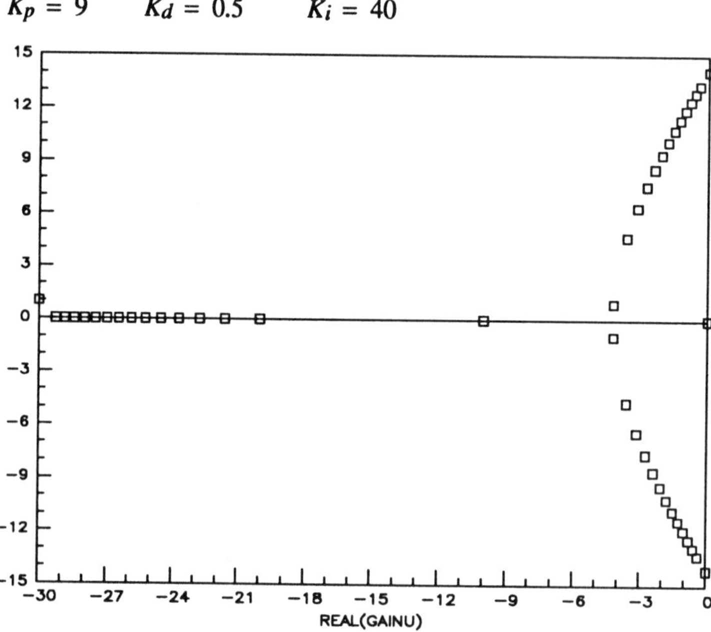

Figure 7-2 Uncompensated root locus for Example 7.1.

The open loop Bode plots and the closed loop step response of the system before and after compensation are shown in Figure 7-3. The compensated step response shows a 60% overshoot with a settling time of approximately 1.2 sec. The gain crossover frequency is 11 with a phase margin of 25 degrees. The Ziegler-Nichols program in the Appendix can be used to obtain the compensator.

7.3.2 Analytical Method

As stated previously, the Ziegler-Nichols technique does not allow us to design a PID controller to achieve specific closed loop behavior. An analytical technique can be

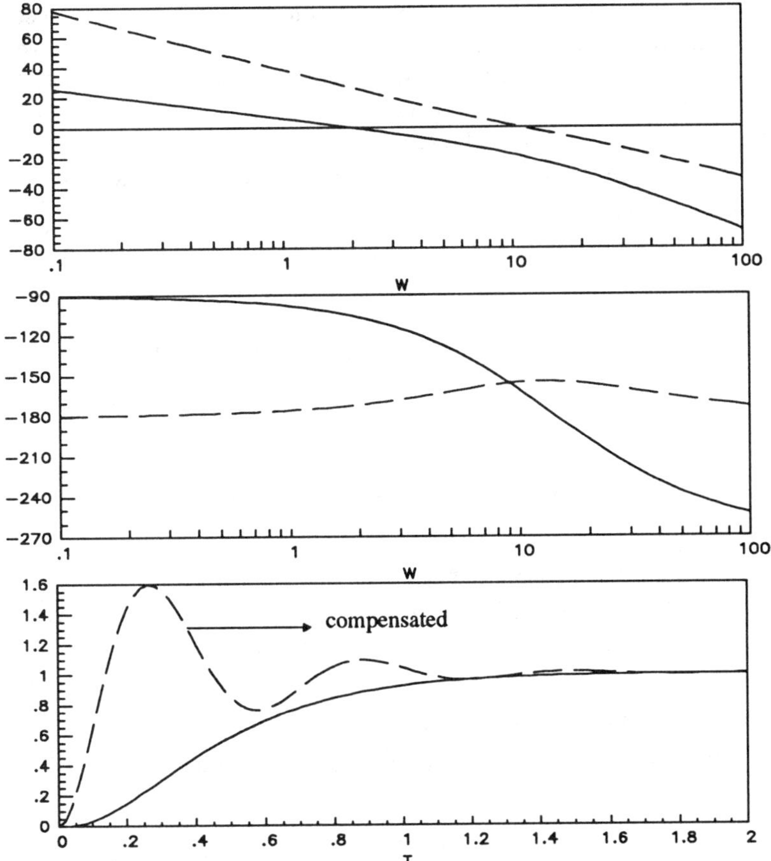

Figure 7-3 Open loop Bode plots and closed loop step response of Example 7.1.

developed to determine the PID parameters given steady state error and performance specifications. The loop gain of a PID controlled system is given by

$$(K_p + K_d\, s + \frac{K_i}{s})\, G(s)$$

If $G(s)$ is a type n plant, the compensated system will be type $n+1$. The error constant is equal to the inverse of the steady state error and is given by

$$K_{n+1} = s^n K_i\, G(s)\,|_{s=0} = \frac{1}{e_{ss}}$$

For a given steady state error specification, we find K_i from the preceding equation. From time domain specifications such as overshoot and settling time, we determine the required closed loop damping ratio and natural frequency. We know from the first section of this chapter that the closed loop natural frequency corresponds to the open loop gain crossover frequency (ω_{gc}) and that the desired PM can be found from the closed loop damping ratio. Therefore, at $\omega = \omega_{gc}$, the compensated system should have a gain of 1 and phase of $\theta(\omega_{gc}) = -180^o + \text{PM}$.

With this information, remembering that K_i is now known, we can write

$$(K_p + j\omega_{gc}K_d + \frac{K_i}{j\omega_{gc}})\, G(j\omega_{gc}) = 1e^{\,j\theta(\omega_{gc})}$$

which leads to

$$K_p + j\omega_{gc}K_d = \frac{1\, e^{j\theta(\omega_{gc})}}{G(j\omega_{gc})} + \frac{j\,K_i}{\omega_{gc}} = R + jX$$

Hence, we see that $K_p = R$ and $K_d = X/\omega_{gc}$.

The above procedure can easily be programmed. Program 2 (Analytic PID) in the Appendix was used to solve the following example.

Example 7.2 PID Control—Analytical Technique

Consider the plant given in Example 7.1 and repeated here

$$G(s) = \frac{400}{s\,(s^2 + 30s + 200)}$$

The following specifications are given

steady state error to unit ramp input = 0.1
overshoot = 10%
settling time = 2 sec

Because the plant is Type 1, we find the steady state error constant for the PID-plant combination to be

$$K_2 = s\,K_i\,G(s)\,|_{s=0} = 2\,K_i = 1/0.1 = 10 \rightarrow K_i = 5$$

From the overshoot and settling time specifications, we determine that the desired closed loop damping ratio and natural frequency are $\zeta = 0.6$ and $\omega_n = 4$ rad/sec. Therefore, we will specify that $\omega_{gc} = 4$ rad/sec and $PM = 2\sin^{-1}(0.6) = 80$ degrees.

Using the Analytical PID program in the Appendix, we get : $K_p = 2.02$, $K_d = 0.52$.

The Bode plots in Figure7-4 indicate that PM is 80 degrees and the gain crossover frequency is 4 rad/sec as expected. The step response of the closed loop system is shown in Figure 7-5. We see from the step response that we have approximated the required settling time of 2 sec. The overshoot of 22% is larger than the specification, however. This is due to the zeros that the PID controller introduces into the system. It is often the case that a PID controller cannot meet all system specifications, and some trial and error is required.

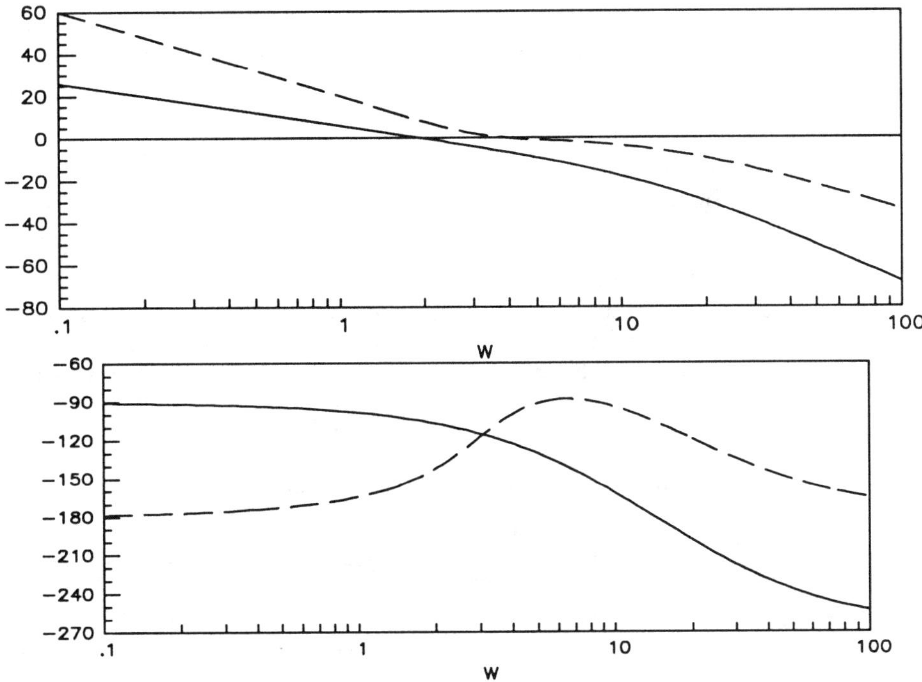

Figure 7-4 Bode plots for Example 7.2.

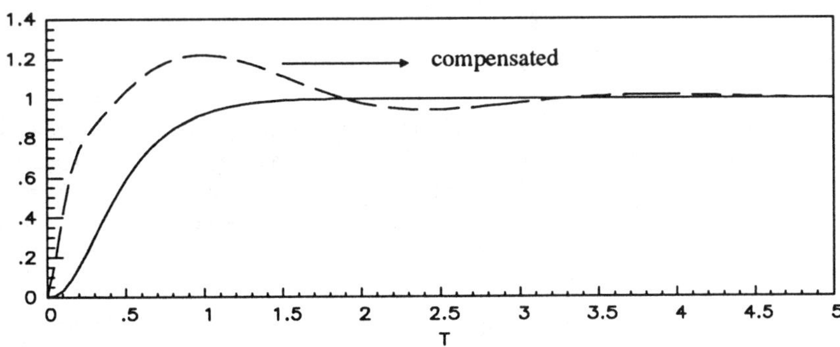

Figure 7-5 Step response for Example 7.2.

7.3.3 PD Control

Because the PD controller is very common, we will discuss it here. Integral control is only used if we want to increase the system type and, thus, reduce steady state errors. The drawback of integral control is that the additional pole at the origin tends to destabilize the system. Conversely, the additional zero added by derivative control usually increases system stability. Therefore, derivative control is often added to feedback systems, especially if increased damping is desired. We will discuss root locus and Bode techniques for PD control in the next section. Here, we will show you the application of an analytical technique to PD design.

Example 7.3 PD Control

Given the plant used in the first two examples, design a PD controller to meet the following specifications:

PM = 45° at $\omega_{gc} = 13.5$ rad/sec.

Note that the PD controller has only two parameters so we cannot meet the same number of specifications as we can with the PID controller. The PID program with $K_i = 0$ can be used for design. The PD coefficients are $K_p = 10$ and $K_d = 0.7$. Figure 7-6 shows that the step response for this PD controlled system has an overshoot of 24% and a settling time of 0.8 sec. The error constant for the compensated system is 20.

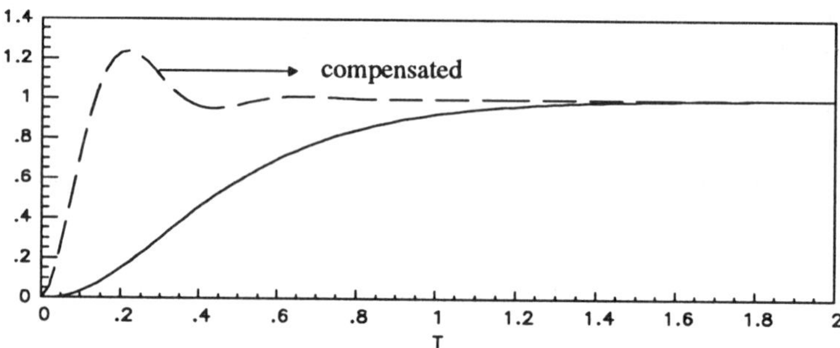

Figure 7-6 Step response for Example 7.3.

Note that we never actually build a pure differentiator ($K_d s$) because of the noise problems inherent in such a device. Rather, the derivative term always has a pole associated with it. In this case, we can treat the PD controller as a lead compensator, as discussed in the next section. PD control is often achieved with a sensor that can directly measure the velocity of the output, e.g., a tachometer. In this case the derivative term is usually placed in a minor feedback loop around the plant as shown in Figure 7-7.

With this configuration, the step response for Example 7.3 is shown in Figure 7-8. We see that the overshoot is now only 10%. The reason for this is that the derivative term in a feedback loop does not create an additional system zero.

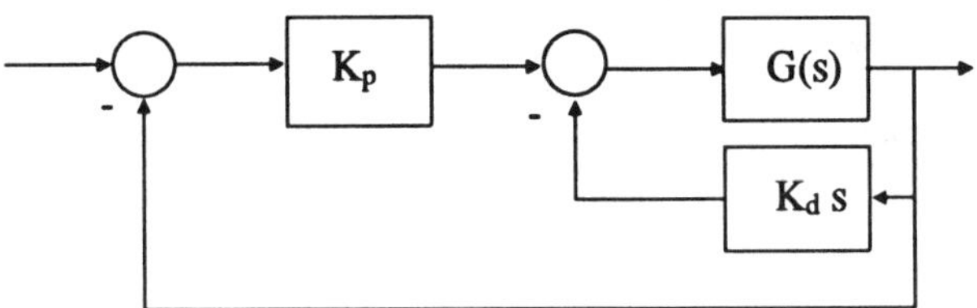

Figure 7-7 PD with tachometer feedback.

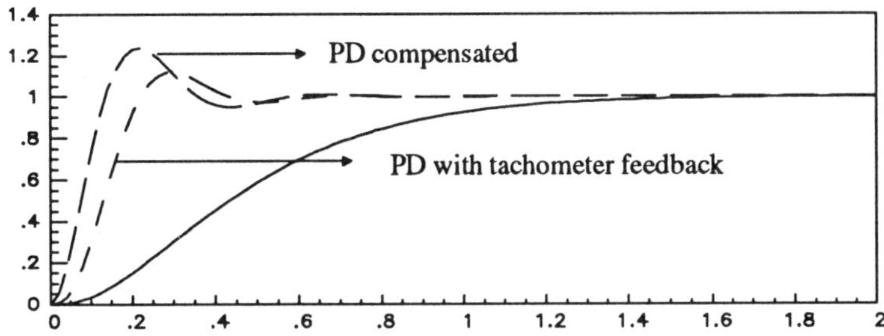

Figure 7-8 Step responses for Example 7.3: uncompensated, using PD, and with the D term in minor feedback loop.

7.4 Lead Compensation

The simplest and most common form of compensation is a filter with one zero and one pole. The general transfer function for this compensator is

$$K(s) = K_c \frac{s+a}{s+b}$$

If the zero occurs before the pole $(a < b)$, $K(s)$ is known as a *lead* compensator. If the pole occurs before the zero $(a > b)$, $K(s)$ is a *lag* compensator. The maximum phase contribution, lead or lag, occurs at $\omega = \sqrt{ab}$.

How does the designer know whether to use a lead or a lag compensator? The answer, of course, is in the system specifications. For example, if the only requirement is to stabilize the closed loop system, then either type of compensation can usually be used (assuming that the plant is stable—for unstable plants, lead compensation must be used). Additional specifications, however, will often lead to a choice of one type of compensation over the other. For example, if a certain ω_{gc} is desired, an examination of the plant Bode plot will immediately determine the compensator type. If the desired ω_{gc} is larger than the plant ω_{gc}, then a lead compensator is needed; if smaller, a lag compensator is needed.

For the lead and the lag compensator, we will describe root locus, Bode and analytical techniques for design. Remember, all of these design procedures assume the plant can be adequately described with a pair of dominant poles. The actual closed loop response will vary somewhat from that predicted from these designs. Always close the loop and simulate the total system; make adjustments as necessary.

All compensators affect the stability, steady state error, and bandwidth of closed loop systems. Lead compensation, in general, increases relative stability by increasing phase margin. For a given system gain, K_c, lead compensators increase steady state error. This is because $a < b$, which means that $K_c\, a/b < K_c$. To decrease steady state error, a large compensator gain must be used. Lead compensators also increase the gain crossover frequency, ω_{gc}. This has the effect of decreasing step response settling time (i.e., increasing system damping). Although this is often desirable, the increase in ω_{gc} also leads to an increase in closed loop bandwidth. This increased bandwidth can result in undesirable signals or noise in the system or instability in systems with time delays (transportation lags).

The following design procedures are to be used as a starting point in a design cycle. They are merely *guidelines* rather than laws or methods that will always work. Not every system can be adequately compensated using simple lead-lag compensators. After all, we are limiting the choice of compensator poles and zeros to the negative real axis, which ensures the compensator itself is always stable. This leaves out compensators with complex poles and zeros or unstable compensators. Although stable compensators are desirable, it is also known that some systems require unstable compensators for closed loop stability. Systems that can be stabilized using stable compensators are called *strongly stable* systems. For systems that cannot adequately be stabilized using classical methods discussed in this chapter, state space or optimal control methods can be used. These more advanced methods are discussed in later chapters. Classical methods, where they are applicable, usually result in low order stable compensators that are adequately designed after a few iterations. It is recommended that you start with these simple compensators before applying more advanced methods that usually result in more complex compensators.

7.4.1 Root Locus Design

Root locus design is based on reshaping the root locus of the system—by adding poles and zeros to the plant—to force the loci to pass through a desired point in the complex plane. The following steps are common to root locus design techniques:

- Determine the desired complex pole location, s_1, from the specifications.
- Locate the compensator zero.
- Determine the compensator pole location using the property that for an s-plane point s_1 to lie on the root locus, the angle of $K(s_1)\, G(s_1)$ must be 180°.
- Does the system gain at s_1 satisfy steady-state error requirement? If not, change s_1 and repeat the design.
- Close the loop and determine if the specifications are met.

There are several procedures in the literature for determining the zero location. Of course, the designer can use his or her experience, and intuition to locate the zero. Dorf [Do89] recommends that the zero be located directly under the desired s-plane point s_1. Ogata [O90], and D'Azzo and Houpis [DH88] describe a more involved geometric procedure that determines both the zero and pole locations.

Select the desired point in the s-plane, s_1, and find $\varphi_c = 180^o - \angle G(s_1)$; the angle that must be contributed by the lead compensator. If φ_c is negative, a lead compensator cannot be designed—go to the lag compensator design. A lead compensator can contribute an angle of approximately 50 to 60 degrees. If more phase lead is required, more than one compensator section can be used. The rest of the procedure is described in Figure 7-9.

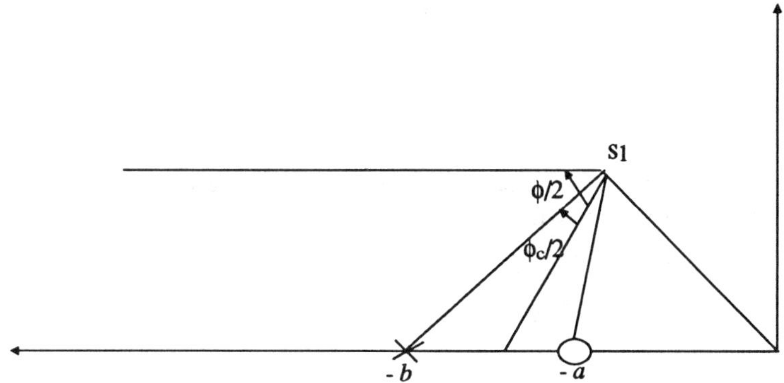

Figure 7-9 Geometric procedure.

Draw a line from the origin to s_1 and a horizontal line from s_1. Find the angle φ formed by these two lines. Bisect this angle. The lines from the desired zero and pole locations are constructed so that each line forms an angle of $\varphi_c/2$ with the bisector. This procedure minimizes the distance between the zero and pole locations. By keeping this ratio close to 1, we minimize the required compensator gain K_c.

7.4.2 Root Locus—Geometric Method

A purely analytical technique can be derived for the geometric procedure that can easily be programmed. The program (No. 2) appears in the Appendix.

- Select desired s-plane location s_1.
- Define $\varphi = \angle(s_1)$ and $\varphi_c = 180^o - \angle G(s_1)$.
- Define $\theta_p = \dfrac{\varphi - \varphi_c}{2}$ and $\theta_z = \dfrac{\varphi + \varphi_c}{2}$.
- Find the pole location from: $p_c = -b = Re(s_1) - \dfrac{\text{Im}(s_1)}{\tan \theta_p}$.

- Find the zero location from: $z_c = -a = Re(s_1) - \dfrac{Im(s_1)}{\tan \theta_z}$.
- Find K_c so that $|K(s_1)\, G(s_1)| = 1$.
- If K_c is too small for steady state error requirements, choose a new s_1 and repeat the procedure.

Example 7.4 Lead Compensation: Geometric Method

As an example of this design procedure, we reexamine the plant used in the previous sections. That is,

$$G(s) = \frac{400}{s\,(s^2 + 30s + 200)}$$

The specifications require

$\zeta = 0.5$ and $\omega_n = 13.5$ rad/sec

These parameters result in a desired s-plane location of $s_1 = -6.75 \pm j\,11.69$. The design procedure described above leads to

$$\varphi = \angle(-6.75 + j\,11.69) = 120^\circ$$

$$\varphi_c = -180 - \angle G(-6.75 + j\,11.69) = 55.8^\circ$$

$$\theta_p = \frac{\varphi - \varphi_c}{2} = 32^\circ$$

$$\theta_z = \frac{\varphi + \varphi_c}{2} = 87.9^\circ$$

$$p_c = -b = Re(s_1) - \frac{Im(s_1)}{\tan \theta_p} = -25.41$$

$$p_z = -a = Re(s_1) - \frac{Im(s_1)}{\tan \theta_z} = -7.16$$

$$K_c = \frac{1}{|G(s_1)\, K(s_1)|} = 13.62$$

The final compensator design for this problem is

$$K(s) = 13.62\,\frac{s + 7.16}{s + 25.41}$$

The step and frequency response are shown in Figure 7-10. It can be seen that the overshoot is now 8% and the settling time is 0.8 sec. The Bode plots show a GM of 15 dB and PM of 60° with the gain crossover frequency at 8. This compares very favorably with the PD design, which resulted in an overshoot of 24% and a PM of 45°. A major difference, however, is that the error constant in the lead compensator design is only 7.68, which is lower than the error constant of 20 obtained with the PD design. Also the higher gain crossover frequency of 13.5 rad/sec results in a faster PD response.

Again, designing to a specific error constant with the root locus techniques is not straightforward. If the error constant of 7.68 that we just obtained is not large enough, we would need to pick a new s-plane point for the design and keep iterating until an acceptable error constant is achieved. There are, however, some analytical methods that may allow the designer to use the root locus technique to design to a specific steady state error requirement.

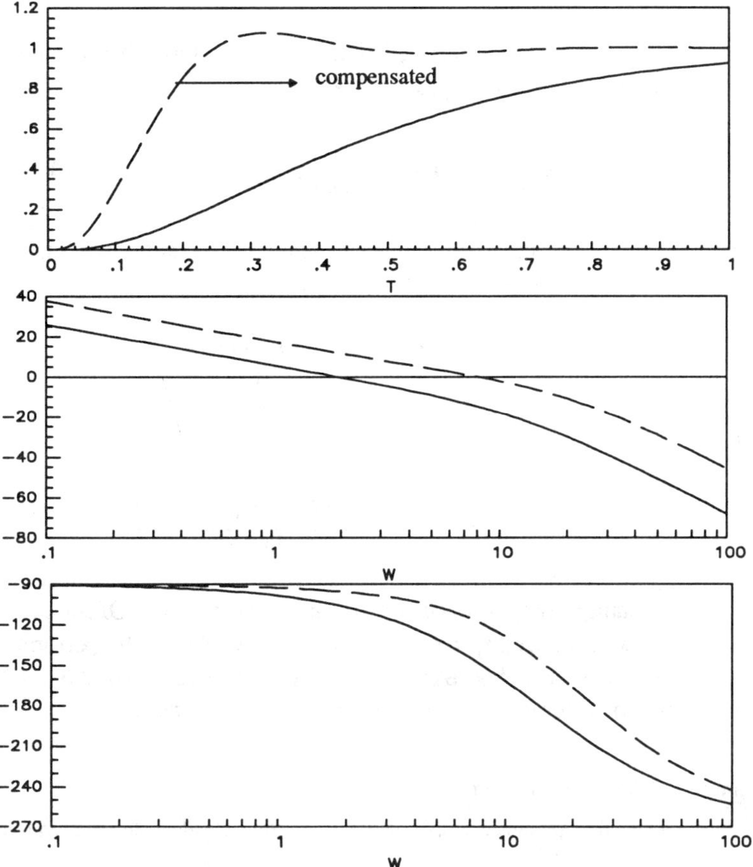

Figure 7-10 Step and frequency responses for Example 7.4.

7.4.3 Root Locus—Analytical Method

We present here an analytical method, modified from [PH88], that can be used to design either lead or lag compensators. For this design, we use the following alternative representation for the compensator

$$K(s) = K_c \frac{s\,\tau_z + 1}{s\,\tau_p + 1}$$

We first choose K_c and the desired s-plane location, s_1, from steady state error and transient specifications. For the compensated system to lie on the root locus

$$K(s_1)\,G(s_1) \;=\; K_c\,\frac{s_1\,\tau_z + 1}{s_1\,\tau_p + 1}\,M_G\,e^{j\theta_G} \;=\; 1\,e^{j\pi}$$

where $G(s_1) = M_G\,e^{\,j\theta_G}$. Because K_c is known, we need to solve the above equation for τ_z and τ_p. If s_l is represented by $s_1 = M_s\,e^{j\theta_s}$, then we have

$$M_s\,e^{\,j\theta_s}\tau_z \;+\; 1 \;=\; \left(\frac{1\,e^{\,j\pi}}{M_G\,e^{\,j\theta_G}K_c}\right)\left(M_s\,e^{\,j\theta_s}\tau_p \;+\; 1\right)$$

This equation can be separated into its real and imaginary parts, resulting in two equations and two unknowns. The solutions of these equations are

$$\tau_z \;=\; \frac{\sin\theta_s \;-\; K_c\,M_G\sin\left(\theta_G - \theta_s\right)}{K_c\,M_G\,M_s\sin\theta_G}$$

and

$$\tau_p \;=\; -\frac{K_c\,M_G\sin\theta_s \;+\; \sin\left(\theta_G + \theta_s\right)}{M_s\sin\theta_G}$$

This technique only works if both τ_z and τ_p are positive. Of course, to design a lead compensator we also need $\tau_p < \tau_z$. In practice, we would usually perform this design for several values of K_c and choose the compensator that gives the best overall performance. A program (No. 4) for this procedure appears in the Appendix.

Example 7.5 Analytical Design

We repeat the previous example, with an additional steady state error requirement. That is,

$$G(s) \;=\; \frac{400}{s\,(s^2 + 30s + 200)}$$

The specifications are

$\zeta = 0.5$, $\omega_n = 13.5$ rad/sec, and velocity error constant of 10.

We will design for $K_c = 5$ and $s_1 = -6.75 \pm j11.69$

We first determine that

$s_1 = -6.75 + j11.69 = 13.49\,e^{j120} = M_s\,e^{j\theta_s}$

$G(s_1) = 0.69\,e^{\,j124.1} = M_G\,e^{j\,\theta_G}$

Using the desired K_c and the values above, we solve for τ_z and τ_p

The compensator for this design is

$$K(s) = 5\frac{0.1s+1}{0.03s+1}$$

Figure 7-11 shows the step and frequency responses for this compensated system. The compensated system has an overshoot of 14% and a settling time of 0.9 sec. We have achieved similar performance as in Example 7.4, but we have a larger error constant here. Note that in Figure 7-11, we have plotted the uncompensated system with the gain of 5 for comparison. The Bode plots show that with the compensator, we have been able to increase both stability margins and speed of response, and reduce the overshoot.

We mention in passing that if this design were repeated with the requirement that $K_c = 10$, a negative τ_p would result. In general, to obtain a final compensator design, we would run the program iteratively for several values of K_c.

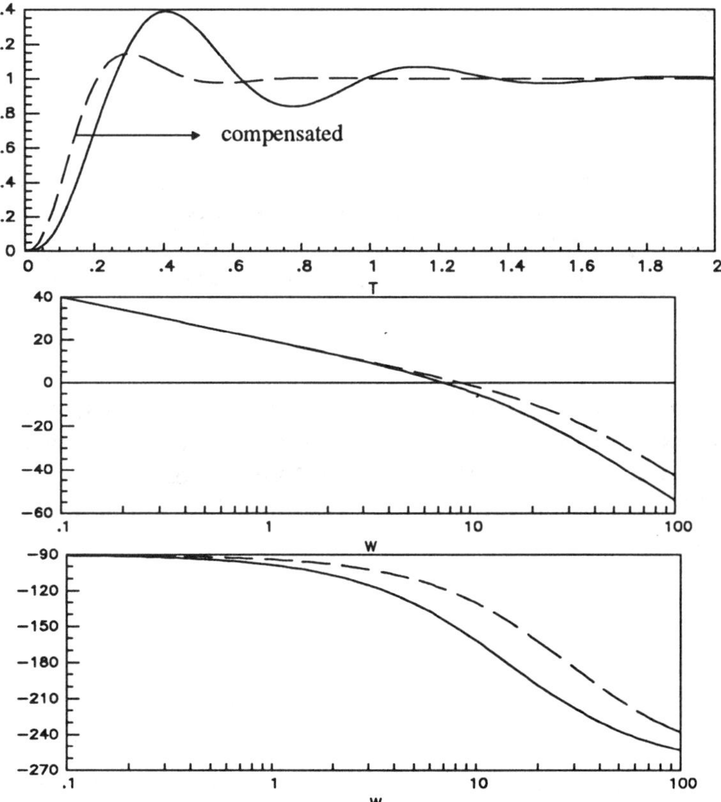

Figure 7-11 Step and frequency responses for Example 7.5.

7.4.4 Lead compensation—Bode Design

The basic idea in Bode design is to shape the open loop transfer function so that it will have desirable low frequency gain (for steady state error or disturbance rejection properties), desirable gain crossover frequency (for speed of response), and adequate stability margins. It is common to parametrize the compensator as shown below for Bode design.

$$K(s) = K_c \frac{\alpha T s+1}{T s+1}$$

In the Bode design method, we first choose the gain to satisfy steady state error requirements. This is one advantage of designs using Bode plots where steady state error specifications can easily be met. Then we satisfy PM requirements and attempt to achieve the desired gain crossover frequency. To use this procedure properly, it is necessary to understand the derivation of the formulas involved. To that end, we will quickly derive the appropriate relationships by considering the phase and magnitude contributions of the compensator

$$K_1(s) = \frac{\alpha T s+1}{T s+1}$$

where $K(s) = K_c K_1(s)$.

Because we would have already chosen K_c to satisfy steady state error criterion, we can exclude it from this discussion. We are only concerned with the phase and additional magnitude that $K_1(s)$ contributes. The phase of this lead compensator is

$$\angle K_1(j\omega) = \tan^{-1} \alpha T\omega - \tan^{-1} T\omega$$

Because we are using this method to achieve the desired PM, we are concerned with the amount of phase lead added by the compensator at the compensated ω_{gc}. For ease of design, we usually try to add the maximum phase lead possible at $\omega = \omega_{gc}$. The frequency at which maximum phase lead occurs can be found by taking the derivative of the above equation and is

$$\omega_{max} = \frac{1}{\sqrt{\alpha}\, T}$$

The maximum phase lead that can be achieved is therefore

$$\angle K_1(j\omega_{max}) = \angle K_1(j\omega_{gc}) = \Phi = \tan^{-1}\sqrt{\alpha} - \tan^{-1}\frac{1}{\sqrt{\alpha}}$$

Finally, a little trigonometry shows that the relationship between α and Φ can be written as

$$\sin\Phi = \frac{\alpha-1}{\alpha+1} \quad \text{and} \quad \alpha = \frac{1+\sin\Phi}{1-\sin\Phi} \quad \text{at} \quad \omega_{max} = \frac{1}{\sqrt{\alpha}\,T}$$

Remember, for this design, we set $\omega_{gc} = \omega_{max}$. The additional magnitude, in dB, contributed by $K_1(s)$ at $\omega = \omega_{max} = \omega_{gc}$, is

$$M = |\,K_1(j\omega_{max})\,|_{dB} = |\,K_1(j\omega_{gc})\,|_{dB} = 10\log\alpha$$

We are now ready to describe the procedure.

First draw the Bode plot using the new gain Kc to satisfy the steady state error requirements. Determine additional phase lead (Φ) needed to satisfy PM requirements. Compute α. Now, knowing that the lead compensator will raise the magnitude by M dB, find the frequency where the uncompensated magnitude is - M dB. This forces the compensated magnitude to have zero dB gain at this frequency. This is the new gain crossover frequency, which is used to compute T. A listing of this procedure is shown below.

- Select K_c to achieve the required error constant.
- Draw Bode plots for $K_cG(j\omega)$, and determine PM for $K_c\,G(j\omega)$.
- Determine additional phase lead required; this is the initial Φ.
- Add a few degrees to the phase just determined to find the working Φ (see below).
- Compute α from $\alpha = \dfrac{1+\sin\Phi}{1-\sin\Phi}$.
- Find the frequency at which the gain of $K_cG(j\omega) = -10\log\alpha$; this frequency will be the compensated ω_{gc}.
- Compute T from $T = \dfrac{1}{\sqrt{\alpha}\,\omega_{gc}}$.
- Draw Bode plots of $K(j\omega)G(j\omega)$ to confirm design.
- Close the loop, and determine appropriate closed loop responses.

The reason that we must add a few degrees to the phase lead needed to obtain the desired PM (fouth bullet) is that the addition of the compensator zero will cause the compensated crossover frequency to increase. This increase in ω_{gc} will result in a smaller PM than calculated per the third bullet. A program (No. 5) for this procedure is available in the Appendix.

It is important to note that with this design procedure, we cannot predetermine the compensated ω_{gc}. We may have to adjust the PM or steady state error requirements if the resultant ω_{gc} is unacceptable.

Example 7.6 Bode Method

As an example of this procedure, we again consider the plant

$$G(s) = \frac{400}{s\,(s^2+30s+200)}$$

The specifications are:

velocity error constant = 10

PM = 45°

The steady state error constant requires $K_c = 5$. The Bode plot for $K_cG(j\omega)$, shown in Figure 7-12, indicates that PM = 32°. Because we want a PM of 45°, the initial $\Phi = 13°$. We add 5° for safety and calculate α as described above to be $\alpha = 1.89$. We now calculate $-10 \log \alpha = -2.77$ dB. Examination of Figure 7-12 shows that this gain occurs at what will become the compensated gain crossover frequency $\omega_{gc} \approx 9$ rad/sec. We now find T as

$$T = \frac{1}{\sqrt{\alpha}\,\omega_{gc}} = 0.08$$

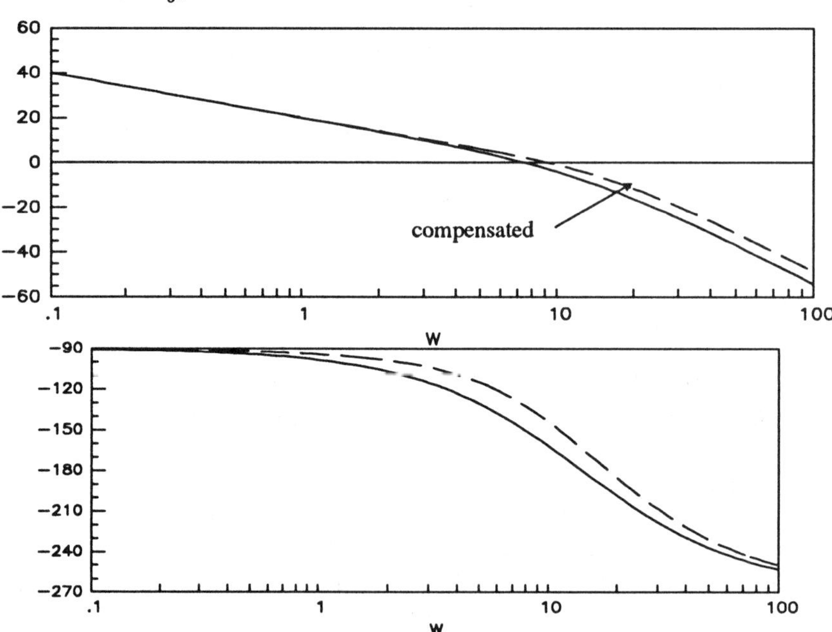

Figure 7-12 Bode plots for Example 7.6.

The compensator is

$$K(s) = 5\,\frac{0.15s+1}{0.08s+1}$$

The compensated PM now is 41°, which is close to the requirement. The step response for the closed loop system is shown in Figure 7-13. The overshoot is 28%, and the settling time is 1.4 sec.

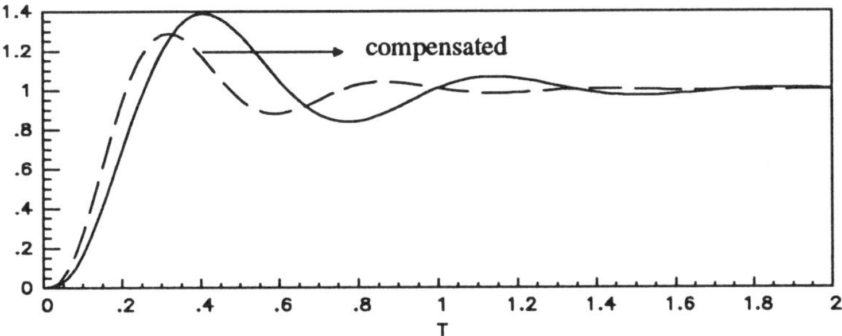

Figure 7-13 Step response for Example 7.6.

7.4.5 Bode Design—Analytical Method

The analytical method described previously for root locus design can be modified and applied to Bode design. In this case, we want the compensated system $K(s)\,G(s)$ to have a gain of 1.0 and a phase of $-180^o + PM$ at $s = j\omega_{gc}$. Assuming the time constant formulation of the compensator, we get

$$K(j\omega_{gc})\,G(j\omega_{gc}) = K_c\,\frac{j\,\omega_{gc}\,\tau_z+1}{j\,\omega_{gc}\,\tau_p+1}\,M_G\,e^{\,j\theta_G} = 1\,e^{\,j(-180+PM)}$$

where M_G and θ_G are the gain (not in dB) and phase of $G(j\omega)$ at $\omega = \omega_{gc}$. This equation can be separated into its real and imaginary parts, resulting in two equations in two unknowns. These equation can then be solved to find

$$\tau_z = \frac{1+K_c\,M_G\cos(PM-\theta_G)}{-\,\omega_{gc}\,K_c\,M_G\sin(PM-\theta_G)} \qquad \text{and} \qquad \tau_p = \frac{\cos(PM-\theta_G)+K_c\,M_G}{\omega_{gc}\sin(PM-\theta_G)}$$

To use these equations, we first determine K_c and draw the Bode plots for $K_c\,G(j\omega)$. We then examine these plots at $\omega = \omega_{gc}$ to find $K_c\,M_G$ and θ_G. Remember that

$K_c M_G$ is the actual magnitude and not the magnitude in dB. Program (No. 6) in the Appendix implements this procedure.

Example 7.7 Bode Analytical Method

Consider our plant

$$G(s) = \frac{400}{s\,(s^2 + 30s + 200)}$$

with the following specifications:

Steady state error to unit ramp input less than 10%
$\omega_{gc} = 14$ rad/sec
PM = 41°

To satisfy the steady state error requirement, we set $K_c = 5$. We examine the Bode plots of $K_cG(j\omega)$, already shown in Fig.7-12. At $\omega = \omega_{gc} = 14$ rad/sec, we find that

$K_c M_G = 0.34$ and $\theta_G = -180^\circ$

Using these values, and the desired ω_{gc} and PM, we get $\tau_z = 0.227$, $\tau_p = 0.038$.

The compensator, therefore, is $K(s) = 5\,\dfrac{0.227\,s + 1}{0.038\,s + 1}$.

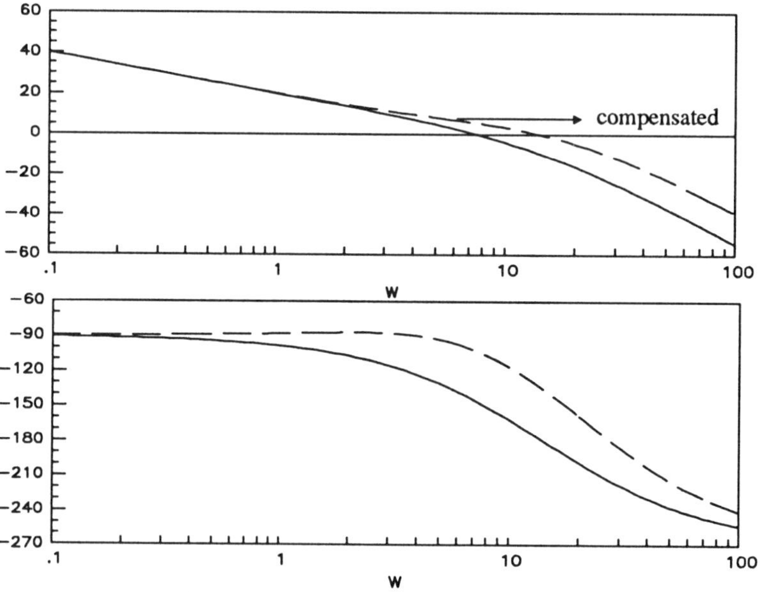

Figure 7-14 Bode plots for Example 7.7.

The Bode plots for the compensated system are shown in Figure 7-14. We see that the required ω_{gc} and PM have been met. The closed loop step response is shown in Figure 7-15. The overshoot and settling time are 19% and 0.9 sec, respectively. This response is similar to that obtained from the first method.

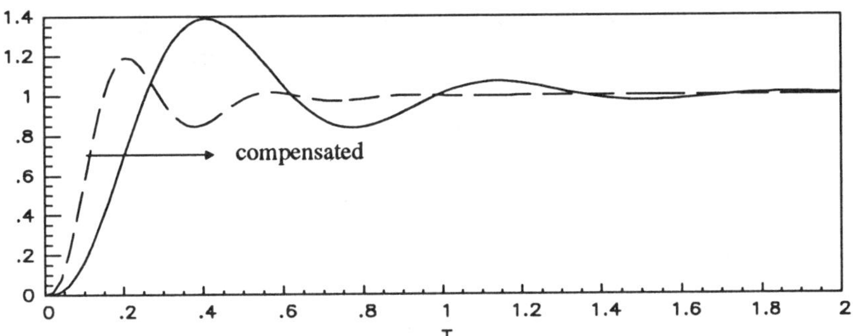

Figure 7-15 Step response for Example 7.7.

Comparison of PD Controller and Lead Compensator

The PD controller discussed in Section 7.3.3 is never actually constructed. Differentiation severely decreases signal to noise ratio and is, therefore, avoided. Rather, the derivative term usually contains a pole to filter out high frequency noise. A more realistic PD controller would be

$$PD(s) = K_p + \frac{K_d s}{sT_d + 1}$$

Combining into a single fraction gives us

$$PD(s) = \frac{K_p T_d s + K_p + K_d s}{T_d s + 1} = K_p \frac{(T_d + K_d/K_p) s + 1}{T_d s + 1}$$

which is the equation for a lead compensator. Hence, PD control is similar to lead compensation where, in the ideal case, the lead compensator pole has been extended to infinity.

7.5 Lag Compensation

In a lag compensator, the pole is smaller than the zero. Because lag compensation adds phase lag to a system, it tends to be destabilizing. For this reason, it is never used if the plant itself is already unstable or has small relative stability margins. However, lag compensation can sometimes be used to increase relative stability by decreasing the system gain. This will be explained in greater detail when we describe Bode plot techniques.

One of the primary uses for lag compensation is to decrease steady state error. This is clearly demonstrated by considering the extreme case of letting the pole in the lag compensator go to zero. In this case, the lag compensator adds an integrator to the system, which increases the system type and, therefore, decreases steady state error. For the general lag compensator, $a > b$, so $K_c\, a/b > K_c$, which leads to a decrease in steady state error.

Lag compensation decreases the gain crossover frequency, ω_{gc}. This leads to systems with slower step responses. Conversely, we often want to limit the closed loop bandwidth to keep extraneous signals out of the control loop. The decreased bandwidth created by the lag compensator would, in this case, be a desirable characteristic.

7.5.1 Root Locus Design

For convenience, we repeat the compensator transfer function

$$K(s) = K_c \frac{s+a}{s+b}$$

The root locus technique is most often used with systems that already satisfy stability and dynamic performance requirements but do not have the necessary steady state error. In this case, the following procedure can be used:

- Determine the desired s-plane location, s_1, from the given specifications.
- Draw the root locus of the plant, $G(s)$.
- Determine the value of K_c that places the root locus at, or near, the desired s-plane location.
- If K_c is too small to meet steady state error requirements, proceed to the next step.
- Choose the ratio of a/b that will yield the desired steady state error.
- Maintaining this ratio, place the pole-zero combination to achieve the desired root locus.
- Check closed loop response.

The next to last step is, of course, the tricky one. There are no formal rules that guarantee success. The following idea, however, is in widespread use: Choose a and b close to each other and yet maintain the required ratio. How can two numbers be very close and yet maintain a ratio such as 10? The answer is to choose them between 0 and 1. For instance, if $b = 0.01$ and $a = 0.1$, they have a ratio of 10, but their total contribution to the time response may be negligible because they almost cancel each other. The main negative effect on time response is that the very small compensator pole will appear as a closed loop pole. This will dominate the settling time of the system. The smaller the pole, the longer the settling time.

Example 7.8 Lag Compensation—Root Locus

Consider the following Type 1 plant

$$G(s) = \frac{10}{s(s+5)}$$

The specifications are: damping ratio of 0.707, steady state error to unit ramp less than 5%.

The point on the root locus that satisfies the damping ratio requirement is $s_1 = -2.5 + 2.5j$. The value of K_c that places the root locus at this point is 1.25. For this value, the error constant is 2.5, which yields a steady state error of 40%.

To reduce the steady state error, we use a lag compensator with the ratio $a/b = 8$. We set the compensator zero (rather arbitrarily) at $a = 0.1$ and compute $b = 0.0125$. The compensator becomes

$$K(s) = 1.25\,\frac{s+0.1}{s+0.0125}$$

The closed loop poles and zero are at $\{\, -0.1037, -2.45 \pm j\,2.45 \,\}$ and $\{\, -0.1 \,\}$. Note that the closed loop zero almost cancels the real closed loop pole, hence, the complex poles are almost dominant and meet the damping ratio requirement. The real closed loop pole causes a larger settling time, however. The closed loop step responses of the system before and after compensation are shown in Figure 7-16. The uncompensated step response was plotted with the gain 1.25 included. This meets the damping ratio requirement but has a larger steady state error. The compensated response has a slightly larger overshoot and longer settling time, but meets the steady state error specification.

7.5.2 Root Locus—Analytical Method

In Section 7.4.3, we showed you an analytical technique for using root locus data to design a lead compensator. Theoretically, this method should also work for lag compensator

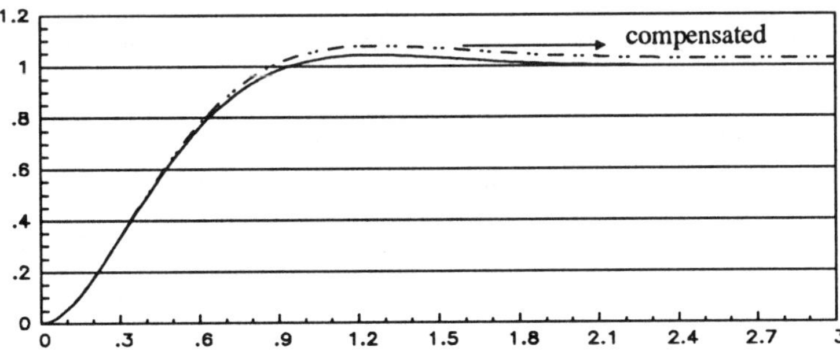

Figure 7-16 Step responses for Example 7.8.

design. We simply plug the relevant data into the equations. In this case, we should find that $\tau_p > \tau_z$. The problem is the typical lag compensator design philosophy that we discussed above and demonstrated in Example 7.8. In this procedure, the original root locus is acceptable and we merely use the lag compensator to increase the steady state error constant. Therefore, at the s-plane point of interest, $\theta_G \approx 180^o$. With this phase, the equations for τ_p and τ_z blow up.

However, if our intent is to use the lag compensator to change ζ and/or ω_n, then we can proceed as follows. Using the time constant form for the compensator

- Choose K_c to meet steady state error requirements.
- Draw root locus for $K_c G(s)$.
- Locate point on s-plane, s_1, that satisfies performance requirements.
- Find M_s and θ_s, where $s_1 = M_s e^{j\theta_s}$.
- Find $K_c M_G$ and θ_G from $K_c G(s_1) = K_c M_G e^{j\theta_G}$, then compute

$$\tau_z = \frac{\sin\theta_s - K_c M_G \sin(\theta_G - \theta_s)}{K_c M_G M_s \sin\theta_G} \quad \text{and} \quad \tau_p = -\frac{K M_G \sin\theta_s + \sin(\theta_G + \theta_s)}{M_s \sin\theta_G}$$

- Draw root locus of $K(s)\,G(s)$ to confirm design.
- Close the loop, and determine time domain response.

Example 7.9 Lag Compensator—Analytical Root Locus

Consider the following plant and specifications.

$$G(s) = \frac{10}{s(s+5)}$$

Steady state error to unit ramp is less than 5%
Closed loop $\zeta = .707$, and $\omega_n = 1.5$ rad/sec

The desired steady state error requires $K_c = 10$. The s-plane point that corresponds to the given ζ and ω_n is $s_1 = -1.06 + j1.06$. The relevant magnitudes and angles are

$M_s = 1.49$ $\theta_s = 135^o$ $M_G = 1.63$ $\theta_G = -150^o$

We finally get $\tau_z = 1.232$, and $\tau_p = 15.104$. Therefore, the compensator is

$$K(s) = 10\frac{1.232\,s + 1}{15.104\,s + 1}$$

The closed loop system has poles at { -1.06 $\pm j$ 1.06, - 2.94 } and a zero at { - 0.81 }.

The step response and Bode plots of the system before and after compensation are shown in Figures 7-17 and 17-18. In the previous example, we showed the uncompensated response that satisfies the time response requirements. In this example, we have shown the uncompensated system with the additional gain of 10; so it satisfies the steady state error specifications. We note, however, that the system is now lightly damped with an overshoot of almost 43% compared with the compensated system, which has an overshoot of 30%. From the Bode plots, we observe that the PM has also increased from 28 to 48 degrees, whereas the gain crossover frequency has decreased from 9.4 to 1.7 rad/sec.

Note that even though the damping ratio is 0.707, the percent overshoot is higher than expected. This is due to the closed loop zero (resulting from the compensator zero) that is to the right of the complex poles, which are not dominant anymore. If this much overshoot cannot be tolerated, the compensator zero should be moved to the left until it almost cancels the real

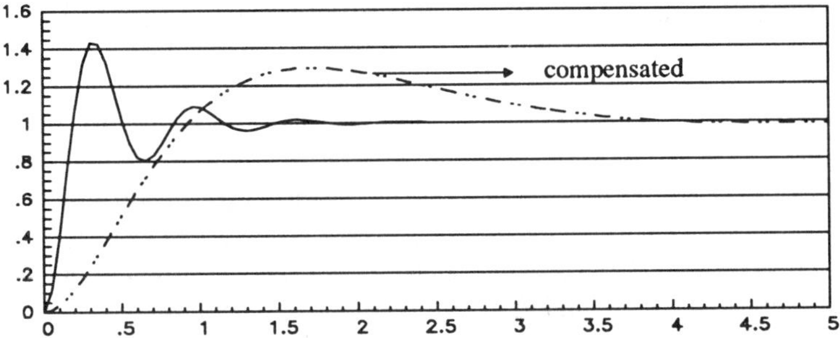

Figure 7-17 Step responses for Example 7.9.

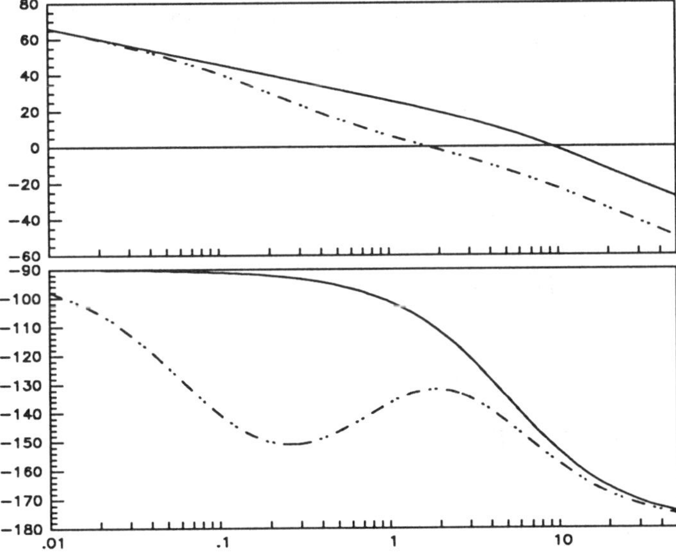

Figure 7-18 Bode plots for Example 7.9.

closed loop pole. The problem is that the location of this pole can not be determined ahead of time. Hence, some trial and error, or another method should be tried.

7.5.3 Lag Compensation—Bode Design

As can be seen from the Bode plots in the previous example, the lag compensator reduces the gain of the system and adds phase lag. Lag compensation is usually used when we wish to reduce the plant gain. This is done either to increase the PM or to lower the closed loop bandwidth. As with the lead compensation technique, the most common Bode method allows the engineer to design to a given steady state error requirement and a desired PM. In this section, we present a method based on Bode plots. A purely analytical technique appears in the next section.

For this method, the most useful form for the lag compensator is

$$K(s) = K_c \frac{1+\alpha Ts}{1+Ts} \qquad \alpha < 1$$

As with lead compensation, we first chose K_c to satisfy the steady state error requirement. The parameters α and T are then found to meet the required *PM*. Before proceeding, let us determine how these parameters affect the gain and phase of the compensator. Evaluating the compensator gain at infinity shows that the maximum reduction in gain is

$$\text{gain reduction in dB} = (GR) = 20 \log \alpha$$

We can also see that at the frequency $\omega = 10/\alpha T$, there is minimal phase contribution from the lag compensator. These facts lead to the following design methodology:

- Determine K_c to satisfy steady state error requirement.
- Draw Bode plots of $K_cG(j\omega)$.
- If the PM is insufficient, find the frequency at which the PM is satisfied (add 5° for safety). This frequency will be the compensated ω_{gc}.
- Find the gain of $K_cG(j\omega)$ at $\omega = \omega_{gc}$. This is the amount of gain that needs to be reduced by the compensator, i.e.,

$$GR = -\,|\,K_cG(j\omega_{gc})\,|_{dB} \;\rightarrow \qquad \alpha = 10^{\,GR/20}$$

- To minimize the phase contribution of the compensator, let $T = \dfrac{10}{\alpha\,\omega_{gc}}$.
- Draw Bode plots of $K(j\omega)\,G(j\omega)$ and confirm design.
- simulate the closed loop system.

The program Bode Lag (No. 7) in the Appendix was used to solve the following example.

Example 7.10 Lag Compensator—Bode Method

Consider the system and specifications in Example 7.9.

We start by choosing $K_c = 10$ to satisfy the steady state error criterion. We now draw the Bode plots of $K_cG(j\omega)$, as shown in Figure 7-19.

A closed loop damping ratio of 0.707 requires a PM of 70°, where we have used the approximation $PM \approx 100\,\zeta$. We add 5 degrees for safety and examine the Bode plots to determine the frequency at which the PM requirement would be satisfied. This gives the compensated $\omega_{gc} \approx 1.2$ rad/sec. Because the gain of $K_cG(j\omega_{gc}) = 24$ dB, we find α and T as $\alpha = 0.063$ and $T = 126.8$.

The lag compensator, therefore, is

$$K(s) = 10\frac{8\,s+1}{126.8\,s+1}$$

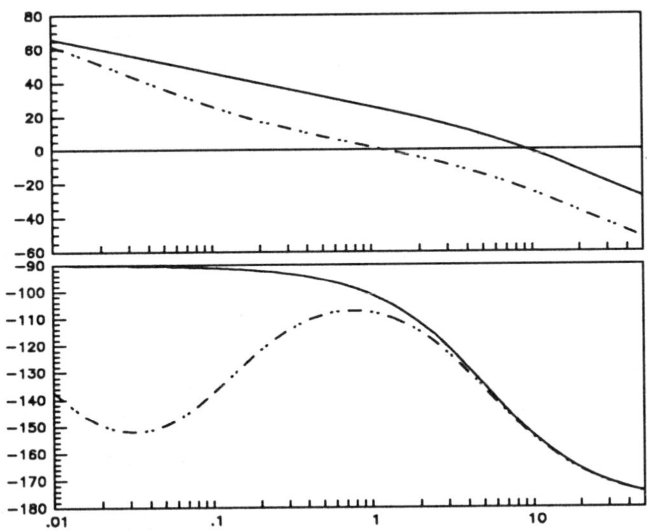

Figure 7-19 Bode plots for Example 7.10.

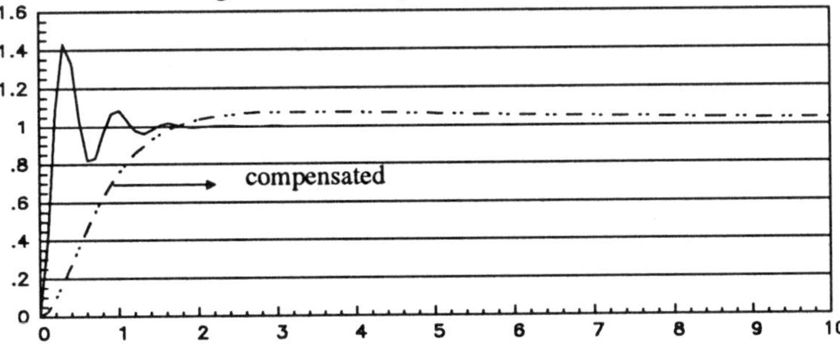

Figure 7-20 Step responses for Example 7.10.

The closed loop poles and zero are { - 0.13, - 2.0, - 2.8 } and { - 0.12 }, respectively. The response is overdamped. The Bode plots and step response are shown in Figures 7-19 and 7-20. We see that the overshoot has decreased from 43% to 5%. The gain crossover frequency is at 1.24 rad/sec with 70 degrees of PM.

Note the phase lag contribution of the compensator and the fact that it occurs at low frequencies. Most of this lag effect is gone when we approach the gain crossover frequency. By the way, this explains why you want to choose small numbers for the compensator pole and zero in the root locus approach. You want to ensure the phase lag occurs at low enough frequencies so it would not adversely affect the PM.

In comparing the root locus and Bode design methods of the previous two examples, we see there is no clear-cut choice of techniques. For this plant and specifications, the root locus design gave us a faster response, but the Bode design gave us less overshoot. For any given problem, we recommend that you use both techniques and choose the compensator that most closely produces the *closed loop* response that you want.

A disadvantage to the preceding technique is that we cannot arbitrarily choose a desired gain crossover frequency. Thus, lag compensation is usually used for adjustments to the steady state error. Lead compensation can then be added to satisfy other performance criteria. Under the right circumstances, however, we can achieve both steady state and transient specifications with a lag design.

7.5.4 Bode Design—Analytical Method

The analytical method previously presented in Section 7.4.5 for Bode lead compensator design can be used, with some restrictions, for lag compensator design. We first repeat the design rules, show an example, and then discuss the limitations of the method.

- Choose K_c to meet steady state error requirements.
- Draw Bode plots of$K_cG(j\omega)$ and determine $K_c\,M_G$ and θ_G at the desired $\omega = \omega_{gc}$.
- For the desired PM, find the pole and zero time constants from

$$\tau_z = \frac{1 + K_c M_G \cos(PM - \theta_G)}{-\,\omega_{gc} K_c M_G \sin(PM - \theta_G)} \quad \text{and} \quad \tau_p = \frac{\cos(PM - \theta_G) + K_c M_G}{\omega_{gc} \sin(PM - \theta_G)}$$

- Draw compensated Bode plots to check design.
- Simulate closed loop response.

Example 7.11 Lag Compensator—Bode Analytical Method

Consider the following plant and specifications

$$G(s) = \frac{10}{s(s+5)}$$

steady state error to unit ramp input of less than 5%

$\omega_{gc} = 2$ rad/sec, and PM = 40°.

We first set $K_c = 10$ and draw the Bode plots for $K_c\, G(j\omega)$; using program No. 6 in the Appendix, we get

$M_G = 0.92$ and $\theta_G = -111.8^o$; the compensator parameters are $\tau_z = 0.81$ and $\tau_p = 8.89$.

The compensator is

$$K(s) = 10\,\frac{0.81\,s+1}{8.89\,s+1}$$

The closed loop poles and zero are { - 0.98 $\pm j$ 1.61, - 3.1430 } and { - 1.22 }, respectively. From the step responses and Bode plots in Figures 7-21 and 7-22, we see that the specifications have been met. The large overshoot is due to the low damping ratio of the complex poles.

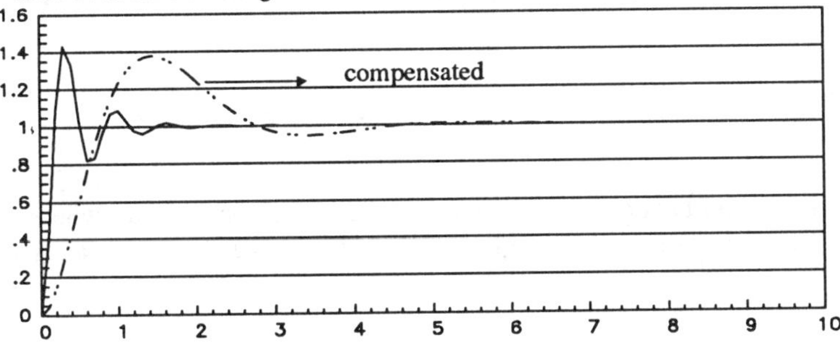

Figure 7-21 Step responses for Example 7.11.

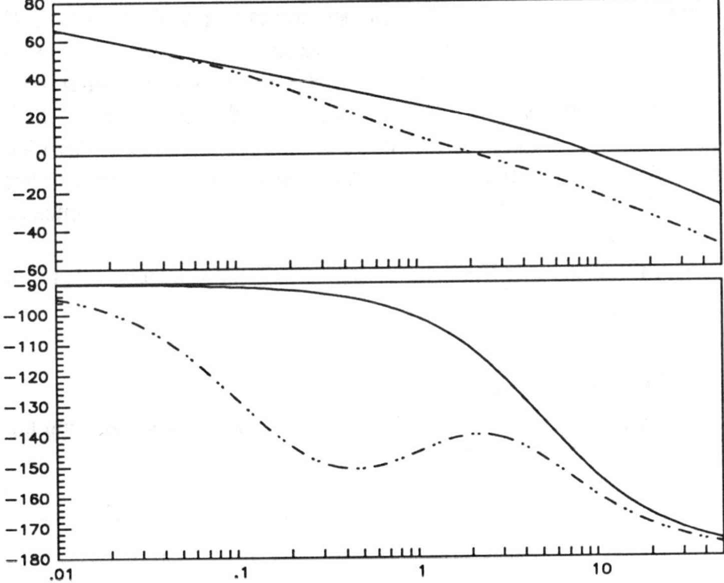

Figure 7-22 Bode plots for Example 7.11.

In the analytical technique, becasue we find the time constants by dividing by the term sin(PM - θ_G), this method blows up if the angle in the sin approaches 180 degrees. There will be instances, therefore, when an arbitrary selection of error constant, ω_{gc}, and PM cannot be achieved. In these cases, you must consider one of these parameters as a variable and iterate the design procedure until an acceptable compensator is found.

We can also modify our programs to compute a set of compensators by using loops and conditional structures, compute all step responses, and choose the one that best meets the criteria. Alternatively, we can use more sophisticated optimization algorithms available in the Optimization Module of MATRIXx to do an optimal design.

Comparison of Lag Compensator and PI Controller

The proportional–integral (PI) controller described in Sections 7.2 and 7.3 can be written as

$$K_p + \frac{K_i}{s} = \frac{K_p s + K_i}{s} = K_p \frac{s + K_i/K_p}{s}$$

We see that a PI controller is a special case of a lag compensator where the compensator pole has been shifted to the origin, i.e., PI approximates lag compensation in the limit.

7.6 General Compensation

For many systems, desired stability and performance specification cannot be accomplished with the PID, lead, or lag compensators we have discussed in the previous sections. In some of these cases, a combination of two or more of these controllers can be used. In other cases, an ad hoc approach is often adopted by the designer. That is, the designer uses her or his experience and insight to choose compensator pole and zero locations, uses the computer to simulate the design, and iterates the design process until an acceptable solution is found. This is where classical design becomes an art, and experience and insight are the best guidelines.

As a final example in this chapter, we will examine a helicopter problem, given in Franklin et al [FPE91].

Example 7.12 Ad hoc Design

Problem 6.17, in Franklin et al [FPE91], gives a state space model for longitudinal motions of a helicopter near hover. The model is

$$\begin{bmatrix} \dot{q} \\ \dot{\theta} \\ \dot{u} \end{bmatrix} = \begin{bmatrix} -0.4 & 0 & -0.01 \\ 1 & 0 & 0 \\ -1.4 & 9.8 & -0.02 \end{bmatrix} \begin{bmatrix} q \\ \theta \\ u \end{bmatrix} + \begin{bmatrix} 6.3 \\ 0 \\ 9.8 \end{bmatrix} \delta$$

$$y = [0\ 0\ 1]\begin{bmatrix} q \\ \theta \\ u \end{bmatrix}$$

where

q = pitch rate

θ = pitch angle of fuselage

u = horizontal velocity

δ = rotor tilt angle

We can use *tform* in MATRIXx to convert from state space to transfer function form.

```
< > S=[A B;C D];
< > [ng,dg]=tform(S,NS)
```

```
DG      =
    1.0000   0.4200  -0.1320   0.9800
NG      =
    9.8000  -4.9000  61.7400
```

This gives us the helicopter transfer function between rotor tilt angle and horizontal velocity.

$$G(s) = \frac{9.8s^2 - 4.9s + 61.7}{s^3 + 0.42s^2 - 0.132s + 0.98}$$

It is clear from the transfer function that this system has both zeros and poles in the RHP. In fact the roots are

```
< > open_pol=roots(dg)
```

```
OPEN_POL     =
-.6500
.1183 + .3678j
.1183 - .3678j
```

```
< > open_zer=roots(ng)
```

```
OPEN_ZER     =
  .2500 + 2.4975j
  .2500 - 2.4975j
```

The system is clearly unstable for all gains. We cannot stabilize this system with any of the methods presented earlier in the chapter. Rather, we adopt an ad hoc approach.

We first cancel the pole at -0.65 with the pole-zero combination $K_1(s) = \frac{s + 0.65}{s + 10}$.

The pole is necessary for realizability so we add it approximately a decade away. We next add a zero at the origin to pull the RHP poles into the LHP. Again we need a pole, so we try the following total compensator

$$K(s) = K_c \frac{s+0.65}{s+10} \frac{s}{s+10}$$

The root locus (zoomed in the vicinity of the origin) for the compensated is shown in Figure 7-23. We achieve maximum stability when $K_c = 2$. Our ad hoc approach here has resulted in the cascading of two lead compensators.

Finally, we close the loop and obtain the step response shown in Figure 7-24.

The output goes to zero because of the compensator zero at the origin. If the step input is considered a disturbance, then this is exactly the response we would want.

In this case, however, we want the rotor tilt angle to control longitudinal speed. We can accomplish this by splitting the compensator into two parts. We use

$$K_1(s) = \hat{K}_1 \frac{s+0.65}{s+10}$$

in the forward path and

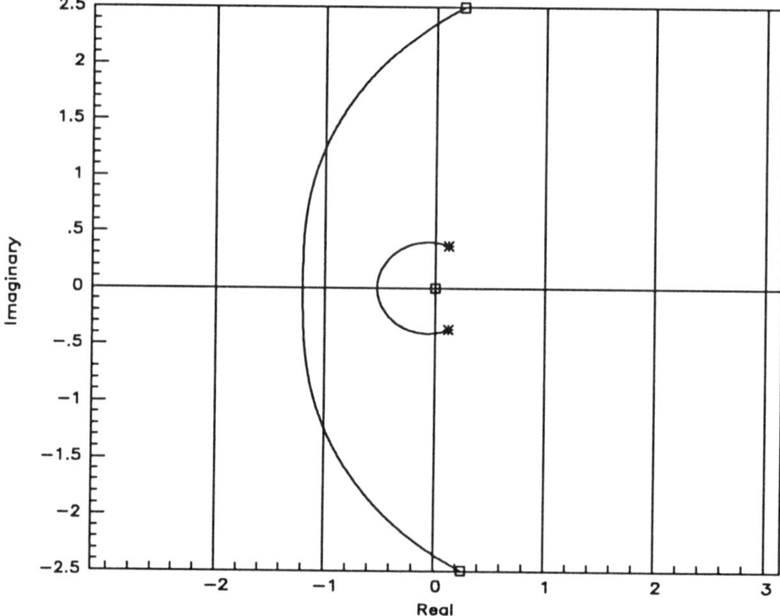

Figure 7-23 Root locus for the compensated system in Example 7.12.

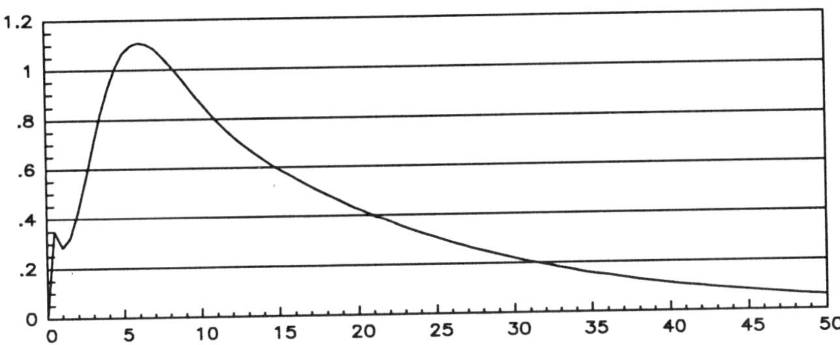

Figure 7-24 Step response for the compensated system in Example 7.12.

$$K_2(s) = \hat{K}_2 \frac{s}{s+10}$$

in the feedback path; note that $K_c = 2 = \hat{K}_1 \hat{K}_2$. We will now select these gains to achieve zero steady state error to a unit step input. This implies that the closed loop transfer function must be 1 at zero frequency, i.e., $T(0) = 1$, where

$$T(s) = \frac{\hat{K}_1 G(s) K_1(s)}{1 + \hat{K}_1 \hat{K}_2 K_1(s) K_2(s) G(s)}$$

Solving for the gains, we get, $\hat{K}_1 = 0.0242$ and $\hat{K}_2 = 82.7206$. The open loop Bode plots and closed loop step response for the modified design are shown in Figures 7-25 and 7-26. You can see that we have achieved a steady state input-output ratio of 1.0 with this design. Any particular steady state ratio between helicopter speed and rotor tilt angle can be achieved with the appropriate selection of the gains as long as their product is 2.

Note that $K_2(s)$ is an approximate differentiator. It can be constructed either from electronic devices such as an op-amps or through the use of an accelerometer mounted to measure longitudinal movement of the helicopter.

The closed loop poles and zeros, shown subsequently, verify closed loop stability.

```
CL_POLES   =

-.1665 + .0000j
-1.0325 + 1.1611j
-1.0325 - 1.1611j
-37.1320 + .0000j

CL_ZEROS   =

.2500 + 2.4975j
.2500 - 2.4975j
-10.0000 + .0000j
```

Measures of relative stability are given by GM and PM shown below.

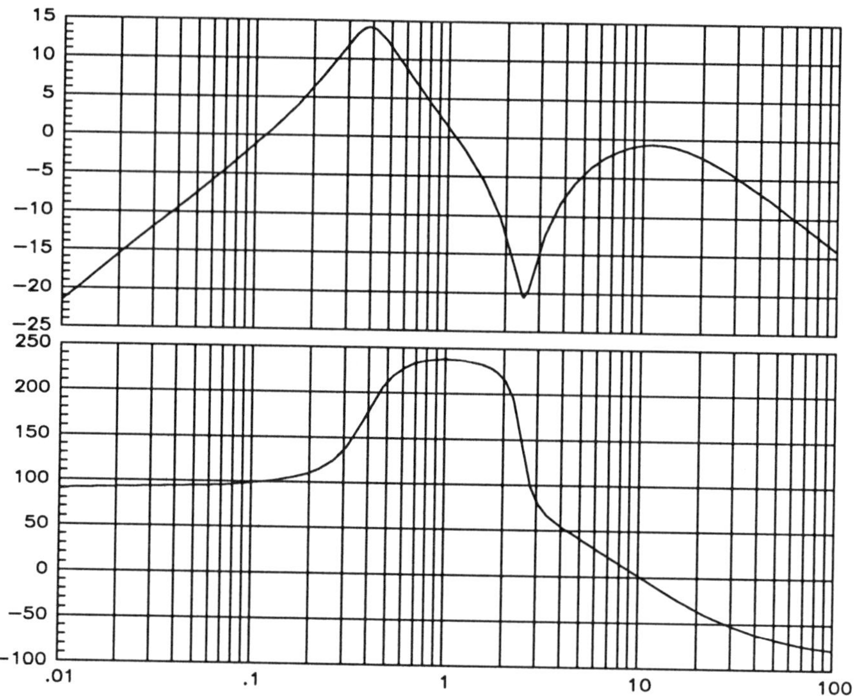

Figure 7-25 Bode plots for the compensated system in Example 7.12.

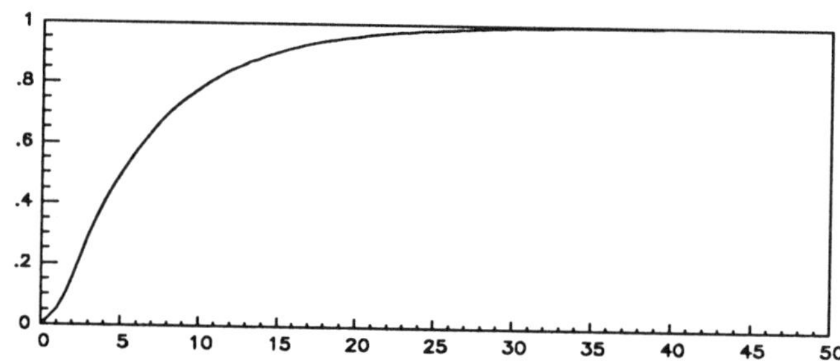

Figure 7-26 Step response for the compensated system with modified gains.

PM =

-80.5185
57.0995

GM =

-14.0641
18.7409

The negative margins are the consequences of RHP poles and zeros in the open loop transfer function. The GM indicates that the system gain can be increased by 18.7 dB or decreased by 14 dB before instability occurs. This conclusion is also verified by the root locus.

7.7 Appendix: Design Programs

1. Ziegler-Nichols Program

```
// Inputs: Km, wm, tf, wi, wf
tf=2.5;wi=.1;wf=100;
poles=rlocus(ng,dg,'nopattern');
kp=0.6*km; kd=kp*pi/(4*abs(wm));ki=kp*abs(wm)/pi;
nk=[kd kp ki]; dk=[1 0];
return
```

2. Analytical PID/PD Program

```
//Requires : ng dg, wgc, pm, Ki
ngv=polyval(ng,jay*wgc); dgv=polyval(dg,jay*wgc); g=ngv/dgv;
  thetar=(pm-180)*pi/180
  ejtheta=cos(thetar)+jay*sin(thetar);
  eqn=(ejtheta/g)+jay*(Ki/wgc)
  x=imag(eqn);
  r=real(eqn);
  Kp=r; Kd=x/wgc
  if Ki <>0, dk=[1 0]; nk=[Kd Kp Ki];...
  else  dk=1; nk=[Kd Kp];end;
return
```

3. Root Locus Lead: Geometric Design Program

```
//[nk,dk]=rllead(ng,dg,s_1)
ngv=polyval(ng,s_1);dgv=polyval(dg,s_1);g=ngv/dgv;
arg_g=atan2(g)*180/pi;
if arg_g > 0; phi_c=180-arg_g; end
if arg_g < 0; phi_c=-arg_g end;  // in this case k < 0 (intro -180)
phi=atan2(s_1)*180/pi ;
theta_z=(phi+phi_c)/2 ;
theta_p=(phi-phi_c)/2 ;
p=real(s_1)-imag(s_1)/tan(theta_p*pi/180)
z=real(s_1)-imag(s_1)/tan(theta_z*pi/180)
nk=[1 -z]; dk=[1 -p];
nkv=polyval(nk,s_1);
dkv=polyval(dk,s_1);
kv=nkv/dkv;
k=1/(g*kv); k=abs(k)
if arg_g < 0;  k= - k;
nk=k*nk;
return
```

4. Root Locus Lead: Analytical Design Program

```
//Requires : ng dg, s1 ,k
//[nk,dk]=anrllead(ng,dg,s1,k)
ngv=polyval(ng,s1);dgv=polyval(dg,s1);g=ngv/dgv;
thetag=atan2(g);thetag_d=thetag*180/pi
mg=abs(g) ; ms=abs(s1)
thetas=atan2(s1);
thetas_d=thetas*180/pi
tz=(sin(thetas)-k*mg*sin(thetag-thetas))/(k*mg*ms*sin(thetag))
tp=-(k*mg*sin(thetas)+sin(thetag+thetas))/(ms*sin(thetag))
nk=[tz 1]
dk=[tp 1]
return
```

5. Bode Lead Design Program

```
// LEAD DESIGN USING BODE
// Requires:  ng, dg, kc, wi, wf,
//you need to find the phase margin of KcG(s) first to determine the
//desired phase margin, dpm
[w,mu,pu]=bode(kc*ng,dg,wi,wf,'noplot');
smo=max(size(mu));ddpm=dpm+5;
phi=ddpm*pi/180
a=(1+sin(phi))/(1-sin(phi))
mm=-10*log(a)/log(10)
for i=1:smo, if mu(i)>=mm, wgc=w(i); end;end;wgc
tt=1/(wgc*sqrt(a)); z=a*tt ;p=tt;
nk=[z 1]
dk=[p 1]
return
```

6. Bode Lead/Lag: Analytical Design Program

```
//Requires : ng dg, wgc ,k , pm
//[nk,dk]=anbdlead(ng,dg,k,wgc,pm)
ngv=polyval(ng,jay*wgc);dgv=polyval(dg,jay*wgc);g=ngv/dgv;
thetag=atan2(g);thetag_d=thetag*180/pi
mg=abs(g)
Tz=(1+k*mg*cos(pm*pi/180-thetag))/(-wgc*k*mg*sin(pm*pi/180-thetag))
Tp=(cos(pm*pi/180-thetag)+k*mg)/(wgc*sin(pm*pi/180-thetag))
nk=[Tz 1]
dk=[Tp 1]
return
```

7. Bode Lag Design Program

```
// LAG DESIGN USING BODE
// Requires:  ng, dg, wi, wf, KC, tf, dpm(desired PM)
[w,mo,po]=bode(Kc*ng,dg,wi,wf,'noplot');
smo=max(size(mo));
ddpm=dpm+5;
i=smo+1;k=0;
while k=0, i=i-1; if po(i)>=-180+ddpm, w1=w(i),aa=mo(i);k=1;end;end
w1
aa
a=10**(-aa/20)
tt=10/(a*w1)
iz=a*tt;ip=tt;
nk=[iz 1]
dk=[ip 1]
return
```

7.8 Problems

7.1 Derive the formulas for the pole and zero location in the root locus geometric method given in Section 7.4.2.

7.2 Derive the formulas for τ_z and τ_p for the root locus analytical method given in Section 7.4.3.

7.3 Derive the formulas for ω_{max}, sin Φ, and Mgiven in Section 7.4.4.

7.4 Derive the formulas for τ_z and τ_p for the Bode analytical method given in Section 7.4.5.

7.5 For each of the following plants, a set of specifications are given. You are to design a cascade compensator to satisfy the specs in each case. You are to use either lead, lag, PID, or combinations of these basic types. If you can not meet the specs using the cascade configuration, try others.

In each case, document your design by providing the following information: the compensator transfer function, closed loop transfer function, closed loop poles and zeros, root locus, open loop Bode magnitude and phase plots, closed loop Bode magnitude plot, closed loop step response, POS, T_r, T_s, M_r, BW, PM, GM.

For practical reasons, the compensators must be proper (if you use PD or PID, either add a high frequency pole to the compensator to make it proper or implement the derivative term in feedback). If you use lead or lag, keep the ratio of the compensator pole and zero to less than 20. If the ratio has to be bigger, split the compensator into stages. The reason for this is that larger ratios might lead to impractical component values when we implement the compensator electronically.

Note: In the following problems, we use the symbol e_{ss} _/ to represent steady state error to a unit ramp input, and the symbol e_{ss} _| for unit step inputs.

a. $G(s) = \dfrac{10\,(s+5)}{(s+15)\,(s^2+8s+20)}$ specs: $e_{ss} \le 10\%$, $\zeta \ge 0.707$

b. $G(s) = \dfrac{1}{s\,(s+1)\,(s+5)}$ specs: $\zeta \ge 0.707$, $T_s \le 4$, $T_r \le 3\ sec$

c. $G(s) = \dfrac{1}{s\,(s+8)^2}$ specs: e_{ss} _/ $\le 5\%$, $\zeta \ge 0.707$

d. $G(s) = \dfrac{1}{(s+1)\,(s+3)}$ specs: e_{ss} _| $\le 1\%$, $POS \le 10\%$, $T_s \le 5\ sec$

e. $G(s) = \dfrac{1}{s\,(s+2)}$ specs: e_{ss} _/ $\le 1\%$, $POS \le 10\%$, $T_s \le 6\ sec$

f. $G(s) = \dfrac{100}{s^2\,(s+10)}$ specs: $POS \le 10\%$, $T_s \le 2\ sec$, $PM \approx 40$ deg

g. $G(s) = \dfrac{1}{s\,(s+1)\,(s+5)}$ specs: e_{ss} _/ $\le 0.1\%$, $PM \approx 45$ deg

h. $G(s) = \dfrac{10}{s^2\,(s+40)}$ specs: $POS \le 15\%$, $PM \approx 45$ deg

i. $G(s) = \dfrac{10\,(s+2)}{s\,(s+0.1)\,(s+10)}$ specs: $POS \le 10\%$, $T_s \le 1\ sec$

j. $G(s) = \dfrac{1}{s\,(s+0.5)}$ specs: e_{ss} _| $\le 1\%$, $\zeta \approx 0.707$, $\omega_n \approx 5$

k. $G(s) = \dfrac{80}{s\,(s+4)}$ specs: $\zeta \approx 0.707$, $\omega_n \approx 10$

l. $G(s) = \dfrac{1600}{s\,(s+4)\,(s+16)}$ specs: e_{ss} _/ $\le 4\%$, $PM \approx 30$ deg

m. $G(s) = \dfrac{60990}{(s+58)\,(s+50)\,(s-50)}$

Specs: POS < 5%, fastest possible response with as much gain and phase margin as you can get.

n. $G(s) = \dfrac{1}{s^2}$ specs: $T_s \le 4\ sec$, $POS \le 30\%$

o. $G(s) = \dfrac{10}{s^2}$ specs: $T_s \le 4\ sec$, $POS \le 20\%$

p. $G(s) = \dfrac{25}{s\,(s+25)}$ specs: e_{ss} $\_\!/ \le 1\%$, $PM \approx 45$ deg

q. $G(s) = \dfrac{1}{s\,(s+1)\,(s+2)}$ specs: e_{ss} $\_\!/ \le 20\%$, $PM \approx 45$ deg

7.6 The inverted pendulum problem is common in control theory. The inverted pendulum is a rod connected via a hinge on its bottom end to a movable cart. We want the pendulum to remain upright. As you will show, however, this system is unstable. The pendulum, therefore, will tend to fall. We wish to control the motion of the cart so that we can keep the pendulum upright. The equations that describe the behavior of this system are nonlinear and are given by

$$\ddot{y} = \frac{1}{(M/m) + \sin^2\theta}\left(\frac{u}{m} + \dot{\theta}^{2} l \sin\theta - g\sin\theta\cos\theta\right)$$

$$\ddot{\theta} = \frac{1}{l\,(M/m) + \sin^2\theta}\left(-\frac{u}{m}\cos\theta - \dot{\theta}^{2} l\cos\theta\sin\theta + \frac{m+M}{m} g\sin\theta\right)$$

where M is cart mass, m is pendulum mass, l is pendulum length, g is acceleration due to gravity, y is cart position, θ is the angle the pendulum makes to the vertical, and u is the control input force acting on the cart.

Because we want to keep the pendulum upright, we are interested in linearizing this model about $\theta = 0$. The linearized state space model for this system is

$$\dot{x} = \begin{pmatrix} 0 & 1 & 0 & 0 \\ 0 & 0 & -mg/M & 0 \\ 0 & 0 & 0 & 1 \\ 0 & 0 & (M+m)g/Ml & 0 \end{pmatrix} x + \begin{pmatrix} 0 \\ 1/M \\ 0 \\ -1/Ml \end{pmatrix} u$$

where the state vector is $x = [y \quad \dot{y} \quad \theta \quad \dot{\theta}]'$

Because all of the states can be directly measured, there are a number of possible output vectors, z

$$z = \begin{pmatrix} \alpha_1 & 0 & 0 & 0 \\ 0 & \alpha_2 & 0 & 0 \\ 0 & 0 & \alpha_3 & 0 \\ 0 & 0 & 0 & \alpha_4 \end{pmatrix} x$$

where α_i is 1 if its corresponding state is being measured and 0 if otherwise.

a. Given the following values: $l = 1\ m$, $M = 1\ kg$, $m = 0.1\ kg$, $g = 9.8\ m/sec^2$, and the fact that we can stabilize this system by measuring only the position of the cart, i.e., $z = [1 \quad 0 \quad 0 \quad 0]\ x$, find the transfer function between the input u and the output y.

b. Show the system is unstable.

c. Design a compensator that will stabilize the system. Find the GM and PM for your design.

d. Find and plot the impulse response of the closed loop system.

e. Design a new compensator that will reduce the settling time, while improving the stability margins of the system if possible.

7.7 Redo the preceding problem with a new pendulum mass, m, of 1kg. Explain any differences in the results of the two problems.

***7.8** In Problem 7.6, we can also easily measure the pendulum rod position. In this case, we have two outputs, so $z = \begin{pmatrix} 1\,0\,0\,0 \\ 0\,0\,1\,0 \end{pmatrix} x$. This is now a one-input two-output system.

a. Find the transfer functions between the input and each output.

b. Find a suitable configuration and design compensator(s) that will stabilize both system outputs. For example, you might consider feeding back the pendulum angle in an inner loop, and feeding back the cart position in an outer loop.

c. Find and plot the impulse responses for your design.

8

State Space Design of Regulator Systems

8.1 Introduction

Control systems can be divided into two broad categories; regulation and tracking. Regulators attempt to maintain a constant system output in the face of internal or external disturbances, plant parameter variation, etc. The thermal control system in your house or apartment attempts to maintain the constant temperature set at the thermostat. Satellite attitude control systems are often designed to maintain a constant angle between transmitting and earth-based receiving antennas. Voltage regulators try to maintain a constant voltage across a load as line voltage or load resistance changes. The primary design criterion for regulators is the desired transient response.

In a tracking system, the output must follow, with minimal error, a prescribed course, represented as a time-varying input. For example, an autopilot might be designed to steer an airplane or ship on a predetermined path. In tracking systems, both the transient response and the steady-state response must fall within certain error bounds.

Because this chapter is concerned only with the design of regulator systems, we will limit our discussion to the control of the transient response. Because a system's transient response is primarily determined by its pole locations, regulator design involves moving the open loop (plant) poles to desired locations by the use of feedback. You are already familiar with the classical design techniques that use the root locus and Bode plot. In these techniques, a compensator (filter) is placed between the feedback signal, measured at the system output and the plant actuator.

In this chapter, we will discuss the use of state space techniques that allows us to place the closed loop poles at desired locations; these methods are known as *pole placement* techniques.

8.2 Pole Placement (State Feedback)

Consider the simple first order system described by

$$\dot{x} = x + u \qquad x(0) = x_0$$
$$y = x$$

where u is the input to the plant actuator. Note that in regulator systems, the external control input is usually set to zero. The pole of this open loop system is 1, indicating that the open loop system is unstable. In state space systems, we usually achieve feedback control by setting the actuator input equal to a gain times the state vector, i.e.,

$$u = -kx$$

Therefore,

$$\dot{x} = x - kx = (1-k)x$$

The closed loop pole is $1-k$, which results in an asymptotically stable system for $k > 1$. In fact, by a suitable choice of k, we can place the closed loop pole anywhere on the real axis.

Let us now consider the second order open loop system.

$$\dot{x} = \begin{bmatrix} 3 & -2 \\ 1 & 0 \end{bmatrix} x + \begin{bmatrix} 1 \\ 0 \end{bmatrix} u$$

This system has poles at $s = 1, 2$ and is, therefore, unstable. Can we use state feedback to place the closed loop poles in the left half plane and stabilize the system? A second order system with the desired closed loop poles located at p_1 and p_2 will have the characteristic equation

$$\Delta_d(s) = s^2 + (p_1 + p_2)\, s + p_1 p_2 = s^2 + \alpha s + \beta$$

If we use state feedback, i.e., $u = -k_1 x_1 - k_2 x_2$ in our unstable system, we obtain the closed loop system

$$\dot{x} = \begin{bmatrix} 3-k_1 & -2-k_2 \\ 1 & 0 \end{bmatrix} x$$

which has the characteristic equation

$$\Delta_c(s) = s^2 + (k_1 - 3)\, s + (2 + k_2)$$

By setting the actual characteristic equation to the desired characteristic equation, we get

$$k_1 = \alpha + 3 \quad and \quad k_2 = \beta - 2$$

Therefore, we can realize any pole locations we desire.

Now, several questions arise. How and why does this kind of feedback control work? Does it work for all systems, and, if not, what are the conditions? Can we get a general formula for the feedback coefficients? Is the method practical ? We will briefly discuss answers to these questions.

Among the many definitions of the concept of "state" we have:

" The state of a system is the minimum amount of information necessary to fully describe the system. That is to say, if the initial state $x(\tau)$ and inputs of the system are known for $t > \tau$, we can predict all future states of the system ".

According to this definition, it is not surprising that state feedback is so effective. After all the system is using all the necessary information to correct itself. This is in contrast to classical control compensation where usually only the output is fed back. Of course, this is just an intuitive argument, and we will make it more rigorous later.

Whether state feedback works for all systems can be seen easily by noticing that when we set coefficients of the two characteristic equations equal to each other, we get several equations in several unknowns. These equations do not always have unique solutions. Also the practicality of state feedback is a more subtle and involved issue that will be discussed in more detail later in this chapter. Let us discuss the general case. Consider the nth order system

$$\dot{x} = Ax + Bu$$
$$y = Cx + Du$$
$$G(s) = C(sI - A)^{-1} B + D = \begin{bmatrix} A & B \\ C & D \end{bmatrix}$$

We say the system is *controllable* if the states can be moved in any direction in the state space using appropriate control inputs. If the system is in modal form, we see that this is equivalent to the ability to move the system modes or poles arbitrarily in the complex plane. Controllability is a property of the pair (A, B) and can be checked by the following fact.

The pair (A, B) is *controllable* if and only if rank of the *controllability matrix*, $\boldsymbol{C}$, is n (n is the system order, i.e., dimension of A). The controllability matrix, $\boldsymbol{C}$, is given by

$$\boldsymbol{C} = [B \;\; AB \;\; A^2B \ldots A^{n-1}B \,]$$

In the preceding, by appropriate control input, we mean state feedback, i.e., $u = -k\,x$. Therefore, if the system is controllable, one can use state feedback to place the poles anywhere in the complex plane. Also we assume that $y = x$, which means that all states are available for measurement and feedback.

It turns out in practice that a weaker notion than controllability is sufficient for most purposes. This notion is called *stabilizability.* It refers to the ability to move only the unstable modes of the system. Therefore, we say a system is *stabilizable* if the unstable modes are controllable, or equivalently, if the uncontrollable modes are stable. The easiest way to check this is to convert the system to modal form, and check each eigenvalue and the corresponding row in the input distribution (B) matrix. The next simple example illustrates the concept.

$$\dot{x} = \begin{bmatrix} 3 & 0 \\ 0 & -1 \end{bmatrix} x + \begin{bmatrix} 1 \\ 0 \end{bmatrix} u \,, \qquad \dot{z} = \begin{bmatrix} 3 & 0 \\ 0 & 1 \end{bmatrix} z + \begin{bmatrix} 1 \\ 0 \end{bmatrix} u$$

Neither of the above systems are controllable. In the first system, the stable mode {-1} is not controllable whereas the unstable mode {3} is controllable. Hence, the system is stabilizable, for instance, by using state feedback control , $u = -k\, x_1$, with $k > 3$, the system is stabilized. In the second system, observe that the unstable mode {1} is not controllable, therefore, the system is not stabilizable. Note that either stability or controllability implies that the system is stabilizable.

Another fact that is important to mention is the transfer function analysis of systems that have controllability problems. It can be proven that in the SISO case, lack of controllability will result in pole-zero cancellation in the corresponding transfer function. So the transfer function of uncontrollable systems is not coprime. The converse of this statement is not true though, i.e., pole-zero cancellation in the transfer function does not necessarily imply uncontrollability. For further details, see [C84], [K80].

Several formulas exist for computation of the state feedback gain (see [K80]). *Ackermann's formula* is an example of one (for SISO systems). Given the desired characteristic equation

$$\Delta_d(s) = s^n + \alpha_1 s^{n-1} + \ \dots \ + \alpha_n$$

$$k = [\,0\,,0\,,\dots\,,1\,]\, C^{-1}\, \Delta_d(A) \qquad \text{where} \qquad \Delta_d(A) = A^n + \alpha_1 A^{n-1} + \dots + \alpha_{n-1} A + \alpha_n I$$

The above formula is not directly suitable for numerical implementation, but various reliable numerical algorithms exist for computation of k. The *poleplace* command in MATRIXx computes k for SISO systems.

```
< > k=poleplace(A,B,cp)
```

cp = desired closed loop poles

For complex poles, only one of the pair must be specified. The choice of poles is arbitrary. Although there are various "optimal" choices, for our purposes now, we select a complex pair to satisfy transient response specifications and place the rest of the poles "far" into the LHP. This is the only choice the designer has to make, and the rest of the design process can be fully automated.

Transfer Function Analysis

It is instructive to apply the classical techniques of root locus and frequency response analysis to our state space compensator design. This is needed for two reasons:
1. Frequently some of the problem specifications are frequency domain specs such as, gain and phase margins, bandwidth, etc., so we do this to verify these specifications.
2. To obtain the resulting compensator transfer function in order to gain more insight into the solution; and compare with an equivalent classical design.

To make this comparison, we first find the open loop transfer function of the state feedback sytem. The plant is represented by

$$\begin{aligned} \dot{x} &= A\,x + B\,u \;\rightarrow\; X(s) = \Phi(s)\,B\,U(s)\,, \quad \text{where} \quad \Phi(s) = (sI - A)^{-1} \\ y &= C\,x + D\,u \;\rightarrow\; Y(s) = (\,C\,\Phi(s)\,B + D\,)\,U(s) = G(s)\,U(s) \end{aligned}$$

$$u = -k\,X\,(\,s) = -k\,\Phi(s)\,B$$

Figure 8-1 shows a block diagram of the zero-input state feedback system. To compute the open loop transfer function, we break the loop at the point indicated (≈), inject a signal at $U(s)$, and measure the response at $U_1(s)$. Therefore, the open loop transfer function is $-\,k\,\Phi(s)\,B$. The equivalent classical open loop transfer function is $G(s)\,K(s)$, where $G(s)$ is the plant, and $K(s)$ is the compensator transfer function. For the loop transfer functions to be equal

$$-\,G(s)\,K(s) = -\,k\,\Phi(s)\,B$$

because $G(S) = C\,\Phi(s)B + D \;\rightarrow\; K(s) = \dfrac{k\,\Phi(s)\,B}{C\,\Phi(s)\,B + D}$

That is, if we build $K(s)$, the classically designed and state space systems will have the same transient behavior. Also, we can apply root locus, Bode and Nyquist analysis to $k\,\Phi(s)\,B$ to determine stability margins, bandwidth, etc. The closed loop transfer function of the state feedback system can be obtained by introducing a reference input v, i.e.,

$$u = -\,k\,x + \overline{N}\,v$$

$$\dot{x} = (A - B\,k\,)\,x + B\,\overline{N}\,v \;\rightarrow\; X(S) = (sI - A + B\,k\,)^{-1}\,B\,\overline{N}\,V(s)$$

$$Y(s) = C\,(sI - A + B\,k\,)^{-1}B\,\overline{N}\,V\,(s) \;\rightarrow\; T(s) = C\,(sI - A + B\,k\,)^{-1}B\,\overline{N}$$

In the above, D is assumed zero (strictly proper plant) to avoid messy formulas. The constant gain $\overline{N}$ can be easily computed to produce zero steady state error for constant reference inputs. Using packed matrix notation (introduced in Chapter 5), we have the open and closed loop transfer functions represented by

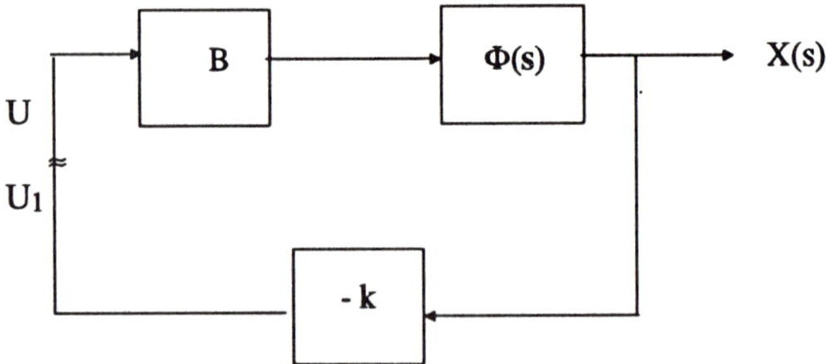

Figure 8-1 State feedback block diagram.

$$SGK = \begin{bmatrix} A & B \\ k & 0 \end{bmatrix} \quad \text{and} \quad ST = \begin{bmatrix} A - B\,k & B\,\overline{N} \\ C & 0 \end{bmatrix}$$

We will be using the above formulas to perform transfer function analysis of our examples within MATRIXx.

Example 8.1 State Feedback Design

The following is the model for the longitudinal motion of a helicopter near hover [FPE91]. The state variables are pitch rate, pitch angle of fuselage, and horizontal velocity, respectively. The control input is the rotor tilt angle. The state equations are

$$\dot{x} = \begin{bmatrix} -0.4 & 0 & -0.01 \\ 1 & 0 & 0 \\ -1.4 & 9.8 & -0.02 \end{bmatrix} x + \begin{bmatrix} 6.3 \\ 0 \\ 9.8 \end{bmatrix} u$$

$$y = [\,0 \;\; 0 \;\; 1\,]\,x$$

The system eigenvalues are found from

```
< > S=[a,b;c,d]; NS=3;eig(a)
```

```
ANS    =
-.6565 - 0.0000j
.1183 + .3678j
.1183 - .3678j
```

Therefore, the system is unstable with a pair of complex poles in the RHP. It is desired to place the system poles at { -1 ± j , -2 }. The control gain vector is obtained from

```
< > cp=[-2,-1+jay];
< > k=polep(a,b,cp)
```

K =
.4706 1 .0627

The open loop transfer function is obtained and used for root locus and Bode analysis; it is given by

```
< > sgk1=[a b;k 0]; nsgk1=ns
< > [w,mc1,pc1]=bode(sgk1,nsgk1,0.1,100);
< > rlocus(sgk1, nsgk1);
```

The root locus and Bode plots are shown in Figures 8-2 and 8-3.

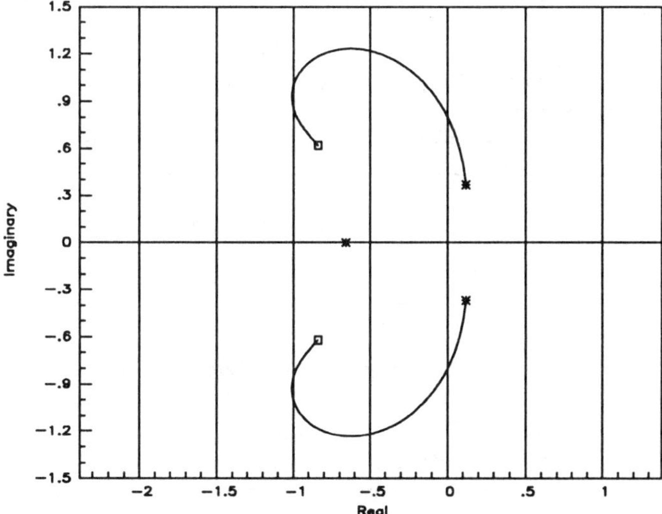

Figure 8-2 Root locus for state feedback design.

The GM and PM are given by

```
< > [gm,pm,wpc,wgc]=margin(w,mc1,pc1)
```

PM =
69.8569

GM =
-19.3071

WGC =
3.6519

WPC =
.8030

You have to be careful interpreting these answers. From the root locus, the system is always stable for high gain; hence, the GM is infinite. Gain reduction margin (GRM), however is -19 dB, i.e., the gain can be reduced by a factor of 10 before instability occurs. It is this margin that the command has produced. The PM is 69 degrees.

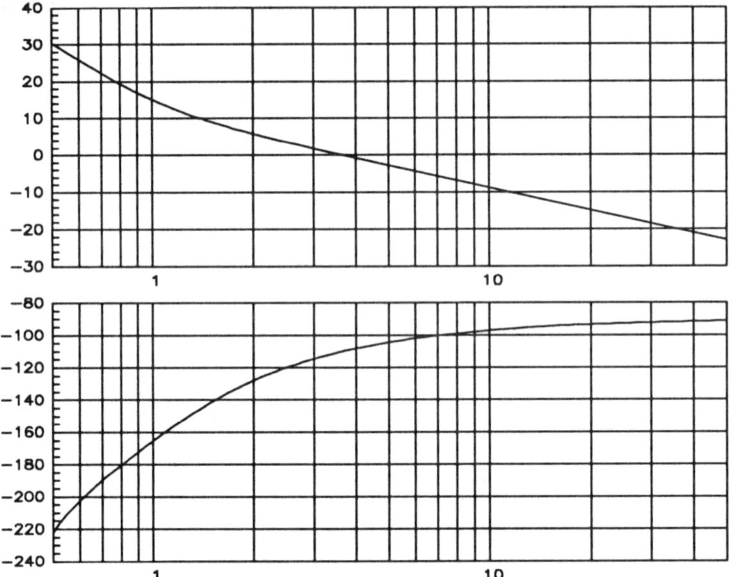

Figure 8-3 Bode plots for state feedback design.

Now we find compensator transfer function *K(s)*. To do that requires inversion of *G(s)*. If *G(s)* is strictly proper, its inverse will be improper and will not have a state space representation; we will use transfer functions indirectly to do this. Note, if we denote *G(s)* by *ng/dg* and *G(s)K(s)* by *ngk/dgk*, we have

$$K(s) = \frac{G(s)\,K(s)}{G(s)} = \frac{ngk/dgk}{ng/dg} = \frac{(ngk)\,(dg)}{(ng)\,(dgk)}$$

We will try to use the *convolve* and *minimal* commands to perform polynomial multiplication and pole zero cancellations to find *K(s)*. If *K(s)* is improper (which it usually is for state feedback), the above will not work and has to be done partially manually (the corresponding commands are commented out in the State Feedback Exec File in the Appendix to prevent error messages).

```
< > [ng,dg]=tform(s,ns);
< > [ngk1,dgk1]=tform(sgk1,nsgk1);
< > nk1=conv(ngk1,dg);
```

```
< > dk1=conv(dgk1,ng);
< > [nk1,dk1]=minimal(nk1,dk1);
< > roots(dk1)
```

ANS =
.2500 - 2.4975j
. 2500 + 2.4975j

```
< > roots(nk1)
```

ANS =
-.8388 + .6215j
-.8388 - .6215j

Hence, $K(s) = \dfrac{0.36\,(s + 0.83 \pm j\,0.62\,)}{s - 0.25 \pm j\,2.49}$ and $G(s) = \dfrac{9.8\,(s - 0.25 \pm j\,2.49)}{(s + 0.65)\,(s - 0.11 \pm j\,0.36)}$

We notice that $G(s)$ has two RHP zeros, and $K(s)$ effectively cancels these and instead puts two zeros in the LHP to pull the RHP poles into the LHP. The result of this is an unstable compensator that is undesirable, because any disturbance or noise at the input of $K(s)$ gets highly amplified and may create saturation problems.

Systems with unstable compensators are only *conditionally stable*. Of course an unstable compensator is not surprising, because, after all, stability of the compensator was not ever used as a constraint on design. Note that we do not build $K(s)$. We implement the design with the state feedback gain k. Finally, notice that $K(s)$ has no classical counterpart. The closed loop transfer function and its poles and zeros are found by

```
< > st1=[a-b*k b;c 0];nst1=ns;
< > clp1=eig(st1,nst1)
```

The preceding command gives eigenvalues of "A" matrix of st1, i.e., the closed loop poles.

CLP1 =
-1.0000 + 1.0000j
-1.0000 - 1.0000j
-2.0000 + .0000j

```
< > clz1=zeros(st1,nst1)
```

The *zeros* command gives zeros of st1, i.e., closed loop zeros.

CLZ1 =
.25000 + 2.4975j
.25000 - 2.4975j

The closed loop poles are indeed in their specified locations. Finally, the step response is found and appears in Figure 8-4. Note, we have scaled the output to eliminate steady state error to step inputs (this is just a lazy way of finding $\bar{N}$!). The percent overshoot is 2.2.

```
< > [t,yc1]=step(st1,nst1,10); yc1=yc1/yc1(100);pos1=max(yc1)
```

POS1 =
2.2114

The design has resulted in a system that is very stable; GM = ∞, GRM = -19 dB, and PM= 70°, with little overshoot, and settling time of about 4 sec. If the states are available for measurement and feedback, this design would be acceptable.

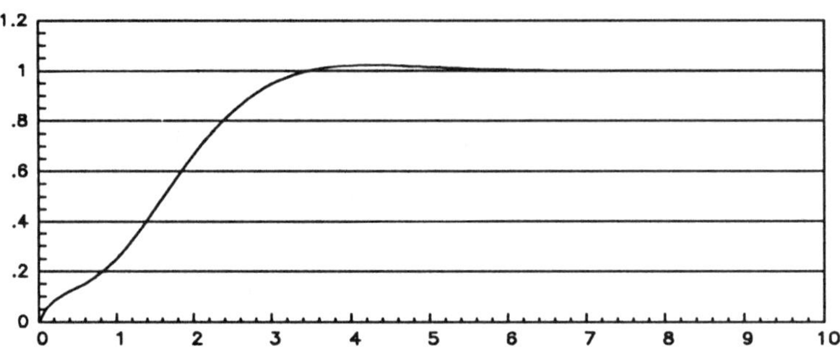

Figure 8-4 Step response for state feedback design.

8.2 Observer Design

The major problem with state feedback is that it is not usually practical! That is, in a typical system with many states, it is simply not possible or practical to sense all the states and feed them back. Constant state feedback requires ideal sensors (infinite bandwidth) for all states, whereas real sensors have limited bandwidth. Sometimes the states are not actual physical variables of the system and as such may not be measurable. Even if the states are actual physical variables, it may not be technologically possible, or economically feasible, to measure all the states. Besides the measurement problem, each feedback loop requires actual hardware (or additional software in computer control), adding to the complexity and cost, and reducing overall reliability of the system. If one sensor fails, the whole system may become unstable. In reality, only certain states or combinations of them are measurable as outputs. Consequently, any practical compensator must only rely on system outputs and inputs for compensation; this is called output feedback.

The concept of the observer is both ingenious and simple. If we do not have the states, is it possible to use system inputs and outputs to estimate the states? The answer is yes. This state estimator is called an "observer" by D. Luenberger, who originally proposed and developed its theory [L64]. The idea is that if we have all system parameters, we can always simulate the model on an analog or digital computer. Even though we do not have access to system states, we have full access to the states of our simulation. Letting $\hat{x}$ denote the state estimates, we have

$$\dot{x} = Ax + Bu\,, \quad x(0) = x_o \qquad \text{and} \qquad \dot{\hat{x}} = A\hat{x} + Bu\,, \quad \hat{x}(0) = \hat{x}_o$$

$$\text{let} \quad \tilde{x} = x - \hat{x} \ \text{ then } \ \dot{\tilde{x}} = A\tilde{x}\,, \quad \tilde{x}(0) = x_o - \hat{x}_o \ \rightarrow \ \tilde{x}(t) = e^{At}\tilde{x}_o$$

Hence, the observer error defined above approaches zero as long as the original system is stable, or the initial conditions of the observer and the system are the same. We do not know the initial conditions of the system, however. If we did, we could have just solved the system equations and computed the states for all time. Therefore, the main problem is estimating the initial conditions of the system. Now note that the above proposed observer is open loop, i.e., it does not use the information provided by the system outputs. It seems reasonable that if we compare the system output with the output of the observer and use it as a correction mechanism, this should stabilize the error dynamics. After all we know that feedback can stabilize unstable systems. So, we propose a closed loop observer

$$\dot{\hat{x}} = A\hat{x} + Bu + L(y - C\hat{x})\,, \qquad \hat{x}(0) = \hat{x}_o$$

Then the state equations for the error system become

$$\dot{\tilde{x}} = (A - LC)\tilde{x}\,, \qquad \tilde{x}(0) = \tilde{x}_o$$

Now if we can choose L such that the eigenvalues of $(A - LC)$ can be arbitrarily placed in the complex plane, our problem is solved. We can guarantee the observer errors to converge to zero for any initial conditions. The above property is the dual of the controllability property and is called *observability*. It is loosely defined as the ability to estimate the system states from a record of output measurements. In the context of our discussion, observability is the ability to place the eigenvalues of $(A - LC)$ arbitrarily by using some gain L. Observability can be mathematically tested by checking the rank of the observability matrix $\boldsymbol{O}$. If the rank is equal to n (dimension of the A matrix), we say the system is observable. The *observability matrix* is defined by

$$\boldsymbol{O} = \begin{bmatrix} C \\ CA \\ CA^2 \\ \cdot \\ \cdot \\ \cdot \\ CA^{n-1} \end{bmatrix}$$

We say that controllability and observability are *dual* notions. By this we mean that if we transpose the C matrix (rank remains the same), and replace A' with A and B' with C, we get $\boldsymbol{O}$. The dual notion of *stabilizability* is called *detectability*. We say a system is *detectable* if the unstable modes are observable or equivalently the unobservable modes are stable.

A consequence of duality is that the same algorithm can be used to solve both problems. For instance, to solve for L, the observer gain, we use the *poleplace* command as shown below

```
< > L=poleplace(A', C',op)
```

where op is the vector of desired observer poles. The observer gain L will be given as a row vector and has to be transposed. The same comments made about the choice of controller poles apply to observer poles also, with the modification that observer poles must be several times faster than controller poles to ensure fast convergence of the estimation process. If the poles are too far in the LHP, values of k and L will be large and may cause saturation problems and even instability; also, the observer bandwidth increases, which causes noise problems. Hence, proper judgment has to be used by the designer.

Now that we know how to estimate the states, let us go back to the control problem. The idea is that we can use the estimated states in lieu of the actual states for state feedback. This renders state feedback practical. How can we guarantee closed loop stability of the overall system, however? After all, we are not using the states but only their estimates. The answer is that there is a separation between the control problem and the observer problem. That is, we can find the controller gain assuming the states are available, and then design an observer to estimate these states and use the estimates in place of the states. The closed loop poles of the system will be the union of the controller poles and observer poles. This result is commonly known as the *Separation Property* and is a cornerstone result of modern control theory. The separation property can be shown by combining the plant, controller, and observer error systems; we get

$$\begin{bmatrix} \dot{x} \\ \dot{\tilde{x}} \end{bmatrix} = \begin{bmatrix} A - Bk & -Bk \\ 0 & A - LC \end{bmatrix} \begin{bmatrix} x \\ \tilde{x} \end{bmatrix}$$

We recall from matrix theory that eigenvalues of a block triangular matrix are the union of the eigenvalues of the diagonal blocks, hence, the separation property.

Transfer Function Analysis

The compensator (combination of state feedback and observer) equation is

$$\dot{\hat{x}} = A\hat{x} + Bu + L(y - C\hat{x})$$

$$u = -k\hat{x}$$

Substituting for u in the observer, taking Laplace transforms and solving for $K(s)$, we get

$$K(s) = k\,(sI - A + Bk + LC)^{-1} L \quad \rightarrow \quad SK = \begin{bmatrix} A - Bk - LC & L \\ k & 0 \end{bmatrix}$$

Note that even though *(A - Bk)* and *(A - LC)* are stable, the compensator matrix *(A - Bk - LC)* may be unstable. This will result in a conditionally stable system as can be seen from the root locus plot in the following example. Other problems with observer based controllers are poor robustness (i.e. sensitivity to parameter uncertainty and variations [DS79]), reduced stability margins compared with state feedback, and compensator complexity. Essentially for an nth order system, we obtain an nth order compensator that may be too complex and expensive. It should be mentioned that some of the above shortcomings can be corrected using modified and more advanced design methods.

The loop transfer function can be obtained by cascading *G(s)* and *K(s)* using the *series* command. The closed loop transfer function is obtained by introducing an external reference input with a gain adjusted to produce zero steady state error to step inputs (*Note*: the *feedback* command can be used to find the closed loop transfer function).

$$u = -K\hat{x} + \overline{N}v$$

$$\begin{bmatrix} \dot{x} \\ \dot{\hat{x}} \end{bmatrix} = \begin{bmatrix} A & -Bk \\ LC & A - Bk - LC \end{bmatrix} \begin{bmatrix} x \\ \hat{x} \end{bmatrix} + \begin{bmatrix} B\overline{N} \\ B\overline{N} \end{bmatrix} v \quad \rightarrow \quad ST = \begin{bmatrix} A & -Bk & B\overline{N} \\ LC & A - Bk - LC & B\overline{N} \\ C & 0 & 0 \end{bmatrix}$$

Example 8.2 Observer Based Design

We will design an observer based controller for Example 8.1. The observer poles are selected to be at $\{-3 \pm 3j, -4\}$, three times faster than the controller poles.

```
< > op=[-3+3*jay  -4];
< > l=polep(a',c',op)
```

```
L  =
5.4664  4.6762  9.5800
```

```
< > l=l';             // L must be a column vector
```

Observer transfer function is

```
< > sk2=[a-b*k-l*c l;k 0];
```

After finding poles and zeros of the compensator, we get

$$K_2(s) = \frac{7.85\,(s + 0.64 \pm j\,0.36\,)}{(s + 14.37\,)\,(s - 0.39 \pm j\,4.07\,)}$$

Comparing $K_2(s)$ with classical lag-lead type compensators, we note that in classical design, compensator poles and zeros are restricted to be on the negative real axis, whereas in state space design, compensator poles and zeros are not restricted and fall anywhere on the complex plane. This extra freedom leads to arbitrary closed loop pole placement, whereas the compensator may turn out to be unstable.

Note: MATRIXx has a command called *lqgcomp* that can be used to compute *K(s)*. It has the following syntax

```
LQGCOMP
Syntax:    [SK,NSK]=LQGCOMP(S,NS,K,L)
             K - Regulator gain matrix.
             L - Observer gain matrix.
```

Now we find the open loop transfer function using the *series* command: *G(s)K(s)*.

```
< > [sgk2,nsgk2]=series(sh2,3,s,3);
< > [w,mc2,pc2]=bode(sgk2,nsgk2,.1,100);
< > rlocus(sgk2,nsgk2, 'nopattern')
```

The root locus and Bode plots are shown in Figures 8-5 and 8-6.

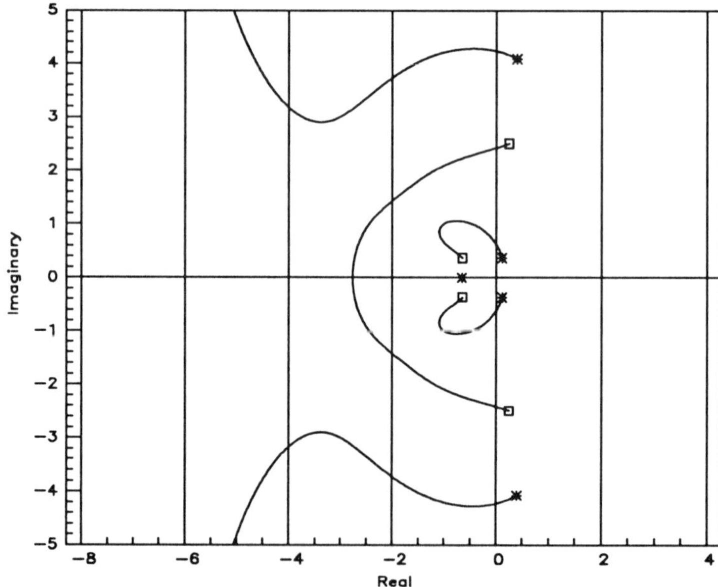

Figure 8-5 Root locus for observer based design.

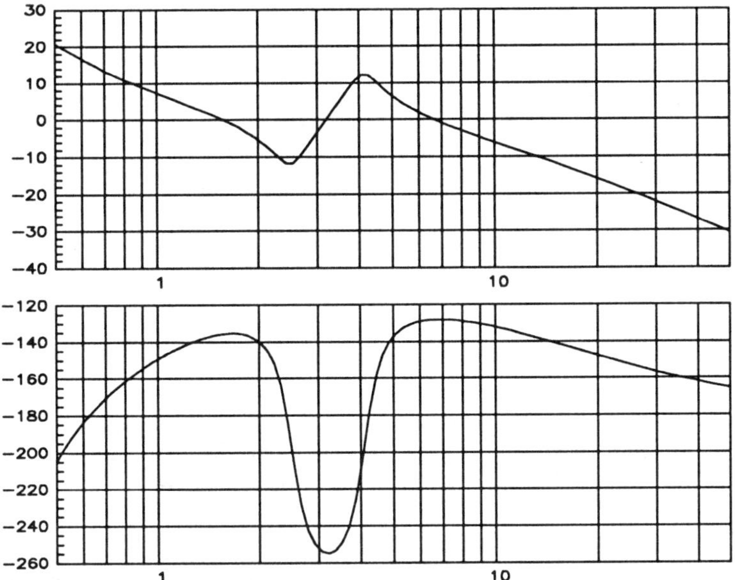

Figure 8-6 Bode plots for observer based design.

Note that the root locus shows the conditional stability of the system. The system becomes unstable for low and high gains. Using interactive root locus we can find the lower and upper limits of gain to be 0.24 and 3.81, resulting in GM of 11.6 dB and GRM of 12.3 dB. The PM is obtained from the Bode plot as 44 degrees. Note that Bode plots for systems with RHP poles and zeros give multiple positive and negative GMs and PMs and as such have to be interpreted carefully. The combination of Nyquist plot and root locus gives the correct answer. The margin command gives the following answer (only the margins are shown).

```
< > [gm2,pm2,wpc2,wgc2]=margin(w,mc2,pc2)
```

```
 PM2    =
 44.3828
 -74.7706
51.7878
 GM2    =
 -15.8048
  11.5472
 -12.1516
```

We will use the *feedback* command to find the closed loop transfer function, *T(s)*, and *eig* and *zeros* commands to find closed loop poles and zeros.

```
< > [st2,nst2]=feedback(s,ns,sk2,ns)
< > clp2=eig(st2,nst2), clz2=zeros(st2,nst2)
```

```
CLP2    =
-1.0000 + 1.0000j
-1.0000 - 1.0000j
-2.0000 +  .0000j
-4.0000 +  .0000j
-3.0000 - 3.0000j
-3.0000 + 3.0000j
CLZ2    =
.2500 + 2.4975j
.2500 - 2.4975j
-14.3751 + .0000j
.3975 + 4.0793j
.3975 - 4.0793j
```

Note that closed loop zeros are the combination of open loop zeros and compensator poles as expected. The closed loop poles are the union of controller and observer poles as expected from the separation property. The step response is given by

```
< > [t,yc2]=step(st2,nst2,10);
< > yc2=yc2/yc2(100);   // to scale the output to get zero steady state error to step
```

The step response is shown in Figure 8-7. We note from the margins that the addition of the observer has reduced the stability margins of the system. The settling time, peak time, and overshoot (2%) are slightly higher in the observer based case.

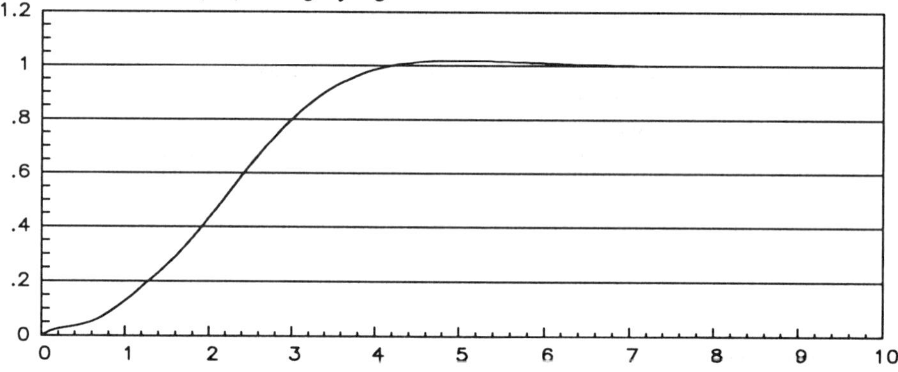

Figure 8-7 Step response for observer based design.

To see how well the observer estimates track the actual states, we will plot the states and estimates together in Figure 8-8. Note that the closed loop system matrix, `st`, is the same ST matrix that is shown before this example. The only difference is that we choose the output matrix, C, as a 6 by 6 identity matrix to pick out all three states and estimates. The initial conditions for the system and observer are chosen as [1, 2, 3] and [-1, -2, -3], respectively.

```
< > st=[[a, -b*k;l*c, a-b*k-l*c], 0*ones(6,1); eye(6), 0*ones(6,1)];
< > [t,x_xhat]=lsim(st,6,ones(100,1),0.02,[1,2,3,-1,-2,-3]);
```

```
< > plot(t,[[x_xhat(:,1:3)],[x_xhat(:,4:6)]],'strip2 nogrid')
```

Note, because the real part of the observer eigenvalues is -3, we expect the observer to converge in about 1.5 sec, which is indeed the case.

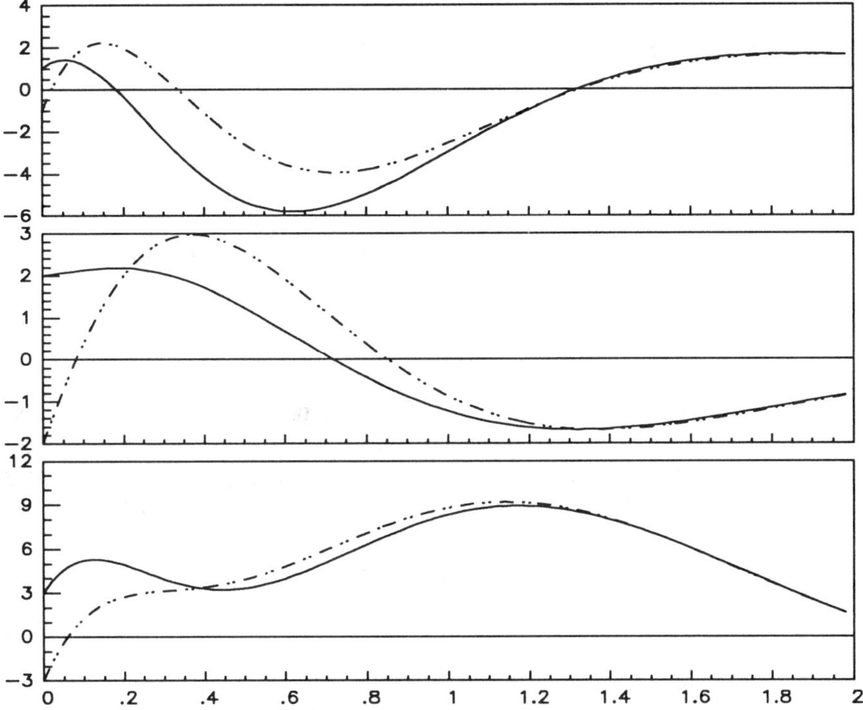

Figure 8-8 Plots of states and observer estimates (solid lines are states; dashed lines are estimates).

8.3 Reduced Order Observer Design

The observer introduced in the previous section has the same order as the system and is referred to as the *full order observer*. If the system has n states and m measurement outputs, it seems redundant to estimate the known states. For instance if $y = x_1$, a full order observer estimates x_1, even though it is clearly unnecessary. Theoretically, all we need is a reduced order observer to estimate the unknown states. This results in an (n-m) dimensional observer, first introduced by D. Luenberger [L64], and referred to as *reduced order* (or *Luenberger*) *observer*. This reduction in order leads to simpler and more economical compensators. If the number of measurements, m, is large, the benefits are substantial.

The derivation of the reduced order observer starts by defining a linear transformation of the states

$$z = Tx\,, \quad \text{where } \dim(T) = (n-m)\times n\,, \quad \text{and } \dim(z) = (n-m)\times 1$$

where T is any matrix such that

$$E = \begin{bmatrix} C \\ T \end{bmatrix} \text{ is nonsingular . Let } E^{-1} = [\,P \mid M\,]$$

Combining y and z, we get

$$\begin{bmatrix} y \\ z \end{bmatrix} = \begin{bmatrix} C \\ T \end{bmatrix} x \quad \rightarrow \quad x = \begin{bmatrix} C \\ T \end{bmatrix}^{-1} \begin{bmatrix} y \\ z \end{bmatrix} = [P \mid M] \begin{bmatrix} y \\ z \end{bmatrix} = P\,y + M\,z$$

If rank $(C) = m$, the above inverse exists. Now, suppose we build a full order observer to estimate z (the observer dimension = dimension of $z = n - m$), then we can clearly generate estimates of x from

$$\hat{x} = P\,y + M\,\hat{z}, \quad \text{where } \hat{z} \text{ is the estimate of } z$$

Therefore, all we have to do is to design an observer to estimate z. To do this, we need to know its dynamics, i.e., a differential equation governing the behavior of z. We obtain a differential equation for z by premultiplying the original state equations by E. This simply corresponds to a change of basis and, hence, a new realization for the system.

$$E\,\dot{x} = EA\,x + EB\,u$$

Substituting for x and E, we get

$$E\,\dot{x} = \begin{bmatrix} C \\ T \end{bmatrix} \dot{x} = \begin{bmatrix} \dot{y} \\ \dot{z} \end{bmatrix} = \begin{bmatrix} C \\ T \end{bmatrix} A\,x + \begin{bmatrix} C \\ T \end{bmatrix} B\,u = \begin{bmatrix} C \\ T \end{bmatrix} A\,[\,P \mid M\,] \begin{bmatrix} y \\ z \end{bmatrix} + \begin{bmatrix} C \\ T \end{bmatrix} B\,u$$

Therefore, we get

$$\begin{bmatrix} \dot{y} \\ \dot{z} \end{bmatrix} = \begin{bmatrix} CAP & CAM \\ TAP & TAM \end{bmatrix} \begin{bmatrix} y \\ z \end{bmatrix} + \begin{bmatrix} CB \\ TB \end{bmatrix} u \stackrel{\Delta}{=} \begin{bmatrix} A_{11} & A_{12} \\ A_{21} & A_{22} \end{bmatrix} \begin{bmatrix} y \\ z \end{bmatrix} + \begin{bmatrix} B_1 \\ B_2 \end{bmatrix} u$$

The differential equation for z is given by

$$\dot{z} = A_{22}\,z + (\,A_{21}\,y + B_2\,u\,)$$

Now, a full order observer for z is designed following the approach in the previous section. Namely, we copy the differential equation for z, replace z by $\hat{z}$, and add an error term for correction.

$$\dot{\hat{z}} = A_{22}\,\hat{z} + (\,A_{21}\,y + B_2\,u\,) + L\,(y - C\,\hat{x}\,)$$

The first term within parentheses is a known quantity and is considered as an input to the observer; the second term is the correction term to stabilize the observer error system. Note that because $[P \mid M]$ is inverse of E, we have $CP = I$ and $CM = 0$, hence,

$$y - C\hat{x} = y - C(Py + M\hat{z}) = y - CPy - CM\hat{z} = y - y - 0 = 0$$

So this correction term provides no correction after all. We recall from classical control that sometimes when output feedback alone is not effective, feeding back the output and its derivative (i.e., rate feedback) may help. Theoretically if y is available, we can assume that its derivatives are also available. Hence, we will instead use the derivative of the measurements as the correction term. The differential equation for y is available from the transformed system equations given above

$$\dot{y} = A_{11}\,y + A_{12}\,z + B_1\,u$$

Collecting all the known quantities on one side and using them as "observer output" for the correction term, we get the sought-after reduced order observer (dim = n - m).

$$\dot{\hat{z}} = A_{22}\,\hat{z} + (A_{21}\,y + B_2\,u) + L\,(\dot{y} - A_{11}\,y - B_1\,u - A_{12}\,z)$$

To show that this observer works, we need to demonstrate that the estimation errors approach zero asymptotically with time. This is verified by showing that the error system is asymptotically stable. By subtracting the differential equation for z from $\hat{z}$, we get the error system dynamics.

$$\dot{\tilde{z}} = (A_{22} - L\,A_{12})\,\tilde{z}$$

The error system contains an undetermined vector L (or matrix in the multi-output case). The question is whether L can be chosen to place the observer eigenvalues arbitrarily (or at least stabilize the error system). Luenberger has shown that observability of the pair (C, A) is equivalent to observability of (A_{12}, A_{22}). Therefore, by duality, L can be chosen to place eigenvalues of the error system anywhere in the complex plane. Also the *poleplace* command can be used to obtain L (SISO case only) by substituting A_{22} for A and A_{12} for C.

```
< > L = poleplace( A22',A12',op)
```

The $\dot{y}$ term in the above observer equation can be eliminated by a simple change of variable. Define w as

$$w \triangleq \hat{z} - L\,y$$

A bit of algebra results in the final form of the reduced order observer

$$\dot{w} = F\,w + D\,y + G\,u$$

$$\hat{x} = M\,w + N\,y$$

where $F \triangleq A_{22} - L\,A_{12}\,,\;\; D \triangleq F\,L + A_{21} - L\,A_{11}\,,\;\; G \triangleq B_2 - L\,B_1\,,\;\; N \triangleq P + M\,L$

Note: In the special case in which C has the following form, T can be selected as

$$C = [\,I_m \;\mid\; 0_{m,n-m}\,] \;\rightarrow\; T = [\,0_{n-m,m} \;\mid\; I_{n-m}\,] \;\rightarrow\; E = I_n$$

In this case, no transformation is needed, and A and B can be directly partitioned to get A_{11}, A_{12}, and other required matrices. Also observe that the measurements appear directly in the output of the observer; hence, measurement noise can pass through the observer, and we conclude that the choice of a reduced order observer has to be made carefully in cases in which noise may be a problem.

The separation property also holds in the reduced order case. It can be derived by combining the closed loop system and error system equations

$$u = -\,k\,\hat{x}\,,\quad \dot{x} = A\,x - B\,k\,\hat{x}\,,\;\text{ it can be shown that }\;\hat{x} = x - M\,\tilde{z}$$

$$\begin{bmatrix}\dot{x}\\ \dot{\tilde{z}}\end{bmatrix} = \begin{bmatrix}A - Bk & BkM\\ 0 & A_{22} - L\,A_{12}\end{bmatrix}\begin{bmatrix}x\\ \tilde{z}\end{bmatrix}$$

Therefore, the closed loop eigenvalues are the union of the controller and observer eigenvalues.

Transfer Function Analysis

The compensator transfer function is derived by substituting for u in the observer equation

$$u = -\,k\,\hat{x} = -\,k\,M\,w - k\,N\,y$$

$$\begin{aligned}\dot{w} &= (\,F - GkM\,)\,w + (\,D - GkN\,)\,y\\ u &= -\,k\,\hat{x} - kN\,y\end{aligned} \quad\rightarrow\quad SK = \begin{bmatrix}F - GkM & D - GkN\\ -\,kM & -\,kN\end{bmatrix}$$

Note that the *lqgcomp* command cannot directly be used in this case; the above formula has to be used instead. The *series* and *feedback* commands can be used, however, to obtain loop transfer and closed loop transfer functions. The closed loop transfer function can be obtained directly by combining the closed loop system and observer equations using an external reference input v

$$u = -k\hat{x} + \overline{N}\,v$$

$$\begin{bmatrix} \dot{x} \\ \dot{w} \end{bmatrix} = \begin{bmatrix} A - BkNC & -BkM \\ DC - GkNC & F - GkM \end{bmatrix} \begin{bmatrix} x \\ w \end{bmatrix} + \begin{bmatrix} B\overline{N} \\ G\overline{N} \end{bmatrix} v \;\rightarrow\; ST = \begin{bmatrix} A - BkNC & -BkM & B\overline{N} \\ DC - GkNC & F - GkM & G\overline{N} \\ C & 0 & 0 \end{bmatrix}$$

Example 8.3 Reduced Order Observer Based Compensator Design

The helicopter example is redesigned using a reduced order observer. It is assumed that the third state variable (i.e., the horizontal velocity) is being measured; hence, we build a second order observer yielding a second order compensator. The observer poles are placed at {-3±j3}. The first step is to choose T. Almost any random matrix will do (as long as E is nonsingular). Then E is inverted, and P and M are peeled off from the inverse of E. Finally, the new realization partitions (A_{11}, A_{12}, etc.) are computed .

```
< > t=[0 1 0 ;1 0 0];
< > e=[c ; t];
< > ei=inv(e);
< > [mm,nn]=size(c);       // dimensions of c are needed to split e^-1
< > p=ei(1:nn,1:mm); m=ei(1:nn,mm+1:nn)
< > a11=c*a*p; a12=c*a*m; a21=t*a*p; a22=t*a*m; b1=c*b; b2=t*b;
```

We are now ready to find observer gain, parameters, and compensator transfer function.

```
< > l=polep(a22',a12',[-3+3*jay]); l=l';
< > f=a22-l*a12; g=b2-l*b1;d=f*l+(a21-l*a11);n=p+m*l;
< > sk3=[f-g*k*m , d-g*k*n ; k*m, k*n]; nsk3=nn-mm
```

After computing poles and zeros of the compensator, we get

$$K_3(s) = \frac{1.56\,(s + 0.714 \pm j\,0.44)}{(\,s - 2.89 \pm j\,5.27\,)}$$

We will find the open loop transfer function next in order to obtain root locus, Bode plots, and stability margins.

```
< > [sgk3,nsgk3]=series(s,ns,sk3,nsk3);
< > [w,mc3,pc3]=bode(sgk3,nsgk3,0.1,100);
< > rlocus(sgk3,nsgk3, 'nopattern')
```

The root locus and Bode plots are shown in Figures 8-9 and 8-10.

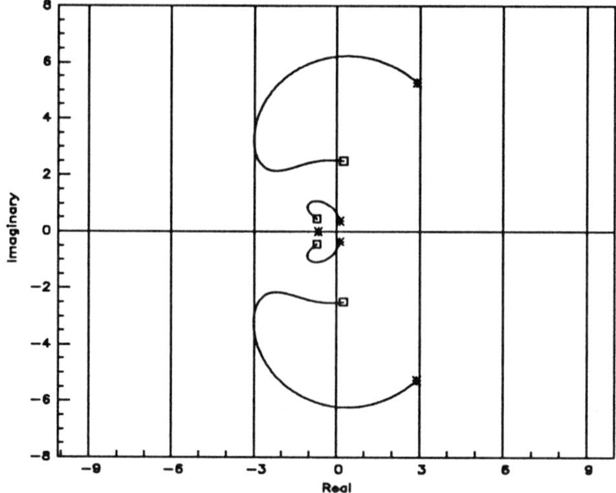

Figure 8-9 Root locus for reduced order observer design.

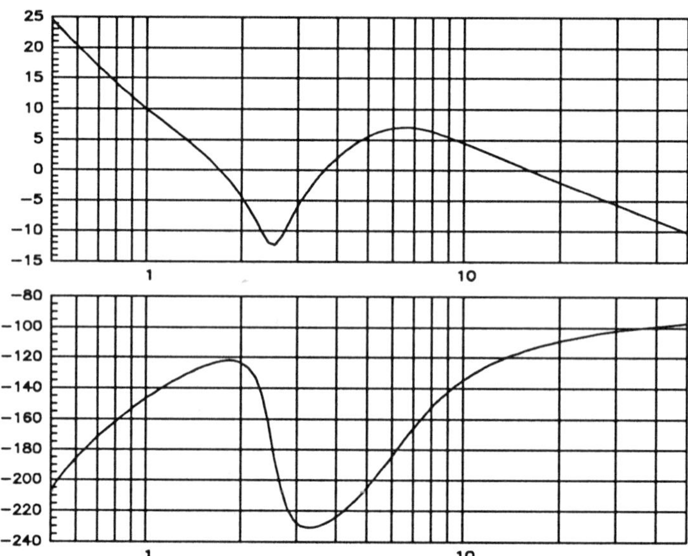

Figure 8-10 Bode plots for reduced order observer design.

Using interactive root locus and the *margin* command, it is verified that the GM is 12.2 dB, and the GRM is -7 dB; so the system is conditionally stable for $0.44 < k < 4.14$.

```
< > [gm3,pm3,wpc3,wgc3]=margin(w,mc3,pc3)
```

```
PM3 =
57.1651
-48.6265
65.5654
GM3 =
-18.9375
12.2086
-7.0039
```

Compared with the full order case, PM and GM have increased, but the GRM is better in the full order case. We next obtain the closed loop transfer function, its poles and zeros, and step response, shown in Figure 8-11.

```
< > [st3,nst3]=feedback(s,ns,sk3,nsk3);
< > [t,yc3]=step(st3,nst3,10); yc3=yc3/yc3(100);
< > clp3=eig(st3,nst3), clz3=zeros(st3,nst3), pos3=max(yc3)
```

```
CLP3 =
-1.0000 + 1.0000j
-1.0000 - 1.0000j
-2.0000 + .0000j
-3.0000 - 3.0000j
-3.0000 + 3.0000j
CLZ3 =
.2500 + 2.4975j
.2500 - 2.4975j
2.8907 + 5.2744j
2.8907 - 5.2744j
```

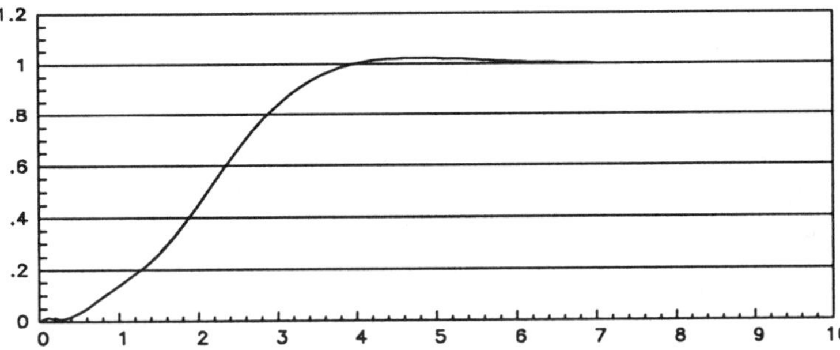

Figure 8-11 Step response for reduced order observer design.

The presence of the observer will result in performance degradation because of incorrect observer initial conditions. To see this, we will use the *lsim* command to find the step response with nonzero initial conditions [1,2,3,1,2].

```
< > [t,yc33]=lsim(st3,nst3,ones(100,1),0.1,[1 2 3 1 2]);
```

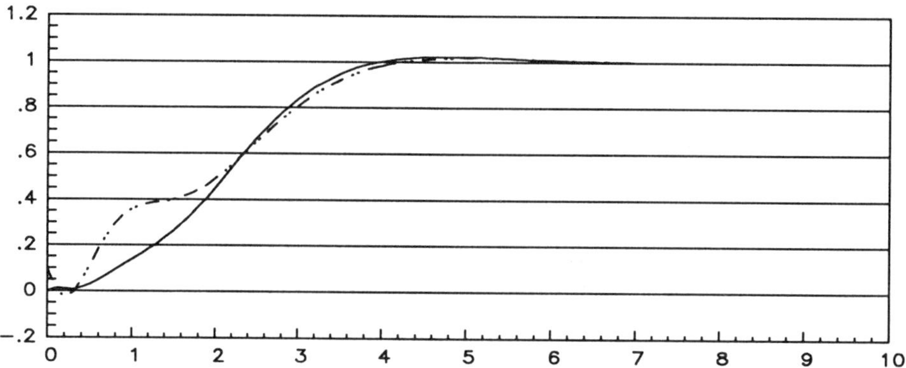

Figure 8-12 Step response for reduced order observer with nonzero initial conditions.

The step response is shown in Figure 8-12. For your convenience, the *execfiles* used to perform the designs in this chapter are included in the Appendix.

Finally, we plot the states and estimates together. Recall that the closed loop system equations are (with no input)

$$\begin{bmatrix} \dot{x} \\ \dot{w} \end{bmatrix} = \begin{bmatrix} A - BkNC & -BkM \\ DC - GkNC & F - GkM \end{bmatrix} \begin{bmatrix} x \\ w \end{bmatrix}$$

Because, $\hat{x} = N\,y + M\,w = N\,C\,x + M\,w$, we can peel out the states and estimates by computing the simulation output matrix from

$$\begin{bmatrix} x \\ \hat{x} \end{bmatrix} = \begin{bmatrix} I & 0 \\ N\,C & M \end{bmatrix} \begin{bmatrix} x \\ w \end{bmatrix}$$

We now choose the system initial state as $x(0) = x_o = [\ 1, 2, 3]$, and the observer initial state as $[\ -1, -2, -3]$. The initial conditions of w are computed from

$$w = z - L\,y = T\,x - L\,C\,x \quad \rightarrow \quad w(0) = (T - L\,C)\,x(0)$$

```
< > a_cl= [a-b*k*n*c, -b*k*m; d*c-g*k*n*c,  f-g*k*m]
< > b_cl=0*ones(5,1); c_cl=[eye(3), 0*ones(3,2); n*c, m];
< > s_cl=[a_cl, b_cl; c_cl,  0*ones(6,1)]
< > xo=[1; 2; 3];wo=(t*-1*c)*xo
< > [t,x_xhat]=lsim(s_cl,5,0*ones(100,1),0.02,[xo;wo]);
< > plot(t,[x_xhat(:,1:3) x_xhat(:,4:6)],'strip2 nogrid ')
```

The plots are shown in Figure 8-13. The observer converges in about 1.6 sec. Note, the third state is exact, because it is not estimated.

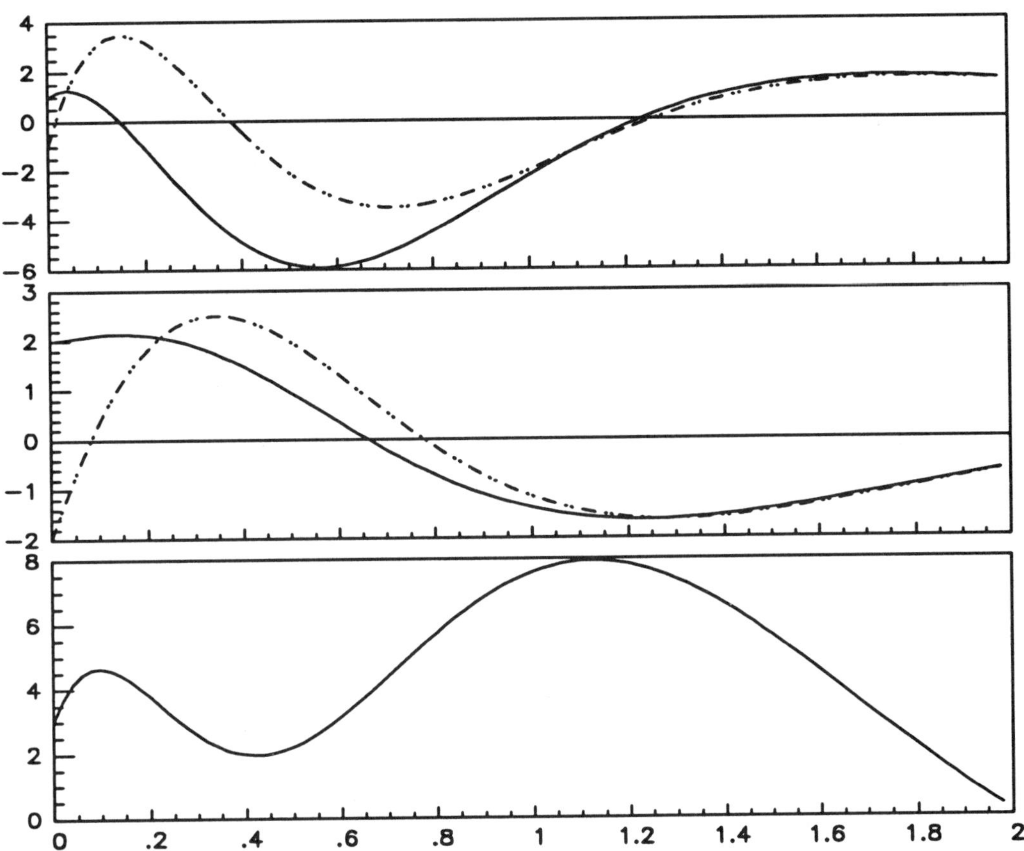

Figure 8-13 Plots of states and estimates using a reduced order obsever (solid lines are states).

8.4 Comments Regarding State Space Design

The techniques discussed in this chapter are very powerful and have expanded the range of problems that can be solved. We would like to discuss briefly some of the advantages and limitations of pole placement here.

The main advantage, as the name implies, is arbitrary pole placement. No matter where the open loop poles and zeros are, we can arbitrarily place the closed loop poles. This gives us a good deal of control over time response of systems. If all the states can be sensed and fed back economically, state feedback can usually provide an easy and adequate design. Otherwise, observers can be implemented to estimate the states. Observers increase the complexity of the system, and they add to the overall cost. More components, more connections, or more lines of code in the digital case translate into less reliability and increased maintenance costs. From a control design viewpoint, observers generally reduce the stability margins. They may also introduce RHP poles or zeros, resulting in conditionally stable systems that may not be desirable. Reduced order observers also generally have a higher bandwidth, making the system more susceptible to high frequency noise. Therefore the choice between full or reduced order observers has to be made carefully. In general, several designs must be performed and time response, stability margins, conditional stability, bandwidth, compensator order, component counts, reliability, sensitivity, etc have to be compared.

Time response depends not only on closed loop poles but also on closed loop zeros; as you may have noticed, we have no control over the zeros. It is also possible to modify our techniques to achieve zero placement, but the procedures become somewhat involved in state space [FPE91]. Transfer function based algebraic techniques are also available that allow simultaneous pole and zero placement. These methods are discussed in Chapter 10. Another disadvantage is that the compensator has the same dimension as the system. This may not be necessary. For example, a large order system may be compensated adequately using low order lead-lag type classical compensators. Therefore, classical techniques should be tried at the first stage. If the results are not satisfactory, try state space methods. Also, advanced model reduction methods are available (MATRIXx includes some of these algorithms; see the manual or use the *what* command). These algorithms allow lower order compensators with some performance degradation.

Two other important issues that were not discussed in this chapter are selection of poles and MIMO (multivariable) systems. The issue of pole selection is discussed in Chapter 10.

Regarding multivariable systems, although techniques discussed in the present chapter apply theoretically, the issues are more complex. The control and observer gains are matrices in this case. If the system has n states, and p inputs, the control gain matrix k will have $p*m$ elements. Selecting n eigenvalues gives n constraints, so we have $p*n$ equations in n unknowns with an infinite number of solutions. Control gain k is no longer unique. Similar situation exists for the observer problem. In fact the *poleplace* command only solves the SISO case. So, how do we select a unique gain?

There are several possibilities. One solution is to use the extra degrees of freedom to place both closed loop system eigenvalues and eigenvectors. This is usually called *eigen-structure assignment* and has found some applications in aerospace control problems [DH88]. Another solution is to find the optimal control gain. A special case of this approach, which is very popular and has found many applications in multivariable systems, is the *LQR/LQG* approach. MATRIXx has several commands relating to *LQR/LQG*, which are available in the Robust Control Module.

Finally, it must be noted that because state space methods are time domain design techniques, frequency domain specifications such as stability margins can not usually be met as specified. In fact, an observer based compensated system can be dangerously close to instability or very sensitive to model uncertainties [DS79]. The lack of robustness of these techniques must be taken seriously because models are rarely perfect. A recent solution to this problem is to apply state space based algorithms and methods that improve system robustness. These methods are generally called *robust control*. Refer to [M89], [F87], [BPDGS91], and [CS91] for these more advanced methods.

8.5 Appendix: Design Programs

1. State Feedback Design Exec File

```
// The following parameters must be previously defined:
//a,b,c,dd,ns,cp,wi,wf,tf,
k=polep(a,b,cp)
sgk1=[a b;k 0];
[w,mc1,pc1]=bode(sgk1,ns,wi,wf);pause;erase;
rlocus(sgk1,ns);pause;erase;
[ng,dg]=tform(s,ns);
[ngk1,dgk1]=tform(sgk1,ns);
nk1=conv(ngk1,dg);
dk1=conv(dgk1,ng);
//[nk1,dk1]=minim(nk1,dk11);
display(' the compensator zeros are');roots(nk1)
display(' the compensator poles are ');roots(dk1)
st1=[a-b*k b;c 0];
[t,yc1]=step(st1,ns,tf);yc1=yc1/yc1(100);
pos1=((max(yc1)-yc1(100))/yc1(100))*100;
display(' the pos is ');pos1
display(' the closed loop poles are');
clp1=eig(st1,ns)
display('the closed loop zeros are');
clz1=zeros(st1,ns)
return
```

2. Full Order Observer Based Design Exec File

```
// The following parameters must be previously defined:
//a,b,c,dd,ns,op,k,wi,wf,tf.
l=polepl(a',c',op);l=l'
s=[a b ; c dd];
[sk2,nsk2]=lqgcomp(s,ns,k,l);
compp2=eig(sk2,nsk2);compz2=zeros(sk2,nsk2);
display(' the compensator poles are ')
compp2
display(' the compensator zeros are ')
compz2
[sgk2,nsgk2]=series(sk2,nsk2,s,ns);
[w,mc2,pc2]=bode(sgk2,nsgk2,wi,wf);pause;erase;
rlocus(sgk2,nsgk2);pause;erase;
[st2,nst2]=feedback(s,ns,sk2,nsk2);
display(' the closed loop poles are ');clp2=eig(st2,nst2);
display(' the closed loop zeros are ');clz2=zeros(st2,nst2)
[t,yc2]=step(st2,nst2,tf);yc2=yc2/yc2(100);
```

```
pos2=(((max(yc2)-yc2(100))/yc2(100)))*100
[t,yc22]=lsim(st2,nst2,ones (100,1),.1,xo);
yc22=yc22/yc22(100);plot(t,yc22]);pause;eras;
return
```

3. Reduced Order Observer Based Design Exec File

```
// The following parameters must be previously defined:
//a,b,c,dd,ns,cp,opr,xor,wi,wf,tf
k=polep(a,b,cp);
inquire T ' enter T such that [c ; t] is nonsingular'
e=[c;t]; ei=inv(e);
[mm,nn]=size(c);
p=ei(:,1:mm); m=ei(:,mm+1:nn);
a11=c*a*p; a12=c*a*m; a21=t*a*p; a22=t*a*m; b1=c*b; b2=t*b;
lr=polep(a22',a12',opr); lr=lr'
f=a22-lr*a12; g=b2-lr*b1;d=f*lr+(a21-lr*a11);n=p+m*lr;
sk3=[f-g*k*m,d-g*k*n;k*m,k*n];nsk3=nn-mm;
compp3=eig(sk3,nsk3)); compz3=zeros(sk3,nsk3);
display(' the compensator poles are'); compp3
display(' the compensator zeros are'); compz3
[sgk3,nsgk3] =series(s,ns,sk3,nsk3);
rlocus(sgk3,nsgk3); pause; erase;
[w,mc3,pc3]=bode(sgk3,nsgk3,wi,wf); pause; erase;
[st3,nst3]=feedback(s,ns,sk3,nsk3);
[tt,yc3]=step(st3,nst3,10); yc3=yc3/yc3(100);
pos3=(((max(yc3)-yc3(100))/yc3(100)))*100
[tt,yc33]=lsim(st3,nst3,ones(100,1),.1, xor); yc33=yc33/yc33(100);
plot(tt,yc33);pause;erase;plot(tt,[yc3 yc33]);pause;eras;
display(' the closed loop poles are '); clp3=eig(st3,nst3)
display(' the closed loop zeros are '); clz3= zeros(st3,nst3)
return
```

8.6 Problems

8.1 Consider the system represented in state space form by $\{A, B, C, D\}$.

$$A = \begin{bmatrix} 0 & 1 & -1 \\ -2 & -3 & 0 \\ \beta & 1 & 1 \end{bmatrix}, \quad B = \begin{bmatrix} 1 \\ 0 \\ 0 \end{bmatrix}, \quad C = [0 \;\; 0 \;\; 1], \quad D = 0$$

a. For what values of β is the system controllable?

b. For what values of β is the system observable?

c. Find the transfer function of the system.

d. For what values of β is the system stabilizable?

e. For what values of β is the system detectable?

8.2 Consider the following plant:

$$A = \begin{bmatrix} 0 & 1 & 0 \\ 0 & 0 & 1 \\ 2 & 0 & -1 \end{bmatrix} \quad , \quad B = \begin{bmatrix} 1 \\ 2 \\ 0 \end{bmatrix} \quad , \quad C = [1 \ \ 0 \ \ 0] \quad , \quad D = 0$$

a. We want to place the closed loop poles at { -10, -1+j, -1-j }. Find the state feedback gain vector.

b. Obtain the equivalent transfer function of the compensator, root locus, Bode plots and closed loop step response. Tabulate the step response features (POS, T_p, T_s), phase and gain margins.

c. Design a full order observer. Choose observer poles at { -40, -4+j4, -4-j4 }. Repeat part b.

d. Design a reduced order observer. Choose observer poles at { -4+j4, -4-j4 }. Repeat part b.

e. Repeat part c with the observer poles at { -40, -1, -2 }.

f. Repeat part d with the observer poles at -1, -2.

Note: in parts e and f, the observer poles are chosen at the plant zeros. It is known that such a choice increases the robustness of the system. Because PM and GM are classical measures of robustness (protection against uncertainty), compare the margins in all cases. Does the choice of observer poles in parts e and f really improve the margins?

8.3 Consider the inverted pendulum described in Problem 7.5.

a. Find the eigenvalues of the linearized system. Is the system stable?

b. Determine the controllabilityof the system.

c. Determine the observability of the system if only the cart position is measured.

d. Determine the observability of the system if only the pendulum angle is measured.

e. Given the following values: $l = 1\ m$, $M = 1\ kg$, $m = 0.1\ kg$, $g = 9.8\ m/s^2$, use the *poleplace* command to find the controller gain that will place the closed loop poles at -1, -3, -2+2j, -2-2j. Obtain the root locus and Bode plots of the compensated system. Find the stability margins, GM and PM.

f. If we use full state feedback ($z = x$), find and plot $y(t)$ and $\theta(t)$ for the closed loop system if the pendulum is displaced by 0.01 radians, i.e., $\theta(0) = 0.01$.

8.4 Suppose in the preceding problem, we can only measure the cart position.

a. Design a full order observer to estimate the states. Select the observer poles at {-6+6j, -6-6j, -10, -20 }.

b. Obtain the root locus and Bode plots of the compensated system. Find the stability margins, GM and PM.

c. Find and plot $y(t)$ and $\theta(t)$ for the closed loop system if the pendulum is displaced by 0.01 radians, i.e., $\theta(0) = 0.01$.

8.5 Repeat Problem 8.4 using a reduced order observer with poles at { -6+6j, -6-6j, -10 }. Compare the results of the three designs: full state feedback, observer, reduced order observer.

8.6 A problem that is similar to the pendulum problem is the attempt to balance a wedge in the inverted position. Hsu and Wendlandt [HW91] examined this problem by constructing a wedge with an internal balancing mechanism. In their final design choice, the internal balancing mechanism was provided by controlling the position of a mass sliding along the wedge sides. We reproduce here their final set of equations, which include the actuator and sensor dynamics (we do not include the A/D and D/A conversion constants). The non-linear equations are

$$[5.53 + 14.38\,(0.25 + x^2)]\,\ddot{\theta} + 28.76\,x\,\dot{x}\,\dot{\theta} - 141.7\sin\theta + 99.61\,x\cos\theta = 0$$

$$18.79\ddot{x} + 305.17\dot{x} - 14.38x\,\dot{\theta}^2 + 99.61\sin\theta = 2.22\,u$$

where θ is the angle the wedge makes with the vertical axis, x is the position of the sliding mass, and u is the voltage control input. The linearized equations are

$$\dot{q} = \begin{pmatrix} 0 & 0 & 1 & 0 \\ 0 & 0 & 0 & 1 \\ 15.54 & -10.93 & 0 & 0 \\ -5.31 & 0 & 0 & -16.24 \end{pmatrix} q + \begin{pmatrix} 0 \\ 0 \\ 0 \\ 1.96 \end{pmatrix} u$$

$$y = \begin{pmatrix} 57.29 & 0 & 0 & 0 \\ 0 & 29.9 & 0 & 0 \end{pmatrix} q$$

where the state vector is given by $q = [\theta, x, \dot{\theta}, \dot{x}\,]'$

a. Discuss the controllablity and observability of the system.

b. Find a state feedback controller to place the closed loop eigenvalues at { -0.7 + 1.8j, -0.7 - 1.8j, -5, -20 }. Obtain the root locus and Bode plots of the compensated system, and determine its stability margins.

c. Assuming full state feedback, find the response of the system to an initial angular displacement of 0.1 rad in the wedge angle.

9

Digital Control

9.1 Introduction

Many of today's control systems use digital computers to provide the compensation that was discussed in the previous two chapters. A typical digital control system is shown in Figure 9-1. Usually, a continuous error signal is digitized by an analog-to-digital converter (ADC). The on-board computer processes this signal to provide a control signal to the plant. Because most plants are continuous, the computer's output is passed through a digital-to-analog converter (DAC).

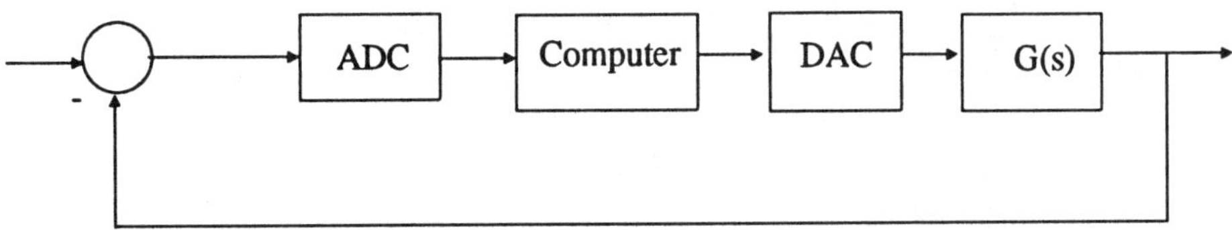

Figure 9-1 Digital control system.

As in continuous control systems, the control engineer must design compensators for digital control systems. The compensator is then realized as a set of difference equations programmed into the computer. Design techniques for digital systems parallel those developed for continuous systems. Compensators for single-input single-output systems can be designed with transform techniques that use the root locus or Bode plot. As we shall see, however, design of digital systems is more complicated than the corresponding continuous system design. We will first review some basics of discrete-time systems analysis.

9.2 Difference Equations

Dynamic behavior in a continuous system is described with differential equations. Dynamic behavior in a digital system is described with difference equations. For example, a second-order difference equation might be

$$y\,[(k+2)T] - 0.7y\,[(k+1)T] + 0.1y\,[kT] = 10\,x\,[(k+2)T]$$

Difference equations are very easy to program. We can rewrite the above as

$$y\,[(k+2)T] = 0.7y\,[(k+1)T] - 0.1y\,[kT] + 10\,x\,[(k+2)T]$$

To solve this equation, we only need two registers. We initialize these registers with $y(0)$ and $y(1)$ and then write a generic program that is similar to

```
STORE Y(0) IN REGISTER A
STORE Y(1) IN REGISTER B
1  Y = 10 X - 0.1A + 0.7B
2  STORE B IN A
3  STORE Y IN B
4  RETURN TO 1
```

where each pass through this code provides the latest value of y.

The relationship between a difference equation and a differential equation can be seen by considering the following:

$$\frac{dy}{dt} + 5y = x(t)$$

where the derivative term represents the velocity of the continuous system. Now, how could we measure velocity if we only observed the system's position every T seconds? The simplest method is to assume that velocity is constant between measurements, so that

$$\frac{dy}{dt} \approx \frac{y\,[(k+1)T] - y\,[kT]}{T}$$

If the present measurement is taken at $[(k+1)T]$, then the differential equation can be approximated by

$$\frac{y\,[(k+1)T] - y\,[kT]}{T} + 5\,y\,[(k+1)T] = x\,[(k+1)T]$$

The difference term in this equation is readily apparent. After some rearrangement of terms, we get

$$y\,[(k+1)T] \;-\; \frac{1}{1+5T}\,y\,[kT] \;=\; \frac{T}{1+5T}\,x\,[(k+1)T]$$

which has the typical appearance of a difference equation.

It is clear that the final form of the difference equation depends on the approximation we use for velocity. Later in this chapter we will discuss some other approximations and discuss their advantages and disadvantages.

There are several ways to solve difference equations. We have seen an example of the simplest approach; write a program that determines each successive value of the output by combining past values of the output with the appropriate present and past values of the input. The problem with this method is that closed form solutions are not obtained. This makes it difficult to predict the behavior and stability of the system.

The other methods that can be used to solve difference equations parallel those for differential equations. The solution can be found in the time domain as a sum of natural and forced solutions. Frequency transform techniques can be used. Finally, the system can be modeled with the state space approach and solutions found by convolving the input with the impulse response. We finish this section by finding the natural solutions to first and second order difference equations. This will give us some insight into the stability of digital systems.

Consider the homogeneous first order difference equation with the given initial condition

$$y_{k+1} \;-\; a y_k \;=\; 0 \qquad\qquad y_0 \;=\; 1$$

where the notation y_{k+1} is shorthand for $y\,[(k+1)T]$. The characteristic equation for a difference equation is formed by replacing y_{k+n} with r^n. The characteristic equation for this first order difference equation, therefore, is

$$r \,-\, a \,=\, 0 \quad \text{so} \quad r \,=\, a$$

The natural solution for real roots of the characteristic equation is r^k. The solution for this homogeneous first order difference equation with $y_0 \,=\, 1$ is

$$y_k \;=\; a^k \qquad k = 0, 1, 2, \ldots$$

It can be seen that if the magnitude of a is less than 1, the natural solution returns to 0 and the system is stable. If the magnitude of a is greater than 1, the system is unstable. Note also the interesting behavior for a negative. The system response oscillates (flip-flops between positive and negative values) even though we are dealing with a first order system. This is different from continuous systems, where no oscillations exist in a first order system

A typical homogeneous second order difference equation is

$$y_{k+2} - a\, y_{k+1} + b\, y_k = 0$$

We have not given any initial conditions here because we are only interested in the form of the natural solution. The characteristic equation for this system is

$$r^2 - ar + b = 0$$

The two solutions to the second order characteristic equation can be real and distinct (overdamped), identical (critically damped), or complex (underdamped). The natural solution for these various cases is

$$\text{overdamped:} \quad r = r_1, r_2 \;\rightarrow\; y_k = C r_1{}^k + C_2 r_2{}^k$$

$$\text{critically damped:} \quad r = r_1, r_1 \;\rightarrow\; y_k = (C_1 + C_2 k)\, r_1{}^k$$

$$\text{underdamped:} \quad r = \alpha \pm j\beta = R\, e^{j\pm\theta} \;\rightarrow\; y_k = R^k (C_1 \cos\theta k + C_2 \sin\theta k)$$

It is clear from the above that for a stable system the magnitude of r must be less than 1.

9.3 Spectrum of Sampled Signal

A discrete signal can be constructed by sampling a continuous signal. That is, every T seconds, a switch closes for an infinitesimally short time. This results in the signals shown in Figure 9-2, where the discrete signal is given by

$$f^*(t) = f(kT) \quad \text{for } k = \ldots -3, -2, -1, 0, 1, 2, 3, \ldots$$

We can also mathematically model a discrete signal as the product of an impulse train and the original continuous signal (*impulse modulation*). That is

$$f^*(t) = f(t) \sum_{k=-\infty}^{\infty} \delta(t - kT)$$

Because the impulse train is a periodic function, we can represent it with a Fourier series

$$\sum_{k=-\infty}^{\infty} \delta(t - kT) = \frac{1}{T} \sum_{n=-\infty}^{\infty} e^{j(2\pi n/T)t}$$

We can now find the Fourier transform of the sampled signal as

$$F^*(\omega) = \int_{-\infty}^{\infty} (f(t)\ \frac{1}{T} \sum_{n=-\infty}^{\infty} e^{j(2\pi n/T)t})e^{-j\omega t}\ dt$$

After some rearranging, we get

$$F^*(\omega) = \frac{1}{T} \sum_{n=-\infty}^{\infty} \int_{-\infty}^{\infty} f(t)\ e^{-j(\omega - 2\pi n/T)t}\ dt$$

Because the Fourier transform of the original continuous signal is

$$F(\omega) = \int_{-\infty}^{\infty} f(t)\ e^{-j\omega t}\ dt$$

We find the Fourier transform of the sampled signal as

$$F^*(\omega) = \frac{1}{T} \sum_{n=-\infty}^{\infty} F(\omega - 2\pi n/T)$$

Figure 9-3 shows the relationship between the frequency content of the continuous and the sampled signals. You can see that the spectrum of the sampled signal is a periodic (in ω) replication of the continuous spectrum. This can lead to several problems in sampled signals.

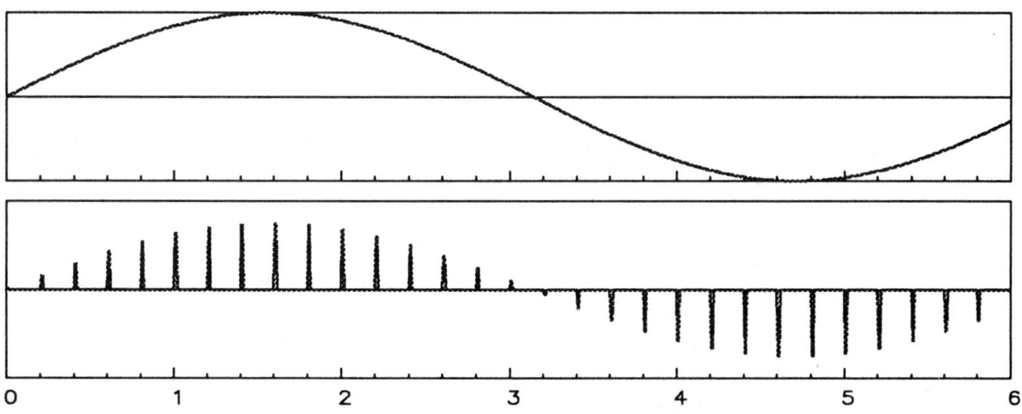

Figure 9-2 A signal and its sampled version.

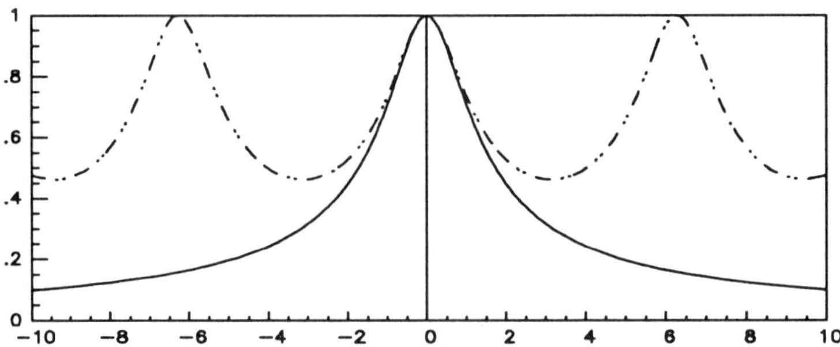

Figure 9-3 Continuous and discrete frequency responses.

Sampling Theorem

A continuous signal can, in theory, be recovered from the sampled signal. This is done by filtering the sampled signal. The output of a low pass filter with appropriate bandwidth is the original continuous spectrum. As the sample rate decreases (sample period increases), however, the separation between succeeding cycles of the sampled spectrum decreases. If $2\pi/T < 2\omega_0$, then we get the picture shown in Figure 9-4. In this case, we cannot reconstruct the original signal with the low pass filter. This leads to the following limit on sample rate

$$\frac{2\pi}{T} > 2\omega_0$$

where ω_0 is the highest frequency of interest in the original signal. This relationship is known as the *Nyquist*, or *Shannon, sampling theorem.*

Aliasing

In practice, of course, we cannot build ideal filters. Also, the spectrum of any real signal never ends abruptly at a given frequency. Unlike the band limited spectrum shown in Figure 9-4, all real spectra extend to plus and minus infinity. This situation is shown in Figure 9-5. There will always be some overlapping between the central lobe and the sidebands of the sampled spectrum. The distortion caused by this overlap is known as *aliasing*. Because we can reduce the amount of overlap by increasing the distance between sidebands, we can reduce aliasing by sampling at a faster rate than the Nyquist rate.

Aliasing causes another problem that cannot be corrected with faster sampling. Noise in a system is often high frequency. In a continuous system, if this noise is outside the control bandwidth, it will not affect the response. When we sample a noisy signal, however, the spectrum of the noise is repeated up and down the frequency axis. That is, if the noise is centered at a frequency ω_D, then the sampled signal will contain the frequencies $\omega_D - 2\pi n/T$. No matter what you choose for the sample period, you will get noise within the control bandwidth.

To avoid the problems associated with side band overlap and high frequency noise, we often precede the sampler with an analog low pass filter. This filter, known as an *anti-aliasing filter*, reduces the high frequency content of a signal, which minimizes the problems we have discussed. If your control system design uses an anti-aliasing filter, you want to be sure to include it in your final simulation.

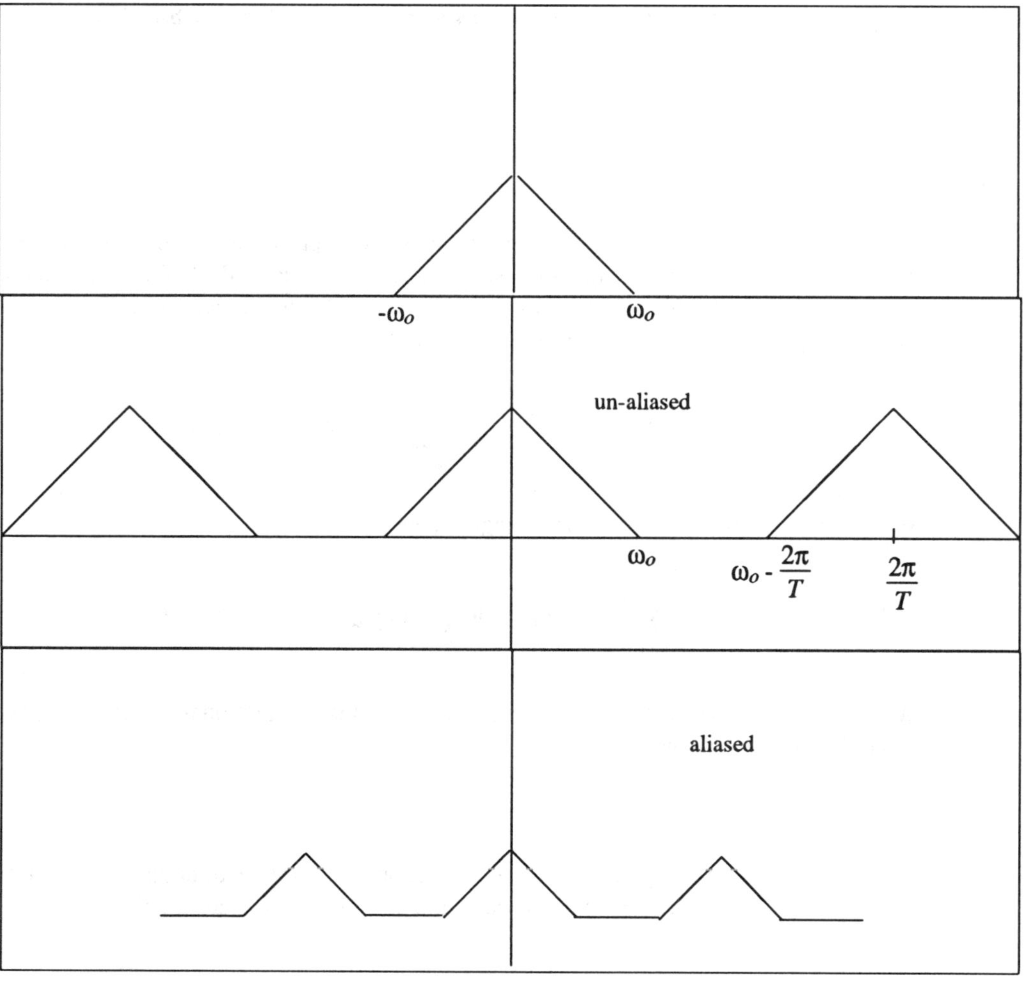

Figure 9-4 Analog frequency response, un-aliased and aliased discrete frequency responses.

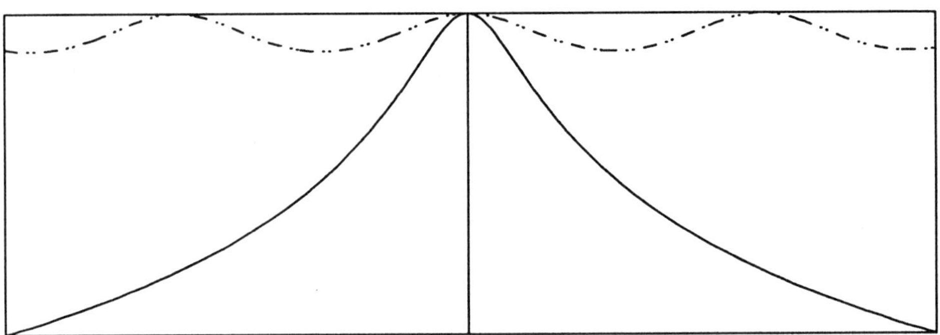

Figure 9-5 Analog and aliased discrete frequency responses of a signal that is not band-limited.

9.4 The *z*-Transform

To apply transform techniques, we need to know the Laplace transform of the discrete signal. To do this, we define again the sampled signal as the product of the continuous signal and the impulse train. Now, however, we assume that the signal starts at $t = 0$. We find the Laplace transform of the sampled signal as follows

$$F^*(s) = \int_0^\infty f^*(t)\, e^{-st} dt = \int_0^\infty \left(\sum_{k=0}^\infty f(kT)\, \delta(t-kT) \right) e^{-st} dt$$

We move the summation outside the integral to get

$$F^*(s) = \sum_{k=0}^\infty \int_0^\infty f(kT)\, e^{-st}\, \delta(t-kT)\; dt = \sum_{k=0}^\infty f(kT)\, e^{-skT}$$

We see that the Laplace transform of a sampled signal is not a rational function of s. We can define a new variable z, however, as

$$z = e^{sT}$$

Using this definition will give us $F^*(s)$ as a function of z. For ease of notation we replace $F^*(s)$ with $F(z)$. We have now defined the z-transform for a sampled signal

$$F(z) = \sum_{k=0}^\infty f(kT)\, z^{-k}$$

Digital control or signal processing textbooks give extended tables of sampled signal, z-transform pairs. Some of the most basic transform pairs are given in Table 9-1 in the Appendix. More important for us is the property of the z-transform that allows us to transform a difference equation into a frequency domain (algebraic) equation

$$f[(k+1)T] \rightarrow z\,F(z) - z f(0)$$

$$f[(k+2)T] \rightarrow z^2 F(z) - z^2 f(0) - z f(1)$$

$$\cdot$$

$$\cdot$$

$$f[(k+n)T] \rightarrow z^n F(z) - z^n f(0) - \ldots - z f(n-1)$$

As an example, we can transform the following zero state difference equation

$$y_{k+3} + 0.3y_{k+2} - y_{k+1} - 0.05y_k = 5x_{k+1} + x_k$$

into the frequency domain equation

$$(z^3 + 0.3z^2 - z - 0.05)\,Y(z) = (5z + 1)X(z)$$

Solving for $Y(z)$ gives us

$$Y(z) = \frac{5z + 1}{z^3 + 0.3z^2 - z - 0.05}\,X(z)$$

Given the z-transform of the input, we can find the output y_k by any number of inverse z-transform methods. For instance, we can use *Partial Fraction Expansion.* It is common practice to first divide $Y(z)$ by z and then perform the expansion. After the expansion coefficients are found, we multiply the result by z. The purpose is to get factors of the form $z / (z - a)$ shown in Table 9-1.

Control engineers, of course, are more interested in system behavior than in specific outputs. System behavior is determined by examining the transfer function, which for this example is

$$H(z) = \frac{Y(z)}{X(z)} = \frac{5z + 1}{z^3 + 0.3z^2 - z - 0.05}$$

A control system composed of blocks of z-domain transfer functions obeys the same principles of cascade parallel and feedback combinations. Mason's rule, likewise, can be applied to such a system.

9.5 Discrete State Space Model

As with continuous systems, we can represent discrete systems with a state space model.

$$x_{k+1} = Ax_k + Bu_k$$

$$y_k = Cx_k + Du_k$$

The z-transform model can be derived from the state space model as follows. First z-transform the state space equations (assuming zero initial conditions)

$$zX(z) = A\,X(z) + B\,U(z)$$

$$Y(z) = C\,X(z) + D\,U(z)$$

Solve for $X(z)$ from the first of these equations

$$(zI - A)\,X(z) = B\,U(z) \quad \rightarrow \quad X(z) = (zI - A)^{-1} B\,U(z)$$

Substitute for $X(z)$ in the output equation

$$Y(z) = C\,(zI - A)^{-1} B\,U(z) + D\,U(z)$$

The transfer function is then given by

$$G(z) = C\,\Phi(z)\,B + D \quad \text{where} \quad \Phi(z) = (zI - A)^{-1}$$

Many of the useful commands in MATRIXx are based on state space models. Therefore, we will often convert between transfer function models and state space models. The relevant commands are *sform*, *split*, and *tform* as discussed in Chapter 5.

9.6 Mapping the s-Plane to the z-Plane

Before we start designing digital compensators, we should examine how digital poles and zeros affect stability and the step response. Because we are already familiar with how pole and zero locations in the s-plane determine stability and step response, we will examine how points in the s-plane map into the z-plane. This mapping is determined by the defining relationship between s and z.

$$z = e^{sT}$$

We first look at the s-plane $j\omega$ axis. On this axis, $s = j\omega$, so, we get

$$z = e^{j\omega T}$$

This function has a magnitude of 1.0 for all ω and an angle of ω*T*. As ω varies from 0 to $2\pi/T$, a circle with a radius of 1.0 is swept out in the *z*-plane. As ω is varied from $2\pi/T$ to $4\pi/T$, we go around the circle again. In fact, the entire infinitely long *j*ω axis in the s-plane is mapped onto the unit circle in the *z*-plane.

We know that the stability region in the *s*-plane is the entire left half of the plane. Because $Re(s)$ in the left hand plane is negative, the mapping is

$$z = e^{(-\alpha + j\omega)T} = e^{-\alpha T} e^{j\omega T}$$

where $Re(s) = -\alpha$. Because $e^{-\alpha T}$ is the magnitude of *z*, and because $e^{-\alpha T} < 1.0$, the left half of the s-plane maps into the inside of the unit circle. Therefore, we can state

"The system is BIBO stable if and only if all poles of $G(z)$ lie inside the unit circle"

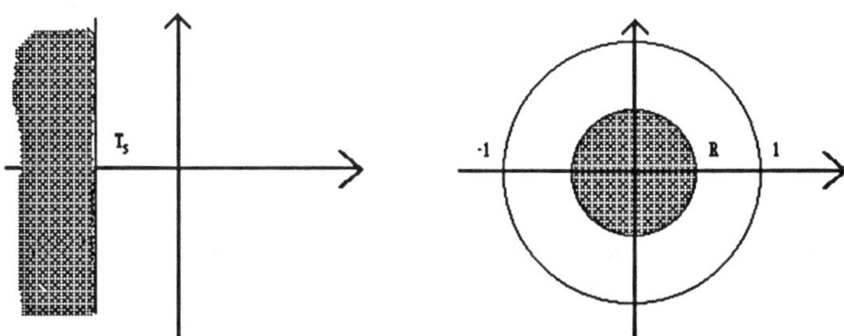

Figure 9-6 Shaded areas represent a region satisfying settling time requirement.

Clearly, poles outside or on the unit circle produce unstable responses. Nonrepeated poles on the unit circle, although not BIBO stable, correspond to marginally stable systems. As with continuous systems, real poles in the z-plane produce overdamped responses, whereas complex poles produce underdamped responses. It is interesting to note the negative real axis in the *s*-plane maps into the real axis from 0 to 1 in the *z*-plane. A digital system with a pole at - 0.5 in the *z*-plane has no corresponding continuous system.

For design purposes, the most important mappings involve the contours for constant T_s, ζ, and ω_n. An example of an *s*-plane and *z*-plane region satisfying settling time less than or equal to a given amount is shown in Figure 9-6.

In the s-plane, points on the settling time contour have a fixed negative real value; i.e.,

$$s = -\sigma + j\,\omega\,, \quad \text{where} \quad T_s \approx 5/\sigma$$

which corresponds to

$$z = e^{-\sigma T}\, e^{\,j\omega T} = R\, e^{\,j\omega T}$$

This contour is a circle of radius R. As R decreases, the settling time decreases.

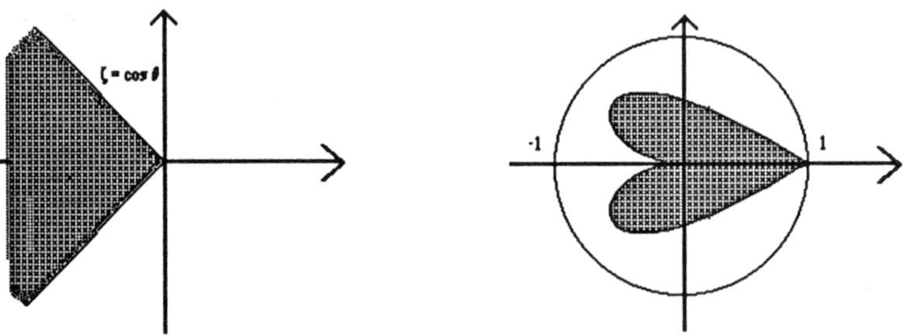

Figure 9-7 Region satisfying damping ratio requirement.

Figure 9-7 shows the s-plane and z-plane region satisfying damping ratio larger than a given amount. Although there is no simple way to formulate equations for these contours, we can point out the following. Because an s-plane root of the second order characteristic equation is given by $s = -\zeta\omega_n + j\sqrt{1-\zeta^2}\;\omega_n$, the corresponding z-plane root is

$$z = e^{-\zeta\omega_n T}\, e^{\,j\sqrt{1-\zeta^2}\,\omega_n T}$$

so

$$|\,z\,| = e^{-\zeta\omega_n T} \;\text{and}\; \theta_z = \sqrt{1-\zeta^2}\;\omega_n T$$

If we fix ζ and let ω_n vary from 0 to π/T, the magnitude of z decreases exponentially while the phase increases linearly. This creates the logarithmic spiral we see for constant ζ in Figure 9-7.

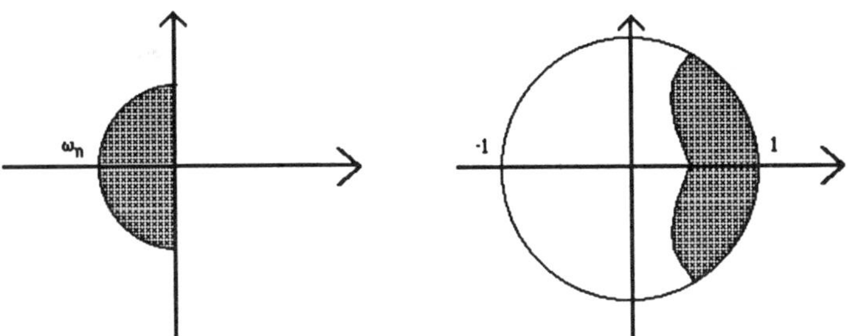

Figure 9-8 Region satisfying natural frequency constraint.

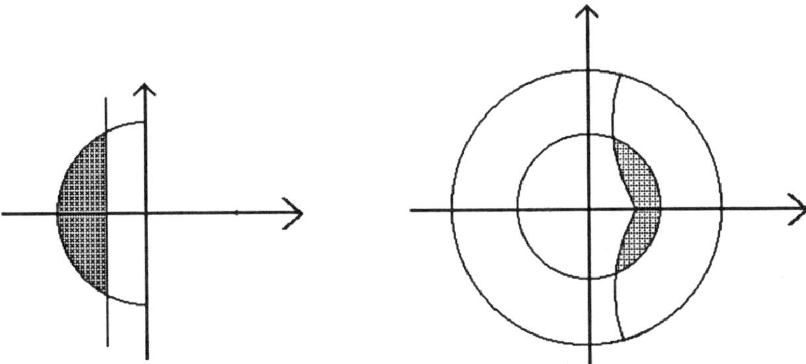

Figure 9-9 Region satisfying settling time and natural frequency constraints.

The contour for constant ω_n is more complicated. Although the magnitude of will still decrease exponentially, the phase is not linearly dependent on ζ. The only easily determined points in the z-plane for this contour occur at $\zeta = 0$ and $\zeta = 1$. The constant contour for ω_n starts on the unit circle at an angle of $\omega_n T$ and ends on the real axis with a magnitude of $e^{-\omega_n T}$. It may help to note that this contour is always perpendicular to the constant ζ contours that it intersects. The region satisfying a constraint for ω_n less than a given amount is shown in Figure 9-8.

A region satisfying settling time and ω_n constraints simultaneously is shown in Figure 9-9.

9.7 System Type and Steady State Error

A z-transform property that is very useful is the final value theorem

$$\textit{Final Value Theorem:} \quad \lim_{k \to \infty} f(kT) = \lim_{z \to 1} (z-1)\, F(z)$$

We can use the final value theorem to find the steady state error constants for a unity feedback digital control system. The error for such a system is

$$E(z) = \frac{1}{1 + G(z)} R(z)$$

where $G(z)$ is the forward path gain, and $R(z)$ is the input to the system. We begin with a discrete step input

$$E(z) = \frac{1}{1 + G(z)} \frac{z}{z - 1}$$

The steady state error is

$$e(\infty) = \frac{1}{1 + G(1)}$$

If $G(1)$ is finite, then this system can track a step with constant error. This is a Type 0 system and we define the error constant K_p so that

$$\text{Type 0:} \quad e(\infty) = \frac{1}{1 + K_p} \qquad K_p = G(1)$$

For a ramp input, $r(t) = kT$, the error is

$$E(z) = \frac{1}{1 + G(z)} \frac{zT}{(z - 1)^2}$$

The final error is

$$e(\infty) = \lim_{z \to 1} \frac{1}{1 + G(z)} \frac{zT}{z - 1}$$

If $G(z)$ has no poles at $z = 1$, then the steady state error will be infinite. If $G(z)$ has one pole at $z = 1$, then the steady state error will be finite and equal to

$$e(\infty) = \frac{T}{(z-1)\,G(z)}\bigg|_{z=1}$$

This is a Type 1 system, and we define the steady state error constant K_v so that

$$\text{Type 1: } e(\infty) = \frac{1}{K_v} \qquad K_v = \frac{(z-1)}{T}\,G(z)\bigg|_{z=1}$$

For a digital unity feedback system, the system type is equal to the number of poles at $z = 1$. We can extend the above procedure to find the error constants for all system types.

$$K_n = \frac{(z-1)^n}{T^n}\,G(z)\bigg|_{z=1}$$

where the system input is $r(k) = \dfrac{(kT)^n}{n!}$, and n is the system type.

An important and simplifying note: If $G(s)$ is digitized using the ZOH equivalence (to be discussed shortly), then $G(s)$ and $G(z)$ have the same error constant. Because this is the usual technique for digitizing a plant model, we can find the plant error constant from the s-plane model.

9.8 Simulation of Digital Control Systems

Digital control systems usually contain both digital and continuous elements. In the frequency domain, digital elements are modeled with the z-transform and continuous elements with the s-transform. We must, therefore, make some compromises to combine these elements into a single systems analysis. Because of these compromises, frequency domain design techniques in digital systems must be verified by a complete time domain simulation of the system. The System Build Module (Chapter 6) allows the user to model the continuous and digital components, including such parameters as finite word length, as they are actually used in the system.

When we model digital systems, we convert continuous transfer functions represented by $G(s)$ into an "equivalent" discrete transfer function $G(z)$. We enclose the word equivalent in quotation marks because it is not possible for a $G(z)$ to match the behavior of the $G(s)$ exactly from whence it was derived. If the digital model produces the same impulse response as the continuous model, it will not match the step response. If it matches the step response, it will not match the impulse response. The frequency response of the digital model never exactly matches the frequency response of the continuous model.

Several techniques exist for discretizing continuous systems. Among them are time response matching (impulse and step), numerical integration methods (Euler backward, forward, and trapezoidal), and others. Each one has its advantages and pitfalls. As mentioned earlier, some preserve the time response, whereas others better preserve the frequency response. From a control view point, stability preservation is very important; some techniques preserve stability, whereas others do not. Techniques that do not preserve the system stability have to be used very cautiously, or misleading simulations will result.

9.8.1 Impulse Invariant Transformation

Impulse invariant transformation converts a continuous system to a discrete one by matching their impulse responses. Consider the continuous transfer function and its impulse response

$$H(s) = \frac{10}{s+5}, \qquad h(t) = 10\, e^{-5t} u(t)$$

The sampled version of this impulse response and its z-transform is

$$h(nT) = 10\, e^{-5nT} u(nT), \qquad H(z) = \frac{10\, z}{z - e^{-5T}}$$

The procedure we use to preserve the impulse response when we represent a continuous plant with a digital model is the following:

Find the impulse response from $H(s)$; let $t = nT$ to convert the continuous response to the discrete response; transform the discrete impulse response into $H(z)$.

The conversion can also be done in state space form. The impulse response of a continuous system and the pulse response of a discrete system are given by

$$h(t) = C\, e^{At} B + D\, \delta(t), \quad h(nT) = C_d A_d^{\,n-1} B_d + (D_d - C_d A_d^{-1} B_d)\, \delta(nT)$$

Now, sample $h(t)$; let $t = nT$ to convert the continuous response to the discrete response; comparing the two responses, we conclude that

$$A_d = e^{AT}, \quad B_d = e^{AT} B, \quad C_d = C, \quad D_d = D + CB$$

In fact, this is how MATRIXx performs this conversion.

9.8.2 Zero Order Hold Equivalence

In practice, a discrete signal never directly drives a continuous filter or plant. The discrete signal is first passed through a digital-to-analog converter (DAC). The DAC produces a continuous output that reflects its discrete input. The simplest and most commonly used

DACs are devices that convert the binary computer output to a voltage level and then hold that level until the computer outputs the next data word T seconds later. This device is known as a zero order hold (ZOH). The output of the ZOH reconstruction of the signal shown in Figure 9-2 is shown in Figure 9-10.

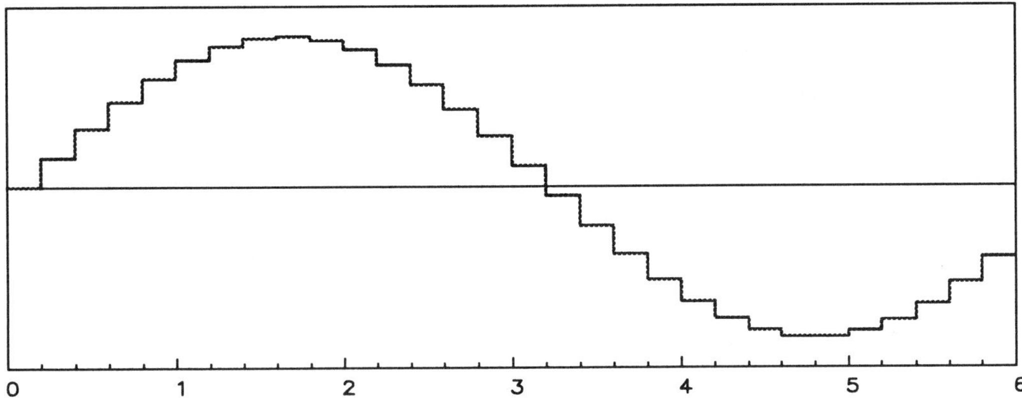

Figure 9-10 ZOH reconstruction of the signal in Figure 9-2.

The zero-order hold creates an output pulse for each input impulse. Because a step is derived from an impulse by integration, we get the ZOH transfer function (Laplace transform of a unit pulse of duration T).

$$\text{ZOH:} \qquad \frac{1 - e^{-sT}}{s}$$

The delay factor resets the integrator before the next impulse comes in. The total transfer function between the switch output and the plant output, therefore, is

$$\frac{1 - e^{-sT}}{s} G(s)$$

Whenever there is a ZOH preceding a plant, we take the z-transform of the above. To find the z-transform of an s-domain transfer function $G(s)$, we perform the following operations:

Find $g(t)$ from $G(s)$, replace t by nT; take the z-transform, which is $G(z)$. We will use this procedure on $G(s)/s$ to find ZOH equivalent transfer function. To do this, we note that

$$Z\left\{\frac{1 - e^{-sT}}{s} G(s)\right\} = Z\left\{\frac{G(s)}{s}\right\} - Z\left\{\frac{e^{-sT}\,G(s)}{s}\right\}$$

The second term in preceding expression is the delayed version of the first term. Because the z-transform of a unit delay is z^{-1}, we finally get

$$G(z)_{ZOH} = (1 - z^{-1})\ \mathbf{Z}\left\{\frac{G(s)}{s}\right\}$$

Consider the following simple example : $G(s) = \dfrac{1}{s+1}$

$$G(z)_{ZOH} = (1 - z^{-1})\ \mathbf{Z}\left\{\frac{1}{s\,(s+1)}\right\}$$

$$L^{-1}\left\{\frac{1}{s\,(s+1)}\right\} = (1 - e^{-t})\,u(t) \;\Rightarrow\; \mathbf{Z}\left\{(1 - e^{-nT})\,u(nT)\right\} = \frac{z\,(1 - e^{-T})}{(z-1)\,(z - e^{-T})}$$

$$G(z)_{ZOH} = (1 - z^{-1})\,\frac{z\,(1 - e^{-T})}{(z-1)\,(z - e^{-T})} = \frac{1 - e^{-T}}{z - e^{-T}}$$

The zero-order hold equivalent is also known as *step invariant*, because it matches the step response of a discrete system to a continuous one. It is by far the most common technique used by control engineers. Table 9-2 shows some simple ZOH equivalents. The discretization can also be obtained in state space (see the exercises). The ZOH state space matrices are given by

$$A_d = e^{AT}, \quad B_d = \int_0^T e^{A\sigma}\,d\sigma\,, \quad C_d = C\,, \quad D_d = D$$

If we use the series expansion of the matrix exponential; perform the integration; and use some matrix algebra, we can show that the discrete B matrix can be easily computed from

$$B_d = A^{-1}\,[\,A_d - I\,]\,B = e^{\begin{bmatrix} A & B \\ 0 & 0 \end{bmatrix} T}$$

The final form requires only matrix operations, and this is how MATRIXx performs the ZOH transformation.

9.8.3 Numerical Integration Methods

To convert analog filters to equivalent digital filters, we are most interested in maintaining the frequency response of the original transfer function. The commonest techniques that attempt to maintain the frequency response of the digitized transfer function can be derived from approximations of the integral or derivative; they are *forward Euler*, *backward Euler*, and *trapezoidal*. With these techniques we replace s everywhere in $H(s)$ with a function of z.

Consider the following situation. We want to know our present position, $y(kT)$, given that we knew where we were T seconds ago and we know the velocity, V, has been constant over this interval. We can then write

$$V = \frac{y[kT] - y[(k-1)T]}{T}$$

We have several choices for V. We can use the velocity at kT seconds, the velocity at $(k - 1)T$ seconds, or the average of the two. The first of these yields the approximation known as backward Euler

$$v[kT] = \frac{y[kT] - y[(k-1)T]}{T}$$

Taking the z-transform of the above

$$V(z) = \frac{z-1}{Tz} Y(z)$$

In the continuous domain, velocity is represented by $sY(s)$. By comparison we can derive a relationship between s and z.

Backward Euler:	$s \approx \frac{z-1}{Tz}$

Using the velocity at $(k - 1)T$ seconds gives us

$$v[(k-1)T] = \frac{y[kT] - y[(k-1)T]}{T} \quad \rightarrow \quad z^{-1} V(z) = \frac{1-z^{-1}}{T} Y(z)$$

and we get

Forward Euler:	$s \approx \frac{z-1}{T}$

Using the average value of the beginning and ending velocity, we get

Trapezoidal:	$s \approx \frac{2}{T} \frac{z-1}{z+1}$

The trapezoidal transformation is known as the *bilinear* or *Tustin's* transformation. Tustin's transformation is the most commonly used technique for converting an analog filter to a digital one.

These transforms can also be done using matrix operations in state space. For example, consider the backward Euler's method. The continuous state space equations in the s-domain are

$$s\,X(s) = A\,X(s) + B\,U(s)$$

Now, replace s by $(z - 1)/Tz$, and apply inverse z-transform to get the approximating difference equation

$$\frac{z-1}{T\,z}X(z) = A\,X(z) + B\,U(z) \quad \rightarrow x\,[(k+1)T] = \Psi\,x(kT) + \Psi\,T\,B\,u\,[(k+1)T]$$

where $\Psi = (I - A\,T)^{-1}$

To obtain a state space representation, we define

$$\eta\,(kT) = x\,(kT) - \Psi\,T\,B\,u\,(kT)$$

Now, rewrite the state equations in terms of the new state, $\eta\,(kT)$

$$\eta\,[(k+1)\,T] = \Psi\,\eta\,(kT) + \Psi^2\,T\,B\,u\,(kT)$$

$$y\,(kT) = C\,\eta\,(kT) + (\,C\,\Psi\,T\,B + D\,)\,u\,(kT)$$

Hence, the discrete state space matrices are

$$A_d = \Psi\,, \qquad B_d = \Psi^2\,T\,B\,, \qquad C_d = C\,, \qquad D_d = C\,\Psi\,T\,B + D\,, \qquad \Psi = (\,I - T\,A\,)^{-1}$$

Matrices for Tustin and forward Euler transformation can also be derived (see the exercises).

9.9 MATRIXx Discrete Commands

Most control system commands in MATRIXx have equivalent discrete versions. The discrete version of these commands usually start with the letter *d*, such as *drlocus*, *dstep*, *dbode*, and others. The syntax and usage of the discrete commands is almost identical to their continuous counterparts. When they are different, we will discuss them in more detail.

```
< > discretize
```

The *discretize* command will convert a continuous system to a discrete one using one of five techniques. It has the following state space and transfer function syntaxes:

The *discretize* command will convert a continuous system to a discrete one using one of five techniques. It has the following state space and transfer function syntaxes:

```
< > sd=disc(s,ns,dt,'type')
< > [numz,denz]=disc(num,den,dt,'type')
```

where we have abbreviated the command. The parameter `dt` is the sampling period. The `type` option allows the user to choose one of five techniques available with this command The available options are *exp*, *ztransform*, *forward*, *backward*, and *Tustin*. The options *exp* and *ztransform* correspond to ZOH and impulse invariant, respectively; the last three are obvious. The default type is *exp* (ZOH).

The discrete impulse (*pulse*) and step response (*dstep*) commands have the following syntaxes:

```
< > [n,hz]=pulse(nz,dz,npts] or pulse(sd,nsd,npts)
< > [n,gz]=dstep(nz,dz,npts) or dstep(sd,nsd,npts)
```

where we have labeled the discrete impulse response as `hz` and the discrete step response as `gz`. All discrete commands produce results at each of N points rather than at specific times or frequencies. If we want to analyze a system from 0 to *tmax* seconds when the sample period is T seconds, then

```
< > npts=1+tmax/T
```

where we assume that *tmax* is an integer multiple of T.

Frequency response of discrete systems can be obtained using the *dbode* command (*dnyquist* and *dnichols* are also available). It has the following syntax.

```
< > [omegaz,db,ph]=dbode(nz,dz,omegazmin,omegazmax,npts)
```

With one exception, this command is identical to the continuous *bode* command. The exception is that the frequency values are not absolute, they are relative to the sample period T. The relationship between the continuous frequency, ω, and the value used in this command is

$$\texttt{omegaz} = \omega T$$

The discrete root locus is *drlocus*. It has the same syntax as its continuous counterpart and the same options are available. The main difference between them is that *rlocus* plots in rectangular coordinates, whereas *drlocus* uses polar coordinates.

The next example compares the step responses of the original continuous model and the digital model that results from impulse and ZOH matching.

Example 9.1 Response of Impulse Matched and ZOH Transfer Function

Use impulse matching and ZOH to convert $H(s)$ to $H(z)$ with $T = 0.1$ sec. Compare the impulse and step responses of $H(s)$ and $H(z)$.

$$H(s) = \frac{10}{(s+2)(s+5)}$$

We first find $h(t)$ and replace t with nT.

$$H(s) = \frac{10/3}{s+2} - \frac{10/3}{s+5} \quad \rightarrow \quad h(t) = \frac{10}{3}(e^{-2t} - e^{-5t})\, u(t)$$

$$h(nT) = \frac{10}{3}(e^{-0.2n} - e^{-0.5n})\, u(nT)$$

We also need the continuous and discrete step responses.

$$g(t) = (1 - \frac{5}{3}e^{-2t} + \frac{2}{3}e^{-5t})\, u(t)$$

$$g(nt) = (1 - \frac{5}{3}e^{-0.2n} + \frac{2}{3}e^{-0.5n})\, u(nT)$$

Returning to the impulse response and taking the z-transform of each exponential and then combining gives us

$$H(z) = \frac{0.707\, z}{z^2 - 1.425\, z + 0.497}$$

Using the *ztransform* type for impulse response matching, we get

```
< > nc=10; dc=[1, 7, 10];
< > [n_ztr,d_ztr]=disc(nc,dc,0.1,'ztransform')
```

```
D_ZTR   =
1.0000  -1.4253   .4966
N_ZTR   =
.7073   .0000
```

We see that this procedure has produced the same numerator and denominator terms that we derived analytically for impulse-invariant transform.You can also verify the following ZOH transform analytically.

```
< > [n_zoh,d_zoh]=disc(nc,dc,0.1)
```

```
D_ZOH   =
1.0000  -1.4253   .4966
```

```
N_ZOH    =
.0398  .0315
```

Before we find the impulse and step response for $H(z)$, we will determine these responses for the continuous $H(s)$. We will not use the *impulse* and *step* commands however. The problem with these commands is that they internally calculate the times at which the impulse and step response are found. These times will not correspond to the times at which the digital response are calculated (every $N\,T$ seconds). To resolve this, we generate the continuous responses by programming the actual impulse and step responses.

First, we determine the number of data points to be used. We can use the *step* or *impulse* commands to find that the continuous system responses settle within 3.5 sec. Because we have set the sample period to 0.1 sec, we get NPTS = 36.

We now determine the continuous impulse (hc) and step (gc) responses from

```
< > i=[0:npts-1]'; hc=10/3*exp(-0.2*i)-10/3*exp(-0.5*i);
< > i=[0:npts-1]'; gc=ones(i)-5/3*exp(-0.2*i)+2/3*exp(-0.5*i);
```

the discrete responses are now found

```
< > [n,h_ztr]=pulse(n_ztr,d_ztr,npts);
< > [n,g_ztr]=dstep(n_ztr,d_ztr,npts);
< > [n,g_zoh]=dstep(n_zoh,d_zoh,npts);
```

If we want to plot these responses as functions of time rather than as function of n, we can define the time vector as

```
< > time=n*0.1
```

The continuous and discrete impulse responses for impulse-invariant case are plotted together in Figure 9-11.

You can see that the match here is exact. Because we derived $H(z)$ from the impulse response of $H(s)$, this is the result we would expect. The continuous and discrete step responses for the

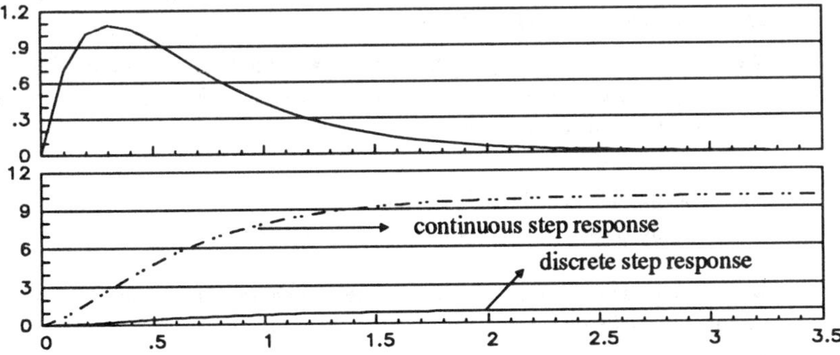

Figure 9-11 Top plot: impulse responses for continuous and impulse invariant method; bottom plot: step responses for the same systems.

impulse-invariant case are also plotted together in Figure 9-11 (bottom plot). The difference in the two responses is striking. Although the settling time has been preserved, the final value of the discrete response is greatly different from the continuous response.

Figure 9-12 shows that the continuous and ZOH equivalent step responses are identical. This digitization technique always produces the same step response as the continuous system.

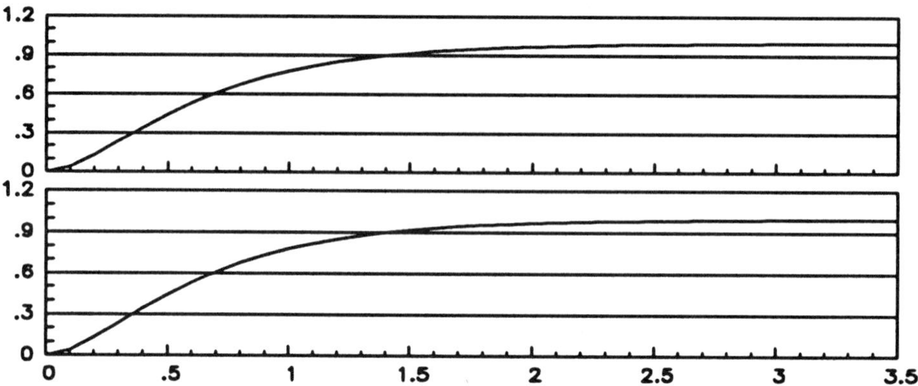

Figure 9-12 Top plot: step response of continuous system; bottom plot: step response for ZOH equivalent discrete system.

The next example compares the frequency response of the ZOH equivalent and the continuous system. As we shall see, the fidelity of the frequency response depends very much on the sample rate.

Example 9.2 Frequency Response of the ZOH Equivalent

Use the ZOH equivalent to digitize $H(s) = \dfrac{10}{s+1}$

for the sample periods $T = 1,\ 0.5,$ and 0.1 sec. Compare the Bode plots for the continuous and three discrete transfer functions.

We again have the problem that to compare a continuous to a discrete Bode plot, we must force both responses to use the same frequency points. We can do this with the state space version of the Bode commands

```
< > [omega,dbc,phc]=bode(s,ns,omega)
< > [omegaz,dbz,phz]=dbode(sd,ns,omegaz)
```

where *omega* and *omegaz* are vectors of the desired frequency points. The discrete frequency vector is given by *omega*T*.

We will determine the Bode plots of the transfer functions from 0.1 to 10 rad/sec in 100 equal steps for the three sampling periods. Because the code is simple, we will skip it.

Note that we plot all magnitudes versus the continuous frequency vector. Figure 9-13 shows the result. Several interesting properties can be seen in the figure. First, the frequency response of the ZOH equivalent depends very much on the sample period. As the sample period decreases, the ZOH equivalent approaches the continuous frequency response. At larger sample periods, the frequency response appears to be cyclical.

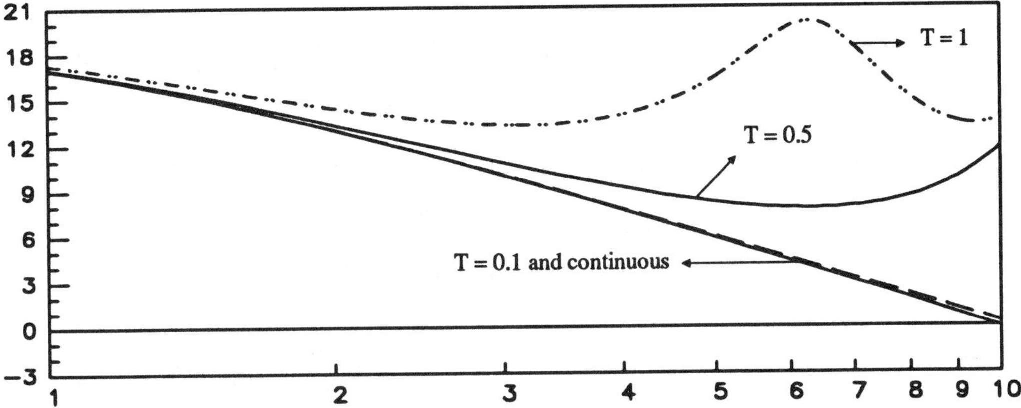

Figure 9-13 Frequency responses of ZOH for T = 1, 0.5, 0.1, and the continuous system.

We have discussed earlier the importance of sampling at a rate greater than the Nyquist rate. For this transfer function, the bandwidth is 1.0 rad/ sec. Therefore, we should sample at least at 2 rad/sec. In other words, the maximum sample period should be

$$T_{\max} = \frac{2\pi}{2} \approx 3.14 \text{ sec.}$$

Even at our slowest sample rate ($T = 1$ sec.), we are still sampling at 3 times the nyquist rate. To achieve a good frequency fit, however, we need to sample at 30 times the sample rate! Clearly, the ZOH equivalence is not good at maintaining the frequency response of the original continuous transfer function.

The cyclical nature of the frequency response of the discrete transfer function is not due to the digitization technique used. It is inherent in all z-transform transfer functions. To see this, consider the simple transfer function

$$H(z) = \frac{1}{z - 0.5}$$

Because $z = e^{sT}$ and $s = j\omega$, we find the frequency response of the discrete transfer function from

$$H_z(\omega) = \frac{1}{e^{j\omega T} - 0.5}$$

The function $e^{j\omega T}$ repeats itself, however, whenever $\omega T = 0,\ 2\pi,\ 4\pi,\ \ldots$ Therefore, the transfer function will repeat itself at the frequency intervals

$$\omega = \frac{2\pi}{T},\ \frac{4\pi}{T},\ \ldots$$

That is, all discrete Bode plots are periodic and repeat at the sample rate $(2\pi/T)$. There is no such thing as a true low-pass digital filter. At best, a digital filter will exhibit its expected behavior only for frequency values significantly less than the sampling rate.

When do we use the ZOH equivalence? We usually use this technique to model a continuous plant. This is because we are most often interested in the time response of the plant. We rarely use the ZOH equivalence to convert a continuous filter to a digital filter. We have seen that this technique does not faithfully reproduce frequency response and we design filters for their frequency response characteristics.

Example 9.3 Comparison of Forward Euler, Backward Euler, and Tustin

Use forward Euler, backward Euler, and Tustin to digitize $H(s)$ for $T = 0.1$ and 1.0 sec. Also obtain the Bode magnitude plots, and compare the results.

$$H(s) = \frac{10}{s+1}$$

The results of the experiment are shown in Figure 9-14 for $T = 0.1$ and Figure 9-15 for $T = 1.0$. For $T = 0.1$, you can see that all three techniques produce filters that closely match the continuous filter. For $T = 1.0$, Figure 9.15 shows that only the Tustin digitization technique produces results that are similar to the continuous filter. We again point out that $T = 1.0$ sec for this filter is not that large. Because the continuous filter has a bandwidth of 1.0 rad/sec, the Nyquist sampling rate is 2.0 rad/sec ($T = 3.14$ sec). We are, therefore, sampling at 3 times the Nyquist rate.

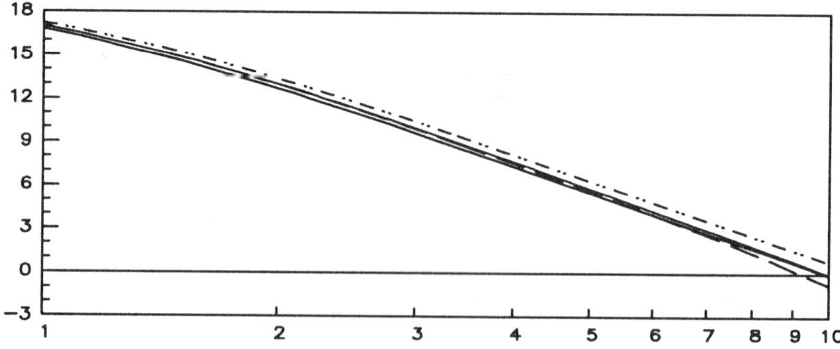

Figure 9-14 Frequency responses of analog and digital filters for $T = 0.1$.

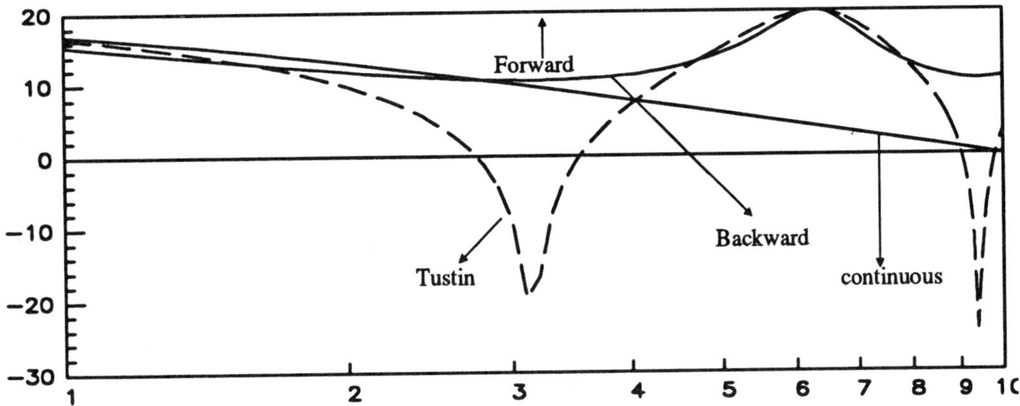

Figure 9-15 Frequency responses for $T = 1$.

We can draw the conclusion that for very fast sample rates (T very small), then any digitization technique can be used. For slower sample rates, use Tustin's approach.

There are some additional points to consider when comparing these three techniques. The first point is that the forward Euler technique is not always stable. Consider the stable continuous filter

$$H(s) = \frac{1}{s+1} \quad \rightarrow \quad \text{pole} = -1$$

The forward Euler transformation is

$$H(z) = \frac{T}{z-1+T} \quad \rightarrow \quad \text{pole} = 1 - T$$

If T is greater than 2, the discrete pole lies outside the unit circle, and the filter response will be unstable. Forward Euler can produce a numerically unstable system from a stable continuous system. This is only a problem for slow sample rates.

It is instructive to solve for z from each of the transformation techniques.

$$\text{forward Euler:} \quad z = 1 + sT$$

$$\text{backward Euler:} \quad z = \frac{1}{1-sT}$$

$$\text{Tustin:} \quad z = \frac{1 + sT/2}{1 - sT/2}$$

The forward Euler is actually the first two terms in the Taylor series expansion of the exponential (remember $z = e^{sT}$). The Tustin transformation is the *Pade* approximation to the exponential.

We know that the $j\omega$ axis in the s-plane maps into the unit circle in the z-plane. Neither of the Euler techniques preserves this mapping. The Tustin technique does, however. To see this, let $s = j\omega$ in the Tustin approximation

$$z = \frac{1 + j\omega T/2}{1 - j\omega T/2}$$

From this equation we find the magnitude and phase as

$$|z| = 1 \quad \text{and} \quad \theta_z = 2 \tan \omega T/2$$

As ω increases, the phase increases while the magnitude stays constant at 1.0. Thus, a unit circle is swept out.

Figure 9.15 shows that even Tustin's is not perfect. You can see that the continuous and Tustin derived discrete filter have slightly different bandwidths. This problem is known as *warping*.

9.10 The Warping Problem

Consider the following continuous filter with a bandwidth of a.

$$H(s) = \frac{1}{s/a + 1}$$

The Tustin's transformation of this filter yields

$$H(z) = \frac{1}{\frac{2}{T}\frac{z-1}{z+1}\frac{1}{a} + 1}$$

To find the frequency response of the digital filter, we let $z = e^{j\omega T}$. Before we return to $H(z)$, let us examine

$$\frac{z - 1}{z + 1} \rightarrow \frac{e^{j\omega T} - 1}{e^{j\omega T} + 1}$$

If we factor out $e^{j\omega/2}$ from the numerator and denominator, we get

$$\frac{z-1}{z+1} \rightarrow \frac{2j\sin \omega T/2}{2\cos \omega T/2} = j\tan\frac{\omega T}{2}$$

For $s = j\omega$, our discrete filter becomes

$$H_z(\omega) = \frac{1}{j\left(\frac{2}{T}\tan\omega\frac{T}{2}\right)\frac{1}{a}+1}$$

Because the bandwidth of a first order filter is the frequency at which the imaginary term equals the real term, we get the bandwidth of the discrete filter as

$$\omega_{BW} = \frac{2}{T}\tan^{-1}\left(\frac{aT}{2}\right)$$

This formula gives us the relationship between the continuous and discrete equivalent bandwidths. As we sample faster and faster, T gets smaller and smaller. Because the arctan of a small number is equal to that number, we conclude that at a high sample rate, the discrete filter has the same bandwidth as the continuous filter. For the lower sample rates we often use in control systems, however, the digitized filter can have a significantly different bandwidth from the original continuous filter.

9.10.1 Prewarping

The warping problem has been addressed by *prewarping* the continuous filter before we digitize. This is done by replacing a in $H(s)$ with $\bar{a}$, where $\bar{a}$ is defined as

$$\textit{prewarping:}\quad \bar{a} = \frac{2}{T}\tan\frac{aT}{2}$$

If we replace the original continuous filter with

$$H_{pw}(s) = \frac{1}{s/\bar{a}+1}$$

and then apply Tustin's transformation to this filter, the resulting discrete filter will have the same bandwidth as the original $H(s)$.

Note that if we apply prewarping to a filter $H(s)$ to get $H_{pw}(s)$

$$H(s) = \frac{K}{s+a}, \qquad H_{pw}(s) = \frac{K}{s+\bar{a}}$$

and then use Tustin's, we will get the correct bandwidth. We have changed the low frequency gain, however. To avoid this, we divide through by a and apply prewarping to

$$H(s) = \frac{K/a}{s/a + 1} \quad , \quad H_{pw}(s) = \frac{K/\bar{a}}{s/\bar{a} + 1}$$

Example 9.4 Tustin's with Prewarping

Use Tustin's with prewarping to digitize $H(s)$ for sample periods of 0.5 and 1.0 sec.

$$H(s) = \frac{10}{s+2}$$

We first divide through by 2 to get

$$H(s) = \frac{5}{s/2 + 1}$$

For $T = 0.5$ sec, we get , $\bar{a}_1 = \frac{2}{0.5} \tan\frac{2 \times 0.5}{2} = 2.1852$. Hence, we digitize

$$H_1(s) = \frac{5}{s/2.1852 + 1} \quad \rightarrow \quad H_1(z) = 1.7665\frac{z+1}{z-0.2934}$$

For $T = 1.0$ sec, we get, $\bar{a}_2 = \frac{2}{1} \tan\frac{2}{2} = 3.1148$. So we digitize

$$H_2(s) = \frac{5}{s/3.1148 + 1} \quad \rightarrow \quad H_2(z) = 3.0449\frac{z+1}{z+0.2180}$$

Figure 9-16 shows the Bode plots for the continuous $H(s)$ and the digitized versions of the two prewarped transfer functions. As predicted, all three plots have the same bandwidth. It is

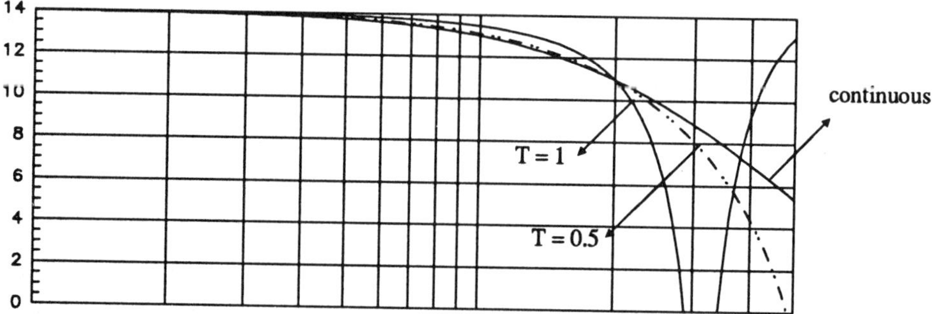

Figure 9-16 Frequency responses for Tustin using prewarping.

clear, however, that the complete frequency responses for the three transfer functions are quite different.

The procedure we have just derived for prewarping is not so easily applied when digitizing higher order transfer functions. Do we prewarp each pole and zero? Do we try to maintain the center frequency of a band-pass filter, or the bandwidth, or both? The bottom line is that we can force a digitized version of a continuous transfer function to match the original transfer function at a single frequency only. We either have to live with the rest of the digitized frequency response; play with the parameters of the continuous transfer function before digitizing; or design the filter directly in the z-plane.

The best solution is to design the filter, or compensator, directly in the z-plane. This we will do in the next section. However, control engineers are still often faced with the task of replacing an analog compensator with its digital equivalent. The following modification, known as *critical frequency prewarping*, provides a reasonable method for doing this.

9.10.2 Critical Frequency Prewarping

Let us revisit the Tustin approximation for s

$$s \approx K \frac{z-1}{z+1}$$

where $K = 2/T$ in the standard approximation (for example, the one used by the *disc* command).

We state the problem as follows: Can we find a K so that that at a specific frequency the above approximation becomes exact. The frequency we choose is one that we determine is critical to our filter design, i.e., $\omega = \omega_c$. Letting $s = j\,\omega_c$

$$j\,\omega_c = j K \tan \frac{\omega_c T}{2}$$

Clearly, if we choose

$$K = \frac{\omega_c}{\tan \omega_c T/2}$$

$H(s)$ and $H(z)$ will be identical at $\omega = \omega_c$.
The critical frequency prewarping technique, therefore, is

$$\textit{Critical Frequency Prewarping:}\ s \rightarrow \frac{\omega_c}{\tan \omega_c T/2} \, \frac{z-1}{z+1}$$

Note that as T gets small, this transformation approaches the regular Tustin's approximation.

The next example will show the use of critical frequency warping in digitizing a notch filter. Before we show this example, we need to discuss how to implement this technique in MATRIXx. The *disc* command only provides the standard Tustin approximation. We can fool this command into using warping as follows. The *disc* command with the *tustin* option uses

$$s \rightarrow \frac{2}{T}\frac{z-1}{z+1}$$

whereas, we want $s \rightarrow \dfrac{\omega_c}{\tan \omega_c T/2}\dfrac{z-1}{z+1}$

In the normal use of the *disc* command, the actual sample period is used. There is nothing to prevent us from using a different value, say T_w, in the command. That is, we prewarp the sample period. Comparing the two approximations for s, we can derive the following (ω_c is the critical frequency, and T is the actual sample period)

$$T_w = \frac{2}{\omega_c} \tan \frac{\omega_c T}{2}$$

Example 9.5 Critical Frequency Pre-warping

For the sample period $T = 0.1$ sec, digitize the notch filter

$$H(s) = \frac{s^2 + 0.2s + 100}{s^2 + 10s + 100}$$

We note the notch occurs at 10 rad/sec, which becomes our critical frequency. We will obtain the unwarped digital notch filter at $T = 0.1$ sec and the prewarped filter at $T_w = 0.1093$ sec, and show their frequency responses.

The digital filter for T = 0.1 is given by

```
DZ1    =
  1.0000  -.8571   .4286

NZ1    =
   .7200  -.8571   .7086
```

Prewarping at the critical frequency results in the following filter

```
DZ2    =
  1.0000  -.7606   .4077

NZ2    =
   .7098  -.7606   .6979
```

Figure 9-17 shows the plots of the original and digitized magnitudes. Only with critical frequency prewarping have we achieved the goal of maintaining the notch frequency. Note however, that we cannot control the bandwidth or other parameters with this (or any) digitization technique.

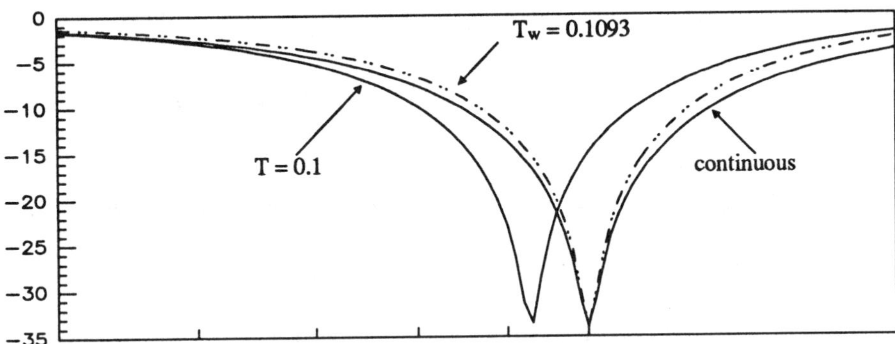

Figure 9-17 Frequency responses of analog and digital notch filters.

9.11 Digital Compensators

There are several methods for designing digital compensators.

1. Conversion of a classically designed continuous compensator into an equivalent digital compensator.
2. Direct design of a digital compensator using frequency transform techniques.
3. Direct design of a digital compensator using state-space techniques.

As we have seen in the previous sections, great care must be taken with the first method. Conversion of a continuous compensator to a digital compensator is most often accomplished with Tustin's with or without prewarping. At very high sample rates, these techniques have proved very effective. At lower sample rates, however, this conversion usually creates unexpected problems. This happens because the digital compensator has significantly different response characteristics than the original continuous compensator.

Design in the z-plane more often allows the designer to incorporate the effects of the sample period. The most useful technique here is the root locus. We have already seen that frequency response plots of z-domain transfer functions are not as well behaved as their continuous counterparts. Later, however, we will introduce another transformation, the w-transform, which will allow us to use Bode plots for digital design.

9.11.1 Proportional-Integral-derivative Control

The proportional-integral-derivative controller (PID), introduced in Chapter 7, is as effective in digital systems as it is in continuous systems. In fact, it is the most popular and commercially available controller used in the process industry. The integral controller increases the system type, which reduces steady state error. The derivative controller increases the damping and, hence, the stability of the system. The most common discrete PID controller has the following form

$$PID \qquad K_p + K_D \frac{(z-1)}{zT} + K_I \frac{zT}{z-1}$$

In this formulation, velocity is found as the difference between present and past value divided by the sample period, $(1 - z^{-1})/T$. The integral term assumes that we are finding the area under a constant value over the period T.

The Ziegler-Nichols method, described in Chapter 7, can also be used here. Do not forget to include the sample period in the controller formulation.

First, set $K_d = K_I = 0$ and then increase the proportional gain until the system just oscillates (i.e., closed loop poles on the unit circle in the z-plane). The proportional gain is then halved, and the other two gains are calculated as

$$K_p = 0.6\,K_m \qquad K_D = \frac{K_p \pi}{4\,\omega_m} \qquad K_I = \frac{K_p\,\omega_m}{\pi}$$

where K_m is gain at which the proportional system oscillates and ω_m is the oscillation frequency. The oscillation frequency can be found from the angle of the pole which crosses the unit circle, i.e., $\omega_m = \theta/T$. The oscillation frequency can also be found by running a closed loop step response with $K_p = K_m$.

Note that this technique does not design to any specifications. Rather, Ziegler and Nichols found that this design procedure provided "good" behavior for process controllers.

Example 9.6 PID Design with Ziegler-Nichols

Design a digital PID controller for $G(s)$ with a sample period of $T = 0.25$ sec.

$$G(s) = \frac{10}{s(s+2)}$$

Remember to always use the ZOH equivalent to digitize a plant. We then run a root locus on $G(z)$ to determine K_m and ω_m. Finally, we calculate the PID controller parameters and run a step response.

Using root locus, we find that for a gain of 1.75, the poles are at

```
Z1    =
.5716 + .8199j
.5716 - .8199j
```

The magnitude of these poles is 0.9995, which is almost on the unit circle. We can compute the frequency of oscillation from

```
< > wm=atan2(z1(1))/T
```

WM =
3.8480

The PID parameters are

KP = 1.0500
KD = .2143
KI = 1.2861

We now run a step response for this PID design. The result of the step response is shown in Figure 9-18. The PID controller produces a system with an overshoot of 90% and a settling time of 4.5 sec.

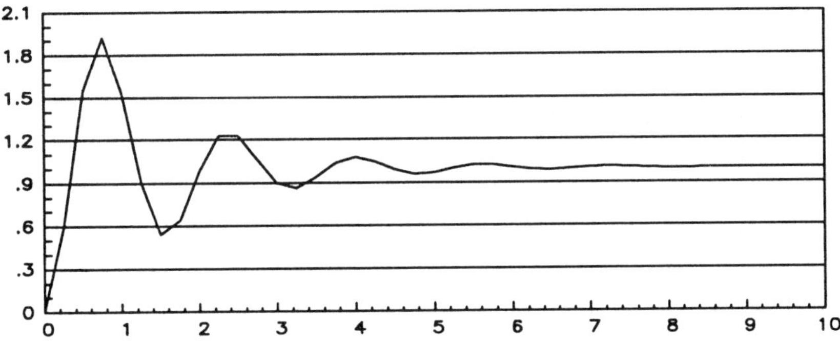

Figure 9-18 Step response of Ziegler-Nichols design.

9.11.2 PID—Analytical Technique

The analytical technique we discussed in Chapter 7 was based on phase margin calculations. This procedure will not work easily here. We can derive a new analytical procedure, however, that is based on the root locus technique.

We first determine K_I from the steady state error requirement. Next, we determine the desired z-plane point, z_1, from the time domain specifications. If z_1 is to be on the root locus, then

$$\left(K_p + K_D \frac{z_1 - 1}{z_1 T} + K_I \frac{z_1 T}{z_1 - 1} \right) G(z_1) = -1$$

Because K_I and z_1 are known

$$K_p + K_D \frac{z_1 - 1}{z_1 T} = -\frac{1}{G(z_1)} - K_I \frac{z_1 T}{z_1 - 1}$$

The preceding is a complex equation. Equating the real and imaginary parts of the equation, results in two equations in two unknowns. Let R and X denote the real and imaginary parts of the right hand side of the preceding equation and define

$$\alpha + j\beta = \frac{z_1 - 1}{z_1 T}$$

We find that

$$K_D = X / \beta \qquad , \qquad K_p = R - \alpha K_D$$

Example 9.7 PID Analytical Design

Given $G(s)$, design a PID controller satisfying the following requirements

$T = 0.25$ sec, $\zeta = 0.707$, and $\omega_n = 1.414$ rad/sec.

Track a unit ramp input with zero steady state error.

$$G(s) = \frac{10}{s(s+2)}$$

The desired s-plane point is $s_1 = -1 + j$. The z-plane location for the pole is given by $z_1 = e^{s_1 T} = 0.7546 + j0.1927$.

Because the plant is Type 1, the PID controller will increase the system to Type 2. Therefore, we have satisfied immediately the only steady state error requirement. This gives us some freedom in choosing K_I. We start with $K_I = 4$. The program for this example appears in the Appendix.

When we check the closed loop poles, we find that they are

-.8545 + 1.2701j
-.8545 - 1.2701j
.7546 + .1927j
.7546 - .1927j

We note that the system has a pair of complex conjugate poles located outside the unit circle (magnitude = 1.53). Therefore, the system is unstable! Has the program failed to place the poles at the desired location? The answer is that the program has not failed; the design has. This is obvious if we compare the closed loop poles to the desired pole location. We have achieved the desired pole location.

This is the problem with these analytical techniques. We can guarantee that one of the system poles will be where we want it to be. We have no control over where the other poles go.

If we rerun the simulation with $K_I = 1$, we do achieve a stable design, as shown in Figure 9-19. The various parameters are $R = 0.5552$, $X = 0.5177$, $\alpha = -0.9764$, and $\beta = 1.2707$. The PID parameters for this design are: $K_p = 0.9531$, $K_D = 0.4074$, and $K_I = 1.0$.

The closed loop poles are now at

.1714 + .7593j
.1714 - .7593j
.7546 + .1927j
.7546 - .1927j

The magnitude of the poles are 0.7784 and 0.7788, verifying a stable design. Note from the step response the large overshoot. This is due to our lack of control over poles and zeros using this technique.

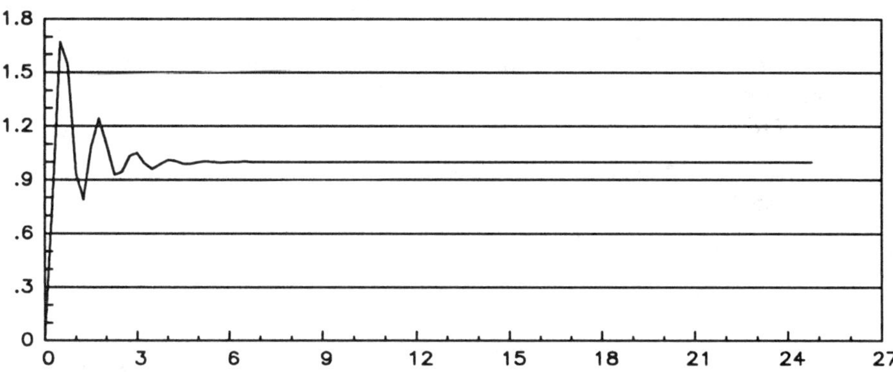

Figure 9-19 Step response of the system using analytical PID design.

9.11.3 Lead-lag Compensation

A discrete lead or lag compensator can be designed with the root locus technique. Because a discrete root locus follows the same mathematics as the continuous root locus, all of the graphical techniques discussed in Chapter 7 should work here. The exception is that the focus is now on the inside of the unit circle in the z-plane rather than on the LHP in the s-plane.

Being limited to working within the unit circle creates some problems. A digital system will go unstable at lower gains than the equivalent continuous system. Also, discrete transfer functions often have more zeros than continuous transfer functions. This makes for a complicated root locus, all of which is squeezed inside a small working area.

To aid in lead (or lag) discrete compensator design, we have developed an analytical technique. Always consider such techniques as starting points in the design. Remember the problem with the PID analytical design. We can guarantee that the root locus will go through the desired z-plane locations, but we cannot guarantee that these will be the dominant poles. The final discrete compensator has the form

$$K(z) = K_c \frac{z+a}{z+b}$$

Because we find steady state error constants for $z = 1$, we can use the steady state error requirement to find K_c. Therefore, we will use the following definition

$$K(z) = \overline{K}\,\frac{\dfrac{z-1}{v} + 1}{\dfrac{z-1}{w} + 1} = \overline{K}\,\frac{\dfrac{\overline{z}}{v} + 1}{\dfrac{\overline{z}}{w} + 1}$$

where $\overline{z} = z - 1$, $a = v - 1$, $b = w - 1$, $K_c = \overline{K}\, w/v$

Now, when $z = 1$, $\overline{z} = 0$, so $\overline{K}$ is the compensator's contribution to the steady state error.

From the transient requirements for the system, we determine s_1, the desired s-plane location. We then use $z_1 = e^{sT}$ to find the z-plane location z_1 and then $\overline{z}_1$. The derivation of this analytical technique follows.

For z_1 to be on the root locus

$$K(z_1)\, G(z_1) = \overline{K}\,\frac{\dfrac{\overline{z}}{v} + 1}{\dfrac{\overline{z}}{w} + 1}\, G(z_1) = -1 \quad \rightarrow \quad \frac{\dfrac{\overline{z}}{v} + 1}{\dfrac{\overline{z}}{w} + 1} = \frac{-1}{\overline{K}\, G(z_1)}$$

If we solve for $1/v$

$$v^{-1} = -\frac{w^{-1}}{\overline{K}\, G(z_1)} - \frac{1}{\overline{z}_1}\left(1 + \frac{1}{\overline{K}\, G(z_1)}\right)$$

Now, because both the compensator pole and zero must be real, v^{-1} and w^{-1} must be real. Therefore, the imaginary terms on both sides of this equation must be 0. Setting the imaginary term of the right side of the equation to 0 and factoring out the real w^{-1} gives us

$$w^{-1} = \frac{-\operatorname{Im}\left(\dfrac{1}{\overline{z}_1} + \dfrac{1}{\overline{z}_1\, \overline{K}\, G(z_1)}\right)}{\operatorname{Im}\left(\dfrac{1}{\overline{z}_1\, \overline{K}\, G(z_1)}\right)} \quad \text{and} \quad v^{-1} = -\frac{w^{-1}}{\overline{K}\, G(z_1)} - \frac{1}{\overline{z}_1\, \overline{K}\, G(z_1)} - \frac{1}{\overline{z}_1}$$

The following example will demonstrate the procedure.

Example 9.8 Digital Lead Compensator Design

Consider the plant $G(s)$, where the sampling period is 0.05 sec. The specifications are steady state error of 20%, $\zeta = 0.5$, and $\omega_n = 14$ rad/sec.

$$G(s) = \frac{400}{s(s^2 + 30s + 200)}$$

The steady state error specification requires an error constant of 5. Because the plant has an error constant of 2, the compensator must contribute 2.5, i.e., $K = 2.5$.

The transient specifications require the s-plane root of $-7 + j12.12$ and predict a settling time of 0.7 sec. The desired z-plane poles are at $0.5792 + j\,0.4014$. The program is given in the Appendix. The compensator is

$$K(z) = 9.9935\,\frac{z - 0.7609}{z - 0.0441}$$

The resulting closed loop poles are at

-.0270 + .0000j
.5792 + .4014j
.5792 - .4014j
.8289 + .0000j

The closed loop zeros are at

-2.6170
.7609
-.1806

All closed loop poles are inside the unit circle, but the system has a zero outside the circle.

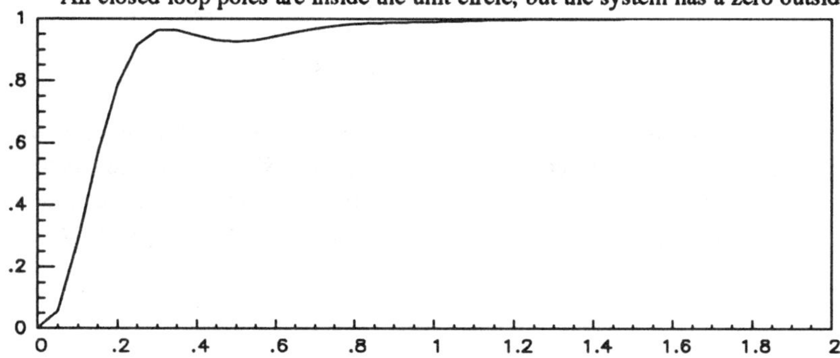

Figure 9-20 Step response for Example 9.8.

Figure 9-20 shows the step response. We have achieved our desired complex poles and a settling time of 1.0 sec. The step response looks quite different from a second order system with dominant poles. As you can see from the pole-zero structure of the system, the complex poles are not dominant in this case.

9.11.4 The *w*-Transform

To this point, we have discussed two methods for designing digital compensators: conversion of a continuous compensator using various transformations; and design in the z-domain. Conversion of a continuous compensator works well when the sample rate is high. The z-domain techniques are preferable at lower sample rates.

The z-domain technique has some disadvantages. For one, all of the design must take place within the limited confines of the unit circle. For another, Bode design techniques that correlate gain crossover frequency and phase margin with closed loop behavior do not apply to the z-transform. These techniques apply to transfer functions whose stability region is the left hand plane.

The *w-transform* is a technique that allows us to apply all s-domain design methods to digital systems. In this technique, we transform $H(z)$ into $H(w)$ using the following variable substitution

$$w = \frac{2}{T}\frac{z-1}{z+1}$$

If this equation looks familiar, it is because it has the same form as Tustin's approximation for s. We already know that Tustin approximation preserves the mapping of the $j\omega$ axis into the unit circle. We can conclude that the w-transform also preserves this mapping. That is, the interior of the unit circle in the z-plane maps into the left side of the w-plane.

All design techniques that we describe in Chapter 7 for $G(s)$ can be applied to $G(w)$. In this procedure, we first use the ZOH approximation to convert the continuous plant $G(s)$ to the discrete plant $G(z)$. We then use the following to convert to $G(w)$

$$z = \frac{1 + wT/2}{1 - wT/2}$$

We now design the compensator using the Bode or root locus techniques discussed in Chapter 7. Finally, we convert the compensator design back to the z-plane. The last step is necessary because we implement digital computers as difference equations.

As an example of converting a continuous plant to the w-plane, consider

$$H(s) = \frac{1}{s + 1}$$

Digitizing with ZOH approximation for $T = 0.5$ sec (using the *disc* command)

$$H(z) = \frac{0.393}{z - 0.607}$$

Continuing with the process, we replace z to get

$$H(w) = \frac{1}{\dfrac{1+0.25w}{1-0.25w} + 1} = \frac{1-0.25w}{1+1.023w}$$

We see that the poles of $H(w)$ and the original $H(s)$ are very close. As we shall see in the next example, this is a function of the sample period. We also note that $H(w)$ has a RHP zero that does not exist in the original $H(s)$. This zero, introduced by the sampling process, is also a function of the sampling period and is common in w-transforms. You must be careful, therefore, when using Bode plots to determine stability of w-plane transfer functions.

MATRIXx does not have a built-in routine for taking w-transforms. We have written a simple program called *z2w* to convert a z-plane transfer function to the w-plane. We can use the *disc* command with the *tustin* option to convert from the w to the z domain.

Example 9.9 The *w*-Transform

Given $H(s)$, Convert to the w-domain using three sample periods, T = 0.5, 0.1, and 0.05 sec. Draw the Bode magnitude plots for the continuous and the three different w-transformed transfer functions.

$$H(s) = \frac{10}{s+5}$$

We first use the *disc* command with the ZOH option to convert to the z-domain and then use the program *z2w* in the Appendix to convert to the w-domain. The results are

$$T = 0.5, \quad H_1(w) = 1.69\,\frac{-w+4}{w+3.393}$$

$$T = 0.1, \quad H_2(w) = 0.49\,\frac{-w+20}{w+4.898}$$

$$T = 0.05, \quad H_3(w) = 0.24\,\frac{-w+40}{w+4.974}$$

We see that as T gets smaller, the w-plane pole approaches the s-plane pole. Also note that all three w-plane transfer functions have the same low frequency gain of 2 as the continuous transfer function. The w-transform always preserves the low frequency gain of $H(s)$.

A big difference in the three transformed functions is the right half plane zero location. As the sample rate gets smaller, the zero moves further and further away from frequencies of interest and will have less effect on the design process.

Figure 9-21 shows the Bode plots for the three w-transformed transfer functions along with the Bode plot for the continuous plant. The fact that there are differences between these plots does not invalidate the use of the w-transform. The w-transform accurately reflects the effect of driving a continuous plant with a sampled signal.

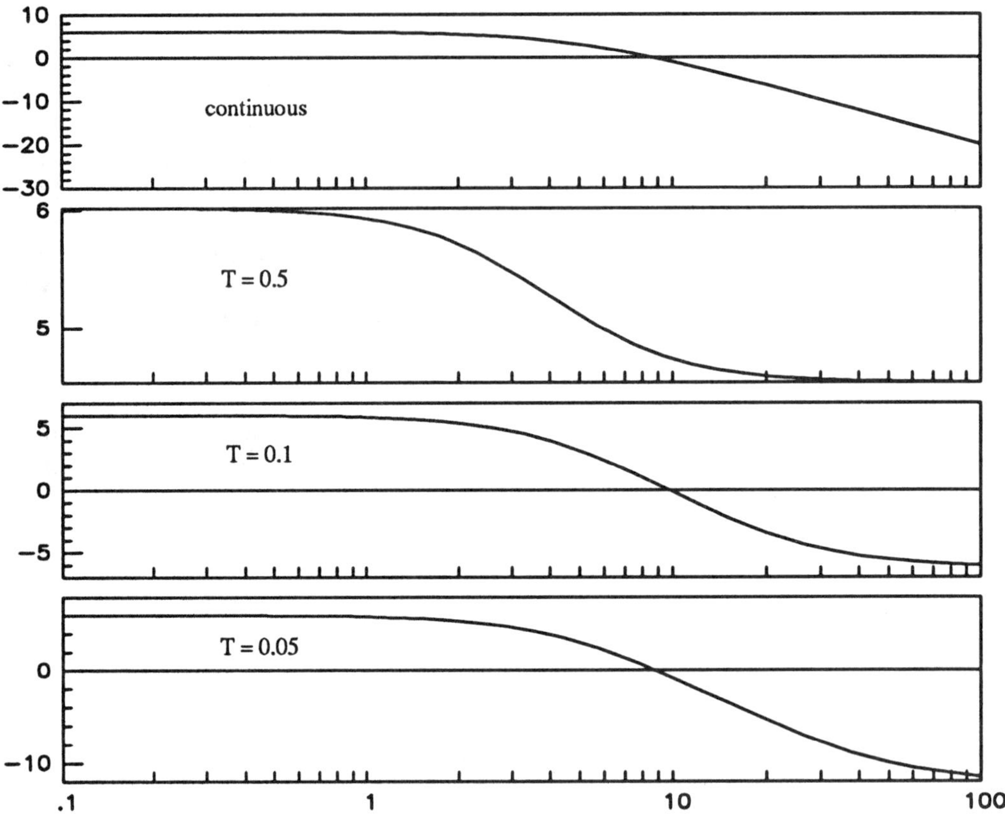

Figure 9-21 Bode plots of an analog transfer function and its w-transform using different sample periods.

Before we use the w-transform for compensator design, we must examine the relationship between s and w in more detail. Remember that transient specifications lead to requirements on the gain crossover frequency when $s = j\omega$. How do we use this information in the w-plane? If we return to the defining relationship for w and let $z = e^{sT}$, we get

$$w = \frac{2}{T}\frac{e^{sT} - 1}{e^{sT} + 1}$$

where both w and s are complex variables. For frequency plots of continuous systems we let $s = j\omega$. In this case, w will be imaginary, and we can let $w = jv$. So

$$jv = \frac{2}{T}\frac{e^{j\omega T} - 1}{e^{j\omega T} + 1} = j\frac{2}{T}\tan\frac{\omega T}{2}$$

After we determine the gain crossover frequency ω_{gc} from the transient specifications for the plant, we determine the w-plane crossover frequency from

$$v_{gc} = \frac{2}{T}\tan\frac{T\omega_{gc}}{2}$$

We then use the standard Bode design techniques to determine the compensator.

Example 9.10 *w*-Transform Design

Use the w-Transform to perform the compensator design for the plant and specification given in Example 9.8.

We will use the analytical Bode design technique described in Chapter 7 (see the Appendix in Chapter 7 for the program). We first discretize the plant with T= 0.05. We then use the w-transform to get the w-plane model for the plant

$$G(w) = \frac{0.0018w^3 - 0.1261w^2 - 6.8186w + 362.176}{w(w^2 + 28.2814w + 181.0898)}$$

The steady state error requirement of 20% requires a compensator gain of 2.5. We also require $\zeta = 0.5$ and $\omega_n = 14$ rad/sec. Translating these to frequency domain implies a PM of 50 degrees and gain crossover frequency of 14 rad/sec. Before proceeding with the design, we must convert the s-plane frequency to the w-plane

$$v_{gc} = \frac{2}{T}\tan\frac{\omega_n T}{2} = 14.6$$

Using the analytical Bode lead program in Chapter 7 gives the following w-plane lead compensator

$$K(w) = \frac{0.4132w + 1}{0.0134w + 1}$$

We now use Tustin transform to convert this back to the z-plane

$$K(z) = \frac{28.5602z - 25.3015}{z + 0.3035}$$

The resulting closed loop poles are at

.2543 + .0000j
.4228 - .6424j
.4228 + .6424j
.9134 + .0000j

The closed loop zeros are

-2.6170
.8859
-.1806

The step response for the compensated feedback system is shown in Figure 9-22. We have achieved an overshoot of 10% and a settling time of 2 sec. Note that the complex poles are not dominant.

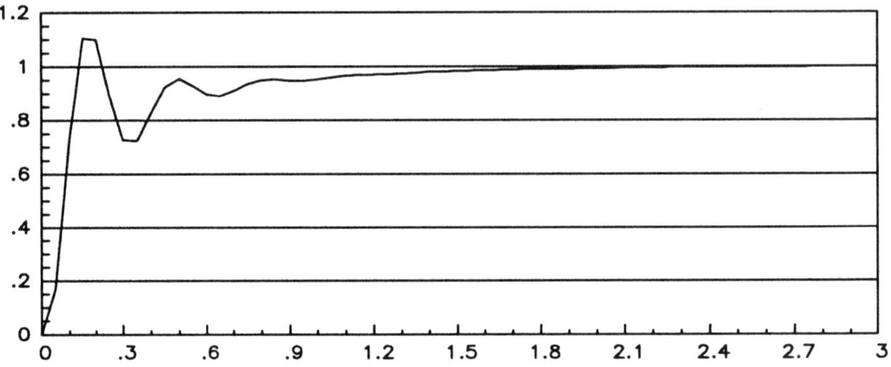

Figure 9-22 Step response for Example 9-10.

Compensator Delay

To this point, we have assumed that there is no delay between the compensator input and output. This is, in fact, never the case. We implement a digital compensator as a difference equation in the computer controller. There will always be some processing delay in the controller. System delays tend to destabilize. Also, we can expect that delays will effect the transient response. Therefore, it is wise to include known delays in the design process. The easiest way to do this is to include the delay in the plant model, i.e., multiply $G(z)$ by $1 / z^n$ for a delay of nT periods, and then proceed with the design.

9.12 Discrete State Space Design

The state space model for a discrete plant is given by

$$x_{k+1} = A x_k + B u_k$$

$$y_k = C x_k + D u_k$$

where the plant poles are the eigenvalues of A. As with continuous systems, we can design compensators for discrete systems using pole placement discussed in Chapter 8, linear quadratic regulator algorithms discussed in Chapter 12, or algebraic design techniques described in Chapter 10. The control input is then given by

$$u_k = -K x_k$$

The *poleplace* command applies in the discrete case without any modifications. The plant is discretized, and the desired poles are chosen within the unit circle (or in the LHP and transformed via the exponential map). Observers are designed similarly, with the exception that the observer equations are difference equations rather than differential equations.

9.13 Appendix

A-1 Programs

1. Analytical PID Design Program

```
//This program calculates the PID parameters kp and kd given ki,
//which is determined from steady state error requirements. It also
//finds closed loop poles, zeros and step response.
//inputs are ng,dg,s1,T,Ki,Tmax(for step analysis)
[sg,nsg]=sform(ng,dg);
[sgd,nsgd]=disc(sg,nsg,t);
[a,b,c,d]=split(sgd,nsgd);
z1=exp(s1*t)
kz1=c*(z1*eye(nsg)-a)\b+d
r=-real(1/kz1+(ki*z1*t)/(z1-1))
x=-imag(1/kz1+(ki*z1*t)/(z1-1))
alpha=real((z1-1)/(z1*t))
beta=imag((z1-1)/(z1*t))
kd=real(x/beta)
kp=real(r-kd*alpha)
nk_pid=[kp*t+kd+ki*t*t, -kp*t-2*kd, kd]
dk_pid=[t, -t, 0]
[sk,nsk]=sform(nk_pid,dk_pid);
[sgk,nsgk]=series(sk,nsk,sgd,nsgd);
[st,nst]=feedback(sgk,nsgk);
clp=eig(st,nst), clz=zeros(st,nst)
npts=1+tmax/t;
[n,y]=dstep(st,nst); time=n*t; plot(time,y);
return
```

2. Digital Lead Design Program

```
// This program requires: g=ng/dg, s1, T, kbar, Tmax
z1=exp(s1*t);
zbar1=z1-1;
[ngz,dgz]=disc(ng,dg,t);
ngz_z1=polyval(ngz,z1);dgz_z1=polyval(dgz,z1);
g_z1=ngz_z1/dgz_z1
w_inv = -imag((1+1/(kbar*g_z1))/zbar1)/imag(1/(kbar*g_z1));
v_inv=-w_inv/(kbar*g_z1) - (1 + 1/(kbar*g_z1))/zbar1;
w=1/w_inv, v=1/v_inv
a=v-1; b=w-1; kc=kbar*w/v;
nk=real(kc*[1 a]);dk=real([1 b]);
[sk,nsk]=sform(nk,dk);
[sd,nsd]=sform(ngz,dgz);
[sgk,nsgk]=series(sd,nsd,sk,nsk);
[st,nst]=feedback(sgk,nsgk);
npts=1+tmax/t;
[n,y]=dstep(st,nst,npts);
time=n*t;
return
```

3. *w*-Transform Program

```
//[nhw,dhw,sw,nsw]=z2w(nhz,dhz,t)
[sd,nsd]=sform(nhz,dhz);
[a b c d]=split(sd,nsd);
t1=eye(nsd) + a;
t2 =eye(nsd) - a;
ad=t1\t2;
bd =-(eye(nsd)+ad)*(t1\b);
cd = c;
dd = -c*(t1\b) + d;
ad=-2*ad/t;
bd=-2*bd/t;
sw=[ad bd;cd dd];
nsw=nsd;
[nhw,dhw]=tform(sw,nsw)
retf
```

A-2 Tables of z-Transform and ZOH Equivalents

Table 9-1 Table of z-Transform Pairs and Properties

f(t)	f(kT)	F(z)
$\delta(t)$	δ_k	1
$u(t)$	$u(kT)$	$\frac{z}{z-1}$
e^{-at}	e^{-aTk}	$\frac{z}{z-e^{-aT}}$
t	kT	$\frac{Tz}{(z-1)^2}$
$\cos \omega T$	$\cos \omega Tk$	$\frac{z(z-\cos \omega T)}{z^2-(2\cos \omega T)z+1}$
$\sin \omega T$	$\sin \omega Tk$	$\frac{z \sin \omega T}{z^2-(2\cos \omega T)z+1}$
$e^{-at} f(t)$	$e^{-aTk} f(kT)$	$F(e^{aT} z)$
$f(t-nT)$	$f((k-n)T)$	$z^{-n} F(z)$
$f(t+nT)$	$f((k+n)T)$	$z^n F(z) - z^n f(0) - \ldots - z f(n-1)$
	$f(\infty)$	$\lim_{z \to 1} (z-1) F(z)$

Table 9-2 Table of Transfer Functions, Their z-transform, and ZOH Equivalents		
G(s)	G(z)	G(z)ZOH
$\frac{1}{s}$	$\frac{z}{z-1}$	$\frac{T}{z-1}$
$\frac{a}{s+a}$	$\frac{az}{z-e^{-aT}}$	$\frac{1-e^{-aT}}{z-e^{-aT}}$
$\frac{a^2}{(s+a)^2}$	$\frac{a^2Tze^{-aT}}{(z-e^{-aT})^2}$	$\frac{Az+B}{(z-e^{-at})^2}$ where $A=1-e^{-aT}-aTe^{-aT}$ and $B=(aT-1)\,e^{-aT}+e^{-2aT}$
$\frac{\omega_n^2}{s^2+2\zeta\omega_n s+\omega_n^2}$	$K\frac{ze^{-aT}\sin bT}{z^2-2e^{-aT}(\cos bT)z+e^{-2aT}}$ where $a=2\zeta\omega_n$, $b=\omega_n\sqrt{1-\zeta^2}$ and $K=\omega_n^2/b$	$\frac{Az+B}{z^2-2e^{-aT}(\cos bT)z+e^{-2aT}}$ where $A=1-e^{-aT}\cos bT-(a/b)\,e^{-aT}\sin bT$ and $B=e^{-2aT}+(a/b)e^{-aT}-e^{-aT}\cos bT$

9.14 Problems

9.1 Solve the following difference equations

a. $y_{n+1}+y_n=-\cos(n\pi)$, $\quad y_0=0$

b. $y_{n+1}-y_n=x_{n+1}-x_n$, $\quad x_n=$ unit step

c. $y_{n+2}+y_n=0$, $\quad y(-1)=0$, $y(-2)=-2$

9.2 Consider the following relaxed system:

$y_n=x_n+0.5\,(x_{n-1}+y_{n-1})$

a. Find the impulse response, h_n.

b. Find the unit step response, y_n.

9.3 Suppose you borrow money from the bank at the rate, β, and make monthly payments of P dollars. Let the initial loan be for L dollars.

a. Find a general formula for your debt, d_n, at start of month n.

b. Find your monthly payments, P, to pay off the loan in N years.

c. Write a program that will compute and tabulate the debt and monthly payments.

d. Find monthly mortgage payments for a \$125,000, 30-year loan at the rate of 9.125%.

9.4 Let y_n denote the step response, h_n the impulse response, and recall that by definition of the transfer function, $H(z)$ is the z-transform of h_n.

a. If the input is a step, find a difference equation relating y_n to h_n. (*Note:* this gives you a way to find the impulse response directly in the time domain from the step response).

b. Show that $y_n = \sum_{m=0}^{n} h_m$ satisfies the above equation.

c. Use -transform to find impulse and step responses for the system $H(z) = \dfrac{z+1}{z-1}$

d. Use the step response in part c and the equation obtained in part a to find the impulse response directly in the time domain.

e. Note that part b gives a direct time domain formula to find the step response from the impulse response. Now use the impulse response in part c to find the step response using the formula given in part b.

9.5 Let y_n and h_n denote unit step and impulse response of an LTI system.

a. Use z-transform to obtain a difference equation relation between h_n and y_n.

b. Using z-transform, find step response of a digital filter satisfying:

$$y_n - y_{n-1} = x_n\,, \qquad y(-1) = 0$$

c. Find the impulse response of the above filter using the relation in part a.

d. Based on the above input-output pairs, what do you think the filter does?

9.6 Find the inverse z-transform of $H(z) = \dfrac{4\,(z-3)}{(z-2)\,(z-1)}$.

9.7 Conside the following so called "running sum":

$$y_n = \sum_{i=0}^{n} h_i$$

a. Write a first order difference equation involving y_n, y_{n-1}, and h_n.

b. Use the equation in part a to find $Y(z)$ in terms of $H(z)$.

c. Use the result in part b to find a general formula for the sum of first n integers.

9.8 Find $F(z)$ if $f(n)$ is given by

$$f(n) = \begin{cases} 1 & n \text{ even} \\ 0 & n \text{ odd} \end{cases}$$

9.9 Derive a general formula for the sum of n squared integers as follows

a. Find Z { k^2 }.

b. Note that y_n satisfies

$$y_n - y_{n-1} = n^2 \quad , \quad y(-1) = 0$$

Solving this difference equation will provide the general formula.

9.10 Consider the following Finite Impulse Response (FIR) filter.

$$y_{k+3} = \frac{1}{4} \sum_{i=0}^{3} u_{k+i}$$

a. Obtain a state space representation {A,b,c,d}.

b. The impulse response of this filter is equal to 0 for values of k > N. Find N (this is why it is called FIR).

9.11 Consider the following system:

$$x(k+1) = A\, x(k) + B\, u(k) \quad \text{where} \quad A = \begin{bmatrix} 3 & -4 \\ 2 & -3 \end{bmatrix}, \quad B = \begin{bmatrix} 1 \\ 0 \end{bmatrix}$$

$$y(k) = C\, x(k) \qquad\qquad C = [1 \quad 0]$$

a. Find the transfer function $H(z)$.

b. Find the impulse response and plot it. Explain the oscillations.

c. Assuming zero initial conditions, find $x(k)$ if $u(k)=\delta(k)$. Also, plot the state sequence in the (x_1, x_2) plane.

d. Assume zero initial conditions, find the step response of the system and plot $y(k)$.

e. Find the step response by solving the state equations directly in time domain assuming zero initial conditions. List $x(k)$ for a few values and plot $x(k)$ in the (x_1, x_2) plane.

9.12 Consider the following system: $T(s) = \dfrac{2\,s^2 + 0.1\,s + 0.4}{s^2 + 0.2\,s + 1}$

Let the sampling period $T = 0.1$ sec. Digitize the system using Euler forward and backward, Tustin, and ZOH approximations. Obtain the step responses and Bode plots over the same range and determine the properties of each transform. Repeat the simulation for $T = 10$ and 0.01 sec.

9.13 Consider the following plant: $G(s) = \dfrac{4}{(s+1)^3\,(s+2)^2}$

a. Find the ZOH equivalent of $G(s)$ for the following sampling periods: $T = 0.5, 1, 4$ sec.

b. Find the poles and zeros $G(z)$. Note that even though $G(s)$ in minimum phase, $G(z)$ may turn out to be nonminimum phase depending on the choice of sampling period.

9.14 In this problem, we study the effects of the various digitization techniques applied to a continuous notch filter. In many control systems we wish to filter out a specific frequency, for example 60 Hz. The following continuous notch filter will provide 40 dB of attenuation at 60 Hz.

$$G(s) = \frac{s^2 + 1.2\pi s + (120\pi)^2}{s^2 + 60\pi s + (120\pi)^2}$$

a. Digitize this continuous filter at a sampling period of $T = 1$ msec using all of the *discrete* options. Show the Bode magnitude plots of the continuous and all of the digitized filters on the same graph.

b. Use the critical frequency warping technique to digitize this filter. Compare the magnitude response of this digitization with the continuous filter.

9.15 Matched pole-zero is another technique used to convert from a continuous to a digital filter. Consider

$$G(s) = 100\frac{s+10}{(s+1)(s+5)}$$

We can digitize this filter by replacing each finite pole or zero term $s + a$ with its discrete equivalent $z - e^{-aT}$, where T is the sample period. It has been found that this technique works best if we also consider the zeros at infinity. That is, if there are n poles and m zeros in the continuous transfer filter, we include the term $(z+1)^{n-m}$ in the numerator of the digital filter. Finally we adjust the digital filter gain so that both digital and continuous filters have the same low frequency gain. This results in

$$GZ(z) = K\frac{(z+1)(z-e^{-10T})}{(z-e^{-T})(z-e^{-5T})} \qquad K = 100\frac{(1-e^{-T})(1-e^{-5T})}{(1-e^{-10T})}$$

where K is chosen so $GZ(1) = G(0)$.

a. Find and display on single graphs, the Bode magnitude and phase plots for the continuous filter and the matched pole-zero for sample periods of $T = 0.5, 0.25, 0.1$ sec.

b. Find and display on a single graph the step responses of the filters in part a.

9.16 We described, in the preceding problem, the matched pole-zero technique for simple pole and zeros. Derive the transformation for a second order pole or zero term

$$s^2 + \zeta\,\omega_n\,s + \omega_n^2$$

a. Digitize the notch filter of Problem 9.15 using the matched pole-zero technique. Compare the magnitude response of this filter with the continuous and critically warped notch filters.

9.17 Consider the following plant: $KG(s) = \dfrac{K}{(s+1)\,(s+2)}$

Assuming a sampling period of 1 sec, use discrete root locus to find the values of K for which the closed loop system remains stable.

9.18 Consider the following plant: $G(s) = \dfrac{2}{s\,(s+1)}$

Let the sampling period be $T = 2$ sec. Design a cascade compensator to achieve a phase margin of 45 degrees. Use w-transform method.

9.19 Consider the plant: $G(s) = \dfrac{1}{s\,(s+4)}$

It is desired that the closed loop system follow unit ramp inputs with less than 5% error, have a bandwidth of at most 7 rad/sec and have a phase margin of at least 45 degrees. Design a cascade compensator using w-transform method. You should select the sampling frequency to be at least 10 times the closed loop bandwidth.

9.20 We described the inverted pendulum in Problem 7.6. We now wish to design a digital controller for this system. Determine the sampling rate by first finding the bandwidth your continuous design. Select the the sample rate to be 10 times this bandwidth.

9.21 The double inverted pendulum is created by hinging a second rod to the top of the rod described in Problem 7.6. A digital controller for this system was presented by [ZZH87]. Their linear model used the six states defined by

$$x = [y, \theta_1, \theta_2 - \theta_1, \dot{y}, \dot{\theta}_1, \dot{\theta}_1 - \dot{\theta}_2]'$$

where y is cart position, θ_1 is the angle the bottom rod makes to the horizontal, and θ_2 is the equivalent angle of the top rod. The difference in the two angles measures the alignment between the rods, which we would like to maintain at a zero angle. The discrete model ($T = 20$ msec) was given as

$$x_{k+1} = \begin{pmatrix} A_{11} & A_{12} \\ A_{21} & A_{22} \end{pmatrix} x_k + b\, u_k$$

$$r_k = C\, x_k$$

where

$$A_{11} = \begin{pmatrix} 1.0 & -2.411E{-}4 & 1.152E{-}5 \\ 0 & 1.003 & -1.77E{-}3 \\ 0 & -3.95E{-}3 & 1.0074 \end{pmatrix}$$

$$A_{12} = \begin{pmatrix} 0.0148 & -3.08E{-}7 & -3.07E{-}7 \\ 2.65E{-}3 & 0.016 & 7.30E{-}3 \\ -3.07E{-}3 & 2.35E{-}5 & 0.016 \end{pmatrix}$$

$$A_{21} = \begin{pmatrix} 0 & -0.0294 & 1.4E{-}3 \\ 0 & 0.4244 & -0.221 \\ 0 & -0.492 & 0.924 \end{pmatrix}$$

$$A_{22} = \begin{pmatrix} 0.858 & -1.20E{-}4 & -4.11E{-}5 \\ 0.323 & 1.00 & 3.21E{-}4 \\ -0.374 & 1.62E{-}3 & 1.00 \end{pmatrix}$$

$$b = (7.53E{-}4, -1.715E{-}3, 1.99E{-}3, 0.0917, -0.209, 0.242)'$$

$$C = (\,I_3 \quad 0\,)$$

a. Find the eignevalues of this system. Is it stable? Is it controllable?

b. Is the system observable for the given C? Find the minimal number of measurements we need to make to still have an observable system.

c. We want the closed loop system to have less than 10% overshoot and settle within 0.5 sec. Use this requirement to derive the desired closed loop dominant pole locations in the z-plane (remember, $T = 20$ msec). Choose four other pole locations and use *poleplace* to design the digital controller gain.

d. Assuming full state feedback, find the discrete pulse response for your closed loop design.

Notes and References

For further information on digital control, refer to [PN90], [FPW90], [Ku80], [O87], [HL85], [K81], [J81], [AW90].

10

Algebraic Design

10.1 Introduction

One of the most intuitive design techniques that appeared on the scene in the 1950's was the algebraic, or analytical, method. The idea was to choose a desired closed loop transfer function and then simply algebraically solve for the compensator. Let $G(s)$ be the plant and $K(s)$ the compensator, and assume unity feedback configuration. The closed loop transfer function is

$$T_c(s) = \frac{K(s)\,G(s)}{1 + K(s)\,G(s)}$$

Assume we are given a desired closed loop transfer function, $T_d(s)$, to be realized. Letting $T_d(s) = T_c(s)$ and solving for the compensator, we get

$$K(s) = \frac{T_d(s)}{G(s)\,[\,1 - T_d(s)\,]}$$

This seems to be the end of our design. As you might have guessed, however, there are some serious flaws with such a simplistic approach. Implicitly assumed in the above approach is that we can realize any desired closed loop response for any plant using a simple unity feedback configuration. This obviously seems farfetched, as you can see by choosing $T_d(s)$ to be equal to 1, the ideal response. It would imply that the system can follow any command input instantaneously with zero error. Note that $K(s)$ would have to be infinite. Therefore, there must clearly be some restrictions to avoid ridiculous results. It turns out that with appropriate restrictions on the compensator and the desired closed loop transfer function it is possible to solve for the compensator algebraically.

Conceptually, the algebraic approach to design differs fundamentally from the classical approach. In the classical approach discussed in Chapter 7, the open loop transfer function is manipulated to achieve desired specifications. The form of the compensator is also restricted to specific lead-lag or PID types. We can meet limited objectives with relatively simple and low order compensators. For instance, in the root locus approach, a pair of complex conjugate poles can be assigned. the location of all other poles and zeros cannot be controlled, however. In essence, we work from inside out (outward approach). The open loop transfer function is shaped, but we have little control over the closed loop transfer function.

In algebraic design, we take the opposite approach. First, we design a desired closed loop transfer function, we then solve for the compensator. Therefore, we take an inward approach. The poles and zeros of the compensator and, hence, the open loop transfer function cannot be controlled. Instead, we have more control over the closed loop poles and zeros. The lack of direct control over the open loop transfer function means we cannot meet any specified stability margin requirements without trial and error.

The ability to assign all poles of the system arbitrarily is reminiscent of state space design. In fact, transfer function analysis of observer based designs led to the revival of the algebraic approach. Most of this chapter is based on the series of articles and books by C. T. Chen [C84, C87a, C87b, CS90a, CS90b] and T. Kailath [K80]. We will use Chen's notation and terminology in most cases.

To see how observer based design leads to a transfer function design, consider the equations of a system with an observer based compensator.

$$\dot{x} = A\,x + B\,u$$
$$y = C\,x$$

$$\dot{\hat{x}} = A\,\hat{x} + B\,u + L\,(\,y - C\,\hat{x}\,)$$

$$u = -K\,\hat{x} + r$$

Taking transforms and solving for $\hat{x}$, we get

$$\hat{x}(s) = (\,s\,I - A - L\,C\,)^{-1}\,[\,B\,u(s) + L\,y(s)\,]$$

Hence, the controller is given by

$$u(s) = -K\,(\,s\,I - A - L\,C\,)^{-1}\,B\,u(s) - K\,(\,s\,I - A - L\,C\,)^{-1}\,L\,y(s) + r$$

We recall that the inverse of a matrix is equal to the ratio of the adjoint over the determinant. Hence we get

$$u(s) = -\left[\frac{L(s)}{A(s)}\,u(s) + \frac{M(s)}{A(s)}\,y(s)\right] + r = \frac{-1}{A(s)}\,[\,L(s)\,u(s) + M(s)\,y(s)\,] + r$$

where $A(s) = \det\,(s\,I - A - L\,C\,)$ and

$$L(s) = \text{Adj}\,[K\,(s\,I - A - L\,C\,)\,B\,]\,, \quad M(s) = \text{Adj}\,[K\,(s\,I - A - L\,C\,)\,L\,]$$

The preceding suggests the *controller-observer* configuration shown in Figure 10-1.

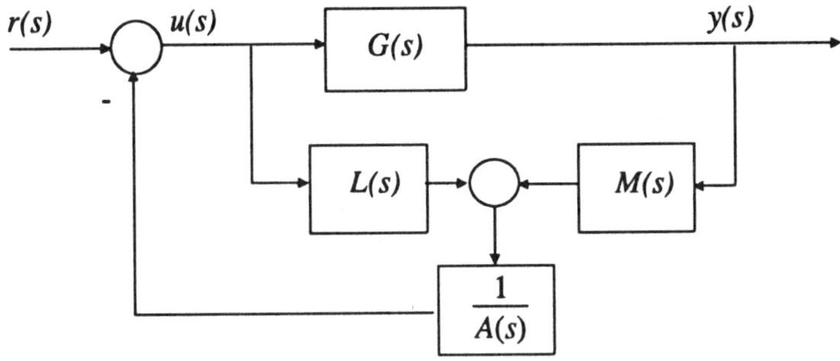

Figure 10-1 Controller-observer configuration.

Now, we turn things around and instead start with the above configuration. The problem can be formulated as

Given the plant $G(s)$, find polynomials $\{ A(s), M(s), L(s) \}$ such that the closed poles are placed at desired locations.

We already know from linear systems theory that this can be done using an nth order compensator (i.e., deg $(A(s))$ = system order = n) as long as the system is completely controllable and observable. Moreover, we know that we can also reduce the compensator order by one corresponding to using a reduced order observer. We will see later that, in addition, we can place the closed loop zeros at desired locations (with some restrictions). We will also study other configurations.

10.2 Design Constraints

To achieve a compensator that works and can be realized physically (or in digital form), we have to place constraints on both the compensator and the desired closed loop transfer function. A desired closed loop transfer function, $T_d(s)$, is said to be *implementable* if there exists a configuration such that the transfer function between r (command input) and y (controlled output) is equal to $T_d(s)$ and meets the following four constraints.

1. The compensators are rational proper transfer functions.
2. The compensated system is well-posed.
3. The compensated system is internally stable.
4. All forward paths from input to output pass through the plant.

The first constraint prevents the occurrence of pure differentiators as compensators. Pure differentiators amplify noise. The higher the noise frequency, the higher the amplification. This is a practical constraint, and most engineers are usually aware of it. The second constraint, well-posedness, ensures that all transfer functions between any pair of inputs and outputs are proper. This ensures that noise entering the system at any point will get filtered out by the system, i.e., the system itself does not act as a differentiator. It should be noted that the first two constraints are independent of each other. For instance, consider *G(s)* and *K(s)* below with unity feedback.

$$G(s) = \frac{s+1}{s-1} \quad \text{and} \quad K(s) = \frac{2-s}{2+s} \quad \rightarrow \quad \frac{G\,K}{1+G\,K} = \frac{(s+1)\,(2-s)}{2\,s}$$

We can see clearly that, even though the individual subsystems are proper, the closed loop system is improper.

The third constraint, internal stability, means that the transfer function between *any pair of inputs and outputs* are stable. Note that this is a stronger condition than stability. It essentially prevents unstable pole-zero cancellations.

The fourth constraint requires all signals pass through the system. If noise occurs at the input and does not pass through the loop, it is directly passed to the output. This condition prevents this from happening. All of the above constraints are reasonable and are usually met in most cases. A design algorithm, however, must be such that it does not violate them.

Consider the following example that blindly solves for a compensator.

$$G(s) = \frac{1}{s^2} \quad \text{and} \quad T_d(s) = \frac{1}{s^2+s+1}$$

We can solve for a feedback compensator to get

$$K(s) = \frac{1}{T_d(s)} - \frac{1}{G(s)} = s+1$$

which is not proper. Solving for a cascade compensator with unity feedback, we get

$$K(s) = \frac{G(s) - T_d(s)}{G(s)\,T_d(s)} = \frac{s}{s+1}$$

Although this is proper, it involves canceling the pole at the origin. The consequence of this is that when the disturbance, *d*, enters between the compensator and the plant, its output will be

$$y(s) = \frac{s+1}{s\,(s^2+s+1)}\,d(s)$$

Hence any constant disturbance will grow unbounded with time and the system is not internally stable.

10.3 Implementable Transfer Functions

Consider a proper plant, G, and a proper stable desired closed loop transfer function, T_d, where

$$G = \frac{N}{D} \quad \text{and} \quad T_d = \frac{N_d}{D_d}$$

Let $rd\,(G) = relative\ degree\ of\ G = degree\ (D) - degree\ (N)$.

A desired closed loop transfer function, $T_d\,(s)$, is said to be *implementable* for the plant, $G(s)$, if there exists a configuration such that the following two conditions are satisfied:

1. *Relative degree condition:* $rd\,(T_d) \geq rd\,(G)$.
2. *Nonminimum phase zero condition:* All RHP zeros of G must be retained in T_d.

For example, consider the following plant and the proposed desired closed loop transfer functions.

$$G(s) = \frac{s-1}{s\,(s-2)}$$

$$T_1 = \frac{1}{s+1}, \quad T_2 = \frac{s-1}{s+1}, \quad T_3 = \frac{s-1}{s^2+2\,s+2}, \quad T_4 = \frac{-2\,(s-1)}{s^2+2\,s+2}$$

We see that T_1 violates condition 2, T_2 violates condition 1, whereas T_3 and T_4 are both implementable using some configuration. Note that T_4 corresponds to a Type 1 system, whereas T_3 is Type 0. It is also possible to track ramp inputs with zero steady state error (i.e., Type 2 system) by adding an additional zero to T_3 or T_4, but this would violate the first condition unless an additional pole is added.

10.4 Selection of Desired Closed Loop Transfer Function

The main step in the algebraic design is the appropriate choice of the desired closed loop transfer function. In fact, once this is determined, a simple program (similar to the ones provided in the Appendix) can produce the compensator. In general, several candidate transfer functions must be tested by simulation to come up with the final choice.

One approach is to choose a pair of dominant complex conjugate poles to meet transient step response requirements. The other poles and zeros can be chosen to satisfy steady state error specifications subject to implementability conditions. Careful attention must be made to the role of zeros, because they will affect the response (see Chapter 1). In fact, after adding poles and zeros to meet these conditions, transient response properties may be lost. The location of the complex poles will have to be changed, and the whole process must be iterated to meet all objectives. One may wonder whether there exists a "best" location for the poles and zeros. The answer is "yes", depending on what one means by "best". This question has been answered many years ago by the control and filter community. Towards this end, we will present ITAE and Symmetric Root Locus methods later.

Other factors exist that one must consider in different situations. One is the problem of saturation and control energy. Most control systems contain electromechanical components. Mechanical components have physical limits on their behavior. One can pull a spring so much before it breaks. An electronic amplifier will saturate once its input passes certain levels. It may also get too hot. All of these properties will introduce undesirable nonlinearities into the system. This is related directly to control energy. For instance, one may be designing a disc drive controller for a laptop computer and then realize later that the motor needed is larger than the computer itself !

One way to check the control signal levels required is to compute the following transfer function

$$\frac{y}{r} = T_c \quad \text{and} \quad \frac{y}{u} = G\,, \quad \text{then} \quad \frac{u}{r} = \frac{T_c}{G} = T_u$$

Hence, for a given command input r, one can compute or plot u, to see if its maximum and minimum values violate any constraints on u. If u is monotonically decreasing, its maximum value can be computed using the Initial Value Theorem of Laplace Transform.

$$u(0+) = \lim_{s\to\infty} s\,U(s) = \lim_{s\to\infty} s\,R(s)\frac{T_c(s)}{G(s)} = \lim_{s\to\infty} \frac{T_c(s)}{G(s)} \quad \text{for a unit step input}$$

For example, for the previous plant G and T_3 and T_4 , we compute

$$u(0^+) = \lim_{s\to\infty} \frac{T_3}{G} = \lim_{s\to\infty} \frac{s\,(s-2)}{s^2+2\,s+2} = 1$$

$$u(0^+) = \lim_{s\to\infty} \frac{T_4}{G} = \lim_{s\to\infty} \frac{-2\,s\,(s-2)}{s^2+2\,s+2} = -2$$

These numbers imply that the control signals will be bounded by 1 for T_3 and 2 for T_4.

Insight from results in optimal control theory indicate that the further the poles are pushed into the LHP, the higher is the control energy required. The Symmetric Root Locus (SRL) technique (to be discussed shortly), allows us to trade off control energy with speed of response.

Another issue is stability margin. Because concepts of gain and phase margin are based on open loop transfer function quantities, and we work with closed loop transfer functions here, meeting these requirements is difficult. One possibility is to use the formula for PM in Chapter 1, namely,

$$PM = 2 \sin^{-1} \frac{1}{2\,|T(j\omega_{gc})|}$$

Keep in mind that the above formula is for second order systems and the gain crossover frequency is unknown. If the bandwidth is specified, however, it could be used as an estimate of the gain crossover frequency and used in the above formula. Then the poles may be chosen to satisfy the phase margin requirement for the first iteration.

10.5 Optimal Transfer Functions: ITAE and Symmetric Root Locus

The problem of optimal transfer functions for a given response has been studied and solved in the 1950s. Suppose we want to design a filter of a given order that would track a unit step input with minimum error. The usual definition of error, $e(t)$, is the difference between input and output. One way to minimize the error is to minimize the area under it over all time. Mathematically, we define a *cost function,* which we attempt to minimize.

$$J = \int_0^\infty e(t)\, dt$$

Now, if the error is both positive and negative, the areas will cancel each other, resulting in zero cost despite large errors. One remedy is to use the absolute value of the error. This is called the Integral of the Absolute Error (IAE) criterion. Another option would be to use the square of the error, the Integral of Square Error (ISE), criterion. This has the additional property of putting more emphasis on larger errors. Another popular measure is the Integral of Time Multiplied Absolute Error (ITAE) criterion

$$J = \int_0^\infty t\, |e(t)|\, dt$$

ITAE has the advantage of putting more emphasis on steady state errors rather than transient errors. Note that t acts as a weighting factor. During transients, the value of t is small, whereas in steady state, t is very large, so error is heavily penalized in steady state.

ITAE turns out to be the most selective criterion, so it is the one used most often. Tables of transfer functions of different orders, tracking step, ramp, and parabolic inputs with associated plots for different criteria are available. Some control systems books have partial tables or plots for ITAE. See [C87] and [FPE91]. For example, a third order Type 1 ITAE transfer function is given by

$$T_d(s) = \frac{\omega_0^3}{s^3 + 1.75\,\omega_o\, s^2 + 2.15\,\omega_0^2\, s + \omega_0^3}$$

The value of ω_0 can be chosen to meet other requirements such as control energy. The ITAE program in the appendix contains the numerator and denominator coefficients for systems of Type 0, 1, and 2. Example 10.3 will demonstrate the use of ITAE approach.

Another approach to obtain a desired closed loop transfer function is to use basic results from optimal control, in particular, the SISO version of the LQR problem (discussed in Chapter 12). Briefly, the approach uses a variation of the ISE criterion. The LQR objective function considered is

$$J_{LQR} = \int_0^{\infty} [\, q\,(\, y(t) - r(t)\,)^2 + u(t)^2\,]\; dt$$

where we are trying to minimize the weighted energy of the tracking error and control. The parameter q allows us to trade off control energy against tracking error. Large values of q will place a heavy penalty on tracking error, resulting in a damped system with large control signals (possibly causing saturation problems). Small values of q will reduce control energy but will result in larger transient errors. The problem can be mathematically solved in the time or frequency domains. Once the optimal control is found and applied to the system, the optimal closed loop transfer function of the system can be obtained. It can be shown that controllers designed using the LQR approach will always be stabilizing.

The optimal closed loop transfer function corresponding to the LQR criterion for a unit step reference input (i.e., $r(t) = 1, t > 0$) is given by

$$T_{LQR} = \frac{q\,N(0)}{D_o(0)}\,\frac{N(s)}{D_o(s)} \quad \text{and} \quad G_e(s) = \frac{e(s)}{u(s)} = \frac{N(s)}{D(s)}$$

where $G_e(s)$ is the transfer function between control input and tracking error.

The polynomial $D_o(s)$ is the optimal characteristic polynomial and is the solution of

$$D_o(s)\, D_o(-s) = D(s)\, D(-s) + q\, N(s)\, N(-s)$$

Finding $D_o(s)$ from the preceding is called *spectral factorization* and is not an easy problem in general. We note, however, that if we divide the preceding equation by $D(s)D(-s)$, we get

$$D_o(s)\,D_o(-s)=0 \;\rightarrow\; 1+q\,\frac{N(s)\,N(-s)}{D(s)\,D(-s)} = 1+q\,G_e(s)\,G_e(-s)=0$$

The above is essentially the root locus form for the parameter q, where the appropriate transfer function is $G_e(s)G_e(-s)$. Because poles and zeros of this transfer function are symmetric with respect to the imaginary axis, its root locus will be symmetric about the same axes. The root locus is also symmetric with respect to the real axis, hence, the Symmetric Root Locus (SRL) will be doubly symmetric about both axes and the origin.

To use SRL, the root locus of the appropriate transfer function is obtained. There are two possibilities, 0 degree or 180 degree root loci. The appropriate root locus is the one that produces no poles on the imaginary axis (note that LQR will always be stabilizing). For example, consider

$$G_e(s)=\frac{(s+1)}{s\,(s+2)} \;\rightarrow\; G_e(s)\,G_e(-s)=\frac{(s+1)}{s\,(s+2)}\;\frac{(-s+1)}{(-s)\,(-s+2)}$$

or

$$G_e(s)\,G_e(-s)=\frac{-(s+1)\,(s-1)}{s^2\,(s+2)\,(s-2)}$$

You can verify that the 0 degree root locus will produce the correct result. Once the root locus is obtained, the optimal closed loop poles will correspond to the stable branches of the loci (the LHP ones). We can then select desired poles along these branches and choose q accordingly. Example 10.4 will demonstrate the procedure.

10.6 Unity Feedback Configuration

Unity Feedback Configuration (UFC) allows arbitrary pole placement for stable plants. Let us introduce the following transfer functions

$$G(s)=\frac{N(s)}{D(s)},\quad K(s)=\frac{B(s)}{A(s)},\quad T_d(s)=\frac{N_d(s)}{D_d(s)}$$

where G, K, and T_d stand for the plant, compensator, and desired closed loop transfer function respectively. Setting the resulting closed loop transfer function equal to the desired one, we get (the dependence on s is suppressed)

$$T_d=\frac{N_c}{D_c}=\frac{B\,N}{A\,D+B\,N}$$

Equating the denominators, we get the *UFC Design Equation.*

$$\boxed{A\,D + B\,N = D_d}$$

Note that the numerator is fixed by N and B, where B is found by solving from the Design Equation. This implies that, in general, assigning closed loop zeros is not possible using UFC. Because tracking properties (steady state errors to polynomial type inputs) depend on the coefficients of both the numerator and denominator of the closed loop transfer function, these requirements cannot be met in general.

Solving the Design Equation

The Design Equation is a polynomial equation, with the unknowns A and B. Similar equations appear in number theory, where we try to solve for integer unknowns. For instance, consider

$$2x + 3y = 8 \quad \rightarrow \quad x = 1 \;,\; y = 2$$

The above equation is called the *Diophantine Equation* in number theory (the solution is not as simple as it first appears). Because polynomials and integers share many algebraic properties, polynomial equations of the same form are also called by the same name. To get a feel for this equation, let us try a simple example.

Suppose the following plant is given, and we desire to move its poles to $\{-1 \pm j\}$, i.e.,

$$G = \frac{N}{D} = \frac{1}{s\,(s+1)} \quad \text{and} \quad \frac{N_d}{D_d} = \frac{1}{s^2 + 2s + 2}$$

The Design Equation becomes

$$A\,(s^2 + s) + B = s^2 + 2\,s + 2$$

If the compensator is a constant, i.e., A and B are constants, the above has no solutions. Trying polynomials of degree one for A and B, we get

$$A(s) = a_0 + a_1\,s \;, \quad B(s) = b_0 + b_1\,s$$

$$(\,a_0 + a_1\,s)\,(s^2 + s) + (b_0 + b_1\,s) = s^2 + 2\,s + 2$$

multiplying out and equating coefficients of equal power, we get four equations and four unknowns

$$\begin{bmatrix} 0 & 1 & 0 & 0 \\ 1 & 0 & 0 & 1 \\ 1 & 0 & 1 & 0 \\ 0 & 0 & 1 & 0 \end{bmatrix} \begin{bmatrix} a_0 \\ b_0 \\ a_1 \\ b_1 \end{bmatrix} = \begin{bmatrix} 2 \\ 2 \\ 1 \\ 0 \end{bmatrix} \rightarrow \begin{bmatrix} a_0 \\ b_0 \\ a_1 \\ b_1 \end{bmatrix} = \begin{bmatrix} 1 \\ 2 \\ 0 \\ 1 \end{bmatrix} \rightarrow K(s) = \frac{B}{A} = s + 2$$

As you can see, the equation has a solution, but the compensator is improper. Note that the system is second order, the compensator is first order, so in the absence of pole zero cancellations, we should expect the closed loop transfer function to be third order. We also note from the Design Equation, that unless the right hand side is third order, the coefficient, a_1 will always be zero. Hence, it is clear that to obtain a proper compensator, we should desire a third order polynomial for $D_d(s)$. Toward that end, we introduce a third pole at { -3 } and solve for the compensator to get

$$K(s) = \frac{4s + 6}{s + 4}$$

This corresponds to a lead compensator, and could have been obtained using root locus design.

The above example demonstrates several points. First, polynomial Diophantine equations can be reduced to a set of simultaneous algebraic equations. Second, these equations do not always have unique solutions. Third, even when the equations have solutions, they do not necessarily result in proper compensators. Under mild conditions, however, it is possible to guarantee existence of a proper compensator to achieve arbitrary pole placement. These conditions are presented below.

Assume that the plant transfer function, G, is strictly proper ($deg\,(N) < deg\,(D) = n$) and *coprime* (i.e., there are no pole-zero cancellations), then there exists a compensator, K, of order (n - 1), for any desired characteristic polynomial, D_d, of order ($2n$ - 1).

The general solution of the Diophantine equation is given below.

$G = \dfrac{N}{D}$ where

$$D(s) = D_n s^n + D_{n-1} s^{n-1} + \ldots + D_0 \;, \quad N(s) = N_n s^n + N_{n-1} s^{n-1} + \ldots + N_0 \,, \quad N_n = 0$$

and $K = \dfrac{B}{A}$ where

$$B(s) = B_{n-1}s^{n-1} + \ldots + B_1 s + B_0\,, \quad A(s) = A_{n-1}s^{n-1} + \ldots + A_1 s + A_0$$

and

$$D_d(s) = F_{2n-1}s^{2n-1} + \ldots + F_1 s + F_0$$

Multiplying the appropriate terms and equating coefficients of equal power leads to the following set of simultaneous equations

$$S(N,D)X = F$$

where

$$S(N,D) = \left[\begin{array}{cc|cc|c|cc} D_0 & N_0 & 0 & 0 & & 0 & 0 \\ D_1 & N_1 & D_0 & N_0 & \ldots & . & . \\ . & . & . & . & & . & . \\ . & . & . & . & \ldots & 0 & 0 \\ D_n & N_n & D_n - 1 & N_n - 1 & & D_0 & N_0 \\ 0 & 0 & D_n & N_n & & D_1 & N_1 \\ . & . & 0 & 0 & \ldots & . & . \\ . & . & . & . & & . & . \\ 0 & 0 & 0 & 0 & & D_n & N_n \end{array}\right]$$

and

$$X = \begin{bmatrix} A_0 \\ B_0 \\ A_1 \\ B_1 \\ . \\ . \\ A_{n-1} \\ B_{n-1} \end{bmatrix}, \quad F = \begin{bmatrix} F_0 \\ F_1 \\ F_2 \\ . \\ . \\ . \\ F_{2n-2} \\ F_{2n-1} \end{bmatrix}$$

The matrix $S(N,D)$ is called the *Sylvester matrix* and has order $2n$. It is a well known fact in algebra that the Sylvester matrix is nonsingular if and only if the polynomials (N,D) are coprime. Note that in SISO systems, coprimeness of the plant transfer function is equivalent to controllability and observability. Therefore, the same condition that allows arbitrary pole placement using state feedback also allows pole placement using the polynomial or algebraic approach. This is the link between the state space and the transfer function approach.

The next example shows the application of this approach. The Appendix contains a program that was used to solve the example.

Example 10.1 Unity Feedback Configuration

Consider the system transfer function used in the lead design Example 7.4. It is repeated here for your convenience.

$$G(s) = \frac{400}{s\,(s^2 + 30\,s + 200)} = \frac{400}{s\,(s + 10)\,(s + 20)}$$

It is desired to place the dominant poles at $s_1 = -\,6.75 \pm\, j\,11.69$. Because the plant is third order, we can find a proper compensator by choosing five poles. We therefore choose three additional poles arbitrarily at { - 10, - 15, - 20 }. We next use the UFC program in the Appendix to solve for the compensator. The result is

```
B     = 6.83   205    1366.6
A     = 1.00  28.50  384.71
```

Hence, the compensator is

$$K(s) = \frac{6.83\,(s + 10)\,(s + 20)}{(s + 14.25 + j\,13.47)\,(s + 14.25 - j\,13.47)}$$

We note that the compensator cancels the plant poles at {- 10, - 20}, and replaces them with complex poles.

The resulting closed loop transfer function becomes

$$T_c = \frac{2733.3\,(s + 10)\,(s + 20)}{(s + 10)\,(s + 20)\,(s + 15)\,(s + 6.75 \pm\, j\,11.69)} = \frac{2733.3}{(s + 15)\,(s + 6.75 \pm\, j\,11.69)}$$

The resulting step response and Bode plots are shown in Figures 10-2 and 10-3. We get a GM of 12 dB, PM of 59 degrees, 9% overshoot and 14% steady state error to unit ramp input. This is close to what we obtained using root locus lead design with a first order compensator.

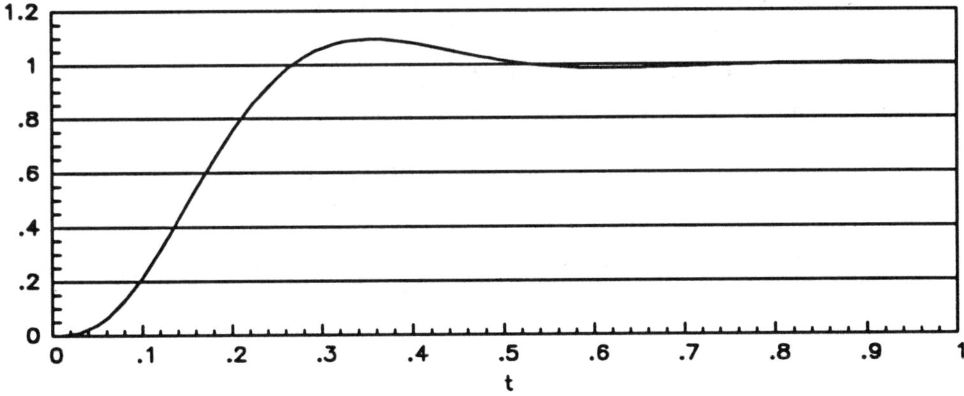

Figure 10-2 Step response for Example 10.2.

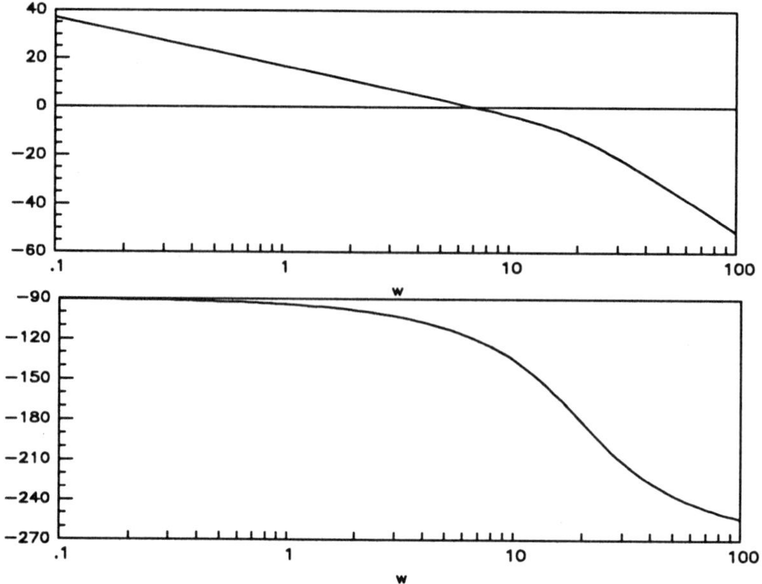

Figure 10-3 Bode plots for Example 10.1.

Example 10.2 UFC Design of the Helicopter Problem

We now solve the helicopter problem introduced in Chapter 8. The plant transfer function is

$$G(s) = \frac{9.8\,(s - 0.25 \pm j\,2.49)}{(s - 0.118 \pm j\,0.367)\,(s + 0.656)}$$

The dominant poles are placed at $\{ -1 \pm j \}$ with additional three poles at $\{ -2, -4, -5 \}$. Using our program, we get

```
B    =  1.9210   2.6381   1.2193
A    =  1.0000  -6.2459  48.1889
```

$$K(s) = \frac{1.92\,(s + 0.68 \pm j\,0.4)}{(s - 3.12 \pm j\,6.19)}$$

Although the compensator is unstable, there has not been any unstable pole-zero cancellations. The resulting closed loop transfer function is

$$T_c(s) = \frac{18.82\,(s - 0.25 \pm j\,2.49)\,(s + 0.68 \pm j\,0.4)}{(s + 1 \pm j)\,(s + 2)\,(s + 4)\,(s + 5)}$$

The design meets all design constraints, mainly that the RHP zeros are retained, and the relative degree is 1. Note that even though the plant has both RHP poles and zeros, it is still possible to find a suitable unity feedback compensator to place the poles arbitrarily. The step response and Bode plots are shown in Figures 10-4 and 10-5. We get a GM of 13 dB, GRM of - 8.5 dB, PM of 55 degrees, 37% overshoot, and 6% steady state error to unit step input.

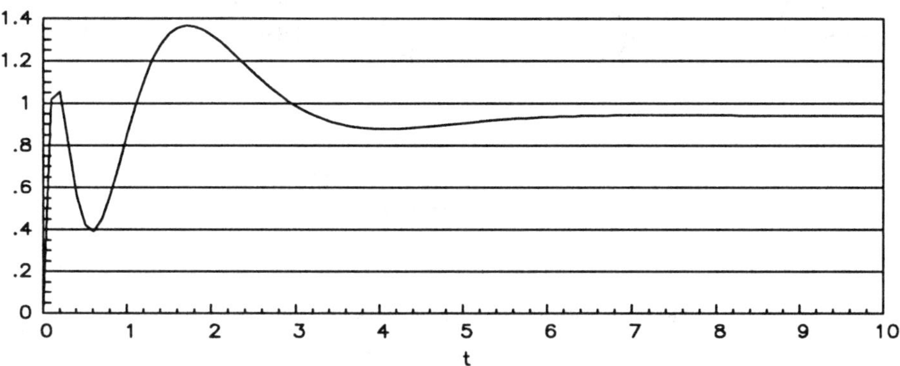

Figure 10-4 Step response for Example 10.2.

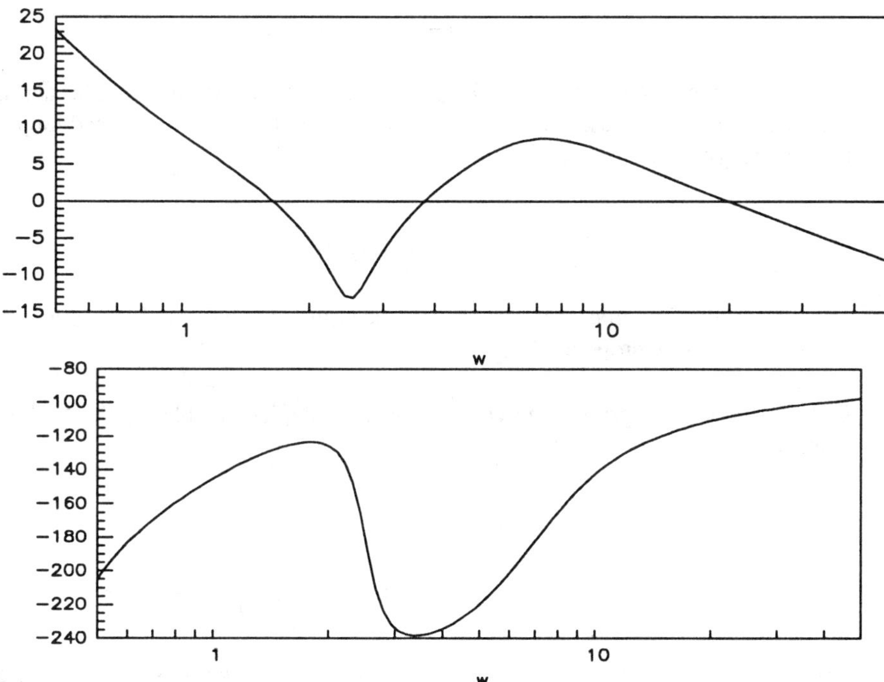

Figure 10-5 Bode plots for Example 10.2.

10.7 Two-Parameter Configuration (RST Compensator)

The *two-parameter* configuration (also known as the *RST* compensator) is shown in Figure 10-6.

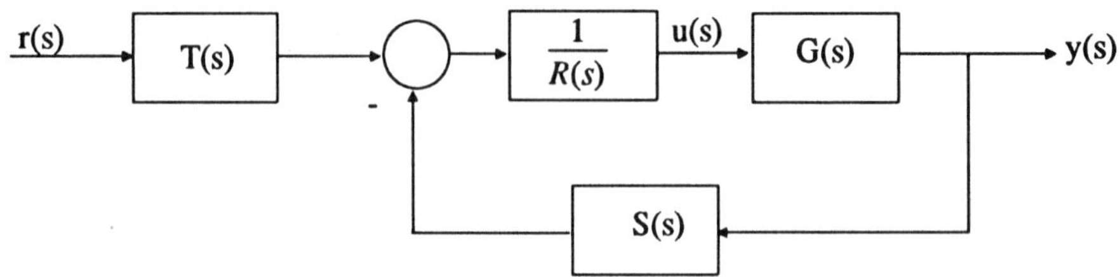

Figure 10-6 Block diagram of RST configuration.

It is a general configuration capable of arbitrary pole and zero assignment. The compensator equation is given by

$$R(s)\,u(s) = -\,S(s)\,y(s) + T(s)\,r(s)$$

where the name *RST* follows from the parameterization of the compensator and is fairly standard in the adaptive and digital control literature. The resulting closed loop transfer function is given by

$$T_c = \frac{N\,T}{S\,N + R\,D}$$

The following procedure guarantees realization of any desired closed loop transfer function for strictly proper and coprime plants.

Given *G(s)*, strictly proper and coprime, and an implementable $T_d\,(s)$, find a proper compensator to realize $T_d\,(s)$.

Solution: Consider

$$T_d\,(s) = \frac{N_d}{D_d} \qquad \text{and let} \qquad \frac{T_d}{N} = \frac{N_d}{D_d N} \triangleq \frac{N_p}{D_p}$$

Now check the degree of D_p. If deg $D_p = p < 2n - 1$, where n is deg D, introduce a stable polynomial, $\bar{D}_p$, of degree $2n - 1 - p$, otherwise set $\bar{D}_p = 1$. Multiply the numerator and denominator of the above by $\overline{D}_p$. Note that because this polynomial will be canceled, it is important that it be stable. We now have

$$T_d = \frac{N N_p \overline{D}_p}{D_p \overline{D}_p} \quad \text{letting } T_d = T_c, \text{ we get } \frac{N_p \overline{D}_p}{D_p \overline{D}_p} = \frac{T}{SN + RD}$$

Equating numerator and denominator terms determines the final Design Equations

$$\boxed{\begin{array}{l} T = N_p \overline{D}_p \\ SN + RD = D_p \overline{D}_p \overset{\Delta}{=} F \end{array}}$$

Note that the degree of F is $2n$ - 1 and that of R and S is n - 1. Observe that the Design Equation is a Diophantine equation, and can easily be converted to the following form.

$$S(N, D)X = F$$

where
$$X = \begin{bmatrix} R_0 \\ S_0 \\ R_1 \\ S_1 \\ \cdot \\ \cdot \\ R_{n-1} \\ S_{n-1} \end{bmatrix}, \quad F = \begin{bmatrix} F_0 \\ F_1 \\ F_2 \\ \cdot \\ \cdot \\ \cdot \\ F_{2n-2} \\ F_{2n-1} \end{bmatrix}$$

Realization of RST Compensator

Because the resulting RST compensator is in transfer function form, a question that may arise is how the compensator is actually realized. The answer is that the compensator is realized as one unit, i.e., as a system with two inputs and one output in state space form. We have

$$u = \begin{bmatrix} \frac{T}{R} & -\frac{S}{R} \end{bmatrix} \begin{bmatrix} r \\ y \end{bmatrix} = K(s) \begin{bmatrix} r \\ y \end{bmatrix} \quad \rightarrow \quad K(s) = \frac{1}{R} [T \quad -S]$$

To obtain the state space realization of *K(s)*, we use the *sform* command. For example, if *R*, *S*, and *T* are second order polynomials, we enter

```
< > den=R; num=[T(1)   -S(1)   T(2)   -S(2)   T(3)   -S(3)];
< > [SK,NSK]=sform(num,den,2)
```

Refer to Chapter 5 for interpreting multi-input multi-output transfer functions.

The next example illustrates the procedure. The example was solved using the RST and ITAE programs in the Appendix.

Example 10.3 RST Compensator: ITAE Approach

We consider the following transfer function $G(s) = \dfrac{(s-1)}{s\,(s-2)}$

The above system has appeared in several papers and books and is well known for being difficult to control. It is an example of a system that requires an unstable compensator for stabilization. None of the traditional classical techniques apply to this plant. State space and the algebraic approach can easily handle this plant, however.

The first step is finding an appropriate desired closed loop transfer function. We will use the ITAE approach for demonstration. The transfer function must have relative degree of at least 1 and must retain the plant's RHP zero. We select a third order Type 1 transfer function (this will result in $\overline{D}_p = 1$).

$$T_d\,(s) = \frac{(s-1)\,(-\,\omega_0^3)}{s^3 + 1.75\,\omega_0\,s^2 + 2.15\,\omega_0^2\,s + \omega_0^3}$$

The only parameter to be determined is ω_0. One way to choose this is to simulate the step response of the transfer function between r and u, T_d/G and choose the one resulting in smaller magnitudes for u.

After several trials, it appeared that larger values of ω_0 resulted in larger peak magnitudes for the control signal. We selected $\omega_0 = 1$, which ensured that $|u(t)| < 1$.

The compensator parameters are given by

```
R    =  1.00  -6.90
S    =  10.65  -1.00
T    =  -1.00
```

The compensator is realized in state space form as shown below

```
< > num=[-s(1) 0 -s(2) t];den=r;
< > [sk,nsk]=sform(num,den,2)
< > [sk,nsk]=minim(sk,nsk)

NSK    =
    1.
 SK    =
   6.9000   7.9992   .1104
  -9.0615  -10.6500   .0000
```

Hence, the compensator is

$$\dot{w} = 6.9\,w + 7.99\,y + 0.11\,r$$

$$u = -\,9.06\,w - 10.65\,y$$

The step response for y/r and u/r and the Nyquist plots are shown in Figures 10-7, 10-8 and 10-9. The following data are obtained: GM = 1.25 dB, GRM = -1.34 dB, PM = -4.9 deg, and the per-cent overshoot is about 3.8. The closed loop poles are at $\{-0.52 \pm j1.06, -0.708\}$.

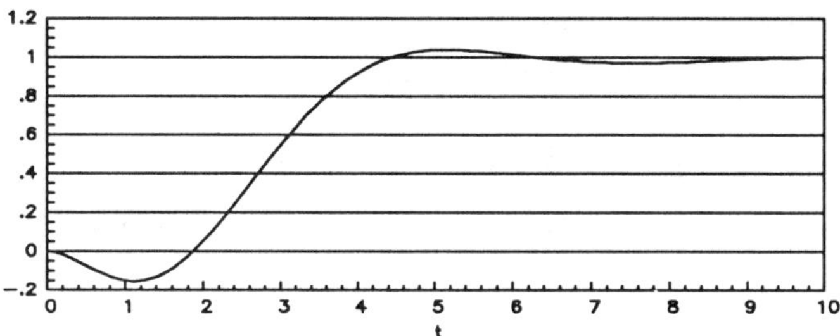

Figure 10-7 Output unit step response for Example 10.3.

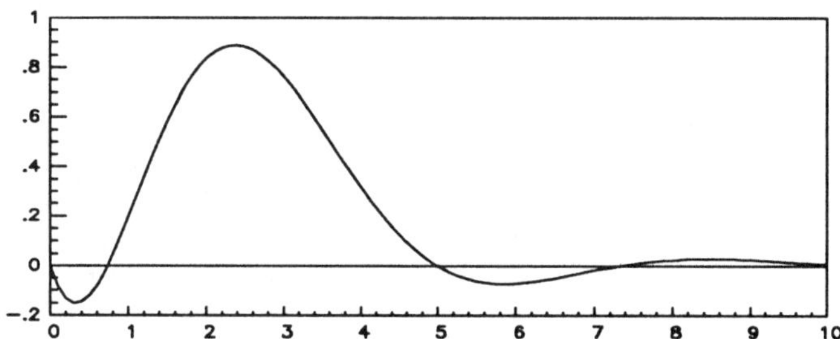

Figure 10-8 Control signal response to a unit step input in Example 10.3.

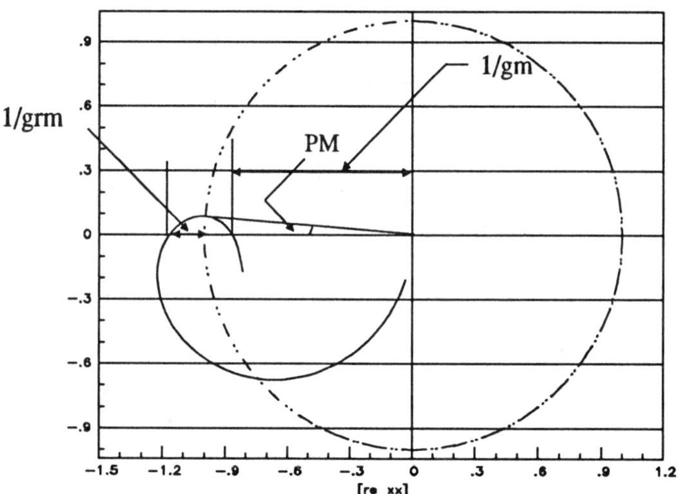

Figure 10-9 Nyquist plot for Example 10.3.

The margins are clearly indicated in the Nyquist plot. It should be pointed out that because of the numerator term, the selected transfer function is not truly ITAE optimal. Tables of ITAE optimal transfer functions do not have any entries with RHP zeros. What we did is very typical in design, namely, we took the available tools and adapted them to our needs to satisfy the specifications as best as possible.

The next example illustrates the SRL approach.

Example 10.4 RST Compensator: SRL Approach

The previous example will be solved using the SRL approach. The first step is to obtain the root locus of

$$G(s)\,G(-s) = \frac{-(s+1)\,(s-1)}{s^2\,(s-2)\,(s+2)}$$

Using interactive root locus, the following three weights were selected $\{q = 0.1, 1, 10\}$. Then, three design iterations were performed where in each case $\overline{D}_p = (s+1)$ was selected. Table 10-1 presents the data of our experiment. The root locus, output step response, control signals, and Bode plots are shown in Figures 10-10 through 10-14. From the data, the following observations can be made. As q increases (control becomes cheaper), closed loop poles are pushed deeper into the LHP, output becomes slightly more damped, control signal magnitudes increase, GM increases, GRM decreases, and PM changes slightly in each case. In Chapter 11, we will argue that some of these effects are expected in general.

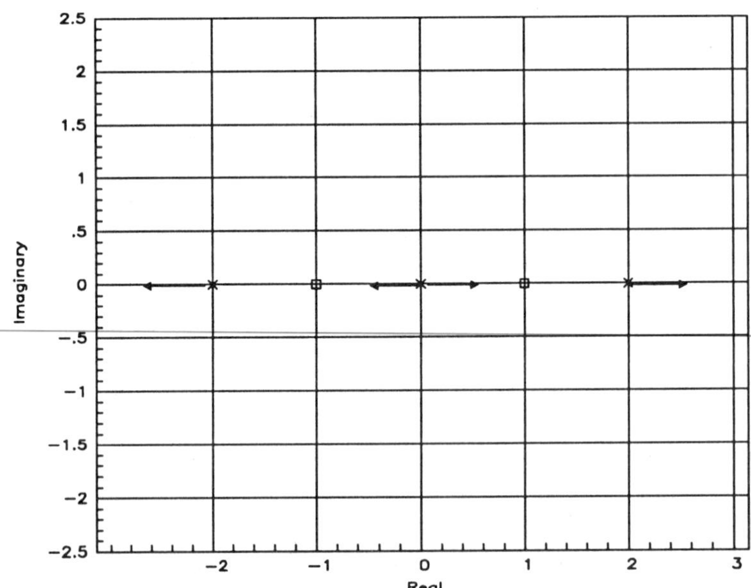

Figure 10-10 Symmetric Root Locus (Arrows have been added for clarity).

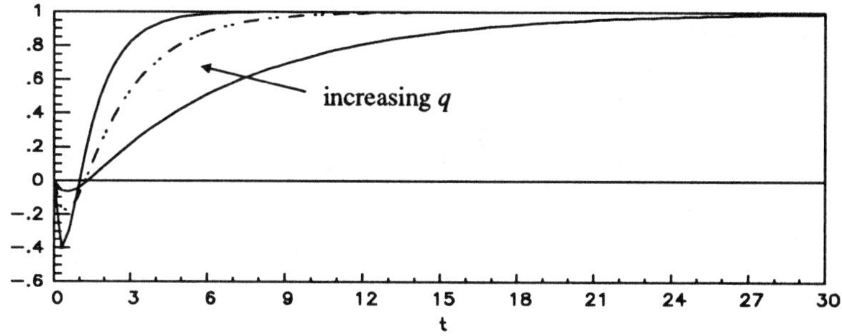

Figure 10-11 Step responses for the SRL example.

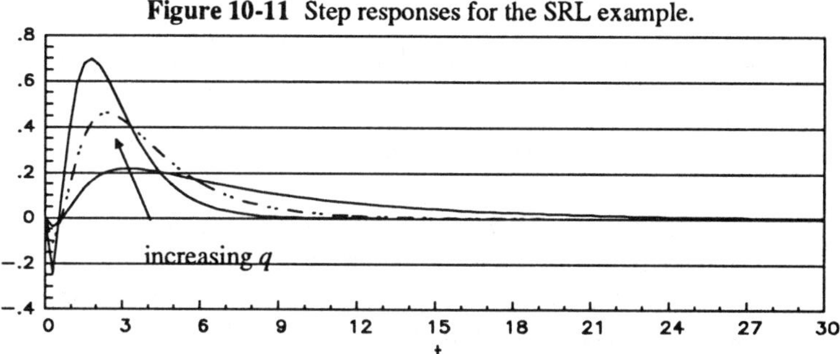

Figure 10-12 Control signal step responses for the SRL Example.

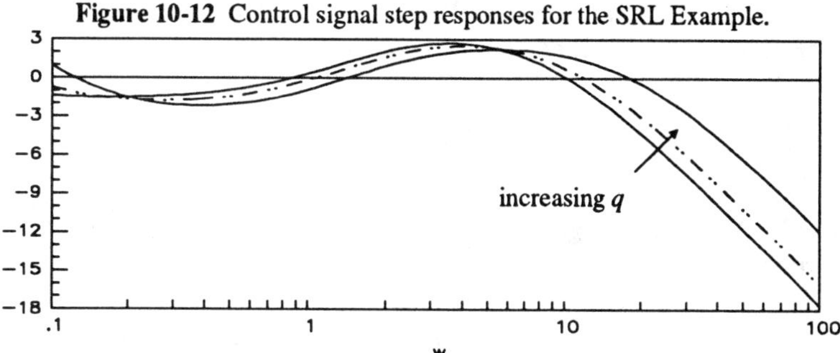

Figure 10-13 Bode magnitude plots for the SRL Example.

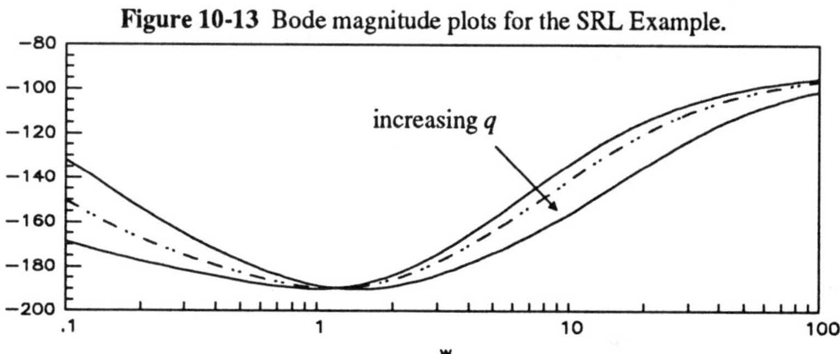

Figure 10-14 Bode phase plots for the SRL Example.

Table 10-1 Results of RST-SRL Design Example

q	Desired Characteristic Polynomial	Closed Loop Poles	Y_{max}	U_{max}	U_{min}	GM	PM	Closed Loop Numerator and Denominator	R S T
0.1	1.00 2.17 .31	-.15 -1.00 -2.01	.98	.21	-.03	1.43 -2.35	-9.74 46.66	-31 .00 .31 1.00 3.17 2.49 .31	1.00 -7.98 13.15 -.31 -.31 -.31
1	1.00 2.64 1.00	-.45 -1.00 -2.18	.99	.46	-.10	1.61 -2.17	-9.51 44.83	-1.00 .00 1.00 1.00 3.64 3.64 1.00	1.00 -10.29 15.93 -1.00 -1.00 -1.00
10	1.00 4.50 3.16	-.86 -1.00 -3.63	.99	.69	-.27	1.95 -2.00	41.76 -10.11 41.75	-3.16 .00 3.16 1.00 5.50 7.67 3.16	1.00 -18.34 25.84 -3.16 -3.16 -3.16

10.8 Plant Input/Output Feedback Configuration

The Plant Input/Output Feedback configuration (IOC), is precisely the configuration that results from an observer based state feedback design. Therefore, arbitrary pole placement is possible. Using the polynomial approach simplifies the problem of zero assignment. This might be the only advantage over direct state space design. Of course, for implementation purposes, the compensator is converted to state space form.

The block diagram corresponding to the IOC is shown in Figure 10-1. As we can see the resulting closed loop transfer function is given by

$$T_c(s) = \frac{NA}{AD + LD + MN}$$

The following procedure guarantees realization of any desired closed loop transfer function for proper and coprime plants.

Given $G(s)$ strictly proper and coprime, find a compensator to realize $T_d(s)$. In addition, we also assume that the relative degree $(T_d(s))$ = relative degree $(G(s))$

Solution : Consider

$$Td(s) = \frac{N_d}{D_d} \qquad \text{and let} \qquad \frac{T_d}{N} = \frac{N_d}{D_d N} \triangleq \frac{N_p}{D_p}$$

Now check the degree of N_p. If deg $N_p = p < n - 1$, introduce a stable polynomial, $\bar{D}_p$, of degree $n - 1 - p$, otherwise, set $\bar{D}_p$ equal to 1. Multiply the numerator and denominator of the above by $\bar{D}_p$. Note that because this polynomial will be canceled out, it is important that it be stable. We now have

$$T_d = \frac{N N_p \overline{D}_p}{D_p \overline{D}_p} \quad \text{letting } T_d = T_c, \quad \text{we get } \frac{N_p \overline{D}_p}{D_p \overline{D}_p} = \frac{A}{A D + L D + M N}$$

Equating numerator and denominator terms determines the final Design Equations

$$\boxed{\begin{aligned} &A = N_p \overline{D}_p \\ &L D + M N = D_p \overline{D}_p - A D \triangleq F \end{aligned}}$$

The polynomial $\overline{D}_p$ plays the same role as the observer characteristic polynomial. Hence, the same judgment for choosing observer eigenvalues can be used to determine roots of $\overline{D}_p$. Also note that the compensator order will be $(n - 1)$, so this actually corresponds to a reduced order observer design. Finally, we note that the Design Equation is similar to the RST compensator, hence, the solution is given by

$$S(N, D) X = F$$

where

$$X = \begin{bmatrix} L_0 \\ M_0 \\ L_1 \\ M_1 \\ \cdot \\ \cdot \\ L_{n-1} \\ M_{n-1} \end{bmatrix}, \quad F = \begin{bmatrix} F_0 \\ F_1 \\ F_2 \\ \cdot \\ \cdot \\ \cdot \\ F_{2n-2} \\ F_{2n-1} \end{bmatrix}$$

The next example illustrates the procedure.

Example 10.5 Input/Output Configuration: Helicopter Problem

The design problem discussed in Example 8.3 will be reexamined here. We will show that we get the same compensator here using the IOC algebraic approach. The example was solved using the Input/Output program in the Appendix; partial outputs of that program are displayed below. The plant transfer function is

$$G(s) = \frac{9.8\,(s - 0.25 \pm j\,2.49)}{(s - 0.118 \pm j\,0.367)\,(s + 0.656)}$$

We first need to select a desired transfer function. For comparison, we will choose the final closed loop transfer function of Example 8.3. Hence the following data is entered (actually the data from that example was first loaded, and then converted to transfer function form; this is what is displayed subsequently).

```
< > DG= [ 1.0000      .4200     -.0060      .0980]
< > NG = [9.8000    -4.9000    61.7400]
< > DD=[1.0000    10.0000    48.0000   112.0000   132.0000    72.0000]
< > ND=1.0D+03 *[.0098     -.0616      .4446     -.5342     2.2335]
```

After forming (N_d/D_dN) and performing pole-zero cancellations, we get N_p and D_p.

```
DP     =
  1.0000  10.0000  48.0000  112.0000  132.0000  72.0000
NP     =
  1.0000  -5.7815  36.1758
```

Note: Because of different algorithmic tolerances, these answers may vary with different hardware platforms. If you do not obtain the same answers, change the tolerance of the *minimal* command (try 1E-2).

Because deg $N_p = p = 2$, then $\overline{D}_p = 1$ and $A = N_p$. After multiplying and subtracting the appropriate polynomials, we get F.

```
F      =
 .0000  15.3615  14.2584  96.6735  132.7836  68.4548
```

Finally, we form the Sylvester matrix, reverse the elements of F, and solve the equation to get L and M.

```
L      =
 1.0D-12 *
 .0000  -.0316   .2264

M      =
 1.5675  2.2387  1.1088
```

The compensator transfer function, in general, is given by (this can be derived by eliminating the feedback from u, see Figure 10-1).

$$K(s) = \frac{M}{L + A}$$

Computing the above, we get

```
< > num_k=m , den_k=a+l

NUM_K    =
 1.5675  2.2387  1.1088
DEN_K    =
 1.0000  -5.7815  36.1758
```

$$K(s) = \frac{1.56\, s^2 + 2.23\, s + 1.10}{s^2 - 5.78\, s + 36.17} = \frac{1.56\,(s + 0.714 \pm j\,0.44\,)}{(s - 2.89 \pm j\,5.27\,)}$$

This is the same compensator obtained using reduced order observer based controller design in Example 8.3.

The advantage of the algebraic approach is that tracking problems (e.g. introducing integral action) can be handled easily by simply modifying the desired closed loop transfer function. Although this can also be done using state space methods, these procedures are more complicated. Chen and Seo, [CS90a] and [CS90b], also discuss how disturbance rejection and internal model principle can be handled using simple modifications of the algebraic approach. The discrete version of the algebraic approach follows identically. Simply replace *G(s)* by *G(z)* where *G(z)* is the pulse transfer function, i.e., the zero-order hold equivalent or other discrete approximations of *G(s)*.

10.9 Appendix: Design Programs

1. Program for UFC Design

This program requires G(s)=ng/dg and D_d. It returns, B and A where K(s) = B / A.

```
//[b,a]=ufc(ng,ng,Dd);
f=Dd;
m=max(size(ng));
nn=max(size(dg));
n=nn-1;            //n is the order of dg;
n2=2*n;            // this is size of f
pad_zer=0*ones(1,nn-m);ng_pad=[pad_zer ng];
//deg of f is 2n-1 where n is the plant order
for i=1:nn;...
    a(i,1)=dg(nn-i+1);...
    a(i,2)=ng_pad(nn-i+1);...
end;
sylv=0*ones(2*n);
for i=1:2:2*n-1;...
     bgnrow=(i+1)/2;...
     sylv(bgnrow:bgnrow+n,i:i+1)=a;...
end;
for i=1:n2;...
    delta(i)=f(n2-i+1);...
end;
x=sylv\delta;
a=0*ones(1,n);
b=0*ones(1,n);
for i=1:2:2*n-1;...
     r=(i-1)/2;...
     a(n-r)=x(i);...
     b(n-r)=x(i+1);...
end;
retf;
```

2. Program for RST Compensator Design

This program requires G(s)=ng/dg, and the desired closed loop transfer function, T_d =Nd / Dd It returns the polynomials R, S and T.

```
//[rr,ss,tt]=RST(ng,dg,nd,dd);
ngdd=conv(ng,dd);
[np,dp]=minimal(nd,ngdd);
m=max(size(dg));
pad_zer=0*ones(1,m-max(size(ng)));
ng_pad=[pad_zer ng];
n=m-1;            //n is the order of dg
p=max(size(dp))-1;     //p is the order of dp
if p < 2*n-1;...
   ndpb=2*n-1-p;...
   display('PLEASE ENTER YOUR DP-BAR- OF ORDER');ndpb,...
   inquire dpbar
   ELSE dpbar=1;...
end;
tt=conv(np,dpbar);
f=conv(dp,dpbar);
mt=2*n; // mt is size of f
//deg of f is 2n-1 where n is the plant order
for i=1:m;...
     col1_2(i,1)=dg(m-i+1);...
     col1_2(i,2)=ng_pad(m-i+1);...
end;
sylv=0*ones(2*n);
for i=1:2:2*n-1;...
     bgnrow=(i+1)/2;...
     sylv(bgnrow:bgnrow+n,i:i+1)=col1_2;...
end;
for i=1:mt;
    f_rev(i)=f(mt-i+1);...
end;
x=sylv\f_rev;
rr=0*ones(1,n);
ss=0*ones(1,n);
for i=1:2:2*n-1;...
    j=(i-1)/2;...
    rr(n-j)=x(i);...
    ss(n-j)=x(i+1);...
end;
retf
```

3. Program for Input/Output Design

This program has the same inputs as RST, but will return the Input/Output compensator parameters L, M, and A.

```
//[l,m,a]=io(ng,dg,nd,dd);
ngdd=conv(ng,dd);
[np,dp]=minimal(nd,ngdd);
n=max(size(ng)); m=max(size(dg));
n=m-1;          //n is order of dg; m is the size of dg (vector)
p=max(size(np))-1;
if p<n-1;...
   ndpb=n-1-p;...
   display('please enter your dp-bar- of order');ndpb,...
   inquire dpbar 'make sure that poles of dpbar are in LHP';...
   else dpbar=1;...
end;
a=conv(np,dpbar);
ftemp1=conv(dp,dpbar);ftemp2=conv(a,dg);
nft1=max(size(ftemp1));nft2=max(size(ftemp2));
ftemp2=[0*ones(1,nft1-nft2) ftemp2];
f=ftemp1-ftemp2;
mt=2*n;
//deg of f is 2n-1 where n is the plant order
//mt is size of f
pad_zero=0*ones(1,m-max(size(ng)));
ng_pad=[pad_zero  ng];
for i=1:m;...
    col_12(i,1)=dg(m-i+1);...
    col_12(i,2)=ng_pad(m-i+1);...
end;
sylv=0*ones(2*n);
for i=1:2:2*n-1;...
     bgnrow=(i+1)/2;...
     sylv(bgnrow:bgnrow+n,i:i+1)=col_12;...
end;
for i=1:mt;...
    f_rev(i)=f(mt-i+1);...
end;
x=sylv\f_rev;
l=0*ones(1,n);
m=0*ones(1,n);
for i=1:2:2*n-1;...
     r=(i-1)/2;...
     l(n-r)=x(i);...
     m(n-r)=x(i+1);...
end;
retf;
```

4. ITAE Program

This program requests order, type, and w, and will output the corresponding ITAE transfer function.

```
// [nt,dt]=itae(ord,typ,w)
   w2 = w**2;
   w3 = w**3;
   w4 = w**4;
   w5 = w**5;
typ1 =[ 0        0        0         0         1        w;
        0        0        0         1         1.4*w    w2;
        0        0        1         1.75*w    2.15*w2  w3;
        0        1        2.1*w     3.4*w2    2.7*w3   w4;
        1        2.8*w    5.0*w2    5.5*w3    3.4*w4   w5 ];
typ2 =[ 0        0        0         1         3.2*w    w2;
        0        0        1         1.75*w    3.25*w2  w3;
        0        1        2.41*w    4.93*w2   5.14*w3  w4;
        1        2.19*w   6.5*w2    6.3*w3    5.24*w4  w5 ];
typ3 =[ 0        0        1         2.97*w    4.94*w2  w3;
        0        1        3.71*w    7.88*w2   5.93*w3  w4;
        1        3.81*w   9.94*w2   13.44*w3  7.36*w4  w5 ];
if typ = 1,...
   dt=typ1(ord,(6-ord):6);nt=dt(1,(ord+1));...
end;
if typ = 2,...
   dt=typ1((ord-1),(6-ord):6);nt=dt(1,ord:(ord+1));...
end;
if typ = 3,...
   dt=typ2((ord-2),(6-ord):6);nt=dt(1,(ord-1):(ord+1));...
end;retf;
```

10.10 Problems

Note: Problems 10.1-10.8 are adapted from the papers by Chen and Seo, [CS90a], and [CS90b].

10.1 Internal Model Principle.

Consider the plant

$$G(s) = \frac{2}{s\,(s^2 + 0.25\,s + 6.25)}$$

The desired closed loop transfer function is

$$T_d(s) = \frac{20}{(s + 10)\,(s^2 + 2\,s + 2)}$$

a) Design an RST compensator (choose the observer poles at -20, and -40).

b) Find and plot the step response of the system.

c) Suppose a step disturbance, d, is introduced such that plant input is the compensator output plus the disturbance. Find the transfer function, $H(s)$, between the disturbance and the plant output y.

d) Find the condition imposed on the compensator parameters to achieve disturbance rejection, i.e., $H(0)=0$.

e) We can achieve disturbance rejection by increasing the order of the compensator. In this problem, this can be done by increasing the order of the observer:

Choose $\overline{D}_p = (s+20)^3$

Now, find the new RST compensator parameters.

f) Verify tracking and disturbance rejection properties of the system by finding unit step responses to the reference input and the disturbance.

10.2 Consider the same plant as in the previous problem. The desired closed loop transfer function in this case was chosen according to the dominant pole criteria.

a) Design an ITAE optimal desired closed loop transfer function satisfying the actuator magnitude constraint of $|u(t)| \leq 10$ for all $t \geq 0$.

b) Repeat the design using the SRL approach.

c) Plot step responses for the ITAE, SRL, and the dominant pole transfer function of the previous problem. Compare the three responses in terms of speed of response and overshoot.

d) Which technique gives the best response for this plant ?

10.3 Consider the plant

$$G(s) = \frac{s-1}{s\,(s-2)}$$

a) Design an ITAE optimal closed loop transfer function satisfying the actuator limits: $|u(t)| \leq 10$

b) Repeat the design using the SRL approach.

c) Obtain the step responses and compare the results.

10.4 Consider the plant

$$G(s) = \frac{s+3}{s\,(s-1)}$$

In each of the following cases, we would like to achieve zero steady state error to unit step inputs and satisfy actuator magnitude constraint of $|u(t)| \leq 10$.

a) Design an optimal transfer function, $T_{d1}(s)$, using SRL approach.

b) Design an ITAE optimal transfer function, $T_{d2}(s)$.

c) Design a second order transfer function, $T_{d3}(s)$, with a damping ratio of 0.9 and natural frequency of 28.

d) Consider the following Type 1 transfer functions:

$$T_{d4}(s) = \frac{100}{s+100}, \quad T_{d5}(s) = \frac{10}{s+10}$$

e) Plot and compare the step responses in each case.

f) Plot and compare the actuator signals in each case.

10.5 Consider the plant in the previous problem.

a) Design a unity feedback compensator to place closed loop poles at { -2, -2±j2 }.

b) Plot the step response of the system. Does the response correspond to what would be expected from the closed loop poles ? If not, explain why.

10.6 Consider the plant in the Problem 10.4, and the following desired closed loop transfer functions.

$$T_{d1}(s) = \frac{600.25}{(s+3)\,(s^2+34.3\,s+600.25)}, \quad T_{d2}(s) = \frac{10\,(s+13)}{s^2+12.7\,s+30}$$

a) Design an RST compensator in each case and compare the designs.

b) Repeat the design using Input/Output Configuration.

10.7 Extension of the RST Configuration.

One restriction imposed in the design for RST was that the desired closed loop transfer function had to be strictly proper. This restriction can be removed by changing one of the design steps. The change is as follows:

If *deg* $\overline{D}_p = p \le 2n$, introduce an arbitrary polynomial $\overline{D}_p$ of degree $2n - p$.

Consider the plant $G(s)$,

$$G(s) = \frac{(s+1)^2}{s\,(s+3)}$$

Let the desired closed loop transfer function be $T_d(s) = 1$.

a) Generalize the RST program in the Appendix to handle this more general case.

b) Use your program to design a compensator.

10.8 Choosing $\overline{D}_p(s)$ in the RST compensator

There are various guidelines for choosing observer poles. One is to choose them at least 2 to 3 times faster than the fastest closed loop poles. Another guideline, suggested by recent results in optimal control, is to place the observer poles at the stable plant zeros and the remaining ones far in the LHP.

Consider the plant $G(s)$ and desired closed loop transfer function $T_d(s)$:

$$G(s) = \frac{s+3}{s\,(s-1)}\,, \quad T_d(s) = \frac{10\,(s+13)}{s^2 + 12.7\,s + 30}$$

We would like to study the effects of $\overline{D}_p(s)$ on disturbance rejection properties of the system. Consider the following choices for $\overline{D}_p(s)$

$\overline{D}_{p1}(s) = s+3$, $\overline{D}_{p2}(s) = s+30$, $\overline{D}_{p3}(s) = s+30$

a) Find the RST compensator in each case. Plot and compare the step responses for the transfer functions between disturbance *d(s)* and output *y(s)*, and *d(s)* and plant input *u(s)*.

b) Plot and compare the frequency responses in each case. The appropriate transfer function is *y(s)/d(s)* in all cases.

c) To study the robustness of the designs, in each case, let the plant pole at s = 1 be replaced by $s = a$. In each case, find the range of a over which the system remains stable.

10.9 Consider the plants and the specifications in Problem 7.5, repeat the designs using the algebraic apoproach. Choose any configuration you desire.

10.10 Consider the inverted pendulum problem discussed in Problem 7.6. Design a compensator using the algebraic approach.

Notes and References

The algebraic approach is discussed fully in [C87a]. For a more advanced treatment including proofs, see [C84]. More recent tutorials, and extensions appear in [C87b], [CS90a], and [CS90b]. Evolution of the method from the state space viewpoint appears in [K80]. The method is also treated briefly in [FPE91], and [FPW90].

11

Random Signals and Systems Analysis

11.1 Intoduction

A fundamental problem in control systems engineering is to design a system that performs optimally in an uncertain environment. By an uncertain environment, we mean systems with uncertain models and subject to uncertain, possibly random, disturbances. One method of tackling this problem is to assume a perfect model for the plant and model the disturbances as random noise. This is the approach that evolved during the 1960s and culminated in the Linear Quadratic Gaussian (LQG) solution. Since that time, other approaches have been developed, such as Robust Control, Adaptive Control, Fuzzy Control and Quantitative Feedback Theory.

The estimation problem culminated in the celebrated Kalman-Bucy filter theory, which has found numerous applications in control, communications and signal processing. Because we will be presenting the Kalman-Bucy filter and the LQG solution in the next chapter, and these problems require a background in random processes, we will present a brief introduction to stochastic processes in this chapter. Because the subject of stochastic processes is quite involved and extensive, our discussion will be limited to definitions, terminology, relevant formulas, interpretations, and basic results that are needed for the next chapter. Relevant MATRIXx signal processing commands will also be introduced.

11.2 Stochastic (Random) Processes

A stochastic process is a family of random variables denoted by $x(t,\omega)$. For a fixed time, $t = T$, $x(T,\omega)$ is a random variable called the *sample function*. For a fixed $\omega = \omega_o$, $x(t,\omega_o)$ is a time function called the *realization*. To simplify our notation, we will drop the dependence of $x(t,\omega)$ on ω.

We will denote the probability density function of a process by $p(x(t))$. A process is completely characterized by its density function. If we have several processes, we need their joint density function. There are various statistical measures one can use to describe a process. The *nth moment* of a process is defined by

$$E\ [x^n(t)] = \int_{-\infty}^{\infty} x^n(t)\, p(x(t,\zeta))\, d\zeta$$

The first moment, $n = 1$, is the *mean* (also called *ensemble average* or *expected value*). The second moment is the *mean square value*. The *nth central moment* is defined by $E\ [x(t) - m(t)]^n$, where $m(t)$ is the mean. The second central moment is the *variance*, and its square root is the *standard deviation*. The first moment, or the mean, describes how the process behaves on the average, and the other moments are measures of variability. In most cases, all we may know about a process are its first and second order statistics. Processes that are completely characterized by these statistics are called *second order processes*. Note that in the above definition of ensemble average, we are integrating over random variables. It is also possible to define *time averages* by

$$< x^n(t) > = \lim_{T \to \infty} \frac{1}{2T} \int_{-T}^{T} x^n(t)\, dt$$

For some processes, time averages and ensemble averages are equal. These processes are called *ergodic*. Because, in practice, we can have access to only one realization of the process, it is the time average that we can realistically compute. The ergodicity assumption is almost always made. It simply implies that one sample of the process represents the whole family, and we can replace ensemble averages by time averages when needed.

The *(auto)correlation function* describes how different points in the process are related to each other, i.e., how similar $x(t_1)$ is to $x(t_2)$. It is defined by

$$R_x(t_1, t_2) = E\ [x(t_1)\, x(t_2)]$$

It is roughly a measure of randomness. Loosely speaking, if the correlation function is small, it means the process is "very random". Temporal relation between two processes is measured by their *cross-correlation function* defined by

$$R_{xy}(t_1, t_2) = E\ [x(t_1)\, y(t_2)]$$

The *covariance function* is similar to the correlation function except that the means are subtracted out. It is defined by

$$\mathrm{Cov}(x) = C_x(t_1, t_2) = E\ [(x(t_1) - m_1)(x(t_2) - m_2)]$$

where m_i is the mean of $x(t_i)$. The *cross-covariance* between two processes is defined similarly. The *correlation coefficient* is defined by

$$\rho_{xy} = \frac{Cov(x, y)}{\sigma_x \sigma_y}$$

where σ_x is the standard deviation of x. The correlation coefficient is a scalar quantity bounded by 1. Given two processes, we say they are *statistically independent* if their joint density function is the product of their individual density functions. A process is said to be *stationary* if

$$p(x(t + \tau)) = p(x(t)) \quad \text{for all } t \text{ and } \tau$$

This implies that the density function and all statistics are functions of the time difference, τ, rather than the individual times. This is usually a strong assumption and not needed for second order processes. A weaker assumption one can make is that the process is *stationary in the wide sense* (*w.s.s.*), defined by the following two conditions

$$E[x(t)] = m, \qquad \text{where } m \text{ is constant}$$

$$R_x(t_1, t_2) = E[x(t_1)\, x(t_2)] = R_x(t_1 - t_2) = R_x(\tau), \qquad \text{where } \tau = t_1 - t_2$$

Unless specified otherwise, we assume our processes are second order, ergodic, and stationary in the wide sense.

If the process has zero mean, then $Cov(x) = R_x(\tau)$. For $\tau = 0$,

$$R_x(0) = E[x^2(t)] = \text{mean square value}$$

$$C_x(0) = E[(x - m)^2] = \sigma^2 = \text{variance of } x$$

The most famous stochastic process is the *Gaussian* or *Normal* process. It is so called because its underlying density function is Gaussian (the famous bell shaped curve). A very important property of a Gaussian process is that it is completely characterized by its mean and covariance. The Gaussian assumption is commonly made (as in LQG). In most cases, this assumption is made for mathematical convenience and, in fact, the mean or the variance of the process may not even be known. These quantities may be statistically estimated or even pulled out of a hat to render a rational synthesis method. The numbers can then be changed until some specifications are met, as in the LQG/LTR technique.

If two w.s.s. processes are also independent, then we have

$$R_{xy}(\tau) = E[x(t)]\, E[y(t + \tau)] = m_x m_y$$

The converse of the preceding is only true for Gaussian processes. Two processes are said to be *uncorrelated* if their cross-covariance is identically zero, which implies that

$$E[x(t)\,y(t)] = E[x(t)]\,E[y(t)]$$

Note that this is a weaker assumption than statistical independence. Two processes are said to be *orthogonal* if they are uncorrelated and have zero mean , i.e.

$$E[x(t)\,y(t)] = 0$$

Frequency domain description of w.s.s. stochastic processes are obtained by taking the Fourier transform. The Fourier transform of the correlation function is called the *power spectral density function* (PSD) and is defined by

$$S_x(\omega) = F[R_x(\tau)] = \int_{-\infty}^{\infty} R_x(\tau)\,e^{-j\omega\tau}\,d\tau$$

$$R_x(\tau) = F^{-1}[S_x(\omega)] = \frac{1}{2\pi}\int_{-\infty}^{\infty} S_x(\omega)\,e^{j\omega\tau}\,d\omega$$

We make the following simple but important observation

$$R_x(0) = \text{mean square value of } x = E[x^2(t)] = \frac{1}{2\pi}\int_{-\infty}^{\infty} S_x(\omega)\,d\omega$$

Therefore, the area under the PSD is proportional to the mean square value of the process and represents its average power. It can also be shown that the PSD is an even function of frequency. The *cross-spectral densityfunction*, $S_{xy}(\omega)$, is defined as the Fourier transform of the cross correlation function.

11.3 Vector Processes

Consider the stochastic process $x(t,\omega)$, where x is an n-dimensional vector. The process is characterized by its joint density function for all time. The first and second order statistics for the process are defined by the following, where we will assume ergodicity and stationarity in the wide sense.

The mean is defined component-wise, i.e., it is a column vector where each element is the mean of the individual elements of the process. The (*auto*)*correlation matrix* is defined by

$$R_x(\tau) = E[x(t)\,x'(t+\tau)]$$

We note that diagonal elements of the correlation matrix are the autocorrelation functions, whereas the off-diagonal elements are cross-correlation functions. The *(auto) covariance matrix* is defined by

$$C_x(t) = E\,[(x(t) - m)(x(t) - m)'] = E\,[x(t)\,x'(t)] - m\,m'$$

The diagonal elements of the covariance matrix are the variances of individual elements, and the off-diagonal elements are cross-covariance functions of different elements, i.e.,

$$C_{ii} = \sigma_i^{\,2} \qquad \text{and} \qquad C_{ij} = \rho_{ij}\,\sigma_i\,\sigma_j$$

Note that if the process has zero mean, we have $C_x(t) = R_x(0)$. Also, if the covariance matrix is diagonal, the process is uncorrelated.

A process is said to be *white Gaussian* if its underlying density function is Gaussian and its PSD is constant for all frequencies, or equivalently, its autocorrelation function is an impulse. For our purposes, we will typically assume that stochastic disturbances and measurement noise are zero mean white Gaussian processes. Another important use of white noise is that many processes can be generated by passing white noise through a linear system. We will also adopt the following notation

$\omega \sim N(m,W)$ means that ω is Normal (Gaussian) with mean m and covariance W

11.4 Response of Linear Systems to Random Inputs

Consider the following linear time-invariant system, with transfer function *H(s) and state space representation given by*

$$\dot{x} = A\,x + B\,u$$
$$y = C\,x$$

where $u \sim N(0,V)$. The mean (m) and covariance (P) of the states satisfy the the following differential equations

$$\dot{m} = A\,m \qquad\qquad m(0) = E\,x(0)$$

$$\dot{P} = AP + PA' + BVB' \qquad\qquad P(0) = Cov\,(x\,(0))$$

The above equations describe how uncertainties with respect to initial states and the random input propagate through the system. If there is no random input , i.e. $V = 0$, we still have uncertainty because of the initial states. Assuming the system is asymptotically stable, the mean approaches zero in steady state, and the covariance matrix will satisfy the following algebraic equation called the *Lyapunov Equation.*

$$AP + PA' + BVB' = 0 \quad \rightarrow \quad P = \int_0^{\infty} e^{At} B V B' e^{A't} dt$$

The output covariance matrix is given by

$$Cov(y) = CPC'$$

Frequency domain descriptions in terms of power spectral densities are given by

$$S_x(\omega) = \Phi(j\omega) BVB' \Phi'(-j\omega) \quad \text{, where} \quad \Phi(\omega) = (j\omega I - A)^{-1}$$

$$S_y(\omega) = H(j\omega) S_u(\omega) H'(-j\omega) = H(j\omega) VH'(-j\omega)$$

$$S_{xy}(\omega) = H(j\omega)V$$

Note that if the input is white noise with unit intensity (i.e., $V = I$), then the system frequency response is given by the cross spectral density function. This is sometimes used to identify system dynamics. We can intuitively think of PSD's as transforms of inputs and outputs and the cross spectral density as the stochastic analog of the concept of the transfer function in deterministic systems.

An alternate expression for P in terms of PSD is given by (using *Parseval's Theorem*)

$$P = \frac{1}{2\pi} \int_{-\infty}^{\infty} \Phi(j\omega) BVB' \Phi'(-j\omega) \, d\omega$$

11.5 MATRIXx Commands

The appropriate commands for generating and analyzing random signals, and computing the response of linear systems to random inputs are described next. An example demonstrating the use of the commands will follow.

```
< > random
```

The *random* command in various forms generates random numbers. Typing *rand* by itself returns a random number from a uniform distribution between 0 and 1 (this is the default distribution), *rand (m,n)* returns an *m* by *n* random matrix, and *rand (a)* returns a random matrix with the same size as matrix *a*.

Rand(' normal') switches to a normal distribution with 0 mean and unity variance, *rand ('seed',n)* resets the seed to a value of *n*, and *rand ('seed',0)* resets the seed to 0. This is used when we wish to repeat a series of experiments using the same random numbers.

```
< > fft
```

The *fft* (*Fast Fourier Transform*) command provides an efficient algorithm for computing the *Discrete Fourier Transform* (DFT) of a time domain signal. The definition of an N-point DFT is given by (in the standard definition, the indices of x and X start at zero)

$$X(i+1) = \sum_{k=0}^{N-1} x_{k+1}\, e^{-2\pi j \frac{ik}{N}} \qquad \text{for } i = 0, \ldots N-1$$

The syntax for *fft* is

```
< > xf=fft(x,m,'win')
```

where x is the time domain signal that can be a row or column, real or complex vector. The output, *xf*, is the DFT of x and in general is a complex vector. The length of *xf* will be equal to the length of x if it is a power of 2; otherwise, x will be padded with extra zeros until its length is a power of 2. The integer m is optional, and it is $\log_2$ of the length of the desired fft. The *win* option allows five types of windowing that can be applied to the data before the *fft* is taken. Windowing is used in digital signal processing applications for smoothing the *fft*. The default window is the *Rectangular* or *Box* window, which corresponds to truncation. Because we are dealing with finite sets of data, this corresponds to no windowing.

Note that for real data, the N-point DFT, *xf*, is symmetric around the $(N/2)$ point, so for plotting purposes, it is sufficient to plot the first half of *xf* corresponding to positive frequencies. Recall also that peaks in the plot of DFT indicate the frequency components present in the signal. A rapidly fluctuating signal may have several peaks in the high frequency region. A random signal with periodic components may have a random looking FFT with distinct peaks at the periodic component frequencies.

The inverse DFT transform command *ifft* has the same syntax; the only difference is that the window is applied to the time domain signal after the inverse DFT is obtained.

```
< >  correlate
```

The discrete autocorrelation of an evenly sampled signal is defined by

$$R_x(m) = \frac{1}{N} \sum_{n=0}^{N-m-1} x(n)\, x(n+m) \quad \text{for} \quad 0 \le m \le M-1$$

Note that this is the discrete version of $E\,[x(t)\, x(t+t)]$, where we use sample, i.e., time average. The cross-correlation of two signals x and y are defined similarly. The syntax for the *correlate* command is given by

```
< > [cxy,t]=correlate(x,y,m,dt)
```

In the preceding, x and y are the data sequences with equal lengths of N. The parameter m is the number of points in the correlation sequence that must be less than N and in addition it must be power of 2; otherwise, it will be rounded to the nearest power of 2. The optional parameter *dt* is the sampling period of x and y.

The output *cxy* is the correlation sequence with length m+1. It is important to note that the first $m/2$ points correspond to negative time. To plot the correlation for positive time, use the points at $(m/2) + 1$ to m. For autocorrelation, use x in place of y in the input of the command.

```
< > spectrum
```

The *spectrum* of a signal is defined as the Fourier Transform of the correlation function. The spectrum command computes the DFT of the correlation sequence with a windowing option. It is defined by

$$S_x(\omega) = \sum_{m=-(M-1)}^{M-1} R_x(m)\, w(m)\, e^{-j\omega m}\,, \qquad w(m) = \text{window sequence (optional)}$$

The syntax of the *spectrum* command is given by

```
< > [ sxy,omega]=spectrum(x,y,m,'win')
```

The signals x and y have the same number of points. The length of the correlation sequence is m, a power of 2. The output, *sxy*, has length 2 m, where again the first m points correspond to negative frequencies. The second output, *omega*, is optional and is the vector of normalized frequencies. For autospectrum, set y equal to x.

The spectrum of a signal shows the frequency contents of a signal. A rapidly fluctuating signal may have many high frequency components, and this is indicated by a "high pass" spectrum. Peaks in the spectrum correspond to periodic components in the signal. Both autospectra and crossspectra can be used to estimate the transfer function of a linear time invariant system using the relations below.

$$S_y(\omega) = |H(j\omega)|^2\, S_x(\omega)$$

$$S_{xy}(\omega) = H(j\omega)\, S_x(\omega)$$

Let *sy* and *sx* denote the output and input spectra over positive frequencies: then *h2* is the estimate of the square of the magnitude of the transfer function *h*. Note that the autospectrum is real, and, therefore, this estimate ignores phase information.

```
< > h2=sy./sx; h=sqrt(h);
```

Let *sxy* denote the cross-spectrum between input and output over the positive frequency range; then an estimate of the transfer function *h* is given by

```
< > h=sxy./sx
```

Note that the cross-spectrum is complex, so *h* is complex. To obtain the Bode plot, we need to compute the magnitude of *h* in dB and the phase in degrees. If the input is unit intensity white noise, then *sxy* is the estimate of the transfer function.

```
< > psd
```

The output power spectral density of a linear time invariant system (denoted by PSD earlier) is computed from

$$S_y(\omega) = H(j\omega)\, S_x(\omega)\, H'(-j\omega)$$

Its syntax is given by

```
< > [w,ypsd,yspec]=psd(s,ns,uspec,wmin,wmax,npts)
< > [w,ypsd,yspec]=psd(s,ns,uspec,omega)
```

The *psd* command provides roughly the same kind of information as the *spectrum* command, but the input-output information is different. The *spectrum* command works directly with data vectors (time domain), and computes their auto and crossspectra (frequency domain). The *psd* command works with the system and uses the spectrum of inputs (frequency domain) to generate spectrum of outputs in the frequency domain. It can, therefore, handle multi-input multi-output (MIMO) systems.

For SISO systems, *yspec* is a column vector and *ypsd* is its first element. If the input is white noise, then *uspec* is a constant; otherwise, it is a column vector for colored noise input.

For multi-input systems, the input PSD is a square hermitian matrix. For a system with *p* white noise inputs, *uspec* is a constant matrix of size *p*. For colored noise inputs, it is a matrix with size given by (NPTS , p^2), where NPTS is the number of points (optional: default = 100) . Each row contains elements of the input PSD matrix for a certain frequency. These matrix elements are stacked row by row to form a large row of size p^2. For instance, the first row contains

$$S_{11}(1), S_{12}(1), \dots, S_{1p}(1), S_{21}(1), S_{22}(1), \dots, S_{2p}(1), \dots, S_{p1}(1), S_{p2}(1), \dots, S_{pp}(1)$$

For multi-output systems with *m* outputs, *yspec* is a matrix with size (NPTS , m^2). Its elements are stacked the same way uspec is. The *ypsd* output is also a matrix with size (NPTS, *p*). Each row corresponds to a specific frequency. For instance, the first row contains

$$\text{yspec}_{11}(1), \text{yspec}_{22}(1), \ldots, \text{yspec}_{mm}(1)$$

Note that if we have several filter stages, the output *yspec* of each stage can be used as the input *uspec* of the next stage. In this way we can use the PSD to study noise propagation through a multistage system.

```
< > lyapunov
```

The *lyapunov* command solves the Algebraic Lyapunov Equation (ALE) defined by

$$A'P + PA + Q = 0$$

The above equation appears in several places in control theory. For instance, in stability theory, it is known that for an asymptotically stable LTI system, ALE has a positive definite solution for any given positive definite Q. For steady state stochastic analysis, the solution of ALE describes the state covariance, P, of an asymptotically stable LTI system driven by zero mean white noise input. The syntax of the *lyapunov* command is given by

```
< > P=lyapunov(A,Q )                    // where Q = B V B'
```

Note that V is the input covariance (i.e., the noise intensity). In filtering applications, P may stand for the error covariance and is a measure of filter performance.

```
< > rms
```

The output RMS response and covariance are computed by the *rms* command. Its syntax is given by

```
< > [yrms,ycov]=rms(S,NS,USD)
```

The input intensity matrix , *usd*, is a square symmetric matrix and is optional (default = I). The output covariance matrix, *ycov*, is also a square symmetric matrix and is optional (default = I). It can be computed as ($C P C'$), where P is the state covariance. Recall that the output RMS response is a measure of the average power at the system output. The following example will demonstrate the use of the above commands.

Example 11.1 : Stochastic Analysis

We consider two second order systems with different bandwidths. Both systems are driven by white noise. The following responses are obtained and compared for both systems: time response, Fourier transform of input and outputs, auto-correlation functions, and spectral densities. The systems are given by

$$G_1(s) = \frac{2}{s^2 + 2s + 2}, \qquad G_2(s) = \frac{25}{s^2 + 25\sqrt{2}\,s + 625}$$

The bandwidths of the systems are $\sqrt{2}$ and 25, respectively. It is naturally expected that the first system will filter high frequency noise much better than the second one.

The first step is to set the random number generator to *Normal* for zero mean, unit intensity white noise; we will also reset the seed to zero. The number of points generated is 128, a power of 2, which is required for some of the commands.

```
< > dt=0.01; t=[0:127]'*dt; rand('norm'); rand('seed',0);
< > in1=rand(t);
```

The systems are next defined and converted to state space form.

```
< > n1=2; d1=[1,2,2]; [s1,ns1]=sform(n1,d1);
< > [a1,b1,c1,d1]=split(s1,ns1);
< > n2=625; d2=[1,sqrt(2)*25,625]; [s2,ns2]=sform(n2,d2);
< > [a2,b2,c2,d2]=split(s2,ns2);
```

Next, we will simulate the systems with the noise input.

```
< > [t,y1]=lsim(s1,ns1,in1,dt); [t,y2]=lsim(s2,ns2,in1,dt);
```

The inputs and the responses are shown in Figure 11-1. We observe that the outputs are smoothed versions of the input where `y1` is much smoother than `y2`, this is due to the fact that both systems are low pass with the second system having a higher bandwidth. This is verified by looking at the DFT of the time domain signals.

```
< > in1f=fft(in1); y1f=fft(y1); y2f=fft(y2);
```

The plots of the first 64 points of magnitude of DFT corresponding to positive frequency versus the frequency axis in units of Hertz are shown in Figure11-2 and verify the low pass characteristics of the systems. The absence of any peaks indicates lack of any periodic components. We will compute the autocorrelations next.

```
< > [ruu,t]=correl(in1,in1,128,dt);
< > ryy1=correl(y1,y1,dt); ryy2=correl(y2,y2,dt);
```

The plots are shown in Figure 11-3. Note that the auto-correlations are symmetric about the vertical axis—even function—and the input autocorrelation is almost impulsive (nonideal white noise) and that there is more correlation in the first system than in the second one. This is a measure of variability in the signals. The more fluctuation in a signal, the less correlation between the neighboring points and, hence, the more impulsive looking the autocorrelation appears. We will compute the spectrum of the signals next (the DFT of the correlations)

```
< > suu=spec(in1,in1,128);syy1=spec(y1,y1,128);syy2=spec(y2,y2,128);
```

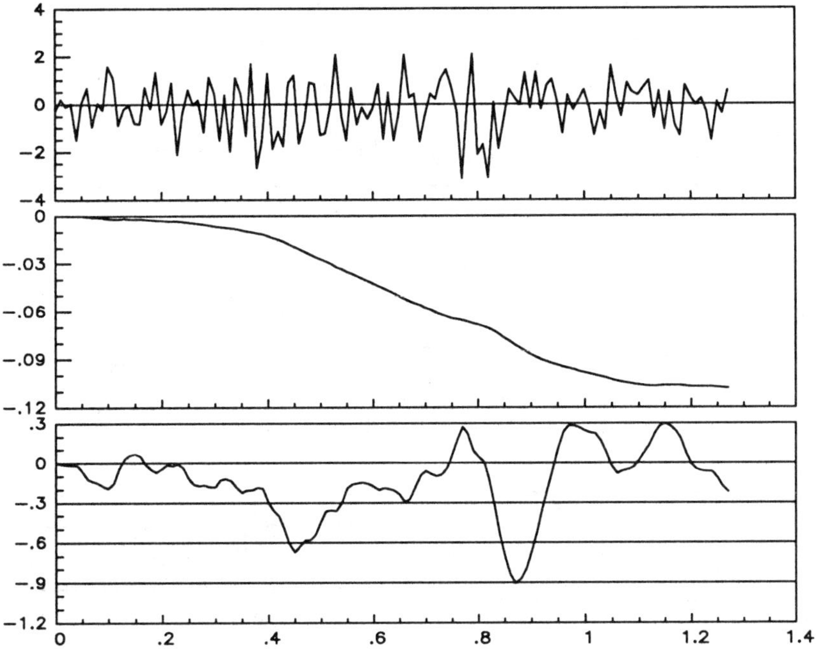

Figure 11-1 Time responses to noise (top plot: noise input; middle plot: y_1 ; bottom plot: y_2).

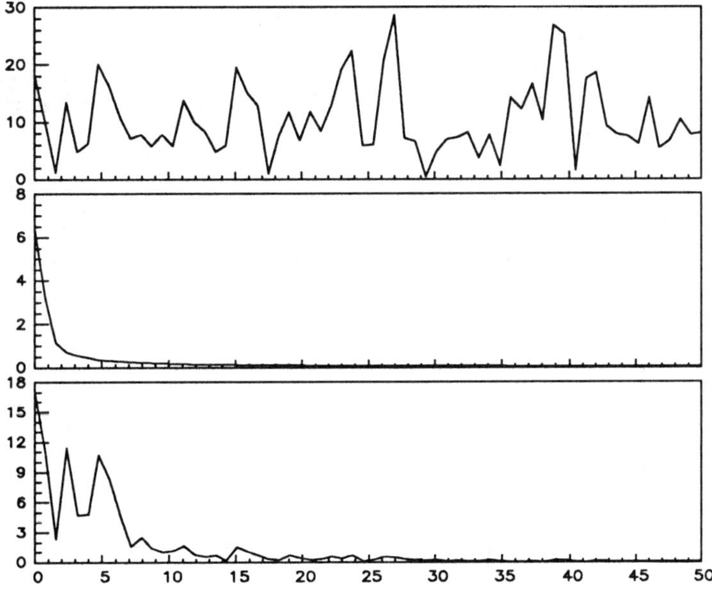

Figure 11-2 FFT of input and outputs (top plot: input fft; middle and bottom plots: ffts of y_1 *and* y_2).

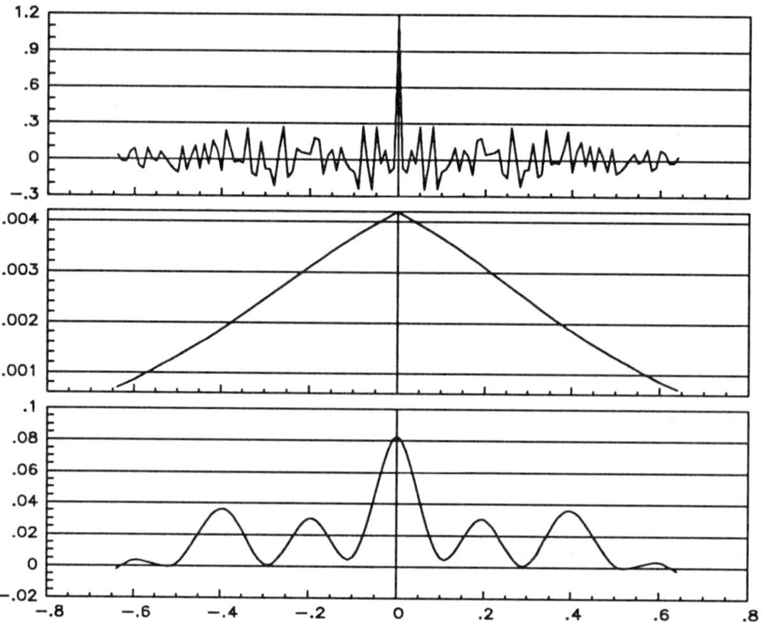

Figure 11-3 Autocorrelations (top plot: input; middle and bottom plots: y_1 and y_2).

The plots for the magnitude of the spectra for positive frequency (i.e. the last 64 points) are shown in Figure 11-4. The plots reconfirm the conclusions from the DFT analysis. Note that the plots are somewhat similar to the DFT plots (the *spec* plots are in dB, whereas the *fft* plots are straight magnitudes). It is is easy to show that (try to observe this from the data)

$$S_x = \frac{1}{N} |X|^2 \quad \text{where} \quad X = DFT\ [x(n)] \quad \text{and} \quad S_x = DFT\ [R_x(m)]$$

The PSD's are computed next. We will also obtain the frequency response of both systems to compare with the PSD results.

```
< > [w,m1,ph1]=bode(s1,ns1,0.1,100);[w,m2,ph2]=bode(s2,ns2,0.1,100);
< > [w,ypsd1,yspec1]=psd(s1,ns1,1,0.1,100);
< > [w,ypsd2,yspec2]=psd(s2,ns2,1,0.1,100);
```

The plots of PSD (converted to dB) and Bode plots are similar again. This is because PSD is the square of the frequency response (a factor of 2 in dB scale).

The state covariance and the output RMS values are then obtained.

```
< > p1=lyap(a1,b1*b1'); p2=lyap(a2,b2*b2')
< > [yrms1,ycov1]=rms(s11,ns1,1); {yrms2,ycov2]=rms(s2,ns2,1);
```

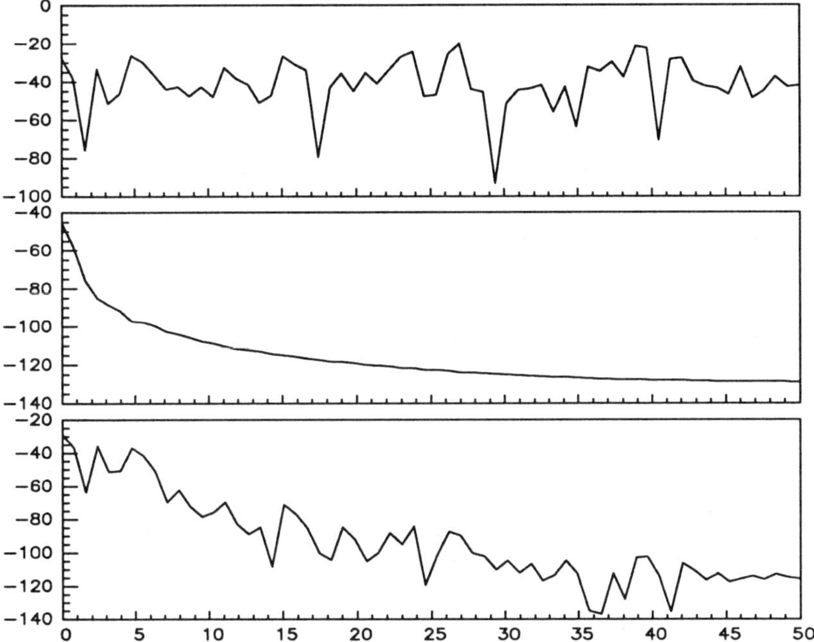

Figure 11-4 The spectra of input and outputs (top plot: input; middle and bottom plots: y_1 and y_2).

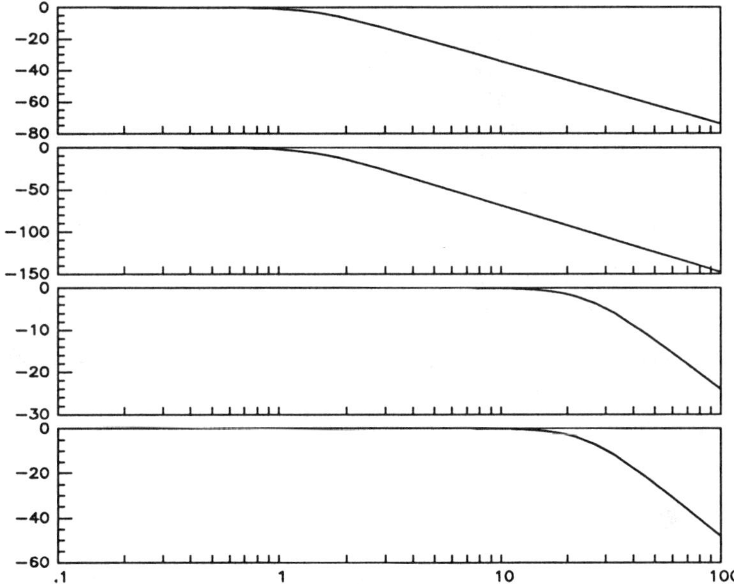

Figure 11-5 Bode magnitude and PSD plots (top two plots: Bode and PSD of first system; bottom two plots: Bode and PSD of second system).

$$P1 = \begin{bmatrix} 0.25 & 0 \\ 0 & 0.125 \end{bmatrix}, \quad P2 = \begin{bmatrix} 0.0141 & 0 \\ 0 & 0 \end{bmatrix}$$

ycov1 = 0.5 , yrms1 = 0.7071 and ycov2 = 8.83, yrms2 = 2.973.

Note that yrms1 is the square root of ycov1, and ycov1 = $C\,P\,C'$. The higher RMS value in the second system indicates the higher average power of noise at the system output.

11.6 Appendix: Example program

```
//This is the program used for Example 11.1
dt=0.01; t=[0:127]'*dt;
rand('norm')
rand('seed',0)
in1=rand(t);
n1=2;d1=[1 2 2];[s1,ns1]=sform(n1,d1);[a1,b1,c1,dd1]=split(s1,ns1);
n2=25*25;d2=[1 sqrt(2)*25 25*25];
[s2,ns2]=sform(n2,d2);[a2,b2,c2,dd2]=split(s2,ns2);
[t,y1]=lsim(s1,ns1,in1,dt);[t,y2]=lsim(s2,ns2,in1,dt);
plot(t,[in1 y1 y2],'strip');pause;erase
[w,m1,ph1]=bode(s1,ns1,.1,100,'noplot');
[w,m2,ph2]=bode(s2,ns2,.1,100,'noplot');
in1f=fft(in1); y1f=fft(y1);y2f=fft(y2);
hz=[0:63]'/(63*2*dt);//frequency axis
plot(hz,abs(in1f(1:64)),abs(y1f(1:64)),abs(y2f(1:64)),'strip');
[ruu,tt]=correl(in1,in1,128,dt);ryy1=correl(y1,y1,128,dt);
ryy2=correl(y2,y2,128,dt);
plot(tt,[ruu,ryy1,ryy2 ],'strip');pause;erase;
suu=spec(in1,in1,128);syy1=spec(y1,y1,128);syy2=spec(y2,y2,128);
plot(hz,[abs(suu(65:128)),abs(syy1(65:128)),abs(syy2(65:128)),' ...
strip logy');
p1=lyap(a1,b1*b1');p2=lyap(a2,b2*b2');
[yrms1,ycov1]=rms(s1,ns1,1);[yrms2,ycov2]=rms(s2,ns2,1)
[w,ypsd1]=psd(s1,ns1,1,0.1,100);ypsdb1=20*log(sqrt(ypsd1))/log(10);
[w,ypsd2]=psd(s2,ns2,1,0.1,100);ypsdb2=20*log(sqrt(ypsd2))/log(10);
plot(w,[m1 ypsd1 m2 ypsd2],'log strip');pause;erase;
return
```

Notes and References

For additional information on stochastic analysis, see [Pa91] and [KS72].

12

Linear Quadratic Control

Linear Quadratic Control (LQ) refers to a body of techniques developed since the 1960s for control systems design. The LQ problem itself is an important subset of the powerful machinery of optimal control. The plant is assumed to be a linear system in state space form, and the objective function is a quadratic functional of the plant states and control inputs. The problem is to minimize the quadratic functional with respect to the control inputs subject to the linear system constraints. The advantage of LQ formulation of problems is that they lead to linear control laws that are easy to implement and analyze. There are many variations and extensions of this problem, some of which will be discussed below.

We will restrict our attention to regulator type problems. The system is assumed to be at equilibrium, and it is desired to maintain the equilibrium—or set-point—despite disturbances. Hence, the objective is to minimize the effects of disturbances on the system. This is to be contrasted with tracking or servomechanism type problems, where the goal is to track a given reference or external input. It can be shown that tracking problems can be converted to regulator type problems.

We will primarily consider the steady state case. In this case the optimization horizon is allowed to extend to infinity. It is known that in this case the control law is a linear time invariant function of the states or outputs of the system. Finite horizon type problems lead to linear time varying controllers that are more difficult to implement and analyze.

12.1 The Linear Quadratic Regulator Problem

Consider the linear system and the quadratic objective function (or cost function)

$$\dot{x} = A\,x + B\,u$$
$$y = C\,x$$

$$J = \frac{1}{2}\int_0^T (x'Q\,x + u'R\,u)\,dt$$

The problem is to minimize J with respect to $u(t)$. This known as the linear quadratic regulator (LQR) problem. A simple interpretation of the cost function is as follows. If the system is scalar (i.e., first order), the cost function becomes

$$J = \frac{1}{2} \int_0^T (q x^2 + r u^2)\, dt$$

Now we see that J represents the weighted sum of energy of the state and control. If r is very large relative to q, the control energy is penalized very heavily. This physically translates into smaller motors, actuators and amplifier gains needed to implement the control law. Likewise if q is much larger than r, the state is penalized heavily resulting in a very damped system that avoids large fluctuations or overshoots in system states. In the general case, Q and R represent respective weights on different states and control channels. Note that the main design parameters are Q and R. How these are chosen will be dealt with later, but in general several design iterations are necessary to obtain a stable optimal system with "good" response. Note that we require that Q be symmetric positive semidefinite (written as $Q \geq 0$) and R symmetric positive definite ($R > 0$) for a meaningful optimization problem.

12.1.1 LQR Solution Using the Minimum Principle

Optimal control problems can be solved using a variety of techniques. Among them are *Euler-Lagrange* equations, *Hamilton-Jacobi-Bellman* theory, and *Pontriagin's minimum principle.* We will present the latter.

To arrive at the *minimum principle*, we must first form the so-called *Hamiltonian*

$$H(x, \lambda, t) = \frac{1}{2}(x'Q x + u'R u) + \lambda' (Ax + Bu)$$

The minimum principle states that the optimal control and state trajectories must satisfy the following three equations:

$$\dot{x} = \frac{\partial H}{\partial \lambda}, \qquad x(0) = x_o \qquad \text{state equations}$$

$$-\dot{\lambda} = \frac{\partial H}{\partial x}, \qquad \lambda(T) = 0 \qquad \text{costate or adjoint equations}$$

$$\frac{\partial H}{\partial u} = 0$$

Using rules for differentiation of matrices and vectors, the preceding equations for the LQR case become:

$$\dot{x} = A\,x + B\,u \qquad x(0) = x_o$$

$$-\dot{\lambda} = Q\,x + A'\lambda \qquad \lambda\,(T) = 0$$

$$u^* = -R^{-1}\,B'\,\lambda \qquad \text{u* is the optimal control}$$

The above coupled linear differential equations form a *two point boundary value problem (TPBVP)*, which because of mixed boundary conditions is difficult to solve numerically. Note that R has to be positive definite for its inverse to exist. Substituting the optimal control into the state equation we get

$$\begin{bmatrix} \dot{x} \\ \dot{\lambda} \end{bmatrix} = \begin{bmatrix} A & -B\,R^{-1}B' \\ -Q & -A' \end{bmatrix} \begin{bmatrix} x \\ \lambda \end{bmatrix} \triangleq H \begin{bmatrix} x \\ \lambda \end{bmatrix}$$

The above matrix, H, is called the *Hamiltonian* matrix and plays an important role in LQR theory. It turns out, however, that we do not have to solve the *TPBVP* after all. To see this, let us make the following substitution:

$$\lambda = P\,x$$

Differentiating both sides with respect to time and substituting for λ we get

$$\frac{d\lambda}{dt} = \frac{dP}{dt}x + P\frac{dx}{dt} = \frac{dP}{dt}x + PA\,x - PBR^{-1}B'P\,x = -Q\,x - A'P\,x$$

The above equation must hold for any x, hence a sufficient condition for optimal control is that P must satisfy

$$-\frac{dP}{dt} = A'P + PA + Q - PBR^{-1}B'P\,, \qquad P\,(T) = 0$$

The above is the celebrated *Riccati* differential equation. It is a *nonlinear* first order differential equation that has to be solved backwards in time. Recall that the *TPBVP* is a *linear* second order differential equation with mixed boundary conditions. It is usually the Riccati equation form of the LQR solution that is used.

The above formulation and solution of the LQR problem is known as the finite time (or finite horizon) problem. It results in a linear *time varying* controller of the feedback form

$$u(t) = -K(t)\,x(t) \quad \text{where} \quad K(t) = R^{-1}B'\,P(t)$$

For the infinite time LQR problem, we let T approach infinity. Of course, now one runs into the question of the convergence of the cost function and, hence, the existence of the optimal controller. Even if the optimal control exists, it does not necessarily result in a stable closed loop system. It turns out that under mild conditions $P(t)$ approaches a constant matrix P (hence $dP/dt \to 0$), and the positive definite solution of the *algebraicRriccati equation (ARE)* results in an asymptotically stable closed loop system.

$$A'P + PA + Q - PBR^{-1}B'P = 0 \qquad (ARE)$$

$$u = -Kx, \qquad K = R^{-1}B'P$$

The exact conditions are the following. The pair (A, B) are stabilizable, $R > 0$, and Q can be factored as $Q = D\,D'$, where D is any matrix such that (D, A) is detectable. These conditions are necessary and sufficient for existence and uniqueness of the optimal controller that will asymptotically stabilize the system.

12.1.2 Generalizations of LQR

The LQR formulation can be generalized along many lines. We mention two of them, namely, cross-product terms in the cost function and regulators with a prescribed degree of stability [AM90].

Cross-product Terms

Consider the more general cost function

$$J = \frac{1}{2}\int_0^\infty \begin{bmatrix} x \\ u \end{bmatrix}' \begin{bmatrix} Q & N \\ N' & R \end{bmatrix} \begin{bmatrix} x \\ u \end{bmatrix} dt = \frac{1}{2}\int_0^\infty (x'Qx + u'Ru + x'Nu + u'N'x)\,dt$$

The above cost function is obtained when nonlinear systems are linearized or a nonlinear cost function is approximated by a quadratic one. It also is used when power input of a system is to be penalized. Another common case is when the cost function contains the term

$$y'y \quad \text{where} \quad y = Cx + Du$$

The appropriate Riccati equation and optimal controller for this general cost function are given by

$$A'P + PA - (PB + N)R^{-1}(PB + N)' + Q = 0$$

$$u = -Kx, \qquad K = R^{-1}(B'P + N')$$

where conditions for existence and uniqueness of the stabilizing optimal control are the following: (A, B) controllable, $(A - BR^{-1}N')$ detectable, and $HH' = Q - NR^{-1}N'$ for some matrix H.

Regulators with Prescribed Degree of Stability

It is possible to design a regulator and prescribe the poles to be located α units to the left of the imaginary axis where α is a positive scalar. This can be done by considering the following modified cost function:

$$J = \frac{1}{2}\int_0^{\infty} e^{2\alpha t}(u'Ru + x'Qx)\,dt$$

It can be shown that the optimal control is given by the same control gain K as the standard LQR where P is the solution of a modified Riccati equation given by

$$(A + \alpha I)'P + P(A + \alpha I) + Q - PBR^{-1}B'P = 0$$

The conditions for existence and uniqueness of the stabilizing optimal control are the same as the standard LQR problem with the exception that A is replaced with $(A + \alpha I)$.

12.1.3 MATRIXx Implementation

The commands *regulator* and *riccati* can solve the LQR problem directly. The syntaxes for these commands are given by

```
< > [ev,k,p]=regulator(A,B,Q,R,N)
< > [ev,k,p]=riccati(S,SQ,NS )
```

where `ev` stands for the optimal closed loop eigenvalues. Inclusion of `P`, the ARE solution, is optional. The main difference between the two commands is the command input structure. Both handle the general cost function formulation with cross product terms. Inclusion of `N`, the cross product weight in the *regulator* command is optional. The term `SQ` in the *riccati* command stands for the two-by-two block matrix in the generalized cost function.

The discrete version of *regulator* is *dregulator* with the same syntax. The discrete version of the *riccati* command has the following syntax:

```
< > [ev,k,p]=riccati(S,SQ,NS,'disc')
```

For discussion of the discrete LQR problem see the references.

Because LQR results in a state feedback controller, we can apply the approach in Chapter 8 to find root locus and Bode plots and find stability margins. A simple program for design and analysis is provided in the Appendix.

12.1.4 LQR Properties with Classical Interpretations

LQR has many desirable properties. Among them are good stability margins and sensitivity properties. We will also discuss the effects of weights in the LQR setting. Most of these properties can be derived using the *return difference inequality* first derived by Kalman [K64].

Return Difference Inequality

The algebraic Riccati equation under mild assumptions can be manipulated to arrive at the following relations.

Return Difference Equality: SISO Case

$$|1 + k\,\Phi(j\omega)\,b|^2 = 1 + |G(j\omega)|^2$$

or

$$|1 + L(j\omega)|^2 = 1 + |G(j\omega)|^2$$

where $L(s)$ is the loop gain given by

$$L(s) = k\,\Phi(s)\,b \qquad \text{where} \qquad \Phi(s) = (sI - A)^{-1}$$

RDE assumes the following : $R = 1$ and $Q = c'c$ and $G(s) = c\,\Phi(s)\,b$

Because the right hand side of the return difference equality (RDE) is always bigger than 1, the following inequalities hold.

Return Difference Inequality: SISO Case

$$|1 + k\,\Phi(j\omega)\,b| \geq 1$$

$$|1 + L(j\omega)| = |J(j\omega)| \geq 1$$

$$|S(j\omega)| \leq 1$$

where $J(s)$ stands for the return difference, i.e., $J(s) = 1 + L(s)$ and $S(s)$ stands for sensitivity, which is defined as the inverse of the return difference (see Chapters 1 and 5).

The preceding return difference inequality (RDI) implies that for all frequencies, the Nyquist plot of the open loop transfer function of an LQR based design always stays outside of a unit circle centered at (-1,0). Because the magnitude of the sensitivity is also always less than unity, the optimal system will have good feedback properties.

The MIMO versions of the above are presented below for completeness.

$$[I + K\,\Phi(j\,\omega)\,B\,]^*R\;[I + K\,\Phi(j\,\omega)\,B\,] = R + B'\,\Phi(j\,\omega)^*\,Q\;\Phi(j\,\omega)\,B$$

$$[I + L(j\,\omega)\,]^*R\;[I + L(j\,\omega)\,] = R + G(j\,\omega)^*\,G(j\,\omega)$$

$$[I + R^{\,1/2}K\,\Phi(j\,\omega)\,B\,R^{\,-1/2}\,]^*[I + R^{\,1/2}K\,\Phi(j\,\omega)\,B\,R^{\,-1/2}\,] \geq I$$

where (*) stands for conjugate transpose and

$$Q = C'C \quad \text{and} \quad G(s) = C\;\Phi(s)\,B$$

LQR Stability Margins

The RDI along with simple geometric arguments can be used to derive the following stability margins for LQR in the SISO case:

1. **GM: [0.5 , ∞)**
2. **PM ≥ 60 °**

Note that the upper GM of infinity and the PM of 60 degrees are actually an overkill Because most systems do not require such large margins. The lower gain margin (GRM) is 0.5 (or -6 dB). One consequence of the infinite GM is the minimum phase property of the loop transfer function *L(s)*. This can be shown in several ways, but simple root locus argument reveals that if the system had not been minimum phase, at least one branch would have had to enter the RHP and approach a zero. Of course in that case, the system would not have infinite upper GM.

High Frequency Roll-off Rate

Consider the complementary sensitivity *T(s)*, which can easilty be shown to be equal to

$$T(s) = I - S\,(s) = -\,k\,(j\,\omega - A + b\,k\,)^{-1}\,b$$

it then follows that

$$\lim_{\omega \to \infty}\; j\,\omega\,T = -\,k\,b = -\,R^{-1}\,b'P\,b\; \leq\; 0$$

The preceding implies that $|T(j\omega)|$ drops as $1/(j\omega)$ in the SISO case, indicating a roll-off rate of - 20 dB per decade at high frequencies. This, of course, affects the noise suppression properties of the optimal system and as such is not very good. It can be argued that this defect is the result of excessive stability margins. It is possible to trade off stability margins with high frequency roll-off rate using variations of LQ techniques known as *frequency shaping* and *loop transfer recovery* procedures [M89].

Time Delay Tolerance

If some time delay of the form $e^{-j\omega\tau}$ is inserted within the loop, we can show that the maximum amount of time delay that the system can tolerate and still remain stable is given by

$$\tau < \frac{\pi}{3\,\omega_x}, \quad \text{where } \omega_x \text{ is the highest gain crossover frequency}$$

Observe that in this case the LQR control gain is no longer optimal. Hence other LQR properties like the stability margins are also lost; only stability is guaranteed.

Tolerance of Sector Nonlinearities

Asymptotic stability of LQR can even be maintained when there are certain sector type time varying nonlinearities inserted at the input of the plant. Sector type nonlinearities (shown in Figure 12-1) are defined by : $\frac{1}{2} + \varepsilon_1 \leq \frac{N(e)}{e} \leq \frac{1}{\varepsilon_2}$

Note that again LQR properties are lost, but stability can be guaranteed.

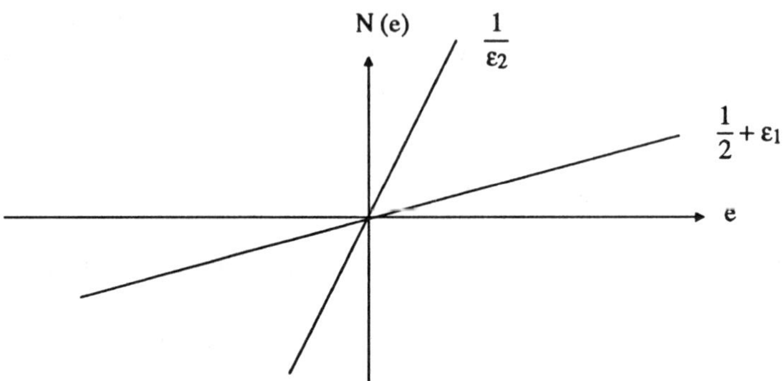

Figure 12-1 Sector type nonlinearity (slopes are shown).

Optimal Root Locus

We will show that a special choice of Q and R allows us to investigate the effects of weights on the location of closed loop poles. Let us assume that Q and R are given by

$$Q = C'C \quad \text{and} \quad R = \rho I \qquad \text{where } \rho \text{ is a positive scalar}$$

the cost function for $D = 0$ becomes

$$J = \frac{1}{2} \int_0^\infty (y'y + \rho\, u'u)\, dt$$

so we are minimizing the system output and control energy. Recall that the Hamiltonian matrix is given by

$$\mathrm{H} = \begin{bmatrix} A & -\frac{1}{\rho} B B' \\ -C'C & -A' \end{bmatrix}$$

The closed loop poles are the eigenvalues of the Hamiltonian matrix, i.e., they are the roots of the following characteristic polynomial $\Delta_c = | sI - \mathrm{H} |$.

After a series of matrix manipulations, we arrive at the following equation.

$$\Delta_c(s) = (-1)^n \Delta(s)\, \Delta(-s)\, | I + \frac{1}{\rho} G(s)\, G(-s)' |, \quad \text{where} \quad \Delta(s) = | sI - A |$$

Limiting ourselves to the SISO case, let us define the following:

n = number of poles, m = number of zeros, with $m < n$, r = *relative degree* = $n - m$, and $G(s) = n(s) / d(s)$.

The above equation simplifies to

$$(-1)^n \Delta_c = \Delta(s)\, \Delta(-s)\, [\, 1 + \frac{1}{\rho} G(s)\, G(-s)\,] = d(s)\, d(-s) + \frac{1}{\rho} n(s)\, n(-s)$$

Note the above has the standard root locus form. It implies the optimal closed loop poles can be obtained from the root locus of $G(s)G(-s)$. Such root loci are generally called *symmetric root locus* (SRL), as you recall from Chapter 10. By increasing ρ, we can minimize control energy. We will discuss the effects of limiting values of ρ.

Minimum Energy Control Case

$$\text{As } \rho \to \infty \quad \Rightarrow \quad (-1)^n \Delta_c(s) \quad \to \quad d(s)\, d(-s)$$

Because the optimal closed loop poles are always in the LHP, we conclude that as the control weighting is increased, the stable open loop poles will remain where they are, and the unstable ones will be reflected across the imaginary axis. This property can be used as a guideline for pole placement.

Cheap Control Case

$$\text{As } \rho \to 0 \quad \Rightarrow \text{closed loop poles} \to \; n(s)\, n(-s) \quad \text{for finite } s$$

Hence, the closed loop poles approach the plant finite zeros or their stable images. For values of s approaching infinity, the closed loop poles will approach zeros at infinity in the famous *Butterworth pattern.*

$$\text{for } |s| \to \infty, \qquad s = \left(\frac{\alpha_m{}^2}{\rho}\right)^{\frac{1}{2r}} e^{\,j\frac{\pi k(r+1)}{2r}} \qquad k = \text{odd integer}$$

where α_μ in the preceding is the coefficient of the highest order term in $n(s)$. We summarize our conclusions in the Table 12-1.

Table 12-1 Summary of Effects of Varying Control Weight on Pole Locations

Control Energy Weight	Open Loop Poles	Closed Loop Poles
Minimum energy control $\rho \to \infty$	Stable poles	Will remain in original place
	Unstable poles	Will be reflected about the imaginary axis
Cheap control $\rho \to 0$	m Poles	Will approach m finite zeros or their stable images
	$(n - m)$ Poles	Will go to zeros at infinity in Butterworth pattern

Example 12.1 LQR Design

We will investigate the solution of Example 8.1, control of longitudinal motion of a helicopter near hover, using LQR design. Moreover, we would like to find out the effects of weighting matrices Q and R on various quantities and also verify the LQR properties we discussed in this section.

Toward this goal, we will separate the effects of Q and R. In one set of simulations, $R = r$, where the scalar parameter r is fixed at a value of { 1 } and $Q = q\,\mathrm{I}$, where the scalar parameter q is allowed to vary over the range { 1, 10, 10^2, 10^3, 10^6 }. In another set, q is fixed at { 1 }, and r is allowed to vary over the same range. Hence, we basically are comparing the cheap control and minimum energy control cases.

The state space equations and the transfer function are repeated below for convenience.

$$\dot{x} = \begin{bmatrix} -0.4 & 0 & -0.01 \\ 1 & 0 & 0 \\ -1.4 & 9.8 & -0.02 \end{bmatrix} x + \begin{bmatrix} 6.3 \\ 0 \\ 9.8 \end{bmatrix} u$$

$$y = [\,0 \;\; 0 \;\; 1\,]\,x$$

$$G(s) = \frac{9.8\,(s - 0.25 \pm j\,2.49)}{(s + 0.65)\,(s - 0.11 \pm j\,0.36)}$$

Case I : $Q = q\mathbf{I}$

We will first investigate the cheap control case, where the ratio r/q approaches zero. The control gain vector, step response characteristics (perccent overshoot, rise time, 2% settling time and peak time), along with stability margin measures (GMs and PMs and their frequencies) are listed in Table 12-2. Note that the control gain tends to increase. This is expected, because the control cost is relatively decreasing so larger gains are used. This may cause saturation problems in practice.

Table 12-2 Data for Varying q $\quad Q = q\,I,\ R = r = 1$

q	Control gain vector	POS Tr Ts Tp	GM PM wgc wpc
1	0.52 4.38 0.99	18.6 1.2 5.2 2.0	-15.8 83.8 12.7 1.9
10	1.12 11.89 3.15	19.0 1.2 5.1 1.9	-22.9 88.2 37.9 2.08
10^2	3.13 35.73 9.98	19.1 1.2 5.1 1.9	-30.8 89.4 117.6 2.2
10^3	9.53 111.15 31.57	19.1 1.2 5.0 1.9	-40.7 89.8 369.6 2.2
10^6	296.36 3489.23 998.39	19.1 1.2 5.0 1.9	-70.6 _ _ 2.2

The PM is larger than 80 degrees in all cases (for $q = 10^6$, there was no gain crossover frequency over the selected range for the Bode plot). The negative GMs indicate by how much the gain can be reduced before instability occurs. It is at least -15 dB and increases with q. Using the gain crossover frequency as an approximate measure of the bandwidth, we observe that as the stability margins increase, bandwidth increases.

Table 12-3 Closed Loop Poles for Varying q $\quad Q = q\,I,\ R = r = 1$

q	1	10	10^2	10^3	10^6
Closed loop poles	-0.73 + 2.14i	-0.73 + 2.17i	-0.73 - 2.18i	-0.73 + 2.18i	-0.73 - 2.18i
	-0.73 - 2.14i	-0.73 - 2.17i	-0.73 + 2.18i	-0.73 - 2.18i	-0.73 + 2.18i
	-12.00	-36.95	-116.547	-368.42	-11650.32

The complex closed loop poles (shown in Table 12-3) approach the stable images of the plant zeros, and the remaining real pole approaches the zero at infinity along a line corresponding to the Butterworth pattern. Because the complex poles are dominant and remain fixed, no appreciable effect on the step response is expected.

The step response and Bode plots of the open and closed loop systems are shown in Figure 12-2. Note the -20 dB roll-off rate of the closed loop magnitude plot at high frequencies.

Case II : $R = r\mathbf{I}$

Now, we will study the minimum energy control case. The ratio of q / r is allowed to approach zero. The values of control gain vector, step response characteristics, and stability margin measures are shown in Table 12-4. Note that, as expected, the gain decreases with higher values of r.

Table 12-4 Data for Varying r				R = r I , Q = I							
r	Control Gain Vector			POS	Tr	Ts	Tp	GM	PM	wgc	wpc
1	0.52	4.38	0.99	18.6	1.2	5.2	2.0	-15.0	0.0	0.0	2.0
10	0.39	1.96	0.31	16.3	1.4	4.6	2.3	-11.8	71.2	5.2	1.6
10^2	0.35	0.98	0.09	12.8	1.8	5.6	2.9	-12.6	61.9	3.1	1.1
10^3	0.28	0.48	0.02	9.9	2.2	7.8	4.1	-14.0	60.5	2.1	0.7
10^6	0.08	0.06	0.0002	0.018	5.4	8.8	9.8	-7.2	60.7	0.2	0.3

The step response characteristics indicate that with larger values of r, the overshoot decreases, whereas all speed of response measures will increase resulting in a well damped and slow system. The margins indicate that the lower GM and PM are pushed to their limits of - 6 dB and 60 degrees with increasing r. The bandwidth decreases as the margins are reduced, but the roll-off rate remains at -20 dB per decade, as shown in the plots of Figure 12-3.

Table 12-5 Closed Loop Poles for varying r			R = r I , Q = I		
r	1	10	10^2	10^3	10^6
Closed loop poles	-0.73 + 2.14i	-0.72 + 1.95i	-0.66 + 1.50	-0.54 + 1.05i	-0.15 + 0.38i
	-0.73 - 2.14i	-0.72 - 1.95i	-0.66 - 1.50	-0.54 - 1.05i	-0.15 - 0.38i
	-12.00	-4.50	-2.27	-1.39	-0.66

The closed loop poles displayed in Table 12-5 verify that with larger values of r, the unstable plant poles at ($0.11 \pm j\,0.36$) are reflected to ($-0.15 \pm j\,0.38$), and the stable pole at (- 0.65) stays close to its original position (- 0.66). The following plots display the basic features of LQR design.

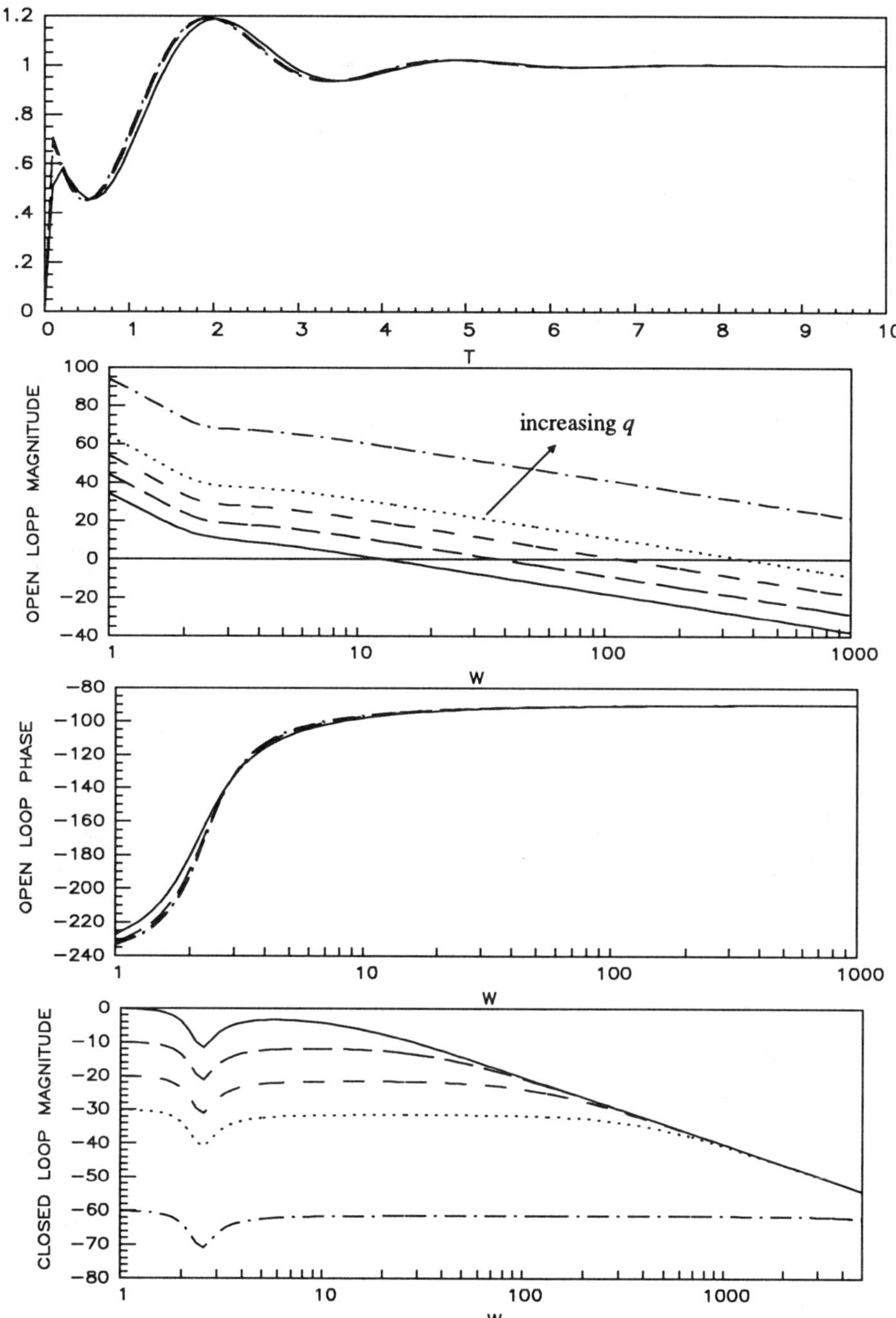

Figure 12-2 Step response, open loop and closed loop Bode plots when q varies.

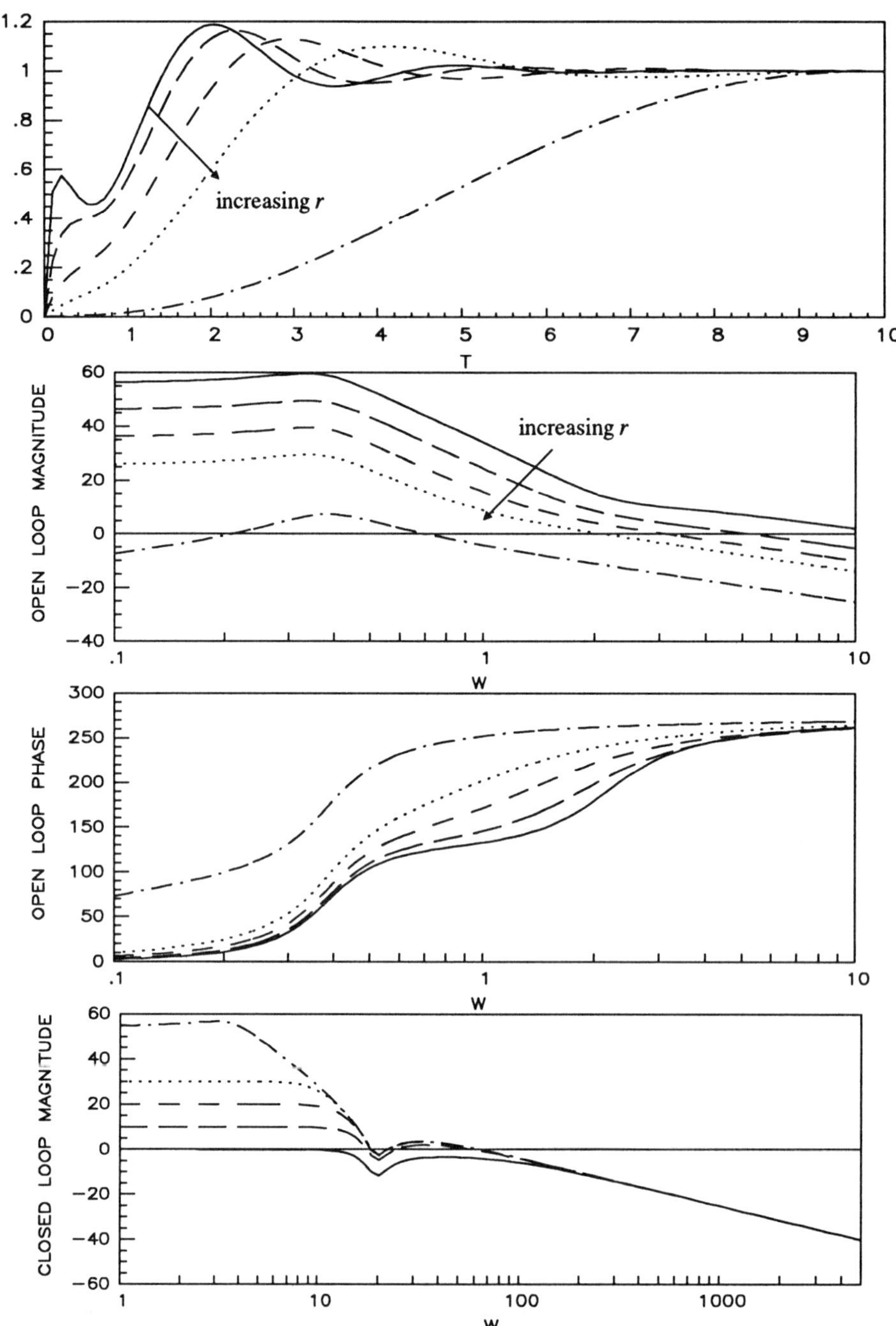

Figure 12-3 Step response, open loop and closed loop Bode plots when r varies.

12.2 Optimal Observer Design—Kalman-Bucy Filter

Estimation theory and the now famous *Kalman-Bucy filter* have a long history and wide variety of applications in control and communications. Our purpose in this section is to briefly describe their use as an integral part of an optimal compensation scheme. The basic premise is that the LQR solution requires that all states be available for feedback. In reality what we have are noise corrupted measurements. The optimal estimation problem is to obtain the best estimate of the states from a record of noisy measurements. It will turn out that under certain assumptions on the system and noise statistics, the optimal estimator (filter or observer) is a linear system that has the same structure as the standard Luenberger observer discussed in Chapter 8. We will first formulate the problem, present the solution, and then show how to implement it.

12.2.1 Problem Formulation and Solution

Consider the system represented in state space form

$$\dot{x} = A\,x + B\,u + \Gamma\,\omega$$

$$y = C\,x + \nu$$

where ω represents random noise disturbance input and ν represents random measurement (sensor) noise. We have to assume some statistical knowledge of the noise processes. It is assumed that both are white Gaussian zero mean stationary processes with known covariances given below.

$$E\{\,\omega(t)\,\} = 0, \qquad \mathrm{E}\{\,\nu(t)\,\} = 0$$

$$E\{\,\omega(t)\,\omega(t+\tau)'\,\} = Q_o\,\delta(t-\tau)$$

$$E\{\,\nu(t)\,\nu(t+\tau)'\,\} = R_o\,\delta(t-\tau)$$

$$E\{\,C\omega(t)\,\nu(t+\tau)'\,\} = 0 \quad \text{for all } t \text{ and } \tau$$

For those unfamiliar with stochastic processes, we refer the reader to Chapter 11 where a brief review with relevant commands are provided.

The problem is to obtain an estimate of $x(t)$ based on noise corrupted measurements such that the variance of the error is minimized. Let us denote the estimate by $\hat{x}(t)$ and the error by $\tilde{x}(t)$ then

$$J_o = E\,[\,\tilde{x}(t)'\,\tilde{x}(t)\,] = \text{error variance}$$

where $\tilde{x}(t) = x(t) - \hat{x}(t)$

The following assumptions are needed to obtain an asymptotically stable minimum variance filter. The pair (C, A) is detectable, the matrix R_o is positive definite, there exists H_o such that $H_o H_o{}' = Q_o$, and (A, H_o) is stabilizable. Under the above assumptions, the optimal estimator (*Kalman-Bucy filter*) is given by

$$\dot{\hat{x}} = A\hat{x} + Bu + L(y - C\hat{x})$$

$$L = \Sigma C' R^{-1}$$

where Σ is found from

$$A\Sigma + \Sigma A' + \Gamma Q_o \Gamma' - \Sigma C' R_o^{-1} C \Sigma = 0$$

It turns out that Σ, the solution of the filter algebraic Riccati equation, is the error covariance. It is known that the trace of the error covariance is the error variance, i.e.

$$tr\,\Sigma = tr\,E[\tilde{x}(t)\tilde{x}(t)'] = E[\tilde{x}(t)'\tilde{x}(t)]$$

Therefore, the trace of Σ indicates how well the filter is performing.

Cross-correlated Noise

One assumption that can be relaxed to obtain a more general filter is the cross correlation between the noise processes. If we assume that the disturbance and measurement noise are correlated, then we can define a general covariance matrix as

$$E\left\{\begin{bmatrix}\omega(t)\\ \nu(t)\end{bmatrix}[\omega(t)' \;\; \nu(t)']\right\} = \begin{bmatrix}Q_o & N_o\\ N_o' & R_o\end{bmatrix}\delta(t-\tau)$$

The solution in this case becomes

$$L = (\Sigma C' + N_o) R_o^{-1}$$

$$A\Sigma + \Sigma A' + \Gamma Q_o \Gamma' - (\Sigma C' + N_o) R_o^{-1} (\Sigma C' + N_o)' = 0$$

Control and Estimation Duality

Close observation of the LQR solution and the optimal estimator solution indicates that the two problems are duals of each other. The duality was also pointed out in Chapter 8, where we discussed pole placement using observers. Duality implies that if we make the following substitutions in the LQR solution, we get the optimal filter solution :

$$A \to A' \;,\; B \to C' \;,\; Q \to Q_o \;,\; R \to R_o \;,\; N \to N_o \;,\; K \to L' \;,\; P \to \Sigma$$

12.2.2 MATRIXx Implementation

The commands *estimator* and *riccati* can be used to solve the optimal estimation problem. The syntax for both commands are given by

```
< > [ev,l,sig]=estimator(A,C,Qw,Rv,Nwv)
< > [ev,l,sig]=riccati(S',SQo,NS)
```

where the inputs correspond to

$$Q_w \delta(t-\tau) = E\{\Gamma \omega(t)\, \omega(t+\tau)' \Gamma'\} = \Gamma Q_o \Gamma'$$
$$N_{wv} \delta(t-\tau) = E\{\Gamma \omega(t)\, v(t+\tau)'\}$$
$$R_v \delta(t-\tau) = R_o$$

The output `ev` stands for the optimal estimator eigenvalues. Inclusion of `sig` and `Nwv` are optional. Because of duality, the *riccati* command uses the transpose of the system matrix `S`, and `SQo` stands for the generalized covariance matrix. The next example illustrates an application of the above commands. Notice that most of the effort is spent on doing a valid simulation and the filter design step is simply an application of the *estimator* command. Following the example, in the next section we will use the optimal estimator to estimate the states and use the estimates in lieu of the actual states for the LQR problem.

Example 12.2 Kalman-Bucy Filter Simulation

We will demonstrate how to simulate a Kalman-Bucy filter using the following system: a double integrator stabilized by a lead compensator.

$$G(s) = \frac{1}{s^2} \quad \text{and} \quad H(s) = \frac{18\,(s+1)}{(s+10)}$$

After cascading the plant with the compensator and closing the loop with unity feedback, we get the system matrix `S`. Splitting `S`, we get

```
< > [a,gamma,c,d]=split(s,ns);
```

We will determine the number of inputs and outputs

```
< > dimgam=size(gamma);noinp=dimgam(2); dimc=size(c); noout=dimc(1);
```

We then reset the random number generator to normal for Gaussian white noise with zero mean and unity variance.

```
< > rand('normal')
```

To simulate the noise response of the system to ω and observe all states, we will modify c to be the identity matrix; c = I and D = 0.

```
< > sx=[a,gamma; eye(ns),0*ones(ns,noinp)];
```

We assume the input noise is a white process with zero mean and a variance of 1 and the measurement noise has variance 0.01. Recall that if

$z=\sigma x$, $x \sim N(0,1)$, then $z \sim N(0,\sigma^2)$; where the notation $N \sim (\mu,\sigma)$ stands for Normal process with mean μ and variance σ.

```
< > ww=1; w=ww*rand(100,noinp);          // variance of w = 1
< > nn=0.1; nu=nn*rand(100,noout);       // variance of nu is 0.01
< > IC=[1,2,3]; [t,x]=lsim(sx,ns,w,0.1,IC);
< > y=x*c'+nu;// adding noise to the output (note the order of multiplication).
```

We will find the filter gain now. Note that $Q_o = 1$, $Q_w = \Gamma Q_o \Gamma'$, and $R_v = 0.01$.

```
< > [ev,l,sig]=estim(a,c,gamma*ww*ww*gamma',nn*nn*eye(noout));
```

```
L =
1.0840
9.0499
0.7854
EV =
- 1.0065 + .0000j
- 10.2766 + 8.6090j
- 10.2766 - 8.6090j
SIG =
.0021  .0059  .0026
.0059  .1089  .0015
.0026  .0015  .0039
```

Now let us take a closer look at the results. The filter form is (note that the control term is zero)

$$\dot{\hat{x}} = A\hat{x} + L(y - C\hat{x})$$

It is known in general that if the measurements are too noisy (R_o large), and the input noise intensity is small (Q_o small), the filter relies on the system model for estimates and chooses L to be small, this results in a slow filter as measured by the location of its eigenvalues. If Q_o approaches infinity, the filter poles approach the stable images of plant zeros. Conversely, if the measurements are good and the input noise intensity is large, the filter relies on the measurements and chooses L to be large, resulting in a fast filter with high bandwidth. In our example, R_o is much smaller than Q_o, so we expect a large L and a fast filter. Indeed, the complex poles of the filter are about three times faster than the system. Note that only the first component of L is large and the rest are much smaller, however. To explain this, take a closer look at the system itself :

$$\begin{aligned}\dot{x}_1 &= x_2\\ \dot{x}_2 &= -18\,x_1 - 10.125\,x_3 + \omega\\ \dot{x}_3 &= 16\,x_1 - 10\,x_2\\ y &= 18\,x_1 - 10.125\,x_3 + \nu\end{aligned}$$

Input noise is fed directly into x_2, so x_2 is quite noisy, but x_1 is the integral of x_2 and x_3 is a filtered version of x_1 and x_2 . We can see that the noise gets filtered heavily by the time it reaches x_3. This is why the first and third components of L are much smaller than the second component. In a sense, the measurements are mainly used to estimate the noisier state and the system model is used to estimate the cleaner states. Inspection of the diagonal elements of Σ (SIG) also indicates poorer performance with respect to the second state (largest component). The plots in Fig. 12-4 also verify the above conclusions. Rewriting the filter equation as

$$\dot{\hat{x}} = (A - L\,C)\,\hat{x} + L\,y$$

gives us the system matrix for the filter. This allows us to find the state estimates using noisy measurements already generated above.

```
< > sf=[a-l*c,l; eye(ns),0*ones(ns,noout)];
< > IC2=[-3,-2,-1]*0.05;   // initial conditions of the filter
< >[t,xhat]=lsim(sf,ns,y,0.1,IC2); //Note the filter input is the measurement y
```

The states and their estimates are plotted as a strip chart in Figure 12-4.

```
< > plot(t,[x,xhat],'noxlabel noylabel nogrid strip2');
```

Note the use of "*strip2*" option, which allows columns of two matrices to be plotted and compared.

12.3 The Linear Quadratic Gaussian Problem

Optimal control of a linear system with respect to the quadratic objective function under incomplete measurements corrupted by white Gaussian noise is generally referred to as the linear quadratci Guassian (LQG) problem. The optimal control is a linear function of the state estimates obtained from the Kalman-Bucy filter. The LQR is a state feedback problem, whereas LQG is an output feedback problem, which is more realistic. The steady state formulation and solution of the problem is presented next.

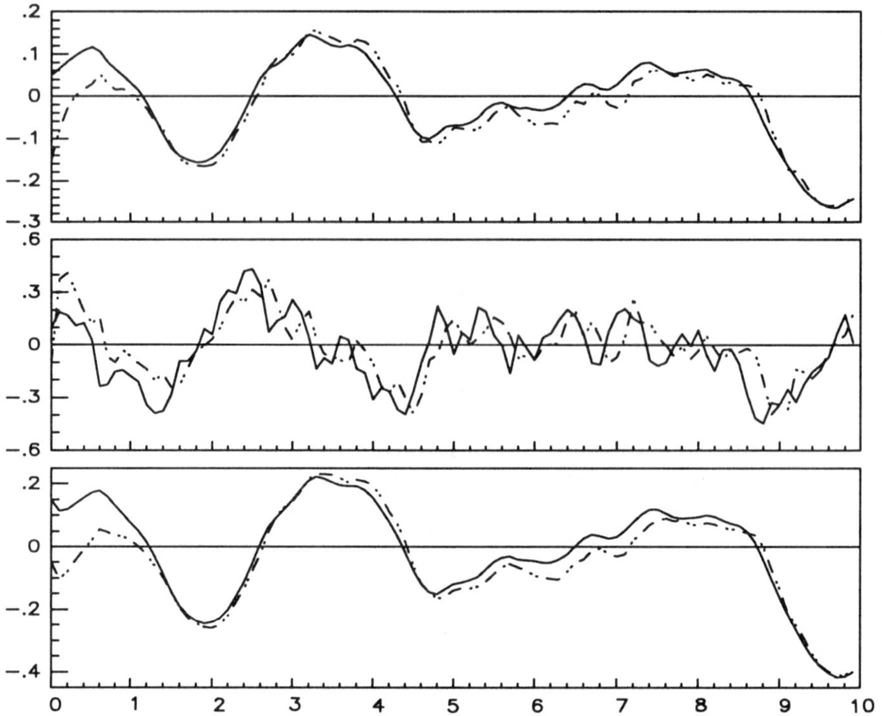

Figure 12-4 Plots of states versus their estimates. The solid lines correspond to the states.

12.3.1 LQG Problem Formulation and Solution

Consider the linear system driven by white Gaussian noise, with noise corrupted measurements, and the quadratic objective function.

$$\dot{x} = A\,x + B\,u + \Gamma\,\omega$$

$$y = C\,x + \nu$$

$$J = \lim_{T \to \infty} \frac{1}{2T}\, E\left\{ \int_{-T}^{T} (x'\,Q\,x + u'\,R\,u)\, dt \right\}$$

The problem is to find the optimal control that will minimize the *average cost*. Note that because the states and the control are both random, the cost function will be random, so we minimize it on the average. Using the same notation and under the same combined assumptions of the LQR and optimal estimation problem, the solution is given by the following:

$$u = -K\,\hat{x}(t)$$

$$K = R^{-1}B'P$$

$$A'P + PA - PBR^{-1}B'P + Q = 0$$

$$\dot{\hat{x}} = A\hat{x} + Bu + L(y - C\hat{x})$$

$$L = \Sigma C' R^{-1}$$

$$A\Sigma + \Sigma A' + \Gamma Q_o \Gamma' - \Sigma C' R_o^{-1} C\,\Sigma = 0$$

Note that the same Riccati equations for the LQR and Kalman-Bucy filter are used here. The solution satisfies the *separation principle* which essentially states that the problem can be solved in two separate stages. This can also be shown by the same procedure described for the observer based compensator design, which is the deterministic version of the problem described here; i.e., the eigenvalues of the closed loop system are the union of the eigenvalues of the controller and the estimator.

$$\text{Closed loop eigenvalues} = \lambda(A - BK) \cup \lambda(A - LC)$$

The generalization of the LQG to the cross correlated noise case with cross terms in the cost function is also straightforward. To study the effects of the four weights $\{Q, R, Qo, Ro\}$, we will consider the following example, that is the LQG version of Example 12.1.

Example 12.3 LQG Design

We will investigate the effects of the four weights $\{Q, R, Qo, Ro\}$ on the time and frequency responses of the helicopter example. The simulations will be done by fixing three of the weights at unity and varying the fourth one over the range $\{1, 10, 10^2, 10^3, 10^6\}$. We will soon see that, in general, LQG does not have the same properties as LQR, and, in fact, most of the LQR properties are lost when a Kalman-Bucy filter is introduced.

It has been well known that uncertainties in the initial state, system input noise and measurement noise increase the overall cost function value and, in fact, these costs can be computed and separated. What was later demonstrated by counterexamples, however, was the fact that the LQR robustness and stability margins are also lost. This renders LQG designs very susceptible to model uncertainties, which are always present; hence, a design based on LQG has to be treated with care and tested for robustness. Doyle and Stein [DS79] also developed a method called *loop transfer recovery* (*LTR*), which allows one to recover LQR properties, asymptotically.

Stability margins measured by GM and PM are computed for each case in this design. In addition, we also compute the following: the minimum distance between the loop gain and the (-1) point, i.e., the minimum of the return difference is also computed as a measure of robustness (denoted by robust stability measure [RSM]); the peak in the closed loop transfer function (resonant peak [M_r]), which can also be used as a measure of relative stability; the control and (the transpose of) filter gain vectors; and closed loop poles.

Most data are truncated by one or two digits to reduce clutter. The plots of open loop magnitude and phase, closed loop magnitude, return difference, and step response are also provided. The programs that generated the data and plots are presented convenience in the Appendix.

Case I : Varying $Q = q$ I

Table 12-6 Data for Varying Q $Q = q$ I						+
q	Gain Margin	Phase Margin	RSM	M_r	Control Gain	Filter Gain
1	-13.5 6.4 -12.8	29.5 -64.0 59.0	0.46	26.1	0.5 4.4 1.0	0.6 0.8 3.9
10	-14.6 6.5 -12.8	31.8 -62.4 67.0	0.49	24.7	1.1 11.9 3.2	0.6 0.8 3.9
10^2	-14.9 6.6 -13.2	32.6 -62.1 72.9	0.50	24.3	3.1 35.7 10.0	0.6 0.8 3.9
10^3	-15.0 6.7 -13.3	32.9 -62.1 75.3	0.50	24.1	9.5 111.2 31.6	0.6 0.8 3.9
10^6	-15.1 6.7 -13.3	33.0 -62.1 76.4	0.51	24.1	296.4 3489.2 998.4	0.6 0.8 3.9

From Table 12-6, we see that increasing q does not have an appreciable effect on any of the stability margins. Control gain increases. Filter gain is, of course, independent of Q. Note that the upper GM is reduced to about 6 (LQR has infinite GM), and the lower GM is between -12 to -15, which is better than LQR. The fact that RSM is smaller than 1 indicates the Nyquist plot enters the unit circle centered at (-1), i.e., the RDI does not apply in the LQG case. This indicates that LQR has better input disturbance rejection properties. The PM varies from 29 to 33 degrees, which is smaller than LQR. The plots are shown in Figure 12-5.

Table 12-7 Closed Loop Poles for Varying Q $Q = q$ I					
q	1	10	10^2	10^3	10^6
Closed loop poles	-2	-2	-2	-2	-2
	-1 + 2i	-1 + 2i	-1 + 2i	-1 + 2i	-1 + 2i
	-1 - 2i	-1 - 2i	-1 - 2i	-1 - 2i	-1 - 2i
	-1 + 2i	-1 + 2i	-1 + 2i	-1 + 2i	-1 + 2i
	-1 - 2i	-1 - 2i	-1 - 2i	-1 - 2i	-1 - 2i
	-12	-37	-117	-368	-11650

Table 12-7 shows that the closed loop poles appear fixed except for one that gets pushed far out into the LHP. The plots indicate a bandwidth of about 2.5 rad/sec and a roll-off rate of 20 dB/dec, which is the same as LQR for this particular system.

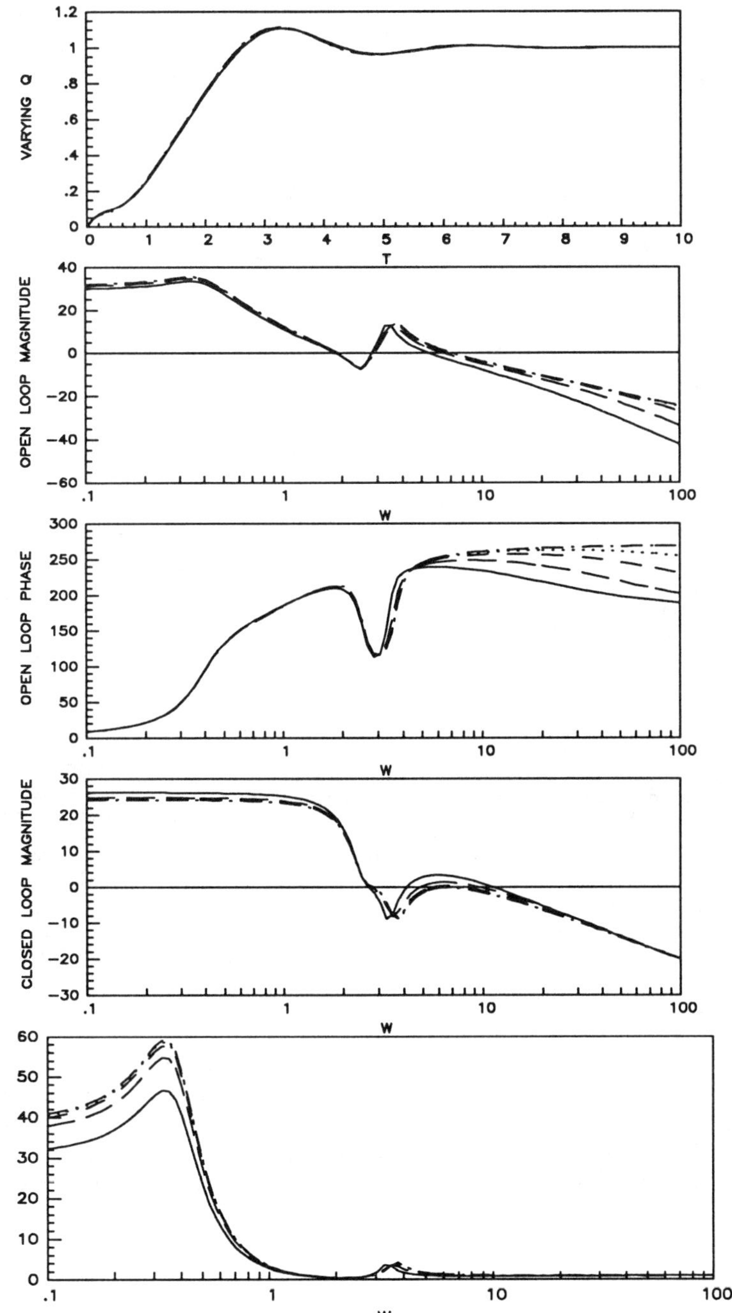

Figure 12-5 Plots of step response, open loop Bode, closed loop Bode magnitude, and return difference for varying q

Case II : Varying $R = rI$

Table 12-8 Data for Varying R $R = rI$,						
r	Gain Margin	Phase Margin	RSM	M_r	Control Gain	Filter Gain
1	-13.5 6.4 -12.8	29.5 -64.0 59.0	0.46	26.1	0.5 4.3 0.9	0.6 0.8 3.9
10	-12.2 5.3	25.0 -84.3 63.6	0.40	29.7	0.3 1.9 0.3	0.6 0.8 3.9
10^2	-10.8 5.6	22.4	0.36	35.3	0.3 0.9 0.09	0.6 0.8 3.9
10^3	-10.4 7.0	23.9	0.38	41.7	0.2 0.4 0.02	0.6 0.8 3.9
10^6	-5.1 13.7	-46.7 38.2	0.65	60.8	0.08 0.06 0.0003	0.6 0.8 3.9

From Table 12-8, we make the following observations. Increasing r reduces the lower GM from -13.5 to -5.1 dB, but increases the upper gain margin from 6 to 13 dB. The PM initially goes down from 29 to 22 but later goes up to 38 degrees. This variation is also indicated by RSM. The control gain decreases (minimum energy control).

Table 12-9 Closed Loop Poles for Varying R $R = rI$					+
r	1	10	10^2	10^3	10^6
Closed loop poles	-1.1 + 1.8i	-1.1 + 1.8i	-1.1 + 1.8i	-1.1 + 1.8i	-1.1 + 1.8i
	-1.1 - 1.8i	-1.1 -1.8i	-1.1 - 1.8i	-1.1 - 1.8i	-1.1 - 1.8i
	-2.1	-2.1	-2.1	-2.1	-2.1
	-0.7 + 2.1i	-0.7 + 1.9i	-0.6 + 1.5i	-0.5 + 1.0i	-0.1 + 0.3i
	-0.7 - 2.1i	-0.7 - 1.9i	-0.6 - 1.5i	-0.5 - 1.0i	-0.1 - 0.3i
	-12	-4.5	-2.2	-1.3	-0.6

Because the closed loop poles (presented in Table 12-9) are the union of the filter and controller poles, we see that because the filter gain is fixed, the first three poles (filter eigenvalues) remain unchanged. The controller poles move toward the stable images of the plant poles. The result is that increasing r will decrease the speed of response considerably. Likewise the bandwidth is also reduced to below 1 rad/sec. The plots for this case, presented in Figure 12-6, show that the high frequency roll-off rate is still about 20 dB/dec.

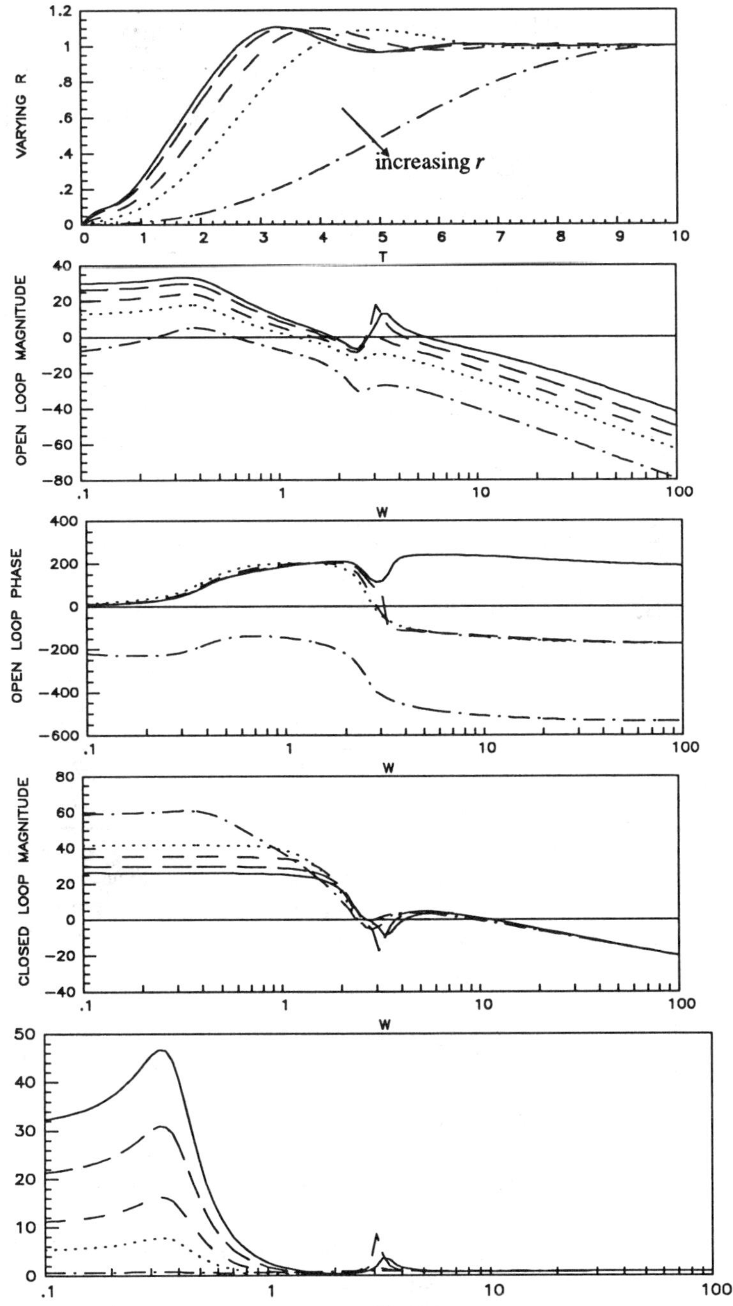

Figure 12-6 Plots of step response, open loop Bode, closed loop Bode magnitude, and return difference for varying r.

Case III : Varying $Q_o = q_o I$

Table 12-10 Data for Varying Q_o $Q_o = q_o I$						+
q_o	Gain Margin	Phase Margin	RSM	M_r	Control Gain	Filter Gain
1	-13.5 6.4 -12.8	29.5 -64.0 59.0	0.4	26.1	0.5 4.3 0.9	0.6 0.8 3.9
10	-14.8 5.9 -7.2	33.5 -46.7 48.0	0.5	22.5	0.5 4.3 0.9	1.2 1.3 4.8
10^2	-16.1 6.2 -4.8	39.8 -36.7 39.4	0.5	18.9	0.5 4.3 0.9	2.2 2.1 5.9
10^3	-20.7 6.8 -3.5	47.1 -30.2 32.5	0.5	15.2	0.5 4.3 0.9	4.2 3.4 7.3
10^6	-40.2 8.5 -1.8	67.5 -21.5 18.2	0.2	14.4	0.5 4.3 0.9	26.0 13.8 14.0

In this case, the lower GM varies from approximately -12 to -1 dB. The upper GM is between 6 and 8 dB. The PM again goes up and then comes down to 18 degrees. This is also verified from the RSM. The rather small margins for large values of q_o is also clear from the step response, which shows wild fluctuations.

Table 12-11 Closed Loop Poles for Varying Q_o			$Q_o = q_o I$		+
q_o	1	10	10^2	10^3	10^6
Closed loop poles	-0.7 + 2.1i	-0.7 + 2.1i	-0.7 + 2.1i	-0.7 + 2.1i	-0.7 + 2.1i
	-0.7 - 2.1i	-0.7 - 2.1i	-0.7 - 2.1i	-0.7 - 2.1i	-0.7 - 2.1i
	-12.0	-12.0	-12.0	-12.0	-12.0
	-1.1 + 1.8i	-1.3 + 2.2i	-1.6 + 2.7i	-2.0 + 3.2i	-4.3 + 5.9i
	-1.1 - 1.8i	-1.3 - 2.2i	-1.6 - 2.7i	-2.0 - 3.2i	-4.3 - 5.9i
	-2.1	-2.5	-3.0	-3.6	-5.6

Table 12-11 shows that the first three closed loop poles are unchanged because the control gain is independent of q_o (Separation property). Filter modal properties are duals of LQR modal properties and show the same pattern. The appropriate transfer function is the transmission between the input noise and the output.

$$G_{KF}(s) = C\,\Phi(s)\,\Gamma = C\,(sI - A)^{-1}\,\Gamma = \frac{-1.4\,(s-7)}{(s - 0.118 \pm j\,0.36)\,(s + 0.65)}$$

For large values of input noise intensity, q_o, m filter poles (at -5.6) approach the stable image of finite zeros of G_{KF} (at 7), and the rest go to zeros at infinity in a Butterworth pattern. For large values of measurement noise intensity, r_o, filter poles approach the stable images of plant poles.

As we increase q_o relative to r_o, the filter places more confidence in the measurements by increasing the gain. This, in effect, produces a faster filter with higher bandwidth. When r_o is increased, the filter deemphasizes the measurements (lower filter gain) and uses the system model for estimation. The filter then trades off speed of response with more filtering action. The plots for this case are shown in Figure 12-7.

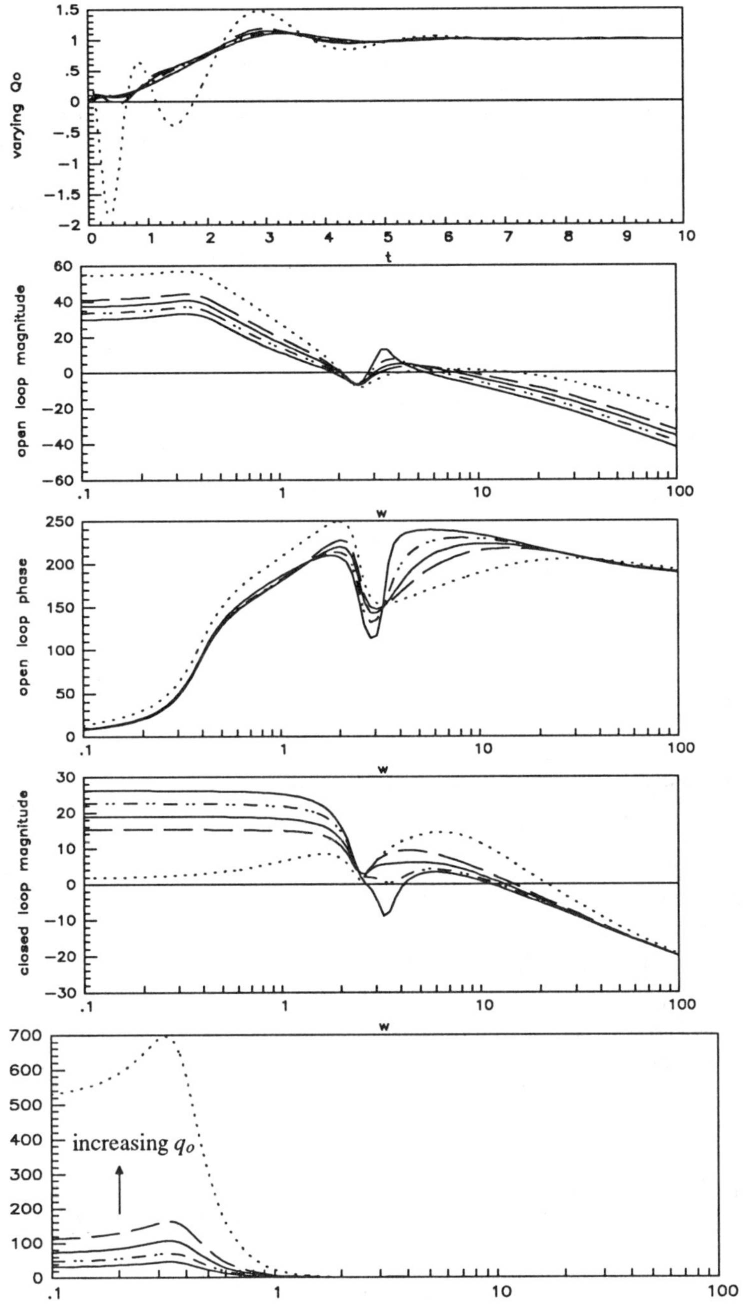

Figure 12-7 Plots of step response, open loop Bode, closed loop Bode magnitude, and return difference for varying q_o.

Case IV: Varying $R_o = r_o I$

Table 12-12 Data for Varying R_o $R_o = r_o$ I						
r_o	Gain Margin	Phase Margin	RSM	M_r	Control Gain	Filter Gain
1	-13.5 6.4 -12.8	29.5 -64.0 59.0	0.4	26.1	0.5 4.3 0.9	0.6 0.8 3.9
10	-12.2 7.0	28.3 -137.1 98.0	0.4	33.5	0.5 4.3 0.9	0.1 0.3 2.5
10^2	-10.8 8.2	33.5	0.5	41.2	0.5 4.3 0.9	0.03 0.1 1.6
10^3	-9.3 11.8	40.7	0.6	49.1	0.5 4.3 0.9	0.001 0.05 1.0
10^6	-5.1 15.8	6-48.4 47.7	0.7	61.1	0.5 4.3 0.9	-0.004 0.01 0.4

As mentioned earlier, the filter poles approach the stable images of plant poles. The PM, upper GM and RSM improve as r_o is increased. Also, the bandwidth and speed of response are reduced. The data are tabulated in Tables 12-12 and 12-13. The plots are given in Figure 12-8.

Table 12-13 Closed loop poles for varying R_o $R_o = r_o$ I					
r_o	1	10	10^2	10^3	10^6
Closed loop poles	-0.7 + 2.1i	-0.7 + 2.1i	-0.7 + 2.1i	-0.7 + 2.1i	-0.7 + 2.1i
	-0.7 - 2.1i	-0.7 - 2.1i	-0.7 - 2.1i	-0.7 - 2.1i	-0.7 - 2.1i
	-12.0	-12.0	-12.0	-12.0	-12.0
	-1.1 + 1.8i	-0.7 + 1.2i	-0.5 + 0.8i	-0.3 + 0.5i	-0.1 + 0.3i
	-1.1 - 1.8i	-0.7 - 1.2i	-0.5 - 0.8i	-0.3 - 0.5i	-0.1 - 0.3i
	-2.1	-1.4	-1.0	-0.7	-0.6

We note that overall, LQG has consistently lower stability margins than LQR. Its sensitivity properties are also worse than LQR. In all cases, in this nonminimum phase example, the closed loop system is conditionally stable. By repeated simulations, one can determine an appropriate choice of weights. it can be shown that by an appropriate choice of weights, it is possible to recover the desirable properties of LQR asymptotically. This is called *loop transfer recovery* (*LTR*). Another extension of LQG design methodology is the choice of frequency dependent weights (*frequency shaped LQG*). From this view point, one can take a purely frequency domain approach to design and control the frequency domain properties of the system in the multivariable case directly.

Other frequency domain techniques for designing robust controllers for multivariable systems are H_∞ and μ–synthesis. It has recently been shown that these methods can be derived from a time domain LQG type approach. Hence, state space algorithms can be used to solve frequency domain MIMO problems. Refer to [M89] and [F87] for an further study. Commands for performing LTR, frequency shaped LQG, H_∞ and μ–synthesis are available in the Robust Control Module of MATRIXx.

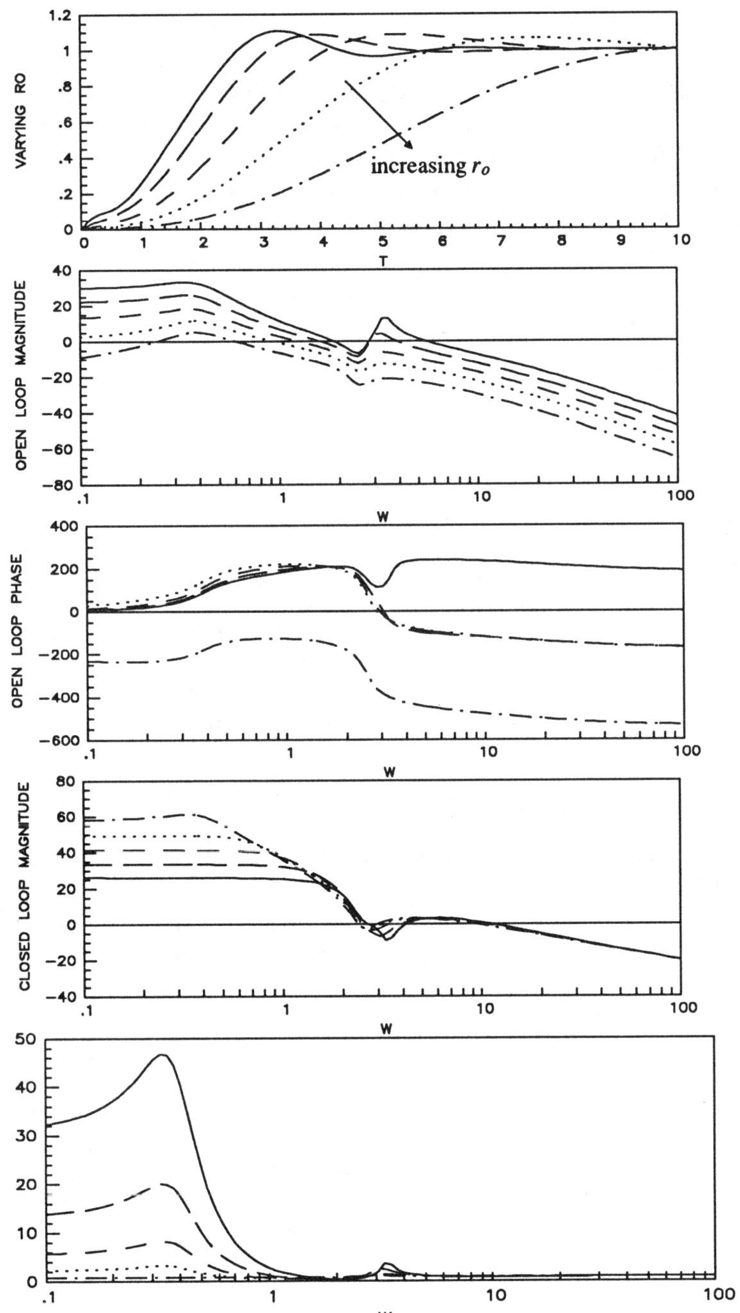

Figure 12-8 Plots of step response, open loop Bode, closed loop Bode magnitude, and return difference for varying r_o.

12.5 Appendix: Design Programs

Programs to generate the data appearing in the tables of this chapter are included in this Appendix. Although it is possible to write one program that will generate all of the data for LQR (LQG) for various cases considered, the data stack and the number of variables used may exceed the memory limitations in earlier versions of MATRIXx. Therefore, a separate program was written in each case. The programs for one case (varying q) are listed below. Programs for other cases will be almost identical.

1. Program to Generate LQR Example Data for Varying q (Example 12.1)

```
//Inputs are: S, NS, A, B, C
bsize=size(b);noinp=bsize(2);csize=size(c);noout=csize(1);
r=1;
for i=1:5;...
qq=[1 10 1e2 1e3 1e6];q=qq(i);...
[eval,gain]=regulat(a,b,q*eye(ns),r);...
sgh=[a b;gain 0*ones(noinp,noinp)];...
st=[a-b*gain b;c 0*ones(noout,noinp)];...
[t,out]=step(st,ns,10);out=out/out(100);...
[woq,mag,phase]=bode(sgh,ns,1,1000,100,'noplot');...
[wcq,cmag]=bode(st,ns,1,5000,100,'noplot');...
kq(i,:)=gain; clpq(:,i)=eval; yq(:,i)=out;...
oq(:,i)=mag; poq(:,i)=phase; cq(:,i)=cmag;...
end;
return
```

2. Program to Compute Margins and Step Response Data for Example 12.1

This program uses data generated by the first program. It also uses the STEPCHAR UDF in Chapter 3 to compute the step response data such as percent overshoot, rise time, etc.

```
for i=1:5;...
sgh=[a b;kq(i,:) 0*ones(noinp,noinp)];...
st=[a-b*kq(i,:) b;c 0*ones(noout,noinp)];...
[gmm,pmm,wpcm,wgcm]=margin(woq,moq(:,i),poq(:,i));...
e=exist('gmm');if e=0, gmm=e, else gmm=gmm';end;...
ee=exist('pmm');if ee=0, pmm=ee, else pmm=pmm';end;...
eee=exist('wgcm'),if eee=0, wgcm=eee, else wgcm=wgcm';end;...
eeee=exist('wpcm'), if eeee=0, wpcm=eeee , else wpcm=wpcm';end;...
gmq(i,:)=gmm; pmq(i,:)=pmm; wgcq(i,:)=wgcm; wpcq(i,:)=wpcm;...
end;
[posq,trq,tsq,tpq]=stepchar(t,yq)
return
```

3. Program to Generate LQG Example Data for Varying *q* (Example 12.3)

```
wi=.1;wf=100; gamma=[1;0;0];
q=[1 10 1e2 1e3 1e6];r=1;qo=1;ro=1;
dimgam=size(gamma);noinp=dimgam(2);dimc=size(c);noout=dimc(1);
for i=1:5;...
[evc,kqq]=regulator(a,b,q(i)*eye(ns),r);...
[evf,lqq]=estim(a,c,gamma*qo*gamma',ro*eye(noout));...
shq=[a-b*kqq-lqq*c lqq;kqq 0*ones(noinp,noout)];...
[sghq,nsgh]=series(s,ns,shq,ns);...
[w,mqq,pqq]=bode(sghq,nsgh,wi,wf,100,'noplot');...
[stq,nsgh]=feedback(s,ns,shq,ns);...
[w,mcqq]=bode(stq,nsgh,wi,wf,100,'noplot');...
fq=freq(sghq,nsgh,w);...
retqq=abs(ones(w)+fq);...
mq(:,i)=mqq; pq(:,i)=pqq; mcq(:,i)=mcqq; retq(:,i)=retqq;...
[gmm,pmm,wpcm,wgcm]=margin(w,mqq,pqq);...
e=exist('gmm');if e=0, gmm=e, else gmm=gmm';end;...
ee=exist('pmm');if ee=0, pmm=ee, else pmm=pmm';end;...
eee=exist('wgcm'),if eee=0, wgcm=eee, else wgcm=wgcm';end;...
eeee=exist('wpcm'), if eeee=0, wpcm=eeee , else wpcm=wpcm';end;...
gmq(i,:)=gmm; pmq(i,:)=pmm; wgcq(i,:)=wgcm; wpcq(i,:)=wpcm;...
rsmqq=min(retqq); rsmq(1,i)=rsmqq;
mrqq=max(mcqq); mrq(:,i)=mrqq;clear mrqq;...
[t,out]=step(stq,nsgh,10);out=out/out(100);...
yq(:,i)=out; kq(i,:)=kqq; lq(:,i)=lqq; clpq(:,i)=eig(stq,nsgh);...
i=i+1;...
end;
return
```

4. Program for LQG Design

This program can be used to design an LQG compenstaor. It computes open loop and closed loop Bode plots, step response, margins, minimum of the return difference, resonant peak, and closed loop poles.

```
// Program inputs:  wi,wf,tf,S,NS,Gamma,Q,R,Qo,and Ro
[a,b,c,d]=split(s,ns);
dimgam=size(gamma);noinp=dimgam(2);dimc=size(c);noout=dimc(1);
[evc,k]=regulator(a,b,q,r);
[evf,l]=estim(a,c,gamma*qo*gamma',ro);
sh=[a-b*k-l*c l;k 0*ones(noinp,noout)];
[sgh,nsgh]=series(s,ns,sh,ns);
[w,m,p]=bode(sgh,nsgh,wi,wf,100,'noplot');
[st,nsgh]=feedback(s,ns,sh,ns);
[w,mc]=bode(st,nsgh,wi,wf,100,'noplot');
f=freq(sgh,nsgh,w);
ret=abs(ones(w)+f);
```

```
[gm,pm,wpc,wgc]=margin(w,m,p);
rsm=min(ret);
mr=max(mc);
[t,y]=step(st,nsgh,tf);y=y/(100);
clp=eig(st,nsgh)
return
```

12.6 Problems

12.1 Repeat Problem 7.5 using LQG. Study the effects of various weights used to optimize the robust stabilty measures (RSM) that were defined in Example 12.3.

12.2 Repeat Problem 7.6 using LQG. Study the effects of various weights used to optimize the robust stabilty measures (RSM) that were defined in Example 12.3.

12.3 Solve the wedge control problem discussed in Problem 8.6 using the LQG approach. Refer to Section 1.6 for a review of feedback properties, and to Section 5.6 for computation of sensitivity and complementary sensitivity matrices. Recall that these quantities are related to disturbance rejection and noise suppression properties of systems. Study the effects of weights on these measures. Do this by obtaining the frequency response of the sensitivity and complementary sensitivity transfer functions using the *freq* command. Use the peak value in these frequency responses as a measure of the size of these responses.

12.4 Repeat the preceding problem using the double inverted pendulum model introduced in Problem 9.21.

Notes and References

For more information about optimal control and the LQ problem, refer to the following texts: [L86a], [K70], [BH75], [KS72], [M89], [SW77], [AM90], AF66], [E84], [O78], and [S86]. Textbooks in the area of estimation and Kalman-Bucy filtering are: [L86b], [AM79], [G86], [BH75] and [M87].

Bibliography

[AF66] M. Athans and P. L. Falb. *Optimal Control.* McGraw-Hill, 1966.

[AH84] K. J. Astrom and T. Hagglund. A Frequency Domain Method for Automatic Tuning of Simple Feeddback Loops. Proc. of the 23rd *Conference on Decision and Control,* Las Vegas, Nevada, 1984.

[AM79] B. D. O. Anderson and J. B. Moore. *Optimal Filtering.* Prentice-Hall, 1979.

[AM90] B. D. O. Anderson and J. B. More. *Linear Optimal Control.* Prentice-Hall, 1990.

[AW90] K. J. Astrom and B. Wittenmark. *Computer Controlled Systems:Theory and Design.* Prentice-Hall, 2nd edition, 1990.

[B91] W. L. Brogan. *Modern Control Theory.* Prentice-Hall, 3rd edition, 1991.

[BH75] A. E. Bryson, Jr. and Y. C. Ho. *Applied Optimal Control : Optimization, Estimation and Control.* Hemisphere Publishing Corporation, 1975.

[BPDGS91] G. J. Balas, A. Packard, J. C. Doyle, K. Glover and R. Smith. Development of Advanced Control Design Software for Researchers and Engineers. Proc. *American Control Conference,* Boston, MA, June 26-28, 1991.

[C84] C. T. Chen. *Linear System Theory and Design.* Holt, Rinehart and Winston, 1984.

[C87a] C. T. Chen. *Control System Design: Coventional, Algebraic and Optimal Methods.* Pond Woods Press, 1987.

[C87b] C. T. Chen. Introduction to Linear Algebraic Method for Control System Design. *IEEE Contr. Syst. Mag.,* vol. 7, no. 5, pp. 36-42, 1987.

[CS90a] C. T. Chen and B. Seo. Application of Linear Algebraic Method for Control System Design. *IEEE Contr. Syst. Mag.,* vol. 10, no. 1, 1990.

[CS90b] C. T. Chen and B. Seo. The Inward Approach in the Design of Control Systems. *IEEE Trans. on Educ.,* vol. 33, no. 3, pp. 270-278, 1990.

[CS91] R. Y. Chang and M. G. Safonov. A Hierarchical Data Structure and New Capabilities of the Robust-Control Toolbox. Proc. *American Control Conference,* Boston, MA, June 26-28, 1991.

[De89] R. A. DeCarlo. *Linear Systems: A State Variable Approach with Numerical Implementation.* Prentice-Hall, 1989.

[Do89] R. C. Dorf. *Modern Control Systems.* Addison-Wesley, 5th edition, 1989.

[DH88] J. J. D'Azzo, C. H. Houpis. *Linear Control Systems: Analysis & Design.* McGraw-Hill, 3rd edition, 1988.

[DS79] J. C. Doyle and G. Stein. Robustness with Observers. *IEEE Trans. Automat. Contr.,* vol. 24, pp. 607-611, 1979.

[E84] T. F. Elbert. *Estimation and Control of Systems.* Van Nostrand, 1984.

[F86] B. Friedland. *Control Systems Design: An Introduction to State -Space Methods.* McGraw-Hill, 1986.

[F87] B. A. Francis. *A Course in H∞ Control Theory.* Springer-Verlag, 1987.

[FPE91] G. F. Franklin, J. D. Powell, A. Emami-Naeini. *Feedback Control of Dynamic Systems.* Addison-Wesley, 2nd edition, 1991.

[FPW90] G. F. Franklin, J. D. Powell, M.L. Workman. *Digital Control of Dynamic Systems.* Addison-Wesley, 2nd edition, 1990.

[F91] A. Feliachi. MS Curriculum National Survey. Proc. *American Control Conference*, Boston, MA, June 26-28, 1991.

[G86] A. Gelb. *Applied Optimal Estimation.* MIT Press, 1974.

[HW91] P. Hsu and J. Wendlandt. The Wedge-A Controller Design Experiment. Preprints, *IFAC Advances in Control Education*, pp. 169-174, 1991.

[H88] J. Hale. *Introduction to Control System Analysis and Design.* Prentice-Hall, 2nd edition, 1988.

[HL85] C. H. Houpis and G. B. Lamont. *Digital Control System-Theory, Hardware, Software.* McGraw-Hill, 1987.

[HSS88] G. H. Hostetter, C. J. Savant, Jr. and R. T. Stefani, *Design of Feedback Control Systems.* Holt, Rinehart and Winston, 2nd edition, 1989.

[J81] R. Jaquot. *Modern Digital Control Systems.* Marcel Dekker, 1981.

[JH85] M. Jamshidi and C. J. Herget eds. *Computer-aided Control Systems Engineering.* Elsevier Science Publishers, 1985.

[K64] R. E. Kalman. When is a Linear Control System Optimal? *Journal of Basic Engineering. Trnas. ASME D*, 86, pp. 51-60, 1964.

[K70] D. E. Kirk. *Optimal Control Theory: An Introduction.* Prentice-Hall, 1970.

[K80] T. Kailath. *Linear Systems.* Prentice-Hall, 1980. Reprinted by permission.

[Ku80] B. C. Kuo. *Digital Control Systems.* Holt, Rinehart and Winston. 1980.

[K81] P. Katz. *Digital Control Using Microprocessors,* Prentice-Hall, 1981.

[K91] B. C. Kuo. *Automatic Control Systems.* Prentice-Hall, 6th edition, 1991.

[KS72] H. Kwakernaak and R. Sivan. *Linear Optimal Control Systems.* Wiley Interscience, 1972.

[L64] D. G. Luenberger. Observing the State of a Linear System. *IEEE Trans. Mil. Electron.*, MIL-8, pp. 74-80, 1964.

[L79] D. G. Luenberger. *Introduction to Dynamic Systems: Theory, Models & Applications.* Wiley, 1979.

[L86a] F. L. Lewis. *Optimal Control.* Wiley, 1986.

[L86b] F. L. Lewis. *Optimal Estimation: With an Introduction to Stochastic Control Theory.* Wiley, 1986.

[M84] R. J. Mayhan. *Discrete-Time & Continuous-Time Linear Systems.* Addison-Wesley, 1985.

[M87] J. Mendel. *Lessons in Digital Estimation Theory.* Prentice-Hall, 1987.

[M89] J. M. Maciejowski. *Multivariable Feedback Design.* Addison-Wesley, 1989.

[MJ73] J. L. Melsa and S. K. Jones. *Computer Programs for Computational Assistance in the Study of Linear Control Theory.* McGraw-Hill, 2nd edition, 1973.

[O78] D. H. Owens. *Multivariable and Feedback Systems.* Peter Peregrinus, 1978.

[O87] K. Ogata. *Discrete-Time Control Systems,* Prentice-Hall, 1987.

[O90] K. Ogata. *Modern Control Engineering.* Prentice-Hall, 2nd edition, 1990.

[Pa91] A. Papoulis. *Probability, Random Variables, and Stochastic Processes.* McGraw-Hill, 3rd edition. 1991.

[P91] G. K. H. Pang. Issues in the Development of the Interactive CACSD package SFPACK. Proc. *American Control Conference,* Boston, MA, June 26-28, 1991.

[PH88] C. L. Phillips and R. D. Harbor. *Feedback Control Systems.* Prentice-Hall, 1988.

[PN90] C. L. Phillips and H. T. Nagle. *Digital Control System Analysis and Design.* Prentice-Hall, 2nd edition, 1990.

[S86] R. F. Stengle. *Stochastic Optimal Control: Theory and Application.* Wiley Interscience, 1986.

[SM67] D. G. Schultz and J. L. Melsa. *State Functions and Linear Control Systems.* McGraw-Hill, 1967.

[SW77] A. P. Sage and C. C. White. *Optimal Systems Control.* Prentice-Hall, 1977.

[TS86] J. M. T. Thompson and H. B. Stewart. *Nonlinear Dynamics and Chaos.* Wiley, 1986.

[ZN42] J. G. Ziegler and N. B. Nichols. Optimum Settings for Automatic Controllers. *Trans. ASME,* pp. 759-768, 1942.

[ZZH87] F. Zu-ren, Y. Zheng-qi and C. Hui-tang. Microprocessor-Based Controller for Double Inverted Pendulum. *IFAC 10th Trennial World Congress,* Munich, FRG, pp. 237-240, 1987.

IEEE Control Systems Magazine, Vol. 10, No. 6, p. 40, Oct.1990.

MATRIXx Command Syntax

Purpose: Element-by-element matrix multiplication.

Syntax: `C=A.*B`

Purpose: Element-by-element right division.

Syntax: `C=A./B`

Purpose: Element-by element left division.

Syntax: `C=A.\B`

Purpose: Kronecker or tensor Product.

Syntax: `C=A.*.B`

Purpose: Kronecker or tensor right division.

Syntax: `C=A./.B`

Purpose: Kronecker or tensor left division.

Syntax: `C=A.\.B`

Purpose: Raise a scalar, vector, or matrix to a power.

Syntax: `C=B**POWER`

Purpose: Temporarily suspend MATRIXx to perform operating system commands.

Syntax: `\\ or $$ or \\operating system command`

Purpose: Absolute value.

Syntax: `C=ABS(A)`

Purpose: Arc-cosine of argument.

Syntax: `C=ACOS(A)`

Purpose: Hyperbolic arc-cosine of argument.

Syntax: `C=ACOSH(A)`

Purpose: Connect two dynamic systems in a feedback loop with augmented inputs and outputs for the feedback path.

```
Syntax: [S,NS]=AFEEDBACK(S1,NS1,S2,NS2)   OR
[S,NS]=AFEEDBACK(S1,NS1,S2)   :constant-gain feedback.   OR
[S2,S2]=FEEDBACK(S1,NS1)      :unity feedback
```

Purpose: Performs approximate maximum likelihood identification on single-input/single-output data.

Syntax: [NUM,DEN,NUMC,FITERR]=AML(Y,U,NUM0,DEN0,NUMC0,P0)

Purpose: Append two dynamic systems in parallel.

Syntax: [S,NS]=APPEND(S1,NS1,S2,NS2)

Purpose: Arc-sine of argument.

Syntax: C=ASIN(A)

Purpose: Hyperbolic arc-sine of argument.

Syntax: C=ASINH(A)

Purpose: Arctangent of argument.

Syntax: C=ATAN(A)

Purpose: 2 argument arctangent.

Syntax: C=ATAN2(Y,X)

Purpose: Hyperbolic arc-tangent of argument.

Syntax: C=ATANH(A)

Purpose: Convert a continuous dynamic system into an internally balanced dynamic form.

Syntax: [SB,SIGMASQ,T]=BALANCE(S,NS)

Purpose: Gain and phase plots of continuous time systems.

Syntax: [OMEGA,DB,PHASE]=BODE(S,NS,OMEGAMIN,OMEGAMAX,NPTS,'OPT') OR
[OMEGA,DB,PHASE]=BODE(NUM,DEN,OMEGAMIN,OMEGAMAX,NPTS) OR
[OMEGA,DB,PHASE]=BODE(S,NS,OMEGA)

Purpose: Check on the size of variables. Very useful for performing syntax checking in MATRIXx command language programming.

Syntax: [A,ERR]=CHK_VAR(A,OPTIONS,ERR_MODE) OR
[A,ERR]=CHK_VAR(A,M,N,OPTIONS,ERR_MODE) OR
[A,B,ERR]=CHK_VAR(A,B,OPTIONS,ERR_MODE) OR

Purpose: Cholesky factorization.

Syntax: C=CHOL(A)

Purpose: Alter the precision of arithmetic operations.

Syntax: CHOP(places)

Purpose: Clear variables or user-defined functions from the MATRIXx data stack.

Syntax: CLEAR * OR
CLEAR VAR1 VAR2 VAR3 ... OR
CLEAR function_name

Purpose: Returns various system times. Very useful in programming and especially in benchmarking.

Syntax: TIME=CLOCK('option')

Purpose: Obtain controllable part of a dynamic system.

Syntax: [SC,NSC,T]=CNTRLABLE(S,NS,TOL)

Purpose: Condition number of a matrix in 2-norm.

Syntax: C=COND(A)

Purpose: Complex conjugate.

Syntax: C=CONJG(A)

Purpose: General input-output interconnection. Constant gain feedback connection.

Syntax: [S,NS]=CONNECT(S1,NS1,K,INGAIN,OUTGAIN)

Purpose: Convolve two polynomials.

Syntax: C = CONV(A,B)

Purpose: Calculate the auto/cross correlation of data.

Syntax: CXY=CORRELATE(X,Y,M)
[CXY,T]=CORRELATE(X,Y,M,DT)

Purpose: Cosine, hyperbolic cosine, cotangent, hyperbolic cotangent, cosecant and hyperbolic cosecant of argument.

Syntax: C=COS(A), COSH(A), COT(A), COTH(A), CSC(A), CSCH(A)

Purpose: Convert a discrete dynamic system into an internally balanced dynamic form.

```
Syntax:        [SB,SIGMASQ,T]=DBALANCE(SD,NS)
```

Purpose: Gain and phase plots of discrete time systems.

```
Syntax:
    [GAIN,DB,PHASE]=DBODE(SD,NS,OMEGANMIN,OMEGANMAX,NPTS,'OPT')  OR
    [GAIN,DB,PHASE]=DBODE(DNUM,DDEN,OMEGANMIN,OMEGANMAX,NPTS)  OR
    [GIAN,DB,PHASE]=DBODE(SD,NS,OMEGAN)
```

Purpose: Define a user-defined function (UDF) or user-defined command (UDC).

```
Syntax:        DEFINE 'filename'   OR
               DEFINE 'filename' 'category'
```

Purpose: Calculate optimal state estimator gain matrix for a discrete time system.

```
Syntax:        [EVAL,KE]=DESTIMATOR(A,C,QXX,QYY,QXY)  OR
               [EVAL,KE,P]=DESTIMATOR(A,C,QXX,QYY,QXY)
```

Purpose: Calculates the determinant of a real or complex square matrix

```
Syntax:        DET(A)
```

Purpose: Removes biases from the columns of a matrix.

```
Syntax:        YD=DETREND(Y)
```

Purpose: Produce a matrix with specified elements on a given diagonal or extract elements from the diagonal of a matrix.

```
Syntax:        B=DIAG(A)  OR
               B=DIAG(A,K)
```

Purpose: Produce a transcript of a MATRIXx session.

```
Syntax:   DIARY('filename')      // to create a session diary
          DIARY('filename',1)     // to create a command diary
```

Purpose: Initial value response of discrete time dynamic system.

```
Syntax:        [N,Y]=DINITIAL(SD,NS,X0,NPTS)
```

Purpose: Convert continuous time dynamic system to discrete time form.

```
Syntax:        SD=DISCRETIZ(S,NS,DT,'TYPE')  OR
               [NUMD,DEND]=DISCRETIZ(NUM,DEN,DT,'TYPE')
```

Purpose: Computing L-infinity norm of the transfer matrix of a discrete-time system.

```
Syntax:        [SIGMA, OMEGA] = DLINFNORM(S, NS, {TOL,{MAXITER}})
```

Purpose: Response of discrete-time system to general inputs.

```
Syntax:        [N,Y]=DLSIM(SD,NS,U,X0)    OR
               [N,Y]=DLSIM(DNUM,DDEN,U)
```

Purpose: Solve a discrete Lyapunov equation.

```
Syntax:        P=DLYAP(A,Q)
```

Purpose: Compute a reduced order form of a discrete-time system.

```
Syntax:        [SR,NSR]=DMREDUCE(SD,NS,KEEP)
```

Purpose: Nichols plot of discrete-time system.

```
Syntax:
[OMEGAN,DB,PHASE]=DNICHOLS(SD,NS,OMEGANMIN,OMEGANMAX,NPTS,OPT)  OR
[OMEGAN,DB,PHASE]=DNICHOLS(NUM,DEN,OMEGANMIN,OMEGANMAX,NPTS,OPT)  OR
[OMEGAN,DB,PHASE]=DNICHOLS(SD,NS,OMEGAN,OPT)
```

Purpose: Nyquist plot of discrete-time system.

```
Syntax:
[OMEGAN,RPART,IPART]=DNYQUIST(SD,NS,OMEGANMIN,OMEGANMAX,NPTS,OPT) OR
[OMEGAN,RPART,IPART]=DNYQUIST(DNUM,DDEN,OMEGANMIN,OMEGANMAX,NPTS,OPT)
[OMEGAN,RPART,IPART]=DNYQUIST(SD,NS,OMEGAN,OPTION)
```

Purpose: Compute power spectral density for discrete system.

Syntax:

```
[OMEGAN,YPSD,YSPEC]=DPSD(SD,NS,USPEC,OMEGANMIN,OMEGANMAX,NPTS)   OR
[OMEGAN,YPSD,YSPEC]=DPSD(SD,NS,USPEC,OMEGAN)
```

Purpose: Compute optimal state feedback gain for discrete-time system.

Syntax:

```
[EVAL,KR]=DREGULATOR(A,B,RXX,RUU,RXU)   OR
[EVAL,KR,P]=DREGULATOR(A,B,RXX,RUU,RXU)
```

Purpose: Plot root locus for a discrete-time single-input single-output system.

Syntax:

```
-- Interactive root locus --
 K = DRLOCUS ( S [ , OPTIONS ] )
 K = DRLOCUS ( S, NS [ , OPTIONS ] )
 K = DRLOCUS ( NUM, DEN [ , OPTIONS ] )
-- Non-interactive root locus --
 EVAL = DRLOCUS ( S, GAIN [ , OPTIONS ] )
 EVAL = DRLOCUS ( S, NS, GAIN [ , OPTIONS ] )
 EVAL = DRLOCUS ( NUM, DEN, GAIN [ , OPTIONS ] )
```

Purpose: Root mean square response of a discrete-time system.

Syntax:

```
YRMS=DRMS(SD,NS,UCOV)
[YRMS,YCOV]=DRMS(S,NS,UCOV)
```

Purpose: Step response of discrete time system.

Syntax:

```
[N,Y]=DSTEP(SD,NS,NPTS)   OR
[N,Y]=DSTEP(DNUM,DDEN,NPTS)
```

Purpose: Eigenvalues of a square matrix.

Syntax:

```
EV=EIG(A)    OR
[V,D]=EIG(A)    OR
EV=EIG(S,NS)
```

Purpose: Calculate optimal state estimator gain matrix for a continuous time system.

Syntax:

```
[EVAL,KE]=ESTIMATOR(A,C,QXX,QYY,QXY)
[EVAL,KE,P]=ESTIMATOR(A,C,QXX,QYY,QXY)
```

Purpose: Invoke user command files.

Syntax:

```
EXECUTE('filename',option)
```

Purpose: Determine the existence of a variable, file, function,or command.

Syntax:

```
E=EXIST('entity','option')
```

Purpose: Leave MATRIXx. Exits a FOR, WHILE or IF structure.

Syntax:

```
EXIT
```

Purpose: Exponential of input.

Syntax:

```
B=EXP(A)    OR
B=EXP(A,'OPTION')
```

Purpose: Produces a matrix with ones on the principal diagonal and zeros elsewhere.

Syntax: `EYE(n)` ... gives an n by n identity matrix. `EYE(m,n)` gives an m by n matrix with ones on the principal diagonal. `EYE(A)` gives a matrix the size of A with ones on the principal diagonal.

Purpose: Connect two dynamic systems ina feedback loop.

Syntax:

```
[S,NS]=FEEDBACK(S1,NS1,S2,NS2)   OR
[S,NS]=FEEDBACK(S1,NS1,S2)     : constant-gain feedback
[S,NS]=FEEDBACK(S1,NS1)        : unity feedback
```

Purpose: Design finite impulse response filter.

Syntax:

```
IR=FFIR(N,BANDS,'OPTION',DENS)    OR
[IR,ERR]=FFIR(N,BANDS,'OPTION',DENS)   OR
[IR,ERR,MAX]=FFIR(N,BANDS,'OPTION',DENS)
```

Purpose: Fast Fourier Transform of input.

```
Syntax:         XF=FFT(X,SIZE,'WIN')
```

Purpose: Infinite impulse response filter design.

```
Syntax:         S=FIIR(N,BAND,RIPPLE,TYPE,APPROX)  OR
                [S,P,Z]=FFIR(N,BAND,RIPPLE,TYPE,APPROX)  OR
                [S,P,Z,DEN,NUM]=FIIR(N,BAND,RIPPLE,TYPE,APPROX)
```

Purpose: Filter propagation and simulation of discrete-time dynamic systems.

```
Syntax:         Y=FILP(SD,U,X0)
```

Purpose: Frequency response of dynamic system. FREQ transforms the A matrix to Hessenberg form prior to finding the frequency response.

```
Syntax:         [OMEGA,H]=FREQ(S,NS,RANGE,option)  OR
                H=FREQ(S,NS,OMEGA,'options')
```

Purpose: Save variables on the data stack in a formatted file.

```
Syntax:         FSAVE 'filename' VAR1 VAR2
```

Purpose: Computes a frequency-shaped state estimator.

```
Syntax:         [EV,SF,NSF]=FSESTI(SA,NS,NSA,QWWA,QVVA,{QWVA})
```

Purpose: Computes a controller from a frequency shaped control law and an estimator.

```
Syntax:         [EV,SCC,NSCC]=FSLQGCOMP(SF,NSF,SC,NSC)
```

Purpose: Computes a frequency-shaped control law.

```
Syntax:    [EV,SC,NSC,SCC,NSCC]=FSREGU(SA,NS,NSA,RXXA,RUUA{,RXUA}
```

Purpose: Filter design by windowing method.

```
Syntax:         IR=FWIN(BANDS,NPTS,'WIN')
```

Purpose: The GET_INFO function would allow procedures to get information that is generally available to the interactive user.

```
Syntax:         VAR=GET_INFO('Subject','Topic')
```

Purpose: Hessenberg form of a matrix.

```
Syntax:         H=HESS(A)   OR
                [P,H]=HESS(A)
```

Purpose: Inverse of a Hilbert matrix.

```
Syntax:         HILB(size)
```

Purpose: Histogram of a matrix.

```
Syntax:         DIST=HIST(A,BREAK)
```

Purpose: Compute inverse Fast Fourier transform of input.

```
Syntax:         X=IFFT(XF,SIZE,'WIN')
```

Purpose: Extract the complex part of the input.

```
Syntax:         Y=IMAG(X)
```

Purpose: Compute the impulse response of a linear continuous time system.

```
Syntax:         [T,Y]=IMPULSE(S,NS,TMAX,NPTS)  OR
                [T,Y]-IMPULSE(NUM,DEN,TMAX,NPTS)
```

Purpose: Find the location of a substring within a string.

```
Syntax:         I=INDEX(STRING,SUBSTRING)
```

Purpose: Linear interpolation and extrapolation of a vector.

```
Syntax:         [YS,ERR] = INTEXT(X,Y,XS);
```

Purpose: Initial value response of continuous time dynamic system.

```
Syntax:         [T,Y]=INITIAL(S,NS,X0,TMAX,NPTS)
```

Purpose: Obtain user input while executing a user-defined function, command file or macro.

```
Syntax:         INQUIRE variable 'prompt-string'
```

Purpose: Compute the inverse of a square matrix.

```
Syntax:         Y = INV(X)
```

Purpose: This command is the opposite of CLEAR. It CLEARs all variables EXCEPT those in the list.

```
Syntax:         KEEP VAR1 VAR2 VAR3 ...
```

Purpose: Transfer control from the UDC, UDF or EXEC file to the keyboard (Not available on IBM PC).

Syntax: `KEYBOARD`

Purpose: Kronecker tensor product.

Syntax: `C = KRON(A,B)`

Purpose: Compute a linearized equivalent to a SYSTEM_BUILD model. Available only with the SYSTEM_BUILD option.

Syntax: `[S,NS] = LIN(DEL,Ue)` OR
`[S,NS] = LIN(T,U)`

Purpose: Line limit on terminal output before prompting user.

Syntax: `LINES(value)`

Purpose: Computing L-infinity norm of a transfer matrix

Syntax: `[SIGMA, OMEGA] = LINFNORM(S, NS, {TOL, {MAXITER}})`

Purpose: Linear interpolation/extrapolation. The output is evenly or logarithmically spaced.

Syntax: `YS = LININT(X,Y,XS,{OPTIONS});`
`[YS,XS] = LININT(X,Y,XMIN,XMAX,{NPTS},{OPTIONS});`

Purpose: Bring data from disk files into working MATRIXx stack.

Syntax: `LOAD 'filename'` OR

Syntax: `LOAD 'filename' A B C`

Purpose: Natural logarithm of argument.

Syntax: `C=LOG(A)`

Purpose: Base 10 logarithm of argument.

Syntax: `C=LOG10(A)`

Purpose: Change the precision and format of results printed at the terminal.

Syntax: `LONG` OR `LONG E`

Purpose: This function solves linear program in the standard form:

minimize C'*X
subject to A*X = B
and X = 0.

It will either report that the problem is infeasible or unbounded, or report the final optimal solutions.

Syntax: `[X,Y,JH,ZH]=LPOPT(A,B,C,ZL,TOL,BETA)`

Purpose: Given a plant and optimal regulator, this function designs an estimator which 'recovers' loop transfer robustness via the design parameter RHO. Plots of singular value loop transfer response are made for the (regulator) and (estimator+regulator) systems.

Syntax:

```
[SC,NSC,EVE,KE,SLTF,NSLTF]=LQELTR(S,NS,QXX,QYY,KR,RHO,WMIN,WMAX,
{NPTS},{OPTION});   OR
[SC,NSC,EVE,KE,SLTF,NSLTF]=LQELTR(S,NS,QXX,QYY,KR,RHO,OMEGA,
{OPTION});
```

Purpose: Produces system matrix for feedback compensator.

Syntax: `[SC,NSC]=LQGCOMP(S,NS,KR,KE)` OR
`[SC,NSC]=LQGCOMP(S,NS,KR,KE,'DIRECT')`

Purpose: Given a plant and optimal estimator, this function designs a regulator which 'recovers' loop transfer robustness via the design parameter RHO. Plots of singular value loop transfer response are made for the (estimator) and (regulator+estimator) systems.

Syntax:

```
[SC,NSC,EVR,KR,SLTF,NSLTF]=LQRLTR(S,NS,RXX,RUU,KE,RHO,WMIN,WMAX,
{NPTS},{OPTION});   OR
[SC,NSC,EVR,KR,SLTF,NSLTF]=LQRLTR(S,NS,RXX,RUU,KE,RHO,OMEGA,
{OPTION});
```

Purpose: Response of continuous-time system to general inputs.

Syntax: `[T,Y]=LSIM(S,NS,U,DELTAT,X0)`

Purpose: Factors from Gaussian elimination.

Syntax: [L,U]=LU(A)

Purpose: Solve a continuous Lyapunov equation.

Syntax: P=LYAP(A,Q)

Purpose: Compute gain and phase margins of a single input, single output continuous-time or discrete-time system.

Syntax: [GNMARGIN,PHMARGIN,FRGN,FRPH]=MARGIN(OMEGA,DB,PHASE)

Purpose: Find the largest value in a matrix or vector.

Syntax: C=MAX(A,value) OR
[C,D]=MAX(A)

Purpose: Perform maximum likelihood parameter identification.

Syntax: [YMAT,P,RSS,JTJ]=MAXLIKE(U,Y,P0,'MODEL',NIT)

Purpose: Places a user-defined menu on the screen.

Syntax: OPTION=MENU(LIST,COLS)

Purpose: Find the smallest number in a matrix or vector.

Syntax: C=MIN(A,value) OR
[C,D]=MIN(A)

Purpose: Finding the minimum distance between the origin and the convex hull formed by the columns of X.

Syntax: G=MIN_DIST(X)

Purpose: Compute the minimal realization of a system.

Syntax: [SMIN,NSMIN,T]=MINIMAL(S,NS,TOL) OR
[NUMMIN,DENMIN]=MINIMAL(NUM,DEN,TOL)

Purpose: This function returns the remainder from the division of the first argument by the second one. If both arguments are integers, then an integral MOD is performed. For real arguments, a real MOD is performed.

Syntax: MOD(A,B)

Purpose: Convert a state space system into modal form.

Syntax: [SM,T]=MODAL(S,NS) OR
SM=MODAL(S,NS)

Purpose: Compute a reduced order form of a continuous system.

Syntax: [SR,NSR]=MREDUCE(S,NS,KEEP)

Purpose: Perform model structure determination

Syntax: [THETA,COR,COV=MSD(X,Y)

Purpose: Nichols plot of continuous-time system.

Syntax:
[OMEGA,DB,PHASE]=NICHOLS(S,NS,OMEGAMIN,OMEGAMAX,NPTS,OPT) OR
[OMEGA,DB,PHASE]=NICHOLS(NUM,DEN,OMEGAMIN,OMEGAMAX,NPTS,OPT) OR
[OMEGA,DB,PHASE]=NICHOLS(S,NS,OMEGA,OPT)

Purpose: Calculate norm of a matrix or vector.

Syntax: NORM(A,TYPE)

Purpose: Nyquist plot of continuous-time system.

Syntax:
[OMEGA,RPART,IPART]=NYQUIST(S,NS,OMEGAMIN,OMEGAMAX,NPTS,OPT) OR
[OMEGA,RPART,IPART]=NYQUIST(NUM,DEN,OMEGAMIN,OMEGAMAX,NPTS,OPT) OR
[OMEGA,RPART,IPART]=NYQUIST(S,NS,OMEGA,OPT)

Purpose: Compute observable part of a system.

Syntax: [SOBS,NSOBS,T]=OBSERVABLE(S,NS,TOL)

Purpose: Generate a matrix containing all ones.

Syntax: ONES(ROW,COLUMN) OR ONES(ROW) OR ONES(matrix)

Purpose: Minimize a general user-defined cost function. The problem can be totally unconstrained or can have one or more constraints including: bounds on the parameters, general equality constraints, and inequality constraints.

Syntax:
```
[P,JH]=OPTIMIZE(PB)    OR
[P,JH,L]=OPTIMIZE(PB,IB)
[P,JH,L]=OPTIMIZE(PB,IB,OP)
[P,JH,L,H,IC]=OPTIMIZE(PB,IB,OP,L0,H0)
```

Purpose: Find orthogonal basis spanning column space of a matrix, i.e., Q'*Q=A

Syntax: `Q=ORTH(A)`

Purpose: This function allows you to pass a command directly to the operating system from MATRIXx. It is similar to the \\ capability except that the string that is passed can be a variable.This function is useful if you are writing procedures that need to perform operating system functions. Interactively, it is simpler to just use \\.

Syntax: `OSCMD('string')`

Purpose: Connect two systems in parallel summing the outputs.

Syntax: `[S,NS]=PARALLEL(S1,NS1,S2,NS2)`

Purpose: Temporarily suspend execution of a user-defined function, command file or macro.

Syntax: `PAUSE`

Purpose: Pseudoinverse of a matrix, i.e., A*C*A=A, C*A*C=C, A*C and C*A are Hermitian.

Syntax: `C=PINV(A,TOL))`

Purpose: Produce two dimensional graphical output.

Syntax: `PLOT(XDATA,YDATA,'options')`

Purpose: Plot 3-D curves and surfaces.

Syntax: `PLOT(XDATA,YDATA,ZDATA,'options')`

Purpose: Calculate state feedback gains via pole placement for single input continuous-time or discrete-time systems.

Syntax:
```
KC=POLEPLACE(A,B,POLES)       ... controller design
KE=POLEPLACE(A',B',POLES)     ... estimator design
```

Purpose: Compute coefficients of the characteristic polynomial of a matrix or vector.

Syntax: `C=POLY(A)`

Purpose: Evaluate the value of a real or complex polynomial in s at a particular (possibly complex) value of s.

Syntax: `H=POLYVAL(P,S)`

Purpose: Output a variable or MATRIX to a file.

Syntax:
```
PRINT 'filename' VAR1 VAR2...VARn
where 'filename' is a legal filename surrounded by quotes and
VAR1...VARn is a list of variable names separated by spaces.
```

Purpose: Multiply all elements of input together.

Syntax: `PROD(X)`

Purpose: Compute power spectral density for continuous system.

Syntax:
```
[OMEGA,YPSD,YSPEC]=PSD(S,NS,USPEC,OMEGAMIN,OMEGAMAX,NPTS)   OR
[OMEGA,YPSD,YSPEC]=PSD(S,NS,USPEC,OMEGA)
```

Purpose: Compute pulse response of discrete time system.

Syntax:
```
[N,Y]=PULSE(SD,NS,NPTS)
[N,Y]=PULSE(DNUM,DDEN,NPTS)
```

Purpose: Principal vector algorithm for computing Jordan forms.

Syntax:
```
ES=PVA(A)
[M,J]=PVA(A)
```

Purpose: Frequency response of dynamic system. PVAFREQ uses PVA to find the Jordan form of the A matrix before computing the frequency response.

Syntax: [OMEGA,H]=PVAFREQ(S,NS,RANGE,option) OR
H=PVAFREQ(S,NS,OMEGA,'options')

Purpose: This user function solves quadratic program in standard form:
minimize X'*Q*X/2 + C'*X
subject to A*X = B , where lower bound <= X <= upper bound.

Syntax: [X,L,JH]=QPOPT(Q,C,PB) OR
[X,L,JH]=QPOPT(Q,C,PB,A,B,TOL)

Purpose: Orthogonal triangular decomposition, i.e, A=Q*R or A*E=Q*R. Q is unitary, R is upper triangular and E is a permutation matrix.

Syntax: [Q,R]=QR(A) OR
[Q,R,E]=QR(A)

Purpose: Solves the general eigenproblem: A*x=lambda*B*x.

Syntax: AB=QZ(A,B) OR
AB=QZ(A,B,'option') OR
[Z,AB]=QZ(A,B,'option')

Purpose: Generate uniform and normal random numbers.

Syntax: RAND(row,column) OR RAND(row) OR RAND(variable)

Purpose: Calculate the rank of a matrix.

Syntax: RANK(A,TOL)

Purpose: Approximate each element of the input by a continued fraction to remove roundoff. Calculate integer rational numbers for the input.

Syntax: X=RAT(A)
[N1,N2]=RAT(A)

Purpose: Estimate of the reciprocal of the condition number.

Syntax: RCOND(A)

Purpose: Extract real part of input.

Syntax: REAL(A)

Purpose: Compute optimal state feedback gain for continuous-time system.

Syntax: [EVAL,KR]=REGULATOR(A,B,RXX,RUU,RXU) OR
[EVAL,KR,P]=REGULATOR(A,B,RXX,RUU,RXU)

Purpose: Modal residues of a continuous or discrete state-space system.

Syntax: [EVAL,RES]=RESIDUES(S,NS) OR
[EVAL,RES]=RESIDUES(S,NS,'MODE')

Purpose: Solve Riccati equation. Using the option 'DISC' solves the discrete Riccati equation.

Syntax: [EV,KC]=RICCATI(S,Q,NS,'DISC')
[EV,KC,P]=RICCATI(S,Q,NS,'DISC')

Purpose: Plot root locus for a continuous-time single-input single-output system.

Syntax:

```
          -- Interactive root locus --
K = RLOCUS ( S [ , OPTIONS ] )
K = RLOCUS ( S, NS, T [ , OPTIONS ] )
K = RLOCUS ( NUM, DEN [ , OPTIONS ] )
K = RLOCUS ( NUM, DEN, T [ , OPTIONS ] )
          -- Non-interactive root locus --
EVAL = RLOCUS ( S, GAIN [ , OPTIONS ] )
EVAL = RLOCUS ( S, NS, GAIN [ , OPTIONS ] )
EVAL = RLOCUS ( NUM, DEN, GAIN [ , OPTIONS ] )
```

Purpose: Perform recursive-least-squares identification on single-input/single-output data

Syntax: [NUM,DEN,FITERR]=RLS(Y,U,NUM0,DEN0,P0)

Purpose: Perform recursive maximum likelihood identification on single-input/single-output data.

Syntax: [NUM,DEN,NUMC,FITERR]=RML(Y,U,NUM0,DEN0,NUMC0,P0)

Purpose: Root mean square response of a continuous-time system.

Syntax: `YRMS=RMS(S,NS,USD)` OR
`[YRMS,YCOV]=RMS(S,NS,USD)`

Purpose: Compute roots of a polynomial.

Syntax: `ROOTS(X)`

Purpose: Round input to nearest integer.

Syntax: `C=ROUND(A)`

Purpose: Initialization of temporary storage for RPEM algorithm.

Syntax: `RPEM('INIT',STRUCTURE,THETA0,P0,CONVRG)`

Purpose: Iteration of RPEM algorithm.

Syntax: `TH=RPEM(Y,U)` OR
`[TH,FI]=RPEM(Y,U)` OR
`[TH,FI,V]=RPEM(Y,U)`

Purpose: Compute row reduced echelon form of a matrix.

Syntax: `C=RREF(A)`

Purpose: Save variables from the data stack to disk in binary form.

Syntax: `SAVE 'filename' VAR1 VAR2...`

Purpose: Schur decomposition of a matrix, where UN*UP*UN'=A. UN is unitary, UP is upper triangular with eigenvalues of A on its diagonal.

Syntax: `UP=SCHUR(A)` OR
`UP=SCHUR(A,OPTION)` OR
`[UN,UP]=SCHUR(A)` OR
`[UN,UP]=SCHUR(A,OPTION)`

Purpose: Secant and hyperbolic secant of argument.

Syntax: `C=SEC(A` AND `A=SECH(A)`

Purpose: Change semi-colon convention for command lines.

Syntax: `SEMI`

Purpose: Connect two state-space systems in series.

Syntax: `[S,NS]=SERIES(S1,NS1,S2,NS2)`

Purpose: Convert to state space form from a transfer-function model of a continuous-time or discrete-time systems.Parameter Q is the number of inputs for MIMO systems (optional).

Syntax: `[S,NS]=SFORM(NUM,DEN,Q)`

Purpose: Change the precision and format of results printed at the terminal.

Syntax: `SHORT` OR `SHORT E`

Purpose: Sine and hyperbolic sine of input.

Syntax: `C=SIN(A)` AND `C=SINH(A)`

Purpose: Simulation of system modeled with SYSTEM_BUILD.

Syntax: `SIM` OR
`Y=SIM(T,U,OPTIONS)` OR
`[TE,YE]=SIM(T,U,OPTIONS)`

Purpose: Insert initial conditions into a SYSTEM_BUILD simulation.

Syntax: `SIMIN(X0)`

Purpose: Extract initial conditions, rates, and outputs from a SYSTEM_BUILD simulation

Syntax: `[X0,XD,Y0]=SIMOUT(U0)` OR
`[XD,Y0]=SIMOUT(U0,X0)` OR
`Y0=SIMOUT(U0,X0)`

Purpose: Solves the indefinite Algebraic Riccati Equation (ARE): A'P + PA - PRP + Q = 0

Syntax: `[P,SOLSTAT]=SINGRICCATI(A, Q, R {,TYPE})`

Purpose: Compute row and column size of input.

Syntax: C=SIZE(A) OR
C=SIZE('A',1)

Purpose: This function lets you specify the size below which the variables will be stored in the stack. The rest of the variables will be stored in files.

Syntax: SIZ_LIMIT(N)

Purpose: Sort columns of a matrix.

Syntax: INDEX=SORT(A) OR
INDEX=SORT(A,'magn')

Purpose: Sort columns of a matrix.

Syntax: AS=SORTVALUE(A)
AS=SORTVALUE(A, 'magn')

Purpose: Calculate the auto/cross spectrum of data.

Syntax: [SXY,OMEGAN]=SPECTRUM(X,Y,M,WIN)

Purpose: Natural cubic spline.

Syntax: YS=SPLINE(X,Y,XS) OR
[XS,YS]=SPLINE(X,Y,RANGE,NPTS)

Purpose: Split a system matrix into its four individual matrices.

Syntax: [A,B,C,D]=SPLIT(S,NS)
[A,B]=SPLIT(S,NS)
A=SPLIT(S,NS)

Purpose: Square root of input.

Syntax: SQRT(A)

Purpose: Staircase form of a system matrix.

Syntax: [SST,T,NCO]=STAIR(S,NS,TOL)

Purpose: Step response of continuous time system.

Syntax: [T,Y]=STEP(S,NS,TMAX,NPTS) OR
[T,Y]=STEP(NUM,DEN,TMAX,NPTS)

Purpose: Convert a number into a string.

Syntax: S=STRING(A)
S=STRING(A,'FORMAT')

Purpose: Sum of all elements in input.

Syntax: SUM(A)

Purpose: Computes singular value decomposition of a matrix, i.e., A=U*S*V'. U and V are unitary and S is the vector of singular values in descending order of magnitude.

Syntax: SV=SVD(A) OR
[U,S,V]=SVD(A)

Purpose: Computes and plots the Singular Values of a continuous system

Syntax: [OMEGA,SVALS]=SVPLOT(S,NS,WMIN,WMAX,{NPTS},{OPTIONS}) OR
[SVALS]=SVPLOT(S,NS,OMEGA,{OPTIONS})

Purpose: Display the syntax of a command, function, or operation.

Syntax: SYNTAX topic

Purpose: Tangent and hyperbolic tangent of argument.

Syntax: C=TAN(A) AND C=TANH(A)

Purpose: Gives transfer function form of a state space system.

Syntax: [NUM,DEN]=TFORM(S,NS)

Purpose: Impulse response of continuous time system.

Syntax: [T,Y]=TIMR(S,NS,RANGE,'MODE')

Purpose: Lower triangle of matrix.

Syntax: C=TRIL(A,K)

Purpose: Trim a SYSTEM_BUILD model.

```
Syntax:        [XT,UT,YT]=TRIM(U)   OR
               [XT,UT,YT]=TRIM(U,U_FREEZE,Y,Y_FREEZE)   OR
               [XT,UT,YT]=TRIM(U,U_FREEZE,Y,Y_FREEZE,X0)
```

Purpose: Upper triangle of matrix.

```
Syntax:        C=TRIU(A,K)
```

Purpose: Display list of applicable MATRIXx and user-defined commands and functions.

```
Syntax:        WHAT   OR   WHAT category
```

Purpose: Display the names of the user-defined and permanent variables on the stack.

```
Syntax:        WHO
```

Purpose: Compute transmission zeros of a continuous or discrete state-space system S.

```
Syntax:    Z=ZEROS(S,NS)   OR
         [Z,K]=ZEROS(S) ... for single-input/single-output systems.
```

Index